Regulating Pre-Implantation Genetic Diagnosis

The successful achievement of pregnancies following pre-implantation genetic diagnosis (PGD) was first reported in April 1990. The technology is often used for patients who are at substantial risk of conceiving a pregnancy affected by a known genetic disorder. However, from this technology other more controversial uses have arisen such as Human Leuhccyle Anligen (HLA)-typing to save the life of a sibling, gender selection for social reasons, the prevention of late-onset diseases, or the prevention of diseases which some people may be genetically predisposed to developing such as breast cancer. The technology surrounding PGD is constantly developing, giving rise to new and unexpected consequences that create fresh ethical and legal dilemmas.

Featuring internationally recognised experts in the field, this book critically explores the regulation of PGD and the broader legal and ethical issues associated with it. It looks at the regulatory situation in a number of jurisdictions including New Zealand, Australia and the United Kingdom, but it also explores a number of themes of wide significance including a historical consideration of PGD and its part in the creation of the 'genetic embryo' as a political tool, the over-regulation of PGD and the ethical difficulties in handling additional unexpected medical information yielded by new technologies. This book will be of particular interest to academics and students of law, medicine and ethics.

Sheila A. M. McLean is the first holder of the International Bar Association Chair of Law and Ethics in Medicine at Glasgow University and is Director of the Institute of Law and Ethics in Medicine at Glasgow University. She has acted as a consultant to the World Health Organization (WHO) and the Council of Europe, and to individual states.

Sarah Elliston is Senior Lecturer at the University of Glasgow. In addition to her work at the University, she has contributed to the work of a number of public and professional organisations. She is the Scottish Case Editor for the Butterworths Medico Legal Reports and writes the medical law section for the Butterworths Scottish Older Client Law Service.

Biomedical law and ethics library
Series Editor: Sheila A.M. McLean

Scientific and clinical advances, social and political developments and the impact of healthcare on our lives raise profound ethical and legal questions. Medical law and ethics have become central to our understanding of these problems, and are important tools for the analysis and resolution of problems – real or imagined.

In this series, scholars at the forefront of biomedical law and ethics contribute to the debates in this area, with accessible, thought-provoking and sometimes controversial ideas. Each book in the series develops an independent hypothesis and argues cogently for a particular position. One of the major contributions of this series is the extent to which both law and ethics are utilised in the content of the books, and the shape of the series itself.

The books in this series are analytical, with a key target audience of lawyers, doctors, nurses and the intelligent lay public.

Available titles:

Human Fertilisation and Embryology (2006)
Reproducing regulation
Kirsty Horsey & Hazel Biggs

Intention and Causation in Medical Non-Killing (2006)
The impact of criminal law concepts on euthanasia and assisted suicide
Glenys Williams

Impairment and Disability (2007)
Law and ethics at the beginning and end of life
Sheila McLean & Laura Williamson

Bioethics and the Humanities (2007)
Attitudes and perceptions
Robin Downie & Jane Macnaughton

Defending the Genetic Supermarket (2007)
The law and ethics of selecting the next generation
Colin Gavaghan

The Harm Paradox (2007)
Tort law and the unwanted child in an era of choice
Nicolette Priaulx

Assisted Dying (2007)
Reflections on the need for law reform
Sheila McLean

Medicine, Malpractice and Misapprehensions (2007)
Vivienne Harpwood

Euthanasia, Ethics and the Law (2007)
From conflict to compromise
Richard Huxtable

Best Interests of the Child in Healthcare (2007)
Sarah Elliston

Values in Medicine (2008)
The realities of clinical practice
Donald Evans

Autonomy, Consent and the Law (2009)
Sheila McLean

Healthcare Research Ethics and Law (2009)
Regulation, review and responsibility
Hazel Biggs

The Body in Bioethics (2009)
Alastair V. Campbell

Genomic Negligence (2011)
An interest in autonomy as the basis for novel negligence claims generated by genetic technology
Victoria Chico

Health Professionals and Trust
The cure for healthcare law and policy
Mark Henaghan

Medical Ethics in China
A transcultural interpretation
Jing-Bao Nie

Law, Ethics and Compromise at the Limits of Life
To treat or not to treat?
Richard Huxtable

Regulating Pre-Implantation Genetic Diagnosis
A comparative and theoretical analysis
Sheila A.M. McLean and Sarah Elliston

Forthcoming titles include:

Bioethics
Methods, theories, scopes
Marcus Düwell

The Jurisprudence of Pregnancy
Concepts of conflict, persons and property
Mary Ford

About the Series Editor
Professor Sheila McLean is International Bar Association Professor of Law and Ethics in Medicine and Director of the Institute of Law and Ethics in Medicine at the University of Glasgow.

Regulating Pre-Implantation Genetic Diagnosis

A comparative and theoretical analysis

Edited by

Sheila A.M. McLean and Sarah Elliston

Routledge
Taylor & Francis Group
LONDON AND NEW YORK

First published 2013
by Routledge
2 Park Square, Milton Park, Abingdon, Oxon OX14 4RN

Simultaneously published in the USA and Canada
by Routledge
711 Third Avenue, New York, NY 10017

Routledge is an imprint of the Taylor & Francis Group, an informa business

British Library Cataloguing in Publication Data
A catalogue record for this book is available from the British Library

Library of Congress Cataloging in Publication Data
A catalog record for this book has been requested

ISBN: 978-0-415-68644-0 (hbk)
ISBN: 978-0-203-09637-6 (ebk)

Typeset in Garamond
by Keystroke, Station Road, Codsall, Wolverhampton

MIX
Paper from responsible sources
FSC www.fsc.org FSC® C004839

Printed and bound in Great Britain by
CPI Antony Rowe, Chippenham, Wiltshire

Contents

Notes on contributors

Peter Braude is Emeritus Professor of Obstetrics and Gynaecology at King's College London. He was formerly Head of the Department of Women's Health at King's College London, and directed the Centre for Pre-implantation Genetic Diagnosis at Guy's and St Thomas Hospital, in the UK. His research group, funded by the Medical Research Council, established the first human embryonic stem cell lines in the UK, and the first internationally to contain the common ΔF508 cystic fibrosis deletion. These and clinical grade lines established recently have been lodged in the UK Stem Cell Bank for use in international research. He served for five years as a member of the Human Fertilisation and Embryology Authority (HFEA), and was chair of the Scientific Advisory Committee for the Royal College of Obstetricians and Gynaecologists (RCOG). He chaired the RCOG expert committee on Umbilical Stem Cell Banking and the Expert Committee advising the HFEA on multiple pregnancies after in vitro fertilisation (IVF). He currently sits on the Committee for the Safety of Blood, Tissues and Organs.

Laura Cabrera is a postdoctoral researcher in bioethics and emergent technologies in the Institute for Biomedical Ethics at Basel University. Laura received a B.Sc. in electrical and communication engineering from the Instituto Tecnológico de Estudios Superiores de Monterrey, in Mexico City; an MA in applied ethics from Linköping University, in Sweden; and a Ph.D. in applied ethics from Charles Sturt University in Australia. Laura's current research focuses on neuroethics as well as ethical issues around human enhancement and emergent technologies.

Tom Campbell is a professor in the Centre for Applied Philosophy and Public Ethics (CAPPE), an Australian Research Council Special Research Centre, Charles Sturt University and University of Melbourne. Publications include: *Adam Smith's Science of Morals* (1971); *Seven Theories of Human Society* (1981); *The Left and Rights* (Routledge & Kegan Paul, 1983); *Justice* (3rd edn, 2010); (with Chris Heginbotham), *Mental Illness: Prejudice, Discrimination and the Law* (1991); *The Legal Theory of Ethical Positivism* (1996); and *Rights: A Critical Introduction* (Routledge 2006).

Donald Chalmers is Distinguished Professor, University of Tasmania and is Director of the Centre for Law and Genetics. He is a Foundation Fellow of the Australian Academy of Law, Chair of the Gene Technology Ethics and Community Consultative Committee, Deputy Chair of the National Health and Medical Research Council (NHMRC) Embryo Research Licensing Committee and Chair of the Data Access Committee of the International Cancer Genome Consortium. He was Chair of the NHMRC Australian Health Ethics Committee (1994–2000); Law Reform Commissioner for Tasmania (1991–7); and Chair of the Australian Red Cross Ethics Committee (2000–10).

Thomas Cleary (LLB (Hons.)), is a graduate of the University of Otago, Dunedin, New Zealand. He is currently studying for a Master's in bioethics and health law.

Sarah Elliston (MA (Cantab.), LLM) practised as a barrister before joining the School of Law at Glasgow University in 1994, where she teaches medical law at undergraduate and postgraduate level. Outside the University, she has contributed to the work of a number of public and professional organisations. This has included membership of Local Research Ethics Committees; a Department of Health Steering Committee on Xenotransplantation; and the Independent Review of the Removal and Retention of Organs at Post-Mortem (Scotland). She is currently a member of the Scottish Transplant Group Ethics Subgroup advising the Scottish Transplant Group, and, through the Group, the Scottish Government Health Directorates, on the implementation of the report of the Organ Donation Taskforce. She has acted as a consultant for professional bodies, such as the British Medical Association (BMA) and the General Pharmaceutical Council, and on research projects. She has published on a range of issues in medical law, including *The Best Interests of the Child in Healthcare* (2007), and is on the editorial board of national and international medico-legal journals, including the *Medical Law Review*.

Mark Henaghan is Dean and Professor of Law at the University of Otago, specialising in family law and a barrister and solicitor of the High Court of New Zealand. Publications include: *Family Law Policy in New Zealand* (3rd edn, 2007) (co-author); *Family Law in New Zealand* (12th edn, 2005) (co-author); *Relationship Property on Death* (2004) (co-author), which won the 2005 J. F. Northey prize for the best law book in New Zealand; *Relationship Property Consolidated Legislation and Analysis* (2001) (co-author); *Care of Children* (2005); and *Health Professionals and Trust: The Cure for Healthcare Law and Policy* (2012). He is a member of the Advisory Group on Assisted Reproductive Technology. Professor Henaghan is an author and member of the Editorial Board for LexisNexis *Family Law Service* and the New Zealand *Family Law Journal*, and author of a number of articles on family law. He is on the editorial boards of *Child and Family Law*

Quarterly and *International Journal of Human Rights*. He is currently engaged in an international study of relocation cases and their impact on the parties and their children, with collaborators from Australia and the UK. He is the Principal Investigator for the Human Genome Research Project, TeKaupapa Rangahau Ira Tāngata – Law, Ethics and Policy for the Future – sponsored by the New Zealand Law Foundation. This project has produced four major reports: *Choosing Genes for Future Children* (2006); *Genes, Society and the Future* (vol. 1) (2007); *Genes, Society and the Future: Genetic Testing of Children* (vol. 2) (2007); and *Genes, Society and the Future* (vol. 3) (2009).

Emily Jackson is Professor of Law at the London School of Economics and Deputy Chair of the HFEA. She is a member of the BMA's Medical Ethics Committee, and a member of the ethics committees of the Royal College of Physicians and the Royal College of Pathologists. Publications include: *Regulating Reproduction* (2001); *Medical Law* (2nd edn, 2009); *Debating Euthanasia* (2011); and *Law and the Regulation of Medicines* (2012).

Martin Johnson is Professor of Reproductive Sciences, University of Cambridge and President of Christ's College. He was Head of Department (1995–9) in the Anatomy Department in Cambridge, and has held honorary positions in Obstetrics and Gynaecology, United Medical and Dental Schools (UMDS) (1991–5); Zoology and Law at La Trobe University (Melbourne, 1993, 2006); Physiology at Sydney University and St Paul's College (1999–2004); and the Indian Institute of Science, Bangalore (1984–9). He was Chair of the British Society for Developmental Biology (1984–9); member of the HFEA (1994–9); the BMA Board of Medical Education (2002); specialist scientific advisor to the Joint Lords and Commons Committee scrutinising the Draft Human Embryos and Tissue Bill (2007); and founding scientific member of the Cambridge Socio-Legal Group (2001–8). Awards include: the Albert Brachet Prize, Belgian Royal Academy of Sciences, Letters and Fine Arts (1989); and King's Fund Prize for Innovation in Medical Education (1993). Publications include: *Essential Reproduction* (6th edn, 2007), winner of the BMA Obstetrics and Gynaecology prize, 2008; *Sexuality Repositioned* (2004) (co-author); *Death Rites and Rights* (2007) (co-author); plus many papers on reproductive science, ethics, law, regulatory practice and medical education. He is currently studying the history of mammalian developmental biology in the UK since 1945, including a study of the early contextual history of PGD.

Sheila McLean was the first holder of the International Bar Association Chair of Law and Ethics in Medicine at Glasgow University. She has been a Vice-Chair of UNESCO's International Bioethics Committee and remains a member of that Committee, and has acted as a consultant/adviser to the WHO, the Council of Europe, the United Nations Educational, Scientific and Cultural Organization (UNESCO) and a number of individual states. She has acted as legal adviser to the House of Commons Select Committee on Science and Technology and the joint House of Lords/House of Commons Committee on the Human Tissue and Embryos Draft Bill. She has held a number of posts external to the University, including founding Chairperson of the Scottish Criminal Cases Review Commission, and has chaired a number of governmental committees, such as the review of the consent provisions of the HFEA 1990; the Independent Review of the Removal and Retention of Organs at Post-Mortem (Scotland); the Working Group on No Fault Liability for Medical Injury (Scotland); and the Expert Panel on Pre-Implantation Genetic Diagnosis (Scotland). She has been elected a Fellow of the Royal Society of Edinburgh, the Royal College of General Practitioners, the Royal College of Physicians (Edinburgh), the Institute of Biology, the Academy of Medical Sciences and the RSA, and has been awarded honorary degrees by the Universities of Edinburgh and Abertay, Dundee. She has acted as an expert reviewer for many of the major grant-awarding bodies and similar organisations both within and outside the UK. She has published extensively in the area of medical law, is on the editorial board of a number of national and international journals, and is regularly consulted by the media on matters of medical law and ethics. In 2005 she was awarded the first ever Lifetime Achievement Award at the Scottish Legal Awards. Her book, *Assisted Dying: Reflections on the Need for Law Reform,* was awarded the Minty Prize of the Royal Society of Authors and the Royal Society of Medicine in 2008.

Kerry Petersen is an associate professor, Law School, La Trobe University, Australia and has been admitted to the Supreme Court of Victoria as a barrister and solicitor. She has been the author and editor of a number of books, articles and book chapters in the areas of medical law, human reproduction law and children's rights. She was awarded an Australian Bicentennial Fellowship by the Menzies Centre, King's College, University of London and was a Visiting Scholar at the Centre for Family Research, Cambridge (2005). She was also a Senior Research Fellow at the University of Glasgow, Scotland (1995–6) and a residential Fellow at the Rockefeller Center, Bellagio, Italy (1994). Kerry has held an Australian Research Council Discovery grant 'The ART of making babies: how human embryo research and assisted reproduction are regulated in Australia and New Zealand' (completed in 2011); and is currently working on an Australian Research Council Discovery grant 'A longitudinal study exploring women's experiences following a prenatal diagnosis of foetal abnormality' with a team from the Murdoch Children's Research Institute. She is a member of the Medico-Legal Society, the Fertility Society of Australia, Women's Health Victoria, and is the lawyer on the Melbourne IVF Human Research Ethics Committee.

Jeanne Snelling is a graduate of the Otago University Faculty of Law, New Zealand. After completing her degree, Jeanne worked as a research assistant for a multidisciplinary independent review group, commissioned by the Ministry of Health, which was charged with examining the safety, efficacy and adequacy of regulation of electroconvulsive therapy in New Zealand. Jeanne then undertook research assistance for Professor Peter Skegg (a specialist in medical law) in relation to the book *Medical Law in New Zealand*, before taking up a position as a research fellow on the Otago University *Human Genome Research Project: Law, Policy and Ethics for the Future*. Jeanne is currently writing her Ph.D. thesis on PGD. Prior to studying law, Jeanne worked as a registered nurse specialising in intensive care.

Anastasia Theodosiou is a clinical medical student at the University of Cambridge (2010–13). She previously obtained a BA (2009) and an M. Phil. (2010) for research into the history of PGD in the Department of Physiology, Development and Neuroscience, Cambridge. She is a supervisor in human reproduction at Downing College, Cambridge, and has a strong academic and professional interest in children's and women's health.

Introduction

Sheila A. M. McLean

Advances in medicine have offered people a range of choices unthought of even by the middle of the last century. The so-called revolutions in human genetics and assisted reproduction – perhaps especially when combined – provide remarkable diagnostic and therapeutic potential. However, these apparent forces for good also raise ethical and sometimes legal questions which can shape the responses of both individuals and states as to how, when and to whom they should be made available. In this book, the focus is on pre-implantation genetic diagnosis (PGD), a technique that – as will be explained later – allows intending parents to identify genetic abnormalities in their *ex vivo* embryos. Since PGD requires that *in vitro* fertilisation (IVF) has been undertaken, some of the issues considered here will also touch on the general ethical and legal debate about assisted reproduction itself.

It is not uncommon for assisted reproductive techniques and technologies (ARTs) to be regulated by the state. Most, albeit not all, Western countries in which such services are available have legislated to control their availability. By and large, the impetus for regulation has come from a desire to respect the embryo of the human species and – albeit indirectly – to protect the child the embryo might become. While no doubt a laudable aim, few if any legislatures seem to have approached this subject with procreative liberty firmly at the forefront of their contemplation. This may seem rather strange, especially given that the history of the last 100 years is littered with egregious state interventions into the freedom of people to make reproductive decisions for themselves, and marked by a robust and largely successful struggle for recognition of the importance of liberty in this highly sensitive and personal area.

It seems unarguable that – for those who wish to – the ability to reproduce and become a parent is of fundamental importance. Not only does the future of humanity depend on human reproduction, the fulfilment of passing on one's genes to future generations and rearing children is, for many, a profoundly important aspect of their own humanity. Sadly, for some people meeting this aspiration is functionally impossible. For many of them, however, modern medicine has the capacity to circumvent the problems of infertility.

However, it may not be entirely surprising that when the birth of Louise Brown, the world's first 'test tube baby', was announced in 1978, the response was at best cautious and at worst condemnatory. Some (often loud and organised) commentary accused doctors of 'playing God', by seeking to circumvent infertility. This opposition often, but by no means always, came from faith groups for whom any such interference in God's plan was anathema. Others have condemned healthcare services for using resources on something that they did not regard as an illness; rather it was said to be a life preference. That people might suffer debilitating psychological trauma as a result of their inability to conceive is, on this argument, dismissed as not being of sufficient seriousness to merit the use of scarce healthcare resources. Others were concerned about the possible effect of the technology on the embryo, and by implication, the ensuing child. Manipulating the embryo was seen as likely to cause harm which would mean that any children born following ART would likely suffer from some disorder or disability. Still others objected to the fact that IVF almost always entails the selection of specific embryos and the storing or destruction of those not chosen for implantation, and of course the whole process was intimately linked to embryo research which generated its own specific objections. Certainly, the UK's Warnock Report (1978) adopted what might be called a precautionary approach when invited to report on the new technologies. The committee, in fact, seemed to have more or less taken it for granted that regulation (legislation) was necessary in this area, without much in the way of argument as to why that should be the case, what principles should inform regulation or what shape the legislation should take.

Not all was doom and gloom, however. For some, the potential of ART was thoroughly to be welcomed as a means of overcoming involuntary childlessness. Over the years, while there are still those who disapprove of ART – usually on grounds similar to those expressed from the beginning – it seems by and large to have been accepted that embryos are not harmed by IVF, nor are they treated carelessly by clinicians or intending parents. A significant number of healthy children have now been born following IVF, providing infertile individuals and couples with a much wanted family.

Of course, like any technology, it was always probable that the techniques available would expand, as well as be refined. Scientists are rarely content to rest on their laurels and the drive to improve the quality of pregnancies and their outcome led, importantly, to the development of the technique of PGD, which is the focus of this book. PGD, while not particularly common, permits couples at risk of transmitting genetic disease to their offspring to have their *ex vivo* embryos examined at a very early stage to detect whether or not they are likely to be affected and (generally) to select for implantation only unaffected embryos. It can also be used for other purposes, such as to create a so-called 'saviour sibling' or select for or against a particular sex, but screening out affected embryos to avoid the birth of children with, sometimes devastating, conditions is by far the most common reason for the use of PGD.

Like IVF, the common response to PGD was to regulate its availability and use. As will be seen in what follows, however, PGD has come to occupy a particularly significant role in the activities of legislators and regulators. While

IVF is now probably seen as a relatively routine part of medical care, and is often regulated relatively loosely, PGD has been a specific focus of regulatory scrutiny; arguably, a focus that is disproportionate to any purported or actual risks or harms associated with it.

It is this regulatory approach that we seek to explore here, by analysing not only the general ethical and legal issues raised by PGD, but also by addressing some of the developments which have seemingly rendered it increasingly controversial. By examining these, we will explore the suggestion that PGD is overly regulated, even in its more obviously contentious applications, such as sex selection. The specific procedure of PGD also allows reflection on the wider principles and policies that underpin ART and reproductive decisions in general.

We are indebted to the Brocher Foundation, Geneva, Switzerland for its generous support of a seminar which allowed us to develop the genesis of this book and to discuss in congenial surroundings the ideas that inform it.

1 Pre-implantation genetic diagnosis: safely born but not designed

Peter Braude

Introduction

The possible uses of assisted conception technology – *in vitro* fertilisation (IVF) – have changed in breadth dramatically since its first intended application and clinical success in 1978: namely, to overcome infertility caused by tubal disease.[1] There has been a rapid expansion in its use for the treatment of infertility, including alleviation of male infertility using intracytoplasmic sperm injection (ICSI).[2] There are now over 50,000 cycles conducted each year in the UK,[3] and in the USA around 150,000.[4] It is estimated that over 3.5 million babies have been born worldwide following IVF.

With the increasing confidence as to its application and safety, the possibility already mooted in press coverage in the early days of IVF – that access to the embryo *in vitro* might provide an alternative means of preventing transmission of genetic disease – has become a reality. Proof of concept that embryos carrying X-linked diseases could be sexed, and only female embryos transferred, thus avoiding the birth of affected males, was demonstrated in 1968.[5] However, it was with the advent of novel molecular technologies such as fluorescence *in situ* hybridisation (FISH) and amplification of deoxyribonucleic acid (DNA) using the polymerase chain reaction (PCR),[6] that the breadth and potential scale of the tests that could be offered became

1 Edwards, R. G., Steptoe, P. C. and Purdy, J. M. 'Establishing full-term human pregnancies using cleaving embryos grown *in vitro*', *British Journal of Obstetrics and Gynaecology*, 87 (1980): 737–56.

2 Devroey, P. and Van Steirteghem, A., 'A review of ten years' experience of ICSI', *Hum Reprod Update*, 10(1) (2004): 19–28.

3 HFEA, Fertility facts and figures 2008, www.hfea.gov.uk/docs/2010-12-8_Fertility_Facts_and_Figures_2008_Publication_PDF.PDF (accessed 10/01/2012).

4 Society for assisted reproduction (SART) Center for Disease Control, Atlanta, www.cdc.gov/art/ART2008/PDF/ART_2008_Full.pdf

5 Gardner, R. L. and Edwards, R. G., 'Control of the sex ratio at full term in the rabbit by transferring sexed blastocysts', *Nature*, 218(5139) (1968): 346–9.

6 Muggleton-Harris, A., Glazier, A., Pickering, S. and Wall, M., 'Genetic diagnosis using polymerase chain reaction and fluorescent in-situ hybridization analysis of biopsied cells from both the cleavage and blastocyst stages of individual cultured human preimplantation embryos', *Human Reproduction*, (10)(1) (1995): 183–92.

apparent as a clinical reality.[7] FISH on the interphase nucleus of a single biopsied cell allowed sexing to be undertaken by amplifying specific sequences on the Y chromosome.[8] Indeed, the first two successful pregnancies achieved after using this method to test embryos coincidentally occurred during the passage of the Human Fertilisation and Embryology Act 1990[9] in the UK, and probably significantly influenced the discussions in the UK Parliament. For the first time parliamentarians and the public could see important medical uses for the technology, rather than relying on speculation and theory. Its successful application in these cases probably facilitated the relatively permissive legislation that exists today in the UK.[10]

The very power of this technology to amplify even the most minute amount of DNA, in itself produced a raft of difficulties of precision – specific and stringent precautions had to be put in place to avoid amplifying extraneous DNA, such as from the operator, in order to prevent false diagnoses. Equally, there was the inherent danger that absence of a signal due to amplification failure could be misinterpreted in diagnosis; for example, in tests for sex-linked disorders, the absence of the appearance of a Y signal could lead to the erroneous assumption that the embryo was female and suitable for transfer, which proved to be the case in the early days of sexing by PCR.[11] By the mid-1990s, the alternative technique of FISH, whereby coloured fluorescent complementary DNA probes could be used to identify highly specific areas within interphase nuclear chromosomes,[12] simplified the means of making a sexing diagnosis,[13] and its application soon expanded to use in translocations[14] and aneuploidy screening using a variety of different probes.[15]

The use of these powerful genetic technologies has expanded horizons, not only in being able to help further in enabling procreation, but also in areas

7 McLaren, A., 'Prenatal diagnosis before implantation: opportunities and problems', *Prenatal Diagnosis*, 5 (1985): 85–90.

8 Griffin, D. K., Handyside, A. H., Penketh, R. J. A., Winston, R. M. L. and Delhanty, J. D. A., 'Fluorescent in-situ hybridization to interphase nuclei of human preimplantation embryos with X and Y chromosome specific probes', *Human Reproduction*, 6 (1991): 101–5.

9 Handyside, A. H., Kontogianni, E. H., Hardy, K. and Winston, R. M. L., 'Pregnancies from biopsied human preimplantation embryos sexed by Y-specific DNA amplification', *Nature*, (344) (1990): 768–70.

10 Arguably, the 2008 amendments to the 1990 legislation have rendered the law less permissive.

11 Wilton, L., Thornhill, A., Traeger-Synodinos, J., Sermon, K. D. and Harper, J. C., 'The causes of misdiagnosis and adverse outcomes in PGD', *Hum Reprod*, 24(5) (2009): 1221–8.

12 Reid, T., Landes, G., Duckowski, W., Klinger, K. and Ward, D., 'Multicolour fluorescence in situ hybridisation for the simultaneous detection of probe sets for chromosomes 13, 18, 21, X and Y uncultured amniotic fluid cells', *Human Molecular Genetics*, 1 (1992): 307–13.

13 Griffin, D. K., Wilton, L. J., Handyside, A. H., Atkinson, G. H. G., Winston, R. M. L. and Delhanty, J. D. A., 'Diagnosis of sex in preimplantation embryos by fluorescent in situ hybridisation', *BMJ*, 306 (1993): 1382.

14 Mackie Ogilvie, C. and Scriven, P. N., 'Preimplantation genetic diagnosis (PGD) for reciprocal translocations', *Prenatal Diagnosis*, 24(7) (2004): 553–5.

15 Munne, S. and Weier, H. U., 'Simultaneous enumeration of chromosomes 13, 18, 21, X, and Y in interphase cells for preimplantation genetic diagnosis of aneuploidy', *Cytogenet Cell Genet*, 75(4) (1996): 263–70.

outside of conventional reproductive biology. These advances also present new ethical and legal dilemmas.

Pre-implantation genetic diagnosis (PGD)

PGD is an early alternative to prenatal diagnosis (PND) and is currently deemed suitable for a small group of patients who are at substantial risk of conceiving a pregnancy affected by a known genetic disorder.[16] To label PGD as it is presently performed as the pursuit of 'designer babies' is to misunderstand its methodology, and the serious and often lethal genetic diseases that can be prevented by its use.

Genetic disease may result from a new mutation in the genes that manifests as disease in an offspring for the first time in the family. More commonly it is passed on by the parents; either via one parent in a dominantly inherited condition, in which case that parent will have, or will develop the disorder, or in a recessively inherited condition where both parents will be carriers of the condition although not manifesting the disease itself. For a child to inherit the condition will require it to inherit a mutated gene from each parent, which would happen approximately one-quarter of the time. Some diseases are sex linked. Here, the mutated gene is carried on the X chromosome, which in females can be balanced by their other (normal) X and hence generally they do not manifest the disease, although they are carriers for it and can pass it on to their children. Should that mutation be inherited by a male child, where the Y chromosome does not carry information to balance it, the boy will be affected by the disease.

A number of factors will influence when and to what extent a mutation might produce disease. In some cases the effect of the mutation may not manifest until late in adult life (such as Huntington's disease (HD)), whereas in others it may appear early in childhood (for example, spinal muscular atrophy), or even *in utero*. It is also possible that the effects of the mutation may be so mild as not to be recognised or, where it is picked up, to be of no concern. In others, its appearance as a disease may be so variable that the detection of a mutation can only convey a susceptibility, rather than a definitive diagnosis that it will occur (e.g. some breast cancer genes).

There is a vast list of genetic conditions caused by gene mutations, for which there is now the technology to enable diagnosis on a single cell, thus making the use of PGD a possibility. However, the application of PGD to each of these conditions may present different and often unique ethical dilemmas; for example, these will be affected by whether the disease will manifest in early death or physical and mental compromise, in which sex and at what age, whether carriers manifest symptoms, and whether there is any treatment for the disease. Besides inheritance of a single gene mutation, it may be the case

16 Lashwood, A., 'Preimplantation genetic diagnosis to prevent disorders in children', *Br J Nurs*, 14(2) (2005): 64–70.

that a whole chromosome is inherited incorrectly resulting in aneuploidy (number imbalance), or only part of a particular chromosome may be abnormal resulting in a chromosomal rearrangement (translocation, deletion, inversion). The effects of aneuploidy or rearrangement can be lethal, or result in identifiable syndromes causing mental and physical disability, or early or late miscarriage. Chromosome aberrations might be sporadic (*de novo*), or result from environmental effects or advancing age, or may be inherited; it is sufficient for one of the couple to pass on the imbalance for it to manifest. In rearrangements, the likelihood that they will be passed on and manifest as disease is highly variable, being dependent on the random nature of meiotic segregation, and the gamete involved in the fertilisation process – egg or sperm. It is generally more difficult for couples to comprehend this inheritance and the unpredictability of whether or not their offspring will be affected,[17] when compared with those disorders where there is a more defined inheritance – one in four, or one in two.

For couples affected by genetic disease the choices are stark. They can play genetic roulette and take the one in four, one in two, or random chance of having a child who manifests the condition. Alternatively, they could take the chance but decide to terminate an affected pregnancy. It may also be possible to substitute one partner's set of gametes – that is, to opt for egg or sperm donation. In some cases, the choice may be to remain childless. PGD provides a further option, meaning that intending parents can choose to have an embryo created *in vitro*, tested before implantation and only those embryos found to be unaffected by the disease made available for replacement into the uterus, with the intention of establishing a pregnancy.

A sample for genetic analysis may be taken from an egg, a cleavage stage embryo, or from the blastocyst – the immediate pre-implantation stage of development (day 5), where the tissues have differentiated into the inner cell mass (ICM) from which the true embryo/foetus will develop, and the surrounding trophectoderm, from which placenta and other extraembryonic tissues will form.

A single cell of the eight or so to which the embryo will have cleaved by day 3 *in vitro*, is easily accessible and removable after a hole is made in the shell (*zona pellucida*) which surrounds each embryo. This can be done by using an acidified medium or a laser. Early evidence suggests that the loss of a blastomere does not harm the embryo, as its further development is still plastic and uncommitted. However, the removal of more than one blastomere may be detrimental to the establishment of a pregnancy.[18] Removal of a portion of the trophectoderm as a

17 Scriven, P. N., Handyside, A. H. and Ogilvie, C. M., 'Chromosome translocations: segregation modes and strategies for preimplantation genetic diagnosis', *Prenatal Diagnosis*, 18(13) (1998): 1437–9.

18 Goossens, V., De Rycke, M., De Vos, A., Staessen, C., Michiels, A. and Verpoest, W. *et al.*, 'Diagnostic efficiency, embryonic development and clinical outcome after the biopsy of one or two blastomeres for preimplantation genetic diagnosis', *Hum Reprod*, 23(3) (2008): 481–92.

biopsy on day 5 has the practical advantage that fewer embryos will be available, as not all fertilised eggs progress to this stage, thus reducing the load on the laboratory. Equally, each of these embryos has better developmental potential to have reached this stage *in vitro*. The disadvantage is that the diagnosis will either have to be made within 24 hours in order to enable use to be made of the limited implantation window (by day 6), or the embryo will need to be frozen for subsequent replacement if that time interval cannot be met.[19] Removal of the first polar body (and preferably also the second polar body) is easily effected at the time of fertilisation, and will reveal information from the maternally transmitted genome.[20] It can also reveal important transmissible meiotic chromosome errors that account for the majority of sporadic aneuploidies.[21]

The clinical results reported for PGD vary, and depend on the type of disease being tested for, the experience of the clinic and, like IVF in general, substantially on the age of the female patient, from whom the eggs are obtained and into whom the embryo(s) are replaced.[22] As might be expected, with recessive disease around 75 per cent of the embryos may be found to have a genetically transferable result (being normal or carrier). Around the same number is likely for sex-linked disorders where molecular technology is used, so allowing unaffected males also to be detected. The pregnancy rate is reduced in sex selection and in dominant disease, where around one in two embryos might be expected not to be transferable, and is even lower for reciprocal translocations where the risk is variable, but where the odds are stacked against normality. At our Centre for Preimplantation Genetic Diagnosis at Guy's Hospital London, only 65 per cent of the embryos from reciprocal translocations are transferable. The odds of a successful pregnancy following transfer are of the same order as those when unbiopsied embryos are transferred for infertile couples using IVF, and depend largely on the quality of the embryo, itself largely dictated by how many eggs were retrieved and fertilised, thus allowing for more choice in selection of the one (or two) healthy embryos for transfer. The outcomes for children born following embryo biopsy for PGD are reassuring, as PGD does not appear to affect development.[23]

19 Schoolcraft, W. B., Fragouli, E., Stevens, J., Munne, S., Katz-Jaffe, M. G. and Wells, D., 'Clinical application of comprehensive chromosomal screening at the blastocyst stage', *Fertility and Sterility*, 94(5) (2010): 1700–6.

20 Verlinsky, Y., Ginsberg, N., Lifchez, A., Valle, J., Moise, J. and Strom, C. M., 'Analysis of the first polar body: preconception genetic diagnosis', *Hum Reprod*, 5(7) (1990): 826–9.

21 Verlinsky, Y., Cieslak, J., Freidine, M., Ivakhnenko, V., Wolf, G. and Kovalinskaya, L. *et al.*, 'Polar body diagnosis of common aneuploidies by FISH', *J Assist Reprod Genet*, 13(2) (1996): 157–62.

22 Harper, J. C., Coonen, E., De Rycke, M., Harton, G., Moutou, C. and Pehlivan, T. *et al.*, 'ESHRE PGD Consortium data collection X: cycles from January to December 2007 with pregnancy follow-up to October 2008', *Hum Reprod*, 25(11) (2010): 2685–707.

23 Liebaers, I., Desmyttere, S., Verpoest, W. De Rycke, M., Staessen, C. and Sermon, K. *et al.*, 'Report on a consecutive series of 581 children born after blastomere biopsy for preimplantation genetic diagnosis', *Hum Reprod*, 25(1) (2010): 275–82.

However, this technology has raised other more controversial uses,[24] some of which are briefly summarised here. While the technology may be well established, and apparently safe, the consequences of its application remain controversial, at least for some.

Saviour siblings

HLA (human leukocyte antigen) typing of embryos is undertaken in order to find one for transfer which has a tissue match to a sibling with a life-threatening genetic or other disorder that might be ameliorated or cured by transplantation of stem cells obtained from the umbilical cord blood of the born child.[25] Considerable hype has surrounded these techniques and they have been the subject of public, regulatory, parliamentary, ethical and legal debate.[26] [27] However their use is limited, partly because of the infrequency of the need – since in many cases matching stem cells may be available from international bone marrow banks – and the poor odds of finding an embryo match (three in eight) when PGD with tissue-typing is required. This is aggravated further by the fact that, when required, it may be by older women as they already have one or more children, and their response to ovarian stimulation is waning. In addition, if the child suffers from an acute illness such as leukaemia, there may not be sufficient time to perform the IVF, type the embryo by PGD and achieve a successful match and a live birth.[28] Notwithstanding this, there have been many clinical successes which have transformed lives,[29] [30] but the long-term personal outcome for the family dynamic is still unexplored, as sensationalised in the novel *My Sister's Keeper.*[31]

Social sex selection

The availability of PGD makes it possible to select embryos based on their sex. While this may be used to avoid the transmission of genetic disease, it could

24 El-Toukhy, T., Williams, C. and Braude, P., 'The ethics of preimplantation genetic diagnosis', *Obstetrician and Gynaecologist*, 10 (2008): 49–54.
25 Rechitsky, S., Kuliev, A., Tur-Kaspa, I., Morris, R. and Verlinsky, Y., 'Preimplantation genetic diagnosis with HLA matching', *Reprod Biomed Online*, 9(2) (2004): 210–21.
26 Sheldon, S., 'Saviour siblings and the discretionary power of the HFEA', *Medical Law Review*, 13(3) (2005): 403–11.
27 www.spuc.org.uk/about/no-less-human/hlaqanda.pdf (accessed 10/01/2012).
28 Samuel, G. N., Strong, K. A., Kerridge, I., Jordens, C. F., Ankeny, R. A. and Shaw, P. J., 'Establishing the role of pre-implantation genetic diagnosis with human leucocyte antigen typing: what place do "saviour siblings" have in paediatric transplantation?', *Arch Dis Child*, 94(3) (2009): 317–20.
29 Van de Velde, H., De Rycke, M., De Man, C., De Hauwere, K., Fiorentino, F. and Kahraman, S. *et al.*, 'The experience of two European preimplantation genetic diagnosis centres on human leukocyte antigen typing', *Hum Reprod*, 24(3) (2009): 732–40.
30 Rechitsky, S., Kuliev, A., Sharapova, T., Laziuk, K., Ozen, S. and Barsky, I. *et al.*, 'Preimplantation HLA typing with aneuploidy testing', *Reprod Biomed Online*, 12(1) (2006): 89–100.
31 Picoult, J., *My Sister's Keeper*, London: Hodder, 2009.

also be used to select embryos purely because of sex, for example for 'family balancing'. In some families there may be a preponderance of children of one sex, where the parents might wish for a child of the other, and the possibility of sex selection through assisted conception technology is a topic of considerable debate.[32 33] Whereas the American Society of Reproductive Medicine does not oppose the use of preconception techniques such as sperm sorting to couples 'who are seeking gender variety in their offspring',[34] neither it nor the American College of Obstetricians and Gynecologists condones the use of PGD for non-medical purposes.[35 36] Where there is a significant preferential desire for a child or children of one sex – usually male such as in the Middle East,[37] China[38] and India[39] – different rules are generally regarded as necessary to avoid the discrimination that a preference for one sex (usually male) over the other would generate. Although opposition to sex selection for non-medical reasons is not universal,[40] it remains impermissible in many jurisdictions and is specifically outlawed by the Human Fertilisation and Embryology Act 2008 in the UK.

Late-onset disease

Some genetic diseases may only manifest late in life, perhaps in the forties or fifties, such as HD. Since there are many years of good life that may be enjoyed prior to the development of symptoms, some question whether it is appropriate to seek to prevent the birth of people who will not become ill until relatively late in life, or whether it can be justified to discard 'affected' embryos on this basis. However, this is not the only issue arising from testing for this condition.

People who are at risk of HD, because they have a parent with the condition, may not themselves know or wish to know whether they will be affected in due

32 Ethics Committee of the American Society of Reproductive Medicine, 'Sex selection and preimplantation genetic diagnosis', *Fertility and Sterility*, 72(4) (1999): 595–8.

33 Savulescu, J. and Dahl, E., 'Sex selection and preimplantation diagnosis: a response to the Ethics Committee of the American Society of Reproductive Medicine', *Hum Reprod*, 15(9) (2000): 1879–80.

34 'Preconception gender selection for non-medical reasons: Ethics Committee report', *Fertility and Sterility*, 75(5) (2001): 861–4.

35 'Committee on Ethics, American College of Obstetricians and Gynecologists. ACOG Committee Opinion No. 360: sex selection', *Obstet Gynecol*, 109 (2007): 475–8.

36 Malpani, A., 'Preimplantation genetic diagnosis for gender selection for family balancing: a view from India', *Reprod Biomed Online*, 4(1) (2002): 7–9.

37 Kilani, Z. and Haj Hassan, L., 'Sex selection and preimplantation genetic diagnosis at the Farah Hospital', *Reprod Biomed Online*, 4(1) (2002): 68–70.

38 Sen, A., 'More than 100 million women are missing', *New York Review of Books*, 37 (1990): 61–8.

39 Malpani, A. and Modi, D., 'The use of preimplantation genetic diagnosis in sex selection for family balancing in India', *Reprod Biomed Online*, 4(1) (2002): 16–20.

40 Robertson, J. A., 'Gender variety as a valid choice: a comment on the HFEA – response to Edgar Dahl's "The presumption in favour of liberty"', *Reprod Biomed Online*, 8(3) (2004): 270–1.

course. However, despite not wishing to have a predictive HD test, they may wish that any children they might have will not be at risk of the condition. Although there are some PGD units which may be willing to undertake non-disclosure testing, this requires not only a secret to be kept by the testing centre, but might also require collusion of the IVF unit in procedures that may be ethically and medically dubious.[41] If they find that all the embryos they have tested are normal, thus making it highly unlikely that the partner thought to be at risk has the disease and thus does not require IVF and PGD, should the woman not become pregnant, the clinic would be bound to recommend further (but unnecessary) treatment as part of the non-disclosure deal. Alternatively, should HD be found, thus conferring a diagnosis on the at-risk partner, a sham replacement would have to be undertaken in order not to reveal the fact, if there were no embryos suitable for transfer. As a result of these difficulties, some units prefer to make the diagnosis by use of genetic linkage to grandparental alleles.[42] In this way, embryos can be excluded from transfer if they contain a pattern indicating transmission from the affected grandparent. However, in this case only half of the linked embryos would be likely to be affected by HD, but all of them, even if they were normal, would be required to be excluded from transfer. This in itself gives some cause for concern. Both approaches have further repercussions. If it is the male partner who is at risk, but does not wish for predictive testing, it is the healthy female partner who will go through rounds of IVF and PGD and possibly remain childless, even if the man has not inherited the gene. The potential unfairness of this scenario is often overlooked, and is one reason for the opposition to non-disclosure or exclusion testing for such conditions. Specific reference to this appears in the Human Fertilisation and Embryology Authority's Code of Practice.

> In exceptional circumstances the centre may offer PGD, but withhold the patient's test results (PGD with non-disclosure). However, this should only be offered under the following conditions:
>
> (a) that patients are given the opportunity to receive genetic counselling on the implications prior to giving consent,
> (b) that protocols are established to limit, as far as possible, the risk of unwanted disclosure to the patients. Centres should consider using a different embryology laboratory from their own, in order to minimise the number of centre staff who know the patient's genetic status, and
> (c) that no dummy embryo transfers are to be performed.[43]

41 Braude, P. R., De Wert, G. M., Evers-Kiebooms, G., Pettigrew, R. A. and Geraedts, J. P., 'Non-disclosure preimplantation genetic diagnosis for Huntington's disease: practical and ethical dilemmas', *Prenatal Diagnosis*, 18(3) (1998): 1422–6.

42 Asscher, E. and Koops, B. J., 'The right not to know and preimplantation genetic diagnosis for Huntington's disease', *J Med Ethics*, 36(1) (2010): 30–3.

43 Eighth edition, www.hfea.gov.uk/code.html (accessed 30/01/2012), para. 10.9.

PGD and second-generation risk

In recessive or sex-linked conditions, gene carriers may not manifest with the condition but can pass on the mutation to their offspring. In recessive diseases, the risk to the next generation only manifests should the person decide to have children with another who is also a carrier of the same condition, albeit not necessarily with the same mutation. Similarly in sex-linked disorders, where the disorder is carried by the woman, but only expresses in male offspring, there may be a request not to replace carrier female embryos, so as to eliminate the risk from the next generation. Once again there may be disquiet about discarding embryos that are essentially normal and will not, or will be very unlikely to, manifest the condition.[44]

Genetic predisposition

The development of certain serious medical disorders has a clear genetic element, for example, breast cancer and polyposis coli leading to colon cancer. Although the presence of the relevant gene may not inevitably lead to the manifestation of disease, as other factors may need to work in concert for it to manifest (penetrate), there may be a desire on behalf of the individual who has seen the devastation and damage that the disorder has wreaked on the family, to request testing in order to avoid transmission of the disease to their offspring. Whereas there may be a strong motivation to request testing – say for BRCA1 (Breast Cancer Gene 1) which is associated with breast and ovarian cancer – to prevent occurrence in daughters, opponents argue that notwithstanding the seriousness of that condition there may be other either less penetrant genes or less serious disorders, that do not justify the discarding of healthy embryos for that purpose.[45]

Pre-implantation genetic screening (PGS)

The most common use of embryo biopsy is not aimed specifically at prevention of the transmission of recurrent genetic disease, but rather at identification of those embryos that carry such severe sporadic chromosome abnormalities that would prevent early development and implantation and lead to infertility or recurrent pregnancy loss. This technique has a flawless logic: if one could exclude from transfer after IVF those embryos likely to have a significant chromosomal imbalance (aneuploidy), then the transfer of euploid embryos should increase the chances of a successful pregnancy.[46] Since sporadic

44 Watt, H., 'Preimplantation genetic diagnosis: choosing the "good enough" child', *Health Care Anal*, 12(1) (2004): 51–60.

45 Braude, P., 'Preimplantation diagnosis for genetic susceptibility', *N Engl J Med*, 355(6) (2006): 541–3.

46 Munne, S., Sultan, K. M., Weier, H. U., Grifo, J. A., Cohen, J. and Rosenwaks, Z., 'Assessment of numeric abnormalities of X, Y, 18, and 16 chromosomes in preimplantation

aneuploidy is known to increase with increasing maternal age (e.g. Down syndrome (DS)), it has been postulated that PGS would be most effective in older women for whom IVF is least effective.

However, despite the plausibility of the theory, the use of cleavage stage biopsy for this purpose has been shown to be unreliable, mainly due to chromosomal variation (mosaicism) between different cells within the same early embryo. PGS relies on the assumption that each cell of the early cleaving embryo is identical, such that the chromosomal make-up of the biopsied cell is representative of the embryo as a whole. This has proved not to be the case and there are significant differences within embryos, thus resulting in diagnostic differences depending on which cell is biopsied.[47] In addition, the number of FISH probes that can be used in any one phase of analysis is limited; thus only a limited number of chromosomes, usually five to nine, might be tested, and loss or gain of any of the others might still result in unexpected (undiagnosed) aneuploid embryos. Thus some embryos may be excluded from transfer inappropriately, reducing the overall chances of a pregnancy. This sporadic risk of the embryo or a cell within the embryo being aneuploid contrasts with inherited aneuploidies or chromosome rearrangements for which PGD is suitable.

The application of modern genetic technology such as comparative genome hybridisation by gene chip arrays, especially if undertaken at the blastocyst stage, could obviate some of the artefact, as all 24 chromosomes can be analysed and more cells can be taken for analysis. However, the use of such technology to test for euploidy will provide far more genetic information than is being sought. Not only is information provided about chromosome number and chromosome breaks, but much more detailed sensitive genetic information is available to be revealed. Specific information about the commonly inherited disorders such as cystic fibrosis and sickle disease will be easy to obtain, but so too will information about genetic predispositions and new mutations. Although it is likely that only a tiny fraction of these will reveal unexpected disorders that will be inherited by the offspring, it is unlikely that the couple will have received genetic counselling appropriate to genetic discoveries ahead of the procedure. Even if they are counselled at the time of diagnosis, they will not have the time to consider the options appropriately, as a decision as to transfer or freezing will need to made immediately. In addition, carrier status may be revealed, which may force choices about whether or not to consider obviating that disorder from the couple's germ line by not replacing embryos that only carry the disorder but may be unaffected with the disease. Herein lies a major difference between PGD and PGS. Whereas in PGD the couple

human embryos before transfer', *Am J Obstet Gynecol*, 172(4 Pt 1) (1995): 1191–9; discussion at pp. 1199–201.

47 Vanneste, E., Voet, T., Le Caignec, C., Ampe, M., Konings, P. and Melotte, C. *et al.*, 'Chromosome instability is common in human cleavage-stage embryos', *Nat Med*, 15(5) (2009): 5777–83.

seek to avoid a specific genetic condition that has affected them, their offspring or other members of their extended family, the move from simply trying to improve IVF outcome for the infertile by using PGS can produce a more complex set of genetic diagnoses and present more difficult decisions about the child that they wish to have. Such information could also reveal unexpected and unwanted information about the parents themselves. For example, within the extraordinary detail available might be the fact that one parent has a late-onset genetic disorder that he or she will in due course suffer from. This information, which was not sought primarily, will likely have a huge impact on the parents themselves and possibly on other members of the family.

The concern is that with automation and reduction in costs, eventually these methods will become the norm and will present society and the professionals involved with ethical difficulties in handling this additional, and usually unexpected, medical information.[48]

Mitochondrial disease

Mitochondrial malfunction has been recognised as a significant cause of a number of serious multi-organ diseases. Although relatively rare, their seriousness and unusual inheritance pattern has made genetically inherited mitochondrial diseases a focus for the application of pre-implantation technology. However, the fact that mitochondrial disease is maternally inherited in a non-nuclear way, presents unique issues that will challenge legal and scientific orthodoxy.

Mitochondria are the energy-producing organelles in the cytoplasm of every mammalian cell and contain small amounts of DNA. The inheritance and regulation of this mitochondrial DNA (mtDNA) is different from information that is inherited as chromosomes in the nucleus of the cell. First, mtDNA is transmitted solely from the mother in the egg (maternally inherited), and second, its usual function is dependent on the amount or nature of the mitochondria in each cell. Mitochondria containing either mutant or normal mtDNA may exist within the same cell (heteroplasmy), or all the mtDNA may all be the same (homoplasmy), either mutant or normal. The severity of most mitochondrial genetic diseases is dictated by the proportion of mutant to normal mitochondria within the cells, and that proportion may deteriorate in favour of disease with time. Thus, many of these diseases may manifest late or may increase in severity with age. There may also be variations in heteroplasmy between tissues, perhaps resulting in specific manifestations of the disease according to the most affected organ or system. The worst forms of mitochondrial disease may be associated with totally abnormal mitochondria; homoplasmic for a particular mutation.[49]

48 Human Genetics Commission, *Increasing Options, Informing Choice: A Report on Preconception Genetic Testing and Screening*, London: HGC, April 2011.

49 Taylor, R. W. and Turnbull, D. M., 'Mitochondrial DNA mutations in human disease', *Nat Rev Genet*, 6(5) (2005): 389–402.

The use of PGD to seek to identify mitochondrial disease aims to measure the proportion of heteroplasmy in the embryonic cell removed as a biopsy, and in so doing avoid replacing embryos with levels which would manifest disease in the resulting child or adult. However, PGD is too new a technique to be certain that the cell removed is always representative of the whole embryo, although early indications suggest that it may be. The diagnostic level for exclusion from transfer is based on the proportion of mutant mtDNA within the biopsy, and will need to be set based on a best estimate of mitochondrial proportions associated with health rather than disease. This may differ for different mutations and different clinical presentations, and this is where PGD for mitochondrial mtDNA differs from PGD that examines well understood patterns of gene inheritance. Apart from variations in penetrance and expression, a nuclear gene disease manifests with a predictable pattern of inheritance (recessive, dominant, X linked) and embryos will, or will not, manifest with the disease depending on whether they do or do not contain the mutation. In mitochondrial genetic disease, however, it may not always be possible to set a precise proportion of heteroplasmy that will guarantee the offspring to be disease free into adult life, but also set high enough still to allow the probability of finding some embryos that fulfil the criteria for safe replacement. Rather than aiming specifically at avoidance of transmission of the mutation and thus disease prevention, PGD for mitochondrial heteroplasmy can only be aimed at risk reduction. Ethical dilemmas and subsequent legal dilemmas may arise where the only embryos available exceed the proportion previously recommended for safe transfer, raising questions such as is it better to remain childless, or should embryos with a slightly higher but unquantifiable risk for later life be transferred and should it be left to the parents, a regulator or the law to make such decisions?

PGD is inappropriate where the proportion of mtDNA is so high as to be virtually complete (homoplasmy for the mutation). In such cases, the only safe way for the couple to reproduce is either by the use of mutation-free donated oocytes, thus avoiding the mutant mtDNA but at the 'expense' of relinquishing also the inheritance of the woman's nuclear DNA, or by transfer of the woman's or the couple's nuclear genetic material (spindle or pronuclei respectively) into fresh ooplasm from a donated oocyte, where transmission of the mutated mitochondria is avoided, but the couple's own character-carrying nuclear DNA is retained. Currently this has only been demonstrated as proof of principle in non-human primates, where healthy live young have been born,[50] or by using reconstituted abnormally fertilised human oocytes to mimic the procedure,[51] which would require the used of donated human eggs and the transfer of the

50 Tachibana, M., Sparman, M., Sritanaudomchai, H., Ma, H., Clepper, L. and Woodward, J. *et al.*, 'Mitochondrial gene replacement in primate offspring and embryonic stem cells', *Nature*, 461(7262) (2009): 367–72.

51 Craven, L., Tuppen, H. A., Greggains, G. D., Harbottle, S. J., Murphy, J. L. and Cree, L. M. *et al.*, 'Pronuclear transfer in human embryos to prevent transmission of mitochondrial DNA disease', *Nature*, 465(7294) (2010): 82–5.

affected couple's pronuclei. In the UK, provision was made for the Human Fertilisation and Embryology Act 1990 to be amended by regulation such that this procedure could be allowed in principle.[52] The fact that this would be the first in human nuclear gene transfer, requires that its appropriateness and safety is fully evaluated before it is implemented as a clinical technique.[53]

Conclusion

Selection of human embryos *in vitro* for transfer after genetic testing is controversial but legal in many countries. While some see this as no different to the selection that inevitably will be made in order to find the 'best-quality' embryo – the one most likely to result in a pregnancy – following IVF for the alleviation of infertility, others view this as eugenic as it involves decisions about genetic appropriateness. Views about the inherent sanctity of life of the embryo at any stage and the corresponding need to protect it from interference or from any form of genetic selection because of past eugenic history may colour the type of legislation in particular countries. Moreover, the long-term effects of biological manipulation of the embryo will require generations for certainty. The difficulties lie in balancing decisions that satisfy a need or wish on behalf of intending parents with the health and well-being of any resulting children. This is somewhat eased by the knowledge that where the genetic disorder is serious enough, avoidance through pre-implantation selection may be the preferable option to either pregnancy termination or the birth of a child suffering from a serious inherited disorder.

52 Section 35A Human Fertilisation and Embryology Act 2008, www.legislation.gov.uk/ukpga/2008/22/part/1/crossheading/mitochondrial-donation (accessed 10/01/2012).
53 Bredenoord, A. L. and Braude, P., 'Ethics of mitochondrial gene replacement: from bench to bedside', *BMJ*, 341 (2010): c6021.

2 The weak moral basis for strong PGD regulation

Tom Campbell and Laura Cabrera

Introduction: the burden of proof

This critique of state regulation of pre-implantation genetic diagnosis (PGD) points to some weaknesses in the reasoning commonly used to support narrow and restrictive regulatory control. It sets out a presumptive case for broad reproductive rights with respect to PGD along the lines that prospective parents should be free to take such steps as they think fit to have what they regard as healthy and capable children, provided this does not cause undeniable harm, to these children or to other people, which is sufficiently serious to outweigh the presumptive case for reproductive freedom. Counter-arguments to this 'liberal' position are then argued to be flawed, or simply too weak to overcome the strong case for reproductive freedom with respect to PGD. A principal theme in the analysis is that moral considerations, which may reasonably be taken into account by those considering whether or not to avail themselves of the opportunities which PGD does, or may in the future, make available to them are erroneously used to make a case for legal restrictions which are based on no more than personal moral preferences, anxieties or dislikes.

'PGD' is adopted here as shorthand for the process of selecting embryos arising from *in vitro* fertilisation (IVF) for implantation in a woman and the intended development and birth of a child, the selection being done on the basis of scientific evidence relating to the genetic constitution of the embryos available for implantation. This distinguishes PGD from both prenatal diagnosis followed by the termination of the pregnancy, and from genetic modification of embryos.

Since the 1980s, PGD has been developed as an alternative option to more conventional and invasive prenatal diagnosis and allows couples to select an embryo on the basis of its genetic make-up and to commence a pregnancy knowing that their baby will not be affected by a specific unwanted genetic condition.[1] Currently, the main indication for PGD is unsuccessful infertility treatment where there is no identifiable cause in the male or female partner, for

1 McLean, S., *Modern Dilemmas: Choosing Children*, Edinburgh: Capercaillie, 2006.

couples where the female partner is of advanced reproductive age,[2] for couples who have had more than three unsuccessful IVF cycles, and for couples who have had unexplained spontaneous miscarriage.[3] Additionally, PGD is now commonly used for therapeutic purposes relating to inherited genetic conditions or chromosome abnormalities that are likely to give rise to serious illnesses or disabilities or premature death. PGD can be performed, in principle, for any genetic condition for which there is sufficient sequence information; thus the list of conditions for which PGD has been performed is growing rapidly.[4] The possible uses of PGD include testing for susceptibility to diseases and to late-onset conditions,[5] as well as sex-linked disorders.[6] It can also be used for human leukocyte antigen (HLA) matching where an existing child of the family is affected by a disorder. It is worth stressing that while PGD reduces risk for the condition for which testing is done, it does not predict congenital malformations or diseases that do not have an identified genetic basis or are not the subject of the inquiry.[7]

PGD is not a routine procedure, as it is neither easy nor inexpensive. In addition to this, it also carries some hazard for the embryos involved.[8] It is, however, a procedure that gives some couples a higher chance of a successful pregnancy than would be the case using only IVF, by facilitating selection of healthier embryos to be implanted, and it provides a less traumatic alternative to the termination of pregnancy where abnormalities have been detected following prenatal diagnosis. Further, although PGD still contributes only a small fraction to prenatal diagnosis generally,[9] it has the potential to reduce the occurrence of many major chromosomal aberrations and monogenic diseases worldwide.

Nevertheless, while most people who have considered the matter agree that employing PGD for assisting IVF and for therapeutic screening of embryos is justifiable, there is some disquiet at the use of PGD for other purposes, such as sex selection and 'enhancement'. The latter term refers to selection based on characteristics that go beyond the scope of securing average health. At present,

2 Staessen, C., Platteau, P. and Van Assche, E. *et al.*, 'Comparison of blastocyst transfer with or without preimplantation genetic diagnosis for aneuploidy screening in couples with advanced maternal age: a prospective randomized controlled trial', *Human Reproduction*, 19(12) (2004): 2849–58.

3 Cram D. and Pope, A., 'Preimplantation genetic diagnosis: current and future perspectives', *JLM*, 15(1) (2007): 36–44. For further discussion, see Chapter 2 in this volume.

4 Zhuang, G. and Zhang, D., 'PGD', *International Journal of Gynecology and Obstetrics*, 82(3) (2003): 419–23, at p. 420.

5 J. Snelling, 'Preimplantation genetic diagnosis for susceptibility conditions: a new frontier or a logical extension?', *JLM*, 16(2) (2008): 263–78.

6 McLean, *Modern Dilemmas*. For further discussion, see Chapter 1 in this volume.

7 Draper, H. and Chadwick, R., 'Beware! Preimplantation genetic diagnosis may solve some old problems but it also raises new ones', *J Med Ethics*, 25 (1999): 114–20.

8 Botkin, J., 'Ethical issues and practical problems in preimplantation genetic diagnosis', *J L Med & Ethics*, 26(1) (1998): 17–28, at p. 18.

9 Handyside, A., 'Celebrating 20 years of preimplantation genetic diagnosis', *BioNews*, July 2010, www.bionews.org.uk/page_67228.asp (accessed 25/10/2010)

sex selection is feasible, and sometimes practised; while enhancement generally speaking is not. However, with respect to enhancement, it is plausible to think that, as scientific knowledge and medical techniques develop, it will become possible to carry out genetic diagnoses relating to factors concerning behavioural and physical characteristics, which would enable embryo selection on the basis of a wide range of social, economic and aesthetic values.[10] There is also the prospect of diagnosis leading on to genetic improvement through modifying the genetic makeup of pre-implantation embryos, but this goes beyond PGD as we have defined it.

The attitudinal ambivalence towards PGD, and the asymmetry between favourable public attitudes towards its use for avoiding the passing on of inherited diseases and the cautious and indeed sometimes hostile public reactions towards its use in seeking improvements on normal human capacities is reflected in the popular media and in the bioethical literature. Philosophers of considerable stature, such as Jurgen Habermas[11] and Michael Sandel[12] have expressed grave doubts about the wisdom and morality of procedures such as PGD, while others, such as Julian Savulescu[13] and Peter Singer have argued that, on the contrary, parents should be permitted – even encouraged – to utilise such opportunities as are available to them to improve the quality of life for their children. Many commentators have noted that the new reproductive technologies give intending parents a wider range of choices, both preconception and prenatal, changing not only the way in which people view procreation and family, but also our conception of disease, prediction, diagnosis, prevention and what counts as desirable traits.[14] As noted by McLean, '[n]o longer is the debate simply focused on whether or not people have rights to assistance in having children; the modern debate is also about what kind of children they may or should have'.[15]

The prospect of sex selection, which is permitted in some jurisdictions, and the anticipation of genetic enhancement through technological intervention, together with broader anxieties about the moral status of embryos and the manipulation of life, have given rise to extreme caution in some countries with respect to the legal regulation of PGD. PGD is prohibited in Ireland, Switzerland and Germany, and in some jurisdictions in which it is medically available, such as the UK, it has been restricted to narrowly defined therapeutic objectives, such as infertility and particular inherited genetic diseases, carried

10 Home, D., 'Customizing conception: a survey of preimplantation genetic diagnosis and the resulting social, ethical, and legal dilemmas', *Duke L. & Tech. Rev*, (2002): E1.

11 Habermas, J., *The Future of Human Nature*, trans Hella Beister and William Rehg. Cambridge: Polity, 2003.

12 Sandel, M., *The Case against Perfection: Ethics in the Age of Genetic Engineering*, Cambridge, MA: Harvard University Press, 2007.

13 Savulescu, J., 'New breeds of humans: the moral obligation to enhance', *Ethics, Law and Moral Philosophy of Reproductive Biomedicine*, 1 (2005): 36–9.

14 Klipstein, S., 'Preimplantation genetic diagnosis: technological promise and ethical perils', *Fertility and Sterility*, 83(5) (2005): 1347–53.

15 McLean, *Modern Dilemmas*, at p. 40.

out for specific purposes in specially licensed facilities. On the other hand, in the United States, where the majority of clinics in the world using PGD operate, there is relatively little regulation.[16]

Regulative regimes such as that in the UK may be regarded as 'bio-conservative' in the sense that they are based on the assumption that alternatives to existing practice require specific and clear justification in terms of traditional medical or scientific assumptions. For the bio-conservative, the burden of proof is very much on those who seek to change the medical status quo with respect to the uses of PGD. 'Bio-conservative' arguments support policies that permit only strong therapeutic reasons for PGD and hold that PGD decisions should be based on medical rather than parental judgement within clearly defined regulative criteria for embryo development and implantation. For the bio-conservative, all further options should be proscribed.

A more radical conservative position on PGD regulation we term 'naturalist'. Naturalism is a form of reactionary bio-conservatism which maintains that it is the duty of us all to accept the outcomes of natural reproductive acts, with the implication that there should be no legally available reproductive choices beyond engaging in natural procreative conduct, in extreme cases forbidding contraception and termination of pregnancies for any reason, and certainly outlawing PGD and other techniques that involve creating embryos, some of which are selected for implantation with the remainder being discarded.

In contrast, the term 'bio-liberal' may be applied to those who would permit a full range of medical and non-medical harms and benefits to be taken into consideration when selecting embryos for implantation after PGD, unless this is judged to be clearly not in the 'best interests' of the children to be born as a result of the procedure. Within these limits, bio-liberals, such as Savulescu, hold that the choice of whether or not to take advantage of PGD is ultimately a matter for intending parents, under procedures which are regulated only for the prevention of evident harms to the future children involved and the quality of the medical procedures in question. This is the position on the regulation of PGD which we identify as the default option; a position, which, we argue, ought to be adopted subject only to clear, convincing and major social considerations arising from the aggregative effects of predicted reproductive choices.

A more radical position is the one adopted by 'transhumanists'. The transhumanist position shows a commitment to improving the genetically influenced capacities of the human individual and of the species to a point which can be said to change or transcend the human condition as we know it.[17] Transhumanists encourage, and may even require, parents and society in general

16 Fahrenkrog, A., 'A comparison of international regulation of preimplantation genetic diagnosis and a regulatory suggestion for the United States', *Transnational Law & Contemporary Problems*, 15(2) (2006): 757–82.

17 Bostrom, N., 'Human genetic enhancement: a transhumanist perspective', *Journal of Value Enquiry*, 37 (2003): 493–506.

to improve the quality of life for future humans generally by using new technologies and techniques of genetic alteration as well as embryo selection. This would permit, so they argue, overcoming genetically inherent human limitations and the improvement of human features beyond what is currently species typical.

These working labels are used to classify the major regulatory positions that may be adopted towards PGD and the sort of normative considerations that underpin them. The framework of the discussion is that, given the present and potential benefits of PGD and taking the moral assumption that reproduction is a private matter, it is our view that there must be a strong moral case in favour of parental choice in such matters as child bearing. Further, there has to be a strong presumption against state regulation with a high evidentiary burden set to displace it; in particular, with regard to regulations that are not based on reasonable precaution relating to the prevention of undeniable harm to the children who are born as a result of such procedures, or the prevention of unacceptable social consequences arising from the cumulative effect of otherwise acceptable individual choices. The gist of the argument is that this burden of proof is not currently met by the generalised attitudes of disquiet and foreboding which have prompted bio-conservative PGD policies involving extensive legal prohibitions. Such considerations may properly guide individuals' own beliefs as to whether they or other people *ought* to avail themselves of the opportunities that PGD may provide, but they are not appropriate when presented as bases for narrow and restrictive state policies. We may not like or approve of 'pushy parents' wanting 'designer babies' but this alone does not justify preventing them from carrying out their reproductive projects with the assistance of such advanced medical technology as they are able to access.

This chapter is not, therefore, an account of regulatory systems in place for PGD but a normative analysis of arguments for and against regulation of one sort or another. It identifies some of the ethical issues that arise in relation to PGD and examines some of the ethical reasons that are given for various types of regulatory regimes for PGD. It is not directly concerned with the moral choices facing potential parents and others involved in PGD; rather, it is directly concerned with the moral reasons for and against regulation. This highlights the gap between norms which are appropriate to guide individual moral choice and regulatory norms which, if adopted, restrict reproductive choices. Given the narrow limits and restrictions – which some people might regard as coercive – involved in bio-conservatism, the presumption is in favour of bio-liberalism. This is even more the case if it is held that reproductive choices are distinctively 'private' in that they bear primarily on the lives and well-being of the persons whose reproductive activities are at stake. This means distinguishing between what virtuous intending PGD parents and others involved would choose and what all such intending parents ought to be legally permitted, or indeed required, to choose. Moving too readily from reflecting on personal and social ideals to deciding on best regulatory practice, neglects to take into account the gap between private morality and public regulation.[18]

There are, of course, connections between the two types of question in that the same type of moral reasons, such as the reduction of suffering, may apply in both the private and the public domain. Such considerations do not, however, have the same moral weight in both private and public matters. The presumption of liberty – based on the moral significance of autonomy for moral agents, the existence of reasonable disagreement on values, and the danger of government power being abused – generates a similar, if not higher, standard of proof to justify reproductive regulation.

On the other hand, regulatory norms have to take into account the problem of aggregation. Thus, even morally acceptable choices for individual intending parents or medical practitioners may have cumulative consequences that require regulation, as with PGD embryo sex selection for non-clinical reasons, where the sum of individual choices may lead to substantial sex imbalances in a society. Here, however, the standard of proof is still high. Forbidding sex selection simply on the basis of a speculative prediction as to sex imbalance we would argue is an unacceptable intervention in reproductive freedom. Nevertheless, significant sex imbalance in a society is a reasonable basis for political intervention due to the degree of suffering that is known to arise where serious sex imbalances exist. What matters here is to distinguish such public policy considerations from the more nebulous concerns expressed in relation to PGD on the basis of such notions as 'reverence for life' and conceptions of 'human dignity', unless these are given clear and concrete meanings that can be subject to reasoned argument.

The right to reproduce

Insisting on the moral importance of preserving and developing reproductive rights does not mean that we must have recourse to any claimed deontological moral insights with respect to absolute and self-evident rights. Indeed, we view rights as part of a discourse that seeks to establish routine working social relationships, rather than to express overriding moral imperatives. The issue is to decide what rights we ought to establish, sustain and develop in our societies through social, political and legal recognition; not what abstract rights we are asserted to have in some pre-social or transcendental moral realm.

Nor can we simply extrapolate from existing reproductive rights, which in most countries involve at least the right not to be prevented from having children and the right to obtain such medical assistance in this matter as they can afford. Having such particular rights does not mean that there should be yet further reproductive rights, such as the right to an abortion, the right to paid parental leave or the right to be cloned. These are matters which require

18 McLean, *Modern Dilemmas*, at p. 124.

further and distinct moral debate in the light of the known facts and the morally relevant factors. Indeed, rights arguments can be suspect in situations of rapid technological change where major social consequences are involved. In these circumstances, rights are better seen as conclusions of complex arguments and not premises which represent compelling moral conclusions. In rapidly developing fields such as reproductive technology, the questions to be raised are about what rights we *ought* to have rather than what rights we *do* have.

Nevertheless, it is clearly relevant to have regard to the moral and factual considerations that have given rise to the acceptance of existing reproductive rights when we come to consider how such rights might be developed in the light of changed circumstances, whether technical, social or economic. Such reflection has to take into account the scope of the putative rights, their conditionality, the nature of the correlative duties that having a right impose on other people, and who it is that should be able to claim, waive or insist on the fulfilment of those duties. The conclusion that there should be a right or collection of rights delineating these parameters, if adopted by social consensus or legislation, establishes a strong, and perhaps an overriding, presumption that the prescribed right-holders are entitled to claim the benefits designated in the right without having to make a case beyond affirming that they have the right in question. Once the right is established, the likes and dislikes and the moral preferences of others are irrelevant to whether or not they are to be treated in accordance with their entitlement: hence, the importance of a rights discourse in a social and political culture. The relevance of rights language arises because of the presumptions it enshrines in favour of individual (and also collective) choice, the strength of the claims that can be made on the conduct of others, and the protection and benefit this can give to the interests of individuals (and groups) to whom the rights are prescribed.

The right to reproduce is deeply embedded in the history of human rights discourse for a number of reasons. (1) Reproduction is something very important to individual human beings. There is a major human interest in being a parent, given that parenthood is something which is of enormous significance to most people. (2) Reproduction is very important for the collectives in which people live and indeed for the human species as a whole. Self-evidently reproduction is a necessary condition for human survival[19] which establishes a presumption against its limitation. (3) Some very nasty things have been done in the cause of tribal, racial and national dominance, and collective efforts to 'improve' the population through compulsory 'eugenic' programmes, including extermination and non-voluntary sterilisation.

As with rights in general, the right to reproduce (or reproductive autonomy) may be negative (either no law preventing reproduction and/or protection against the intervention of others), or positive (someone else has a duty to assist reproduction). Also, the right to reproduce may be specific with respect to such

19 *Skinner* v. *Oklahoma* 316 US 535 (1942).

details as to how much reproduction (one, two or more children), or, like most statements of human rights, largely open-ended as to content. The right to reproduce may be to give birth to a child, or it may be to give birth to a child without defect or as perfect as it can be, or it may include rights to assistance in the nature and the nurture of the children born. In these latter cases, as McLean points out, '[t]hese reproductive rights are rights within reproduction rather than rights to reproduce'.[20] On the other hand, as she adds, 'the protection offered by rights language is first and foremost the right not to have existing capacities to reproduce interfered with by others (particularly the state)'.[21]

Choice between these possible rights formulations, if we are engaging in ethical discussion, cannot be read off from the abstract or existing 'right to reproduce'. What have to be explored are the reasons for and against having certain sorts or formulations of a right to reproduce. Seeing reproductive autonomy as an intrinsic right (that is a right that is grounded in the act itself rather than its consequences beyond the right-holder) and assuming for the moment the interest theory of rights – whereby rights are grounded *inter alia* on the moral significance of the interests in question – means that reproductive autonomy has to be based on the interests of the right-holder. Thus, we can say that there is a very powerful moral reason for ascribing a right to reproduce in the sense of 'to have children'. We only need to contemplate the misery that the denial of that opportunity creates to justify this conclusion. So, there is a good basis for a strong *prima facie* case for the negative right to reproduce. Moreover, given the misery associated with not having the capacity to be a parent, we can see a similar argument for a positive right to reproduce; the only significant difference being the question of who has to bear the cost of or see to facilitating childbirth.

Extending this line of thought to circumstances relating to PGD, we can note that human beings have a major interest in their children not suffering serious illness, disability or premature death. Thus, we can readily move on to accept that there should be a right for potential parents to take such measures as are necessary to prevent these eventualities, and even to be provided with such help as is available to that end, depending on material and technical resources and the financial and opportunity costs deriving from other human needs.

But what of the parental interest in having a clever child? In general this is not nearly as important to parents as the absence of serious illness in their children. It does not, therefore, have anything like the same moral weight. This means that there is no easy extrapolation from the right to have a healthy child to the right to have a clever one, or a handsome one, or a kind and generous one. It may be that historically the right to reproduce, as a simple negative right not to be prohibited or prevented from reproducing, has been uncontroversially

20 McLean, *Modern Dilemmas*, at p. 17.
21 *Ibid.*

absolute, or nearly so. The same cannot be said on behalf of the right to have an 'enhanced' child who is braver, brighter or more beautiful than others. Yet, the desire to have, and the benefits deriving from having, 'better-than-average' offspring, are clear and important enough to justify at least negative rights not to be prevented or forbidden from doing what you can to achieve to this end, provided that it does not involve harming others to a significant extent. Indeed, we are not always involved here in a zero-sum game where enhancement is measured in a relative manner as being better than average. Developing cleverness has justifications beyond producing competitive advantage. A general increase in the intelligence of a whole population has the potential to increase average and not just individual and family well-being. This brings in the reasonable suggestion that there is an interest here which is important enough to justify not only a strongly grounded negative right to pursue what would appear to be a very legitimate interest, but under certain circumstances even a positive right which correlates with a community obligation to make available or subsidise the means required to further these interests. This is what has emerged in minimally affluent societies in relation to the positive right to education, a development that is in line with improving the average general health in newborn children through subsidised prenatal care. However, we also noted that there might be instances of enhanced traits that might bear a cost on society while only benefiting the individual, for instance, by increasing inequality and discrimination. Such cases need to be assessed on a case-by-case basis.

These interest-based considerations are sufficient for establishing a strong *prima facie* case for the right to access PGD for reasons beyond health-related concerns, which is along the lines of the bio-liberal model we have referred to as enhancement. The interests of the potential parent are sufficient to ground a socially and legally protected choice in an area which is 'private' in the twin senses that the interests in question are dominantly those of the individual and they concern the exercise of functions directly involved with the personal capacities of the putative right-holder.

Rights discourse is also closely associated with justifications which point to the capacity of human beings to make choices, particularly moral choices. For neo-Kantian theorists it is the capacity for choice that is at the core of all rights, not only because such capacities are indispensable to claiming and waiving rights but also because many, if not all, rights have to do with 'respecting' other people as agents by not interfering with their choices unless these choices inflict significant harm on others.[22] As a theory of rights, however, this is rather narrow, if only because human beings benefit from the protection of their rights before they are capable of making claims or exercising choice; a point that has particular significance in the reproductive sphere. Moreover, often the point of giving people the choices that are involved in having a right is to enable them to protect their own interests. Nevertheless, given the intrinsic value we ascribe to the capacity to make choices, including value judgements in general and

22 Griffin, J., *On Human Rights*, Oxford: Oxford University Press, 2008, at pp. 32–7.

moral choices in particular, there is an independent 'autonomy' grounding for justifying rights, where the autonomy is not valued for instrumental reasons but for its own sake.

From the autonomy point of view, the right to reproduce is justified by the fact that the decisions whether, when, how and with whom to procreate are clearly important ones with major implications for an individual's personal and public life, and therefore constitute a crucial locus of personal autonomy. This is particularly visible in the hugely important role of reproductive choice. From the non-instrumental autonomy point of view, the right not to reproduce is part and parcel of the right to reproduce, the important thing being whose choice is decisive, not what the choice turns out to be.

To this ideal of freedom of choice in relation to a person's own life is added the particular significance of moral choice with respect to human relationships and in general promoting the well-being of other people. For Kant, this was the highest manifestation of human freedom and the essence of the importance of humans as deserving of 'respect', because they are 'ends in themselves' who ought not to be treated merely 'as means'.[23] While it would seem a serious oversimplification to trace the grounding of all rights, even all fundamental rights, to such moral autonomy, there is no doubt that this distinctive feature of human life as interpreted by Kant, had and still has an important influence on our thinking about rights.

Relating the autonomy basis of rights to PGD adds substantially to the case for bio-liberalism. This is primarily because the existence of PGD increases the range of choices open to the individual and so enhances the role of choice in each prospective parent's life. This is particularly so in view of the general moral significance of the choices to be made, given the responsibilities that flow from parenting.

Objections to the bio-liberal case for parental choice

This part of the chapter argues that there are good reasons for establishing potential parents' rights to access the PGD techniques which become available for (1) increasing available opportunities for a good life by limiting severe impairments and illnesses for future generations; (2) the possibility to improve the quality of human life by selecting certain traits over others; and (3) extending the intrinsic good of enlarging the scope of morally accountable choices on the part of individuals and societies. This means that, until such time as clearly and indisputably harmful consequences of PGD are established as taking place, PGD should not be subject to special regulations. The burden of proof is firmly on those who want to restrict scientific advance, human improvement and freedom of choice by restricting such rights.

23 Kant, I., *Groundwork of the Metaphysics of Morals*, with Introduction by Sally Sedgwick, Chicago: University of Illinois Press, [1785] 2008, at p. 142.

There is, however, a broad range of counter-arguments favouring the strict regulation of PGD. Some of these relate to uncertain or damaging outcomes both to individuals and to society at large. Others cast doubt on the morality of 'engineering' human nature, whatever the outcome may be. While the second category of counter-arguments can often appear rather nebulous and even superstitious, their negative impact on the freedom to access PGD can be seen in the extent to which they are accepted as reasons for having special regulation limiting the use of PGD which would not be accepted in other spheres of public policy. This can be illustrated by analysing some of the arguments on offer.

Consequentialist counter-arguments

An array of consequentialist counter-arguments to bio-liberalism contends that, whatever is intended, there will be seriously harmful results. Some of these relate to the consequences for the families involved, whereas others relate to the social disutility of PGD. Nearly all appear to lack convincing empirical evidence and most depend on controversial personal viewpoints of a sort not normally accepted as decisive with respect to regulatory policy.

Harm within families

It is said that there will be bad consequences for those immediately involved in PGD. For instance, where non-therapeutic selection is permitted, some parents will make really bad choices when they come to select the characteristics of their children to be. The standard example used to establish this case is that of Ms Duchesneau and Ms McCullough, two women who chose to have a child who is deaf.[24] In their case, being deaf themselves, they wanted a child who could share their particular way of life. The common reaction to this case is to say that this was a selfish act since they could have opted for the existence of a child who had the benefit of hearing.

Interestingly, this criticism of the deaf parents depends on that aspect of the bio-liberal view that encourages prospective parents to do what they can to improve the lot of the child to be. The important point at issue here is that there is disagreement about what human capacities are desirable and about how the right-holders should exercise them to enable individuals to make choices that are not dictated by the preferences of other people. Just because others would not choose to have a deaf child does not mean that persons such as Duchesneau and McCullough should not be allowed to make such a choice, even if other people disapprove of it. This is one of the ways in which rights make room for the manifestation of legitimate value pluralism.

24 Sprigg, M., 'Lesbian couple create a child who is deaf like them', *Journal of Medical Ethics*, 28 (2002): 283.

However, pluralism has its limits and rights may properly be circumscribed by requirements designed to obviate undoubted harms, especially to other people. If the consequentialist can provide evidence that bio-liberal rights with respect to PGD will result, not in eugenics but in what might be called 'malgenics' – the selection of dysfunctional traits – then there would be a strong case for having strict controls to overcome this problem. Rights are not immune from consequentialist considerations; indeed most arguments for having rights are themselves consequentialist in nature. The argument that there should be only circumscribed rights to PGD because, otherwise, more harm than good will result has to be taken very seriously. If most deaf people would like not to be deaf, then using PGD to bring more deafness into existence is a concern, despite its controversial status as a disability, and then there are related costs and inconveniences to others which carry some moral weight. Moreover, while it is possible to imagine that some less well-meaning and less informed persons will make what are indisputably unfortunate choices when selecting their 'designer' babies, there is no substantial evidence offered to show that the overall results will be worse for the quality of life of future people under bio-liberalism than under bio-conservativism, even if we share the opinions of the critics as to what constitutes a regression or an advance in human capacities. Parenting is much more likely to be more inclined to 'procreative benevolence' than procreative malevolence.[25] Moreover the desirability of increasing the diversity of human beings, which is illustrated by the deaf parents' example, will be seen as an advantage by those who fear that enhancement liberalism may lead to a dismal uniformity among humankind.[26]

This may be thought to miss the point. The critics' disquiet may not be about the future of their society, or humanity as a whole, but the fate of that single child who was created deaf. Strong regulation should be in place to vet parenting choice, it may be argued, to reduce the incidence of results that are harmful to the child. This takes us to a fundamental error in this sort of reasoning about PGD which distorts disputes about its application. To select an embryo that will result in the birth of a deaf child is not to make a child deaf but to make a deaf child. The child that was born for Duchesneau and McCullough was not made deaf but was selected because s/he was deaf. The wrong, if it was a wrong, was to give life to a deaf child rather than to a hearing one.

With PGD, we are choosing embryo A over embryo B, and not changing B into A. That is to say, we are enabling A to develop into a person but not B. Thus the non-identity factor, which also brings confusion in other reproductive contexts, undercuts the discrimination critique.[27] Given that we are not

25 Savulescu, J., 'Procreative beneficence: why we should select the best children', *Bioethics*, 15(5/6) (2001): 413–23.

26 Home, 'Customizing conception'.

27 See Kavka, G., 'The paradox of future individuals', *Philosophy and Public Affairs*, 11 (1981): 93–112; Parfit, D., 'Future generations: further problem', *Philosophy and Public Affairs*, 11 (1981): 113–72; Roberts M. and Wasserman, D. (eds), *Harming Future Persons: Ethics, Genetics and the Nonidentity Problem*, Dordrecht: Springer, 2009.

altering the characteristics of A, we cannot say that A has a right to be born without trait 'X', as A not having trait 'X' means that it would not be A. The non-identity factor is about the contrast between selecting which person there is to be as against selecting the character, constitution (or identity) of an existing or future person.

Other consequentialist counter-arguments point to alleged disadvantages for family relationships arising from PGD that go beyond selecting out evident handicaps. These criticisms centre on the poor parent–child relationships that arise, it is argued, from encouraging selfish parenting which does not involve loving the child for its own sake. Botkin, for example, has argued that 'this is not because the child would be directly harmed by the biological selection, but because the selection may well come with a stifling set of expectations'.[28] One of the principal protections for human beings against biological predetermination imposed by third parties, including parents, as Khan has noted in reference to cloning, is the lottery of heredity.[29] Further, '[o]ne of the blessings of the relationship between parents and their children is their inevitable difference, which results in parents loving their children for what they are, rather than endeavoring to make them what they want'.[30]

Connected to this argument, Habermas, another bio-conservative, has argued that techniques such as PGD undermine human autonomy because its practice means that children start off in life as their parents choose.[31] This, according to Habermas, means that they cannot be personally autonomous or equal with respect to their parents in the same way as children born as a result of the natural genetic lottery.[32] Habermas's position is that genetic intervention conflicts with autonomy because those born as a result cannot see themselves as 'the sole authors of their own life history'.[33] Further, he argues that PGD introduces an asymmetry between parent and child that is incompatible with human equality.[34]

Although he does not accept the latter two points, Michael Sandel, in *The Case against Perfection*, develops the moral case against genetic manipulation, in which he includes PGD,[35] along similar lines, so as to encompass a general critique of 'hyper parenting'[36] which, in his view erodes 'the appreciation of giftedness'; that is:

> the capacity to accept unreservedly what is given through unmanipulated childbirth: In a social world that prizes mastery and control, parenthood

28 Botkin, 'Ethical issues', at p. 23.
29 Khan, A., 'Cloning, dignity and ethical revisionism', *Nature*, 388 (1997): 320–1.
30 Ibid., at p. 320.
31 Habermas, J., *Between Naturalism and Religion*, Cambridge: Polity, 2008, at p. 203.
32 Ibid., at p. 2.
33 Ibid., at p. 79.
34 Ibid., at pp. 64–5.
35 Sandel, M. J., *The Case against Perfection: Ethics in the Age of Genetic Engineering*, Cambridge, MA: Belknap Press, 2007, at pp. 20–1, 89.
36 Ibid., at pp. 52, 61.

> is a school of humility. That we care deeply about our children, and yet cannot choose the kind we want, teaches parents to be open to the unbidden. Such openness is a disposition worth affirming, not only within families but in the wider world as well.[37]

Apart from the fact that Sandel's case is tentatively made, perhaps due to the lack of scientific evidence to support its anticipations about parental attitudes to 'designed' children, this argument should not be taken seriously as the basis for restricting rights for which, as we have seen, there is strong *prima facie* moral grounding. There is something distasteful about pushy parenting, and the world would certainly be a nicer place if there were less competitiveness and more solidarity generally, but these preferences are not anywhere near strong enough to justify limiting human choices in areas of life that are of vital importance to most people. Our unease at having a say in choosing the characteristics of our children may provide moral grounds for deciding whether or not we personally wish to use the techniques of PGD or making a moral assessment of the conduct of others in this regard, but this is a far cry from adopting legal restrictions that impose our 'disquiet' on others. This is particularly so because the poor parenting relationships and the wider social consequences to which PGD may give rise are currently diminutive in scale and remote in time. Anxieties about what could, in the long run, happen in a competitive world, are a flimsy basis on which to found law unless there are other more immediate factors at work. Here the often repeated mantra that medical science progresses and law follows far in its wake expresses the opposite of a reality in which laws are being introduced to deal with controversial speculations about technically remote prospects.

Harms to society

Similar points can be made about other equally speculative and morally tentative consequentialist objections to bio-liberalism. For example, it is argued that permitting parents to choose to have children without disabilities or with enhanced capacities will result in increased social injustices, with the advantages going to those who can afford to pay for PGD, which is currently an expensive process.[38] To this line of argumentation it can be said, first, that there is no reason to believe that the costs of PGD or similar procedures will not be significantly reduced in due course. Second, if such arguments are contingent upon current costs then the same high costs will result in only slight increases in the currently infinitesimally low use of the procedure, thus threatening no widespread social change of this sort. Moreover, it is unreasonably selective and clearly inconsistent with current social arrangements within liberal capitalism to use an argument based on increased social inequality as a

37 Ibid., at p. 86.
38 Botkin, 'Ethical issues'.

veto on the private use of resources while permitting private schools, private healthcare and private business. This is not to say that considerations of social inequality are not relevant to rights policy, but the case against bio-liberalism in relation to PGD would have to provide evidence that it would be a substantial and ongoing cause of inequality without accompanying benefits, which would put it in a different category to other causes of inequality.

Another suggested unfortunate social consequence of PGD is the stigmatising of persons with disabilities.[39] Disability rights critics challenge the view that the concern in relation to so-called designer babies is a morally distinct question from concerns about prenatal and pre-implantation testing more generally. They argue that, 'by selecting out certain socially undesirable genetic conditions, we are already creating designer babies'.[40] The objection is that designing of any sort is effectively discriminating because it implies that some lives are more worth living than others. By rejecting embryos on grounds of 'negative' characteristics, we devalue persons who have these characteristics. So, they argue, there is no significant difference between selecting to avoid a disability and selecting for enhancement.

King argues in addition that if society had overcome its fears of disability and truly considered disabled people as equal members of the community, there would not be such an interest in prenatal screening and PGD.[41] The argument is that we should combat the social forces which lead us to disvalue some individuals and idealise others. However, others such as Savulescu[42] and Singer[43] have pointed out that a distinction needs to be made between the disabilities and the people living with disabilities. For instance Savulescu has noted that 'selection reduces the former but is silent on the latter'.[44] Singer's theory of 'replaceability' which he relates to prenatal diagnosis, but which applies equally to PGD, is that parents of a disabled foetus have the moral right to replace a defective foetus with a more healthy one who can attain a better quality of life.[45] Singer points out that this does not imply that it would be better if no people were born with severe disabilities, but only that the parents involved should be able to make the decision about what to do if they are the parents of a disabled foetus, and the same would apply to selection before implantation. Nor need selection imply any lack of respect or equal consideration for people with disabilities who are now alive.

Another contingency that runs in the counter-direction to the liberal position is that 'extending PGD will reduce the number of people affected by

39 Karpin, I., 'Choosing disability: preimplantation genetic diagnosis and negative enhancement', *JLM*, 15 (2007): 89–102.
40 Ibid., at p. 99.
41 King, D., 'PGD and the "new" eugenics', *Journal of Medical Ethics*, 25 (1999): 176–82.
42 Savulescu, 'Procreative benificerce'.
43 Singer, P., 'Taking life: humans', in *Practical Ethics*, 2nd edn, Cambridge: Cambridge University Press, 1993, pp. 175–217.
44 Savulescu, 'Procreative beneficence', at p. 191.
45 Ibid.

serious diseases, adversely affecting the funding of research into new treatments for those disorders'.[46] This could be given as a reason for not doing what we can to remove the causes of any disease on the grounds that this will reduce funding for research and care for those with the disease. Thus, there would not appear to be any reason why this argument should be selectively applied to PGD.

The same sort of points can be made against those who point out that PGD provides a new opportunity for sex discrimination. In particular, it is argued that PGD is likely to result in a significant sex imbalance in cultures where boys are preferred to girls. If this were to be the result of the general availability and use of PGD, then it would create a social and economic problem, although the situation could change, for instance, by increasing the perceived value of female children if they were to become relatively scarce within their society. The social and economic disadvantages of a significant sex imbalance could be a powerful reason for limiting PGD for sex selection in certain societies. However, this is not anywhere near an impending situation, even in societies where boy-preferences dominate. Further, there is no evidence of boy preference within cultures where PGD is available, other than to provide sex balance within a family.[47]

The eugenics fear

The easy acceptance of what, on analysis, appear to be rather flimsy arguments in favour of bio-conservatism in relation to PGD may be explicable by reference to deeper fears. One of these is the view that PGD is equivalent to 'eugenics' and eugenics is generally associated with the most horrendous practices of the Nazi regime. Thus, it is said that the potential increase in the frequency and scope of selection based on the genetic constitution of embryos 'will move us to a eugenic world in which children are valued more for their genotype than for their inherent characteristics'.[48]

The force of this sort of rhetoric depends on the association of eugenics with coerced sterilisation. As King points out, 'the key aspect of eugenics is coercion of people's reproductive choices, for social ends, which may include improving the quality of the population, preventing suffering of future generations or reducing financial costs to the state'.[49] The key negative factor here is, of course, the idea of reproductive physical coercion, something which is not associated with PGD, and which runs directly counter to the thesis that there is a strong *prima facie* case for reproductive freedom. At this point in the rhetoric of eugenics, a slippery-slope argument is introduced along the lines that the

46 Snelling, 'Preimplantation genetic diagnosis for susceptibility conditions', at p. 271.
47 Robertson, J., 'Extending PGD: the ethical debate', *Human Reproduction*, 18(3) (2003): 465–71.
48 Ibid., at p. 466.
49 King, 'PGD and the "new" eugenics', at pp. 176–7.

existence of the opportunity to use PGD will lead to various forms of pressure which remove the element of parental choice. The thesis is that intending parents will be 'coerced' into eugenic conduct by public opinion.

This contention would appear to ignore the elementary distinction between legal and physical coercion, on the one hand, and being subject to the pressure of opinion and financial benefit,[50] on the other. Sandel argues that 'the new liberal eugenics' would be parental rather than state driven, but in the case of parents there are choices present which are not there in state-administered programmes. However, bioethicist George Annas has stated that public pressure in favour of PGD could be very problematic for society, especially given advertising, peer pressure and competiveness. Perhaps, as he points out regarding the new genetics, parents who do not take advantage of new reproductive choices will soon be seen as bad or even neglectful parents.[51] Moreover, the argument that 'the state should not be expected to pay for the specialised care of a child with a severe handicap where the parents had declined the offer of prenatal testing',[52] will coerce people into using these procedures. As King further argues, social pressure will be against intending parents not using PGD, because:

> [F]irstly, able-bodied people receive negative images of people with disabilities and general misinformation about what their lives are like. Parents receiving prenatal genetic counselling are rarely put in touch with people who actually live with the genetic disorder in question. Secondly, parents are aware of the material aspects of disability oppression: insufficient welfare provision, lack of access and discrimination.[53]

Therefore intending parents would see PGD as their duty.

By way of comment on this analysis, we note that coming to see something as your duty does not mean that you are being coerced. Also, the pressures in question are much more likely to arise in relation to failure to avoid having handicapped children as opposed to failing to use PGD for enhancement. In any case, the force of the argument depends on the view that public opinion in this matter would be misguided, which begs the case against the value of PGD. Further, an emphasis on bio-liberalism, with its hostility to state intervention, is a more likely restraint on coercive state policies than the bio-conservatism that underlies current state regulation of PGD.

There is no doubt that techniques such as PGD will offer opportunities for parental options that promote entrenched social inequality and opportunities

50 Buchanan, A., Brock, D. W., Daniels, N. and Wikler, D., *From Chance to Choice: Genetics and Justice*, Cambridge, Cambridge University Press, 2000, at pp. 27–70.

51 Annas, G., 'Turning point for the human species: trial lawyers should prepare for the brave new world of genetic research and human cloning', *TRIAL*29, (2001): 27–9.

52 Green, J. M. 'Obstetricians' views on prenatal diagnosis and termination of pregnancy: 1980 compared with 1993', *British Journal of Obstetrics and Gynaecology*, 102 (1995): 228–32.

53 King, 'PGD and the "new" eugenics', at p. 178.

for states to selectively subsidise and even require participation in schemes designed to eradicate inherited diseases and even improve the perceived quality of human beings. Social equality and government non-interference with such personal matters as reproduction are both important factors and of relevance in determining what social and legal rights and duties ought to be developed and put to work. However, social inequality in itself and the prospect of the possibility of government intervention can hardly be taken as decisive moral factors, unless we are dealing with matters which are, in themselves, otherwise morally neutral. In fact this is not the case, for, as is set out, there are powerful *prima facie* moral considerations in favour of reproductive freedom that include the utilisation of PGD at the request of potential parents.

Moreover, it would seem that many of those who consider the various objections to bio-liberalism which we have outlined to be persuasive, also believe or assume that there is a *prima facie* case against PGD; namely, that it is contrary to a proper attitude to nature, to ourselves and our environment. This may in fact be the underlying philosophical framework that is the rational and/or emotional basis for the critique of PGD bio-liberalism.

Bio-naturalism

A possible, and in our view plausible, explanation for the common acceptance of weak moral reasons for strong regulation of PGD may be traced to different views about the proper relationship between the human and the non-human elements in nature. The sense of 'naturalism' employed here refers to having positive respect for, and giving moral weight to, something simply because it is part of nature. Broadly speaking, naturalism is the view that whatever is 'natural' is both admirable and intrinsically good, whatever its content. This is not a position that is consistently held by those who equate nature with whatever happens to exist, since they normally distinguish between what is genuinely natural and that which is a departure from or corruption of nature. At this point there is a commonly made distinction between that part of nature that is human and that part which is not. The common naturalist view is that humans should respect not only the non-human nature but that part of themselves which is 'natural' in the sense of having been given to humans rather than having been created by them.

This analysis of naturalism points to the religious flavour of bio-naturalism, which we refer to as theological naturalism. This view fits easily with the metaphysical belief that 'nature' is made by a God or Gods (who are not themselves part of nature) and that human life is a gift from the God or Gods, perhaps combined with the characteristically Jewish and Christian view that the non-human world is given to humans for their benefit and use.

The theological version of naturalism can be read into the view that PGD is objectionable because it is 'playing God'. On this thesis, reproduction is a gift from God, the product of which should be treated with the greatest respect and unreserved gratitude. This approach is particularly evident in religions which conceptualise God primarily as the creator of the natural world and combine this with the belief that the Creator has a benevolent purpose which may be seen in the operations of what has been created.

There are extensive differences between specific theological views as to what is given by God and should be received with gratitude, and that which is given by God with the purpose that humans should strive, with His help, to change for the better, including some aspects of human nature itself. For instance, ethical objections to the creation of embryos that are then intentionally destroyed or permanently frozen, is based on a version of theological naturalism in which human life, which is a gift of God, begins at conception.

Those who object to pregnancy termination on the basis of the human personhood of the embryo (or foetus) involved have equal reason to object to IVF in so far as it includes the destruction of embryos. On this approach, the fact that the destroyed embryos are not attached to a womb is not a morally relevant difference. In contrast, those who value embryos for their human potential but have no objection to early-stage terminations of pregnancies, provided there are justifying reasons that have a relatively low threshold of moral weight, could consistently accept PGD on a similar basis. Indeed, given the distress and hazards for the pregnant woman that may accompany abortion, PGD can be seen as morally preferable to early-stage abortion undertaken for the same reasons. On the other hand, what might be seen as the relative convenience of PGD over abortion may be thought likely to increase the incidence of embryo destruction which may be considered a negative factor.[54] PGD is likely to involve the destruction of many more embryos, perhaps for less morally compelling reasons. On the other side of the moral calculation, the general objective of PGD is to assist in the birth of a child, which cannot be said of a termination.

If we accept some sort of theological naturalism, the burden of proof not only passes to those who would destroy human embryos but sets the bar so high that the various consequential arguments that would otherwise be morally relevant fade into insignificance. Those who do not share these theological beliefs will, of course, be unmoved by these considerations but are likely to accept the right of such believers to refrain from using or commending PGD. They will, nonetheless, resist this set of religious convictions being used to establish a regulatory system within a secular state. This would be in line with the political acceptance of the use of some types of birth control, the creation of destruction of some embryos in IVF and termination of pregnancy in some circumstances. In these circumstances it might seem strangely inconsistent to oppose PGD while accepting IVF, and to fail to note that in a non-assisted pregnancy many embryos do not survive. Further, even if there is something unacceptably unnatural in creating embryos and disposing of them prior to implantation, it would not seem proportionate to view the destruction of unimplanted embryos as more significant than the alternative means of selection that is involved in prenatal testing and selective termination.

54 Robertson, 'Extending PGD'.

Theological naturalism is discussed here, partly because it is an example of objections to bio-liberalism, but more as an explanation for why some people have an instinctive unease or strong negative feelings about PGD. In so far as this is a correct explanation, it serves to undermine arguments against bio-liberalism on the, no doubt increasingly controversial, basis that theological metaphysics ought not to feature in the formulation of policy in a secular state. It may also serve to explain the too easy acceptance of the relatively weak arguments in favour of bio-conservatism with which this chapter deals.

However, naturalism need not be associated with any religious or metaphysical positions, and instead can be seen as encompassing secular philosophies according to which the natural world, as it is understood from a scientific point of view, is deserving of respect and is important in itself; a view that is characteristic of 'deep environmentalism'. Such secular views are normally conjoined to an extent with the view that particular respect and positive value is appropriately given to life, and specifically to human life. This latter feature depends, of course, on valuations of life, especially human life, not just because it is part of nature but because it has certain particularly significant properties.

The secular versions of naturalism, as Sandel points out,[55] involve a purely moral evaluation of the importance of 'giftedness' in human life, and are concerned broadly speaking with 'disrespecting nature' by 'manufacturing life'. Thus the President's Council on Bioethics in the United States speaks of human reproduction as a 'gift' and argues that any form of selection or manipulation turns the child into a 'manufacture'.[56] This secular naturalism is separable from any consequentialist arguments about human 'flourishing' or the survival of the species. In this vein, Sandel writes:

> I do not mean to rest the case against enhancement on consequentialist considerations, at least not in the usual sense of the term. My point is not that genetic engineering is objectionable simply because the social costs are likely to outweigh the benefits. Nor do I claim that people who bioengineer their children are themselves are necessarily motivated for a desire for mastery, and this motive is a sin no good result could possibly outweigh. I am suggesting instead that the moral stake in the enhancement debate are not fully captured by the familiar categories of autonomy and rights, on the one hand, and the calculation of costs and benefits on the other.
>
> The bigger stakes are of two kinds. One involves the fate of human goods embodied in important social practices – norms of unconditional love and openness to the unbidden, in the case of parenting; the celebration of natural talents and gifts in athletics an artistic endeavors, humility in the face of privilege, and a willingness to share the fruits of good fortune

55 Sandel, *Case against Perfection*, at pp. 27, 93.

56 President's Council on Bioethics, *Beyond Therapy: Biotechnology and the Pursuit of Happiness*, New York: Reganbooks, 2003.

> through institutions of social solidarity. The other involves the orientation to the world that we inhabit, and the kind of freedom to which we aspire.
>
> It is tempting to think that bioengineering our children and ourselves for success in a competitive society is an exercise in freedom. But changing our nature to fit the world, rather than the other way around, is actually the deepest form of disempowerment.[57]

We include this long quotation to illustrate just how thin the naturalistic case is when separated from a distinctly theological metaphysic in which God is the giver of life. It is not that it is totally unpersuasive. Indeed, it has a warmth and humanity of considerable attraction. However, it has the quality of a personal philosophy to which it is difficult to give significant weight in a policy discussion where the policy is to be adopted for a whole community or society. Sandel does not speak much about state coercion but there are indications that he considers it to be a legitimate tool for the support of the 'openness to the unbidden'[58] which he values, and his remarkably unreligious view that we should change our environment but not ourselves, at least not our own nature. This position would require an explicit argument and a clear justification that could be accepted by those who do not share this particular view of the good life. As it is, his approach does not stand up against the *prima facie* case for bio-liberalism as a political position.

Theological and secular versions of bio-naturalism are examples of somewhat intangible ideas relating to imagined psychological reactions to a novel medical technique. Both struggle to give clear content to the nagging unease which each experiences concerning such techniques, without being able to establish firm empirical or *a priori* grounding to their positions, or presenting a convincing picture as to what is more 'natural' about the genetic lottery except that it arises out of the historically normal form of human reproduction.

Conclusion

There are many other arguments that we could have considered in this overview of the regulatory debate concerning PGD. In the future there may be major issues that arise due to unforeseen or unfortunate consequences, such as tragic, horrid and/or dangerous results of attempted genetic techniques that have gone lamentably wrong unintentionally or as the result of mistaken or evil scientific innovations. Then there is the criticism of bio-liberalism to the effect that, if we really endorse liberalism, we should be aware that by selecting and discarding certain traits we are implicitly endorsing a conception of the good life. Hence, as Dekker has argued, this practice cannot be justified in neutral

57 Sandel, *Case against Perfection*, at pp. 96–7.
58 Ibid., at pp. 45, 46, 86.

terms, and liberals should be sceptical of it.[59] True liberalism would seem to allow only the selection of traits that are useful for all conceptions of the good life, but whether it is plausible to agree on which sort of traits fulfil this definition remains something to be seen. On the other hand, we could have considered the argument that PGD regulation seems to involve a shift of reproductive power from women to physicians.[60] Another approach would have been to point out the slippery terminology in which the debate is conducted, with shadowy lines being drawn between therapy and enhancement.

However, we have covered enough ground to reach the tentative conclusion that there are reasons for believing that there is a powerful presumption in favour of bio-liberalism with respect to PGD, but that there could, some way off, be social consequences of the widespread use of PGD for both medical and social enhancement which might have sufficient ethical drawbacks in certain contexts to justify a measure of state control of the uses to which PGD is put. This is not currently the situation, so, unless we arbitrarily deploy a very strong version of the precautionary principle, there is presently no basis for any special or strong regulation of PGD other than that which may be justified with respect to medical practice generally. The moral arguments against PGD regulation may not be as strong as some who use the rhetoric of the 'right to reproduce' may suggest, but they are, nevertheless, of sufficient power to overcome the arguments against bio-liberalism that are currently on offer. It is, therefore, a topic that calls for continuing debate and political attention but not, as yet, for strong and restrictive regulation.

59 Dekker, T., 'The illiberality of perfectionist enhancement', *Medicine, Health Care and Philosophy: A European Journal*, 12(1) (2009): 91–8.

60 Draper and Chadwick, 'Beware!'.

3 PGD and the making of the 'genetic embryo' as a political tool

Martin H. Johnson and Anastasia A. Theodosiou

Introduction*

In 1990, the UK Parliament passed the Human Fertilisation and Embryology Act (HFEA 1990), which, among other provisions, legalised controlled research on human embryos. This Act resulted from six years of public and parliamentary debate, as well as lobbying for and against embryo research. Mulkay[1] has discussed how the pro-research lobby made genetic disease a particular focus of the parliamentary debate.[2] Pro-research lobbyists briefed MPs and the press, emphasising the potential to understand, prevent and even 'greatly reduce the frequency of genetic disorders'.[3] They drew particular attention to the desirability of diagnosing and selecting embryos based on their genetic characteristics, through the technique of pre-implantation genetic diagnosis (PGD), and contrasted this approach as being preferable to manipulating embryos by genetic engineering. Then, Robert Winston's team announced the first clinical pregnancy following PGD to avoid transmission of sex-linked genetic disease just five days before the 1990

* References to archival material are presented in text and in section 1 of the Reference list at the end of the chapter as follows: Material accessed from the MRC records at the National Archives at Kew, Surrey, UK (NA); from the papers of Professor Peter Braude and the Progress Educational Trust held at the London School of Economics Archive (LSE); from the Anne McLaren papers at the British Library (BL); and from Enoch Powell's papers in the Churchill College Archives, Cambridge (CC). These archives contain several hundred unnumbered items, some of which are stored in divisions and sub-series of folders. We cite these sources with a numbered archival code in the order that they appear in the text (NA1–11, BL1, LSE1–8, and CC1–12), and we include in the reference list a short description, date and archival location by division and subdivision, where applicable (e.g. NA1, 1971; Grant application, Edwards, R. G., Steptoe, P.C. 10 Feb.: FD10/161). The second section of Reference list at the end of the chapter includes references to verbatim records of fifty Parliamentary debates from the Hansard database. We cite these debates by year and speaker in the text (e.g. Lord Ennals: Hansard, 1990), and by a complete online database reference in the reference list (e.g. Hansard, 1990; Human Fertilisation and Embryology Bill [HL]. HL Deb. 13 March 1990, vol. 516 cc1476–511).

1 Mulkay, M., *The Embryo Research Debate: Science and the Politics of Reproduction*, Cambridge: Cambridge University Press, 1997.

2 Ibid., at pp. 62–6.

3 Ibid., at pp. 132–3.

Commons vote.[4] Mulkay suggests that this demonstration that research on human embryos really did produce genuine therapeutic benefits influenced parliamentary opinion decisively.[5] Mulkay's work offers a detailed sociological account of the tactics employed by the pro-research lobby between 1985 and 1990. He only hints, however, at the origins of these political arguments, as most of his discussion is based on the parliamentary debates and press commentary accompanying the passage of the HFEA 1990.

In this chapter, we explore how the concept of the 'genetic embryo' emerged as a political tool, and how the transformation of the embryo into a genetic entity affected the outcome of debate. While Mulkay suggests that genetic disease was only a 'minor feature' of the pro-research case until the late 1980s,[6] we have argued recently that it played a critical role from as early as 1985 in structuring both research activities and Parliamentary debates preceding the passing of the HFEA 1990.[7] In this chapter, we trace the history of the genetic embryo from its origins in the 1950s, through pioneering PGD studies in animals from as early as 1965, and in the discussions about prenatal testing and abortion. We suggest that the pro-research focus on genetic disease of the 1980s built on these earlier, often politically driven, discussions. We argue that the genetic embryo that ultimately emerged was a useful political tool, albeit one built on an insecure scientific foundation, and that its utility was due in part to exaggerated pro-research claims that went largely unchallenged.

The concept of the genetic embryo

We introduce the term 'genetic embryo' as a concept that was not simply employed as a political tool by the pro-research lobby, but rather was moulded by public, professional and Parliamentary perceptions of embryo research, *in vitro* fertilisation, PGD, abortion and prenatal testing. Our evidential sources include parliamentary debates and voting patterns, public opinion polls and media reports, scientific papers, and archival letters and documents. The phrase 'genetic embryo' was not actually used in these debates, but has been coined by us to encapsulate a variety of ways in which the genetic make-up of the embryo was a subject of debate and influenced the approach taken to the permissibility of scientific techniques. Use of this term provides a unifying conceptual framework within which to consider (a) the growing research and clinical interest in normal and abnormal genetics in human embryology, and (b) the geneticisation of political arguments in medico-scientific research

4 Handyside, A. H., Kontogianni, E. H., Hardy, K. and Winston, R. M., 'Pregnancies from biopsied human preimplantation embryos sexed by Y-specific DNA amplification', *Nature* 344 (1990): 768–70.

5 Mulkay, *Embryo Research Debate*, at p. 42.

6 Ibid., at p. 63.

7 Theodosiou, A. A. and Johnson, M. H., 'The politics of human embryo research and the motivation to achieve PGD', *Reproductive BioMedicine Online*, 22 (2011): 457–71.

policy and the 1980s' UK embryo research debate. The concept of the genetic embryo can take a variety of forms, ranging from its use with reference to diagnosis, prevention or cure of genetic disease to simply understanding embryo genetics. Moreover, many references are vague about the technological details and social implications of the concepts described, perhaps due to insufficient information, or for strategic reasons. Nonetheless, the genetic embryo provides a common thread, which may be traced from the 1950s to 1990, allowing us to consider the evidence as to why the pro-research lobby came to focus strategically on genetic disease in the embryo research debate.

Early biomedical developments

The period after the Second World War saw the beginnings of the process by which genetics came to occupy its central position in biomedicine by the 1980s. A major practical stimulus to this early genetic research was to understand the impact of radiation-induced genetic damage to the germ line, which assumed particular political salience with the use of the atomic bomb in Japan, the radioactive fallout from atomic testing and the development of atomic energy.[8] However, basic molecular and cytogenetic studies were to prove both complementary and, in the longer term, of more importance to the emergence of the genetic embryo. At the molecular level, the recognition that deoxyribonucleic acid (DNA) was the molecular carrier of genetic information[9] was a key discovery, and was rapidly followed by the findings that each cell of the body carried a full set of DNA/genes[10] that were selectively expressed as mRNA (messerge ribonucleic acid) to generate different cell phenotypes.[11] Cytogenetic studies led to the acceptance of the human karyotype as having 46 chromosomes,[12] agreement on the nomenclature of human chromosomes,[13] and the discovery that chromosomal aneuploidies underlay developmental anomalies such as Down, Turner and Klinefelter syndromes.[14] These latter

8 De Chadarevian, S., 'Mice and the reactor: the "genetics experiment"', *1950s Britain: Journal of the History of Biology*, 39 (2006): 707–35.

9 Watson, J. D. and Crick, F. H., 'Genetical implications of the structure of deoxyribonucleic acid', *Nature*, 171 (1953): 964–7; Watson, J. D. and Crick, F. H., 'Molecular structure of nucleic acids; a structure for deoxyribose nucleic acid', *Nature*, 171 (1953): 737–8; Franklin, R. and Gosling, R., 'Molecular configuration in sodium thymonucleate, *Nature*, 171 (1953): 740–1.

10 Gurdon, J. B., Elsdale, T. R. and Fischberg, M., 'Sexually mature individuals of Xenopus laevis from the transplantation of single somatic nuclei', *Nature*, 182 (1958): 64–5; Gurdon, J. B., 'Adult frogs derived from the nuclei of single somatic cells', *Dev. Biol*, 4 (1962): 256–73; Gurdon, J. B., 'The developmental capacity of nuclei taken from intestinal epithelium cells of feeding tadpoles', *J. Embryol. Exp. Morphol.*, 10 (1962): 622–40.

11 Weinberg, A. M., 2001, 'Messenger RNA: origins of a discovery', *Nature*, 414 (2001): 485.

12 Tjio, J. H. and Levan, A., 'The chromosome number of man', *Hereditas*, 42 (1956): 1–6; Ford, C. E. and Hamerton, J. L., 'The chromosomes of man', *Nature*, 178 (1956), 1020–3.

13 Denver Conference, 'A proposed standard system of nomenclature of human mitotic chromosomes', *Lancet*, 1(7133) (1960): 1063–5.

14 Ford, C. E., Polani, P. E., Briggs, J. H. and Bishop, P. M., 'A presumptive human XXY/XX mosaic', *Nature*, 183 (1959): 1030–2; Ford, C. E., Jones, K. W., Polani, P. E., De

discoveries led Robert Edwards to return to his pioneering 1950s' studies on egg maturation in mouse and human,[15] in an attempt to understand whether the causes of these aneuploidies might reside in abnormalities of meiotic maturation during oocyte development.[16] Indeed, driven by this motivation, it was Edwards who first proposed the idea of PGD in 1965,[17] and went on to demonstrate it in 1968.[18]

PGD and the genetic embryo

Using pre-implantation blastocysts flushed from the excised uteri of pregnant rabbits,[19] Gardner and Edwards biopsied trophoblast and stained it for sex chromatin, providing a reliable method of sexing, which was compatible with further development of the embryo. Following transfer of the biopsied blastocysts to a pseudopregnant female, sex was confirmed anatomically and histologically at full term. Edwards and Gardner addressed the potential for clinical application explicitly, claiming that the scope of experimental embryology could be greatly extended to include the detection of 'autosomally inherited deformities from either parent'.[20]

However, it was not until 1990 that the first clinical demonstration of PGD was achieved at the Hammersmith Hospital, London.[21] Embryos from two couples were sexed, to exclude male embryos at risk of inheriting adrenoleukodystrophy or X-linked mental retardation. Unlike Edwards and Gardner's study in rabbits, human embryos were obtained by IVF and sexed

Almeida, J. C. and Briggs, J. H., 'A sex-chromosome anomaly in a case of gonadal dysgenesis Turner's syndrome', *Lancet*, 1(7075) (1959): 711–13; Jacobs, P. A. and Strong, J. A., 'A case of human intersexuality having a possible XXY sex-determining mechanism', *Nature*, 183 (1959): 302–3; Lejeune, J., Gautier. M. and Turpin, R., 'Étude des chromosomes somatiques de neuf enfants mongoliens', *Comptes Rendus Hebd Seances Acad Sci*, 248 (1959): 1721–2.

15 Edwards, R. G. and Gates, A. H., 'Timing of the stages of the maturation divisions, ovulation, fertilization and the first cleavage of eggs of adult mice treated with gonadotrophins', *J. Endocrinol.*, 18 (1959): 292–304; Edwards, R. G., 'Meiosis in ovarian oocytes of adult mammals', *Nature*, 196 (1962): 446–50; Edwards, R. G., 'Maturation *in vitro* of mouse, sheep, cow, pig, rhesus monkey and human ovarian oocytes', *Nature*, 208 (1965): 349–51; Edwards, R. G., 'Maturation *in vitro* of human ovarian oocytes', *Lancet*, 2 (7419) (1965): 926–9.

16 Johnson, M. H., 'Robert Edwards: the path to IVF' *Reprod BioMed Online*, 23 (2011): 245–62; Johnson, M. H., 'Robert Edwards: Nobel Laureate in Physiology or Medicine', in Prof. Karl Grandin (ed.), *Les Prix Nobel 2010*, Nobel Foundation (www.nobelprize.org), pp. 237–56.

17 Edwards, R. G., 'Maturation *in vitro* of human ovarian oocytes', *Lancet*, 2(7419) (1965): 926–9.

18 Gardner, R. L. and Edwards, R. G., 'Control of the sex ratio at full term in the rabbit by transferring sexed blastocysts', *Nature*, 218 (1968): 346–9.

19 Ibid.

20 Ibid., at p.348.

21 Handyside, A. H., Kontogianni, E. H., Hardy, K. and Winston, R. M., 'Pregnancies from biopsied human preimplantation embryos sexed by Y-specific DNA amplification', *Nature*, 344 (1990): 768–70.

by polymerase chain reaction (PCR) amplification of DNA from a single 8-cell blastomere using Y-chromosome-specific probes.

Both of these demonstrations provided a method for sexing embryos without precluding subsequent development or transfer to a receptive uterus. However, due to species differences, methodological modifications were required before the work of Gardner and Edwards using rabbits could be applied clinically. Human embryos are more difficult to obtain practically and ethically than rabbit embryos, as well as being smaller and less amenable to manipulation. Thus, although human IVF was achieved experimentally in 1969,[22] the first IVF baby was not born until 1978,[23] and IVF was still widely viewed with suspicion until the late 1980s.[24] Furthermore, while rabbit trophoblast biopsy provided 200–300 cells, biopsy of human embryos at the 8-cell stage yielded only one or two cells, necessitating far more sensitive genetic testing techniques. Such single-cell testing became theoretically possible in the late 1970s using micro-enzymatic assays,[25] but these were not applied to PGD in mouse models for ten years[26] and proved problematic in humans.[27] It was not until the development of PCR in the late 1980s[28] that single-cell testing of human

22 Edwards, R. G., Bavister, B. D. and Steptoe, P. C., 'Early stages of fertilization in vitro of human oocytes matured in vitro', *Nature*, 221 (1969): 632–5.

23 Steptoe, P. C. and Edwards, R. G., 'Birth after the reimplantation of a human embryo', *Lancet*, 2(8085) (1978): 366.

24 Theodosiou and Johnson, 'Politics of human embryo research'.

25 Monk, M. and Kathuria, H., 'Dosage compensation for an X-linked gene in preimplantation mouse embryos', *Nature*, 270 (1977): 599–601; Monk, M. and Harper, M. I., 'X-chromosome activity in preimplantation mouse embryos from XX and XO mothers', *Development*, 46 (1978): 53–64; Monk, M. and Harper, M. I., 'Sequential X chromosome inactivation coupled with cellular differentiation in early mouse embryo', *Nature*, 281 (1979): 311–13.

26 Monk, M., Handyside, A., Hardy, K. and Whittingham, D., 'Preimplantation diagnosis of deficiency of hypoxanthine phosphoribosyl transferase in a mouse model for Lesch–Nyhan syndrome', *Lancet*, 2(8556) (1987): 423–5; Monk, M., Handyside, A. H., 'Sexing of preimplantation mouse embryos by measurement of X-linked gene dosage in a single blastomere', *J. Reprod. Fertil.*, 82 (1988): 365–8; Monk, M., 'Pre-implantation diagnosis', *Bioessays*, 8 (1988): 184–9; Monk, M. and Handyside, A. H., 'Sexing of preimplantation mouse embryos by measurement of X-linked gene dosage in a single blastomere', *J. Reprod. Fertil.*, 82 (1988): 365–8; Benson, C. and Monk, M., 'Microassay for adenosine deaminase, the enzyme lacking in some forms of immunodeficiency, in mouse preimplantation embryos', *Hum. Reprod.*, 3 (1988): 1004–9; Holding, C. and Monk, M., 'Diagnosis of beta-thalassaemia by DNA amplification in single blastomeres from mouse preimplantation embryos', *Lancet*, 2(8662) (1989): 532–5.

27 Braude, P. R., Monk, M., Pickering, S. J., Cant, A. and Johnson, M. H., 'Measurement of HPRT activity in the human unfertilized oocyte and pre-embryo', *Prenat. Diagn.*, 9 (1989): 839–50.

28 Saiki, R. K., Scharf, S., Faloona, F., Mullis, K. B., Horn, G. T., Erlich, H. A. and Arnheim, N., 'Enzymatic amplification of beta-globin genomic sequences and restriction site analysis for diagnosis of sickle cell anemia', *Science*, 230 (1985): 1350–4; Saiki, R. K., Bugawan, T. L., Horn, G. T., Mullis, K. B. and Erlich, H. A., 'Analysis of enzymatically amplified beta-globin and HLA-DQ alpha DNA with allele-specific oligonucleotide probes', *Nature*, 324 (1986): 163–6; Mullis, K. B. and Faloona, F. A., 'Specific synthesis of DNA in vitro via a polymerase-catalyzed chain reaction', *Meth. Enzymol.*, 155 (1987): 335–50; Li, H. H., Gyllensten, U. B., Cui, X. F., Saiki, R. K., Erlich, H. A. and Arnheim, N., 'Amplification and analysis of DNA sequences in single human sperm and diploid cells', *Nature*, 335 (1988): 414–17.

embryos became a practical reality.[29] It is these technological hurdles that have provided the conventional explanation as to why PGD took 22 years to be applied clinically.

However, we have argued recently that technological deficit offers an incomplete explanation for the somewhat protracted clinical development of PGD between 1968 and 1990.[30] Thus, while there was very little discussion about, or experimental work on, PGD in humans before the mid-1980s, pre-implantation sexing for commercial incentives was pursued experimentally in cattle and large farm animals in the 1970s and early 1980s, although accuracy and feasibility were not tested on a large scale. Karyotyping, X-linked enzyme micro-assays and immunological detection of a male-specific antigen were each investigated as approaches to PGD that required neither PCR nor embryo biopsies of hundreds of cells.[31] The dearth of human PGD studies in the 1970s and early 1980s suggests a relative lack of interest in overcoming the technological hurdles described. In contrast, the flurry of research and discussion seen between 1986 and 1990 suggests a sudden change in motivation to achieving clinical PGD, which we have ascribed to political events:[32] notably the parliamentary opposition to research on human embryos that greeted publication of the Warnock Report.[33] The potential application of PGD for the detection of genetic disorders became a critical part of the scientific response to this issue.

Abortion legislation in the 1960s: its role in the development of the genetic embryo

Just as the pro-research lobby in the latter half of the 1980s focused on the potential for embryo research to control genetic disease via PGD, so the 1960s' pro-abortion parliamentarians' debates on abortion legislation had highlighted the issue of detecting and terminating abnormal pregnancies. The potential for abortion to prevent the birth of handicapped children was one of two powerful arguments stimulating the passage of the Abortion Act 1967, the other being the desire to eliminate illegal and 'back-street' terminations in the interests of women's health. In the wake of the thalidomide tragedy of the early 1960s,[34] it was seen as 'profoundly shocking' that women were denied easily

29 Handyside, A. H., Pattinson, J. K, Penketh, R. J., Delhanty, J. D., Winston, R. M. and Tuddenham, E.G., 'Biopsy of human preimplantation embryos and sexing by DNA amplification', *Lancet*, 1(8634) (1989): 347–9.
30 Theodosiou and Johnson, 'Politics of human embryo research'.
31 Ibid.
32 Ibid.
33 *Report of the Committee of Inquiry into Human Fertilization and Embryology*, London: HMSO, 1984 (Warnock Report).
34 Lenz, W., 'Kindliche Missbildungen nach Medikament-Einnahme während der Gravidität?', *Dtsch. Med. Wochenschr.*, 86 (1961): 2555–6; Daemmrich, A., 'A tale of two experts: thalidomide and political engagement in the United States and West Germany', *Social Hist. Med.*, 15 (2002): 137–58.

accessible, legal abortions 'even in this extreme case when they knew their baby was likely to be born severely deformed'.[35] At a time when doctors felt that they had '"failed to keep their contract" if the baby was anything but normal',[36] the widespread public and professional attention given to the thalidomide incident 'enabled abortion to be formulated as a public health issue'.[37]

In July 1966, David Steel's Medical Termination of Pregnancy Bill received a majority vote of 223:29 in the Commons. All 15 speakers made specific reference to Clause 1(b) of the Bill, which proposed allowing termination if there was a 'substantial risk that if the child were born it would suffer from such physical or mental abnormalities as to be seriously handicapped'.[38] Out of ten pro-abortion speakers, six accepted this clause 'unreservedly',[39] arguing that the decision 'should be left to the wishes of the mother and the judgement of her doctors' so as to avoid the 'suffering caused to both children and parents by such disasters'.[40] One MP even shared personal experiences, defending his wife's decision to terminate a pregnancy affected by rubella.[41] Pro-abortion speakers cited the endorsement of Clause 1(b) by bodies such as the British Medical Association (BMA) and the Abortion Law Reform Association, as well as a national opinion poll stating that termination on 'these grounds . . . received the highest support from public opinion – 91 per cent'.[42] In contrast, four of the five anti-abortion speakers found Clause 1(b) to be 'utterly repugnant', reminding the House of 'Hitler's conception of a race of perfect physical specimens',[43] and questioning who should judge whether another 'human being's life is worth living'.[44] The remaining four pro-abortion speakers and one anti-abortion MP took a more ambivalent stance, broadly approving of Clause 1(b), but warning of the 'need for caution and for considerable discussion in Committee'.[45]

Aside from the argument of principle, one of the most significant sources of conflict in the 1960s' abortion debates was whether or not foetal abnormality could be diagnosed accurately, or only estimated by risk assessment. Indeed, anti-abortion speakers insisted that such conditions were 'not predictable' or 'diagnosable before birth',[46] while even pro-abortion speakers worried that 'in none of these cases' was there 'anything approaching certainty' that there would be 'abnormality in the child'.[47] Accordingly, parliamentarians referred

35 Lee, E., *Abortion Law and Politics Today*, Basingstoke: Macmillan, 1998, at p. 79.
36 Ibid., at p. 167.
37 Ibid., at p. 79.
38 Steel: Hansard, 1966.
39 Maude: Hansard, 1966.
40 Jenkins: Hansard, 1966.
41 Lyons: Hansard, 1966.
42 Steel: Hansard, 1966.
43 Knight: Hansard, 1966.
44 St. John-Stevas: Hansard, 1966.
45 Abse: Hansard, 1966.
46 Lord Barrington: Hansard, 1967b.
47 Lord Stonham: Hansard, 1965.

Table 3.1 Usage of key words in 14 Commons and Lords debates on abortion (1965–7)

Tag	*Key words*	*Total usage*
Risk	risk	356
Diagnos	diagnose(s); diagnosis; diagnostic	42
Handicap	handicap(s); handicapped; handicapping	219
Abnorm	abnormal; abnormality; abnormalities	177
Deform	deformity/ies; deformed; deformation(s); deforming	167
Defect	defect(s); defective	76
Malform	malformation(s); malformed; malforming	40
Gene	gene(s); genetic(s)	17
Hered/herit	hereditary; heritable; inherited; inheritance	13
Disab	disability; disabilities; disabled; disabling	12
Chromos	chromosome(s); chromosomal	6
Congenital	congenital	5
Amnio	amniocentesis; amniotic fluid; amnion	4
Ultra/sonar	ultrasound; ultrasonography; ultrasonic; sonar	0
Chorio/CVS	chorion biopsy; chorionic villus sampling	0

Note: Parliamentary rhetoric was analysed quantitatively by counting usage of key words electronically. For each of these key words, a suitable 'tag' was chosen to identify usage in different grammatical contexts (e.g. the tag 'diagnos' was used to identify the key words 'diagnosis', 'diagnose(s)' and 'diagnostic'). A reference was counted only if spoken in the context of a genetic or non-genetic characteristic in an embryo or foetus.

far more frequently to risk than to diagnosis, and where the latter term was used, it was often to emphasise the woeful lack of diagnostic techniques (see Table 3.1). In the 14 debates on abortion between 1965 and 1967, there were only four references to amniocentesis, and no explicit references to ultrasound, as prenatal testing was not yet firmly established in clinical practice. As such, risk was mostly discussed in the context of exposure to infectious agents such as rubella, or teratogens like thalidomide, rather than genetic, chromosomal or hereditary factors (Table 3.1).

Thus, the rhetoric of the genetic embryo evoked in the 1980s' embryo research debates was preceded by Parliamentary reference to the 'deformed foetus' in the 1960s. There is evidence that the latter was very effective in securing the passage of the Abortion Act 1967. Despite uncertainty about the limits of medical diagnosis, it was agreed by a majority of 162:73 that abortion on grounds of 'substantial risk' of foetal abnormality should remain in the Bill,[48] setting an important precedent of Parliamentary support for the principle of handicap prevention that was to influence the embryo research debates two decades later. Thus, in 1985, one pro-research speaker cited the Abortion Act 1967 as legal precedent, arguing that Parliament had 'recognised the legitimacy of terminating the prospect of human life for a defective embryo', and so it would be hypocritical to reject embryo research aimed at

48 Hansard, 1967a.

Table 3.2 World Health Organization (WHO)-sponsored CVS registry

	1983	*1984*	*1987*	*1991*
CVS cases	178	3,194	35,538	78,491
Centres	6	43	78	144
Countries	5	14	21	29
Continents	2	3	4	6

Source: based on Milunsky, *Genetic Disorders and the Fetus: Diagnosis, Prevention, and Treatment*, 3rd edn, Baltimore, MD: Johns Hopkins University Press, 1992, p. 124.

preventing such handicaps.[49] Some MPs, like Renee Short, spoke in both the debates on abortion and on embryo research, emphasising in both cases the 'heartbreaking and unaccountable tragedy' of 'congenital abnormality',[50] and the suffering of 'unfortunate . . . disabled children'.[51]

The advent of prenatal diagnosis

Although amniocentesis was pioneered to diagnose sex in 1955,[52] prenatal testing did not become established in clinical practice until after the 1960s' debates. The technique was subsequently expanded to enable diagnosis of dozens of metabolic and genetic disorders.[53] Indeed, data collected by Guy's Hospital indicated that the percentage of mothers aged 40 or more in their region who were tested increased from 12% in 1975 to 18% in 1976, 36% in 1977, and 42% in 1978.[54] The clinical application of amniocentesis increased further following large-scale international clinical trials to assess safety in the late 1970s.[55] Ultrasound was introduced into gynaecological and obstetric practice in the mid-1960s, and its clinical and experimental use rose rapidly throughout the 1970s,[56] until it gained the approval of 'virtually all prenatal diagnosticians'.[57] In the mid-1980s, first trimester chorionic villus sampling

49 Jackson: Hansard, 1985.
50 Short: Hansard, 1985.
51 Short: Hansard, 1966.
52 Serr, D. M., Sachs, L. and Danon, M., 'The diagnosis of sex before birth using cells from the amniotic fluid (a preliminary report)', *Bull. Res. Counc. Isr.*, 5B(2) (1955): 137–8.
53 Burton, B. K., Gerbie, A. B. and Nadler, H. L., 'Present status of intrauterine diagnosis of genetic defects', *Am J Obstet Gynecol*, 118 (1974): 718–46. Elias, S. and Verp, M. S., 'Prenatal diagnosis of genetic disorders', *Obstet Gynecol Annu*, 12 (1983): 79–102.
54 Orlandi, C., Polani, P. and Bovicelli, L., *Recent Advances in Prenatal Diagnosis: Proceedings of the First International Symposium on Recent Advances in Prenatal Diagnosis, Bologna, 15–16 September 1980*: London: Wiley, 1981.
55 Milunsky, A., *Genetic Disorders and the Fetus: Diagnosis, Prevention, and Treatment*, 3rd edn, Baltimore, MD: Johns Hopkins University Press, 1992, pp. 45–7.
56 White, D., *Ultrasound in Biomedicine: Cumulative Bibliography of the World Literature in Ultrasound in Medicine and Biology to 1978*, London: Pergamon, 1982.
57 Turnbull, A. C. and MacKenzie, I. Z., 'Second-trimester amniocentesis and termination of pregnancy', *Br Med Bull*, 39 (1983): 315–21.

(CVS) began to gain clinical popularity (see Table 3.2), as it provided an earlier alternative to second trimester amniocentesis followed by later, and thus more physically and emotionally traumatic, abortions.

By the 1980s, these developments had largely naturalised the concept of intervening in pregnancy to prevent abnormality. Indeed, in 1982, while National Health Service (NHS) clinics performed only 29% of the abortions that took place after 17 weeks (the remainder being carried out by private practitioners), they performed 85% of the late abortions for suspected foetal abnormality.[58] These figures indicate 'the reluctance of most gynaecologists to carry out late abortion[s]', but also the 'special status given to congenital abnormality'.[59] By 1989, the Royal College of Physicians reported that 60–85% of 'informed women at risk' requested amniocentesis in the UK, and that, in areas where screening was routine, the birth rate of babies with neural tube defects had fallen by 60–70%.[60] As such, during the embryo research debates of the 1980s, even many opponents of embryo research wanted 'to see diseases and handicaps eliminated',[61] and were 'at least equally concerned to find cures' as were the pro-research speakers,[62] objecting to the need for destructive embryo research rather than the principle of intervening to select genetically healthy embryos for transfer. Thus, the political and clinical experience with abortion on grounds of handicap prevention from the 1960s onwards likely contributed to the political status and effectiveness of the concept of the genetic embryo in the 1980s.

The genetic embryo and the Medical Research Council

While prenatal testing was becoming increasingly acceptable clinically during the 1970s, the potential to control genetic disease using PGD was initially overshadowed by widespread scepticism and ethical concerns about IVF and embryo research. Indeed, the Medical Research Council (MRC) found research on or transfer of IVF embryos to be unethical, and refused to fund such research until 'they were provided with satisfactory evidence that there would be no increased risk of abnormal offspring'.[63] In 1971, the MRC considered and ultimately rejected a grant application by Robert Edwards and Patrick Steptoe to fund their research on human conception and development *in vitro*, one objective of which was to facilitate development of PGD.[64]

58 *Ciba Foundation Symposium 115, Abortion: Medical Progress and Social Implications*, London: Pitman, 1985, at p. 103.
59 Ibid.
60 Royal College of Physicians, *Prenatal Diagnosis and Genetic Screening: Community and Service Implications/A Report of the Royal College of Physicians*, London: Royal College of Physicians, 1989.
61 Braine: Hansard, 1990b.
62 Hargreaves: Hansard, 1986b.
63 NA1.
64 NA2.

Johnson *et al.* provide a detailed analysis of this decision, explaining that the Council viewed IVF as 'purely experimental rather than as potentially therapeutic, and so set the bar for safety high'. [65] Grant referees John Evans and Roger Short rejected the possibility that embryo sexing could avert the birth of children with sex-linked defects, and found amniocentesis followed by abortion to be 'far simpler' and even 'less hazardous both for the mother and the foetus'.[66] The MRC advocated experiments on non-human primates, but added that only the 'eventual birth, after transfer, of a normal baby' could satisfy them that IVF did not cause abnormalities.[67] Even Anne McLaren, who later played a central role in the pro-embryo-research lobby, publicly expressed concern that 'a malformed baby' might be born if transfers were 'carried out prematurely, through the desire . . . to be first in the field'.[68]

In contrast, Edwards and Steptoe were among the first to recognise the scope for embryo research to prevent, rather than cause, genetic abnormalities. Indeed, they attempted to biopsy and sex human blastocysts in the early 1970s, albeit without success,[69] and suggested that this would be 'an excellent approach to the control of sex-linked mutant genes in man'.[70] In their 1971 grant application to the MRC, they acknowledged research into 'averting the birth of children with certain inherited disorders' as one of their core objectives, along with the 'alleviation of infertility'.[71] These aims were reiterated in a working party report of the British Association for the Advancement of Science,[72] of which Edwards was a member. In addition, a 1972 study by the BMA reported on the potential to 'diagnose certain foetal abnormalities in fertilised ova', and that 'this way might be preferable to termination at 16 weeks' following amniocentesis.[73]

The birth of the first IVF baby in 1978, free from apparent congenital abnormality, 'vindicated Edwards and put pressure on the MRC to justify and reverse a decision that now looked wrong'.[74] While the MRC had previously given 'infertility a low priority compared to population control',[75] the clinical success of IVF 'transformed' the public's 'latent demand for a technological

65 Johnson, M. H., Franklin, S. B., Cottingham, M. and Hopwood, N., 'Why the Medical Research Council refused Robert Edwards and Patrick Steptoe support for research on human conception in 1971', *Hum. Reprod.*, 25 (2010): 2157–74, at p. 2167.

66 NA3.

67 NA 1978. Statement. Ramaswamy, S. [28 July: FD10/161].

68 BL1.

69 Cited in Harper, J. 'Background: introduction to preimplantation genetic diagnosis', *Preimplantation Genetic Diagnosis*, 2nd edn, Cambridge: Cambridge University Press, 2009, pp. 1–10, at p. 3.

70 Edwards, R. G., 'Problems of artificial fertilization', *Nature*, 233 (1971): 23–5.

71 NA2.

72 Jones, A. and Bodmer, W. F, *Our Future Inheritance: Choice or Chance? A Study by a British Association Working Party*, Oxford: Oxford University Press, 1974, at p. 31.

73 Ibid., at pp. 120–1.

74 Johnson *et al.*, 'Why the Medical Research Council refused Robert Edwards and Patrick Steptoe'.

75 Ibid.

solution to the problem of childlessness into an active demand' which the Council could not ignore.[76] In October 1978, the MRC advised 'an urgent review' of policy, 'in light of the recent demonstration of the feasibility of human in vitro fertilisation and embryo transfer, and proposals received by the Cell Board both from Dr Anne McLaren . . . and from Professor R V Short'.[77] The statement from Short, however, referred only to his desire to use 'human spermatozoa to fertilize . . . hamster eggs' in order to study anomalies in haploid sperm nuclei,[78] while McLaren's contribution was somewhat ambivalent. Although she concluded that a policy review 'would be no bad thing', she did not 'see any great urgency' at that time,[79] which implies that the Council's decision to review their previous policy was more influenced by the birth of a healthy IVF baby than by the expert opinion received. However, McLaren did caution that 'we need to be certain' that IVF embryos 'are not abnormal', and stressed that 'the only ethical approach' would be 'to carry out chromosomal and biochemical studies' on pre-implantation embryos, which 'might well also throw light on the aetiology of spontaneous abnormalities of implantation and early development'.[80] Critically, she specified that 'there would be no question' of research embryos being transferred, and so 'no increased risk of abnormal offspring'.[81] Thus, while the fear that IVF might cause anomalies remained, it was suddenly used as a justification to encourage, rather than withhold, support for research on human embryos.

Following the MRC's decision, an MRC Advisory Group met in March 1979, made up largely of reproductive physiologists and clinicians.[82] They concluded that 'scientifically sound research' should be allowed, provided that the aim was 'clearly defined and acceptable', and 'relevant to clinical problems such as contraception or the differential diagnosis and treatment of infertility'.[83] Although they did not specify the study of inherited disease in these conclusions, they did note 'with interest the recent developments of the use of recombinant DNA techniques in the field of prenatal diagnosis . . . which might become relevant' to the 'prevention of inherited disease'. The Advisory Group met again in May 1982, and this time agreed that 'all the available evidence in animals' suggested that there were 'no adverse effects on offspring' born by IVF.[84] Based on this opinion, the MRC, for the first time, encouraged the pursuit of 'a screening device for determining the chromosome constitution of an embryo' in order to avoid genetic disease. This perspective on PGD was offered by none other than John Evans, who, in 1971, had deemed Edwards' suggestion of the

76 Mulkay, *Embryo Research Debate*, at p. 11.
77 NA4.
78 NA5.
79 NA6.
80 NA6.
81 NA6.
82 NA4.
83 NA7.
84 NA8.

same technology to be 'minor', 'complicated and unnecessary'.[85] The increased focus on embryo genetics was reflected in the Advisory Group's expanded membership, which now included the genetics expertise of McLaren, Evans, Polani and Williamson. The Group reiterated that research should be allowed if 'relevant to clinical problems such as contraception and . . . infertility', but wished 'to include . . . the fields of embryology and inherited disease'.[86] That November, the Council published these guidelines in the *British Medical Journal*,[87] providing an important public endorsement of embryo research by a professional scientific body, and formalising the tripartite conception of research to tackle contraception, infertility and genetic disease.

Some of the earliest embryo research projects supported by the MRC focused on this new third aim, including work by Angell *et al.*[88] at the MRC's Reproductive Biology Unit in Edinburgh. This study investigated the 'high failure rate (80%) of implantation' in clinical IVF, and contributed the 'surprising and remarkable finding' that 3/11 embryos tested showed chromosomal defects. They concluded that such defects 'clearly result in early embryo loss',[89] and so used genetic arguments to justify the need for further research to improve the success rate of IVF. Johnson, Braude and Pratt received the first MRC external grant supporting human embryo research in 1983, which aimed 'to draw on the knowledge of the mouse embryo to establish criteria of normal development in the human embryo, and to apply these to detect causes of abnormality and reproductive failure'.[90] These individuals were heavily involved in pro-research lobbying from the mid-1980s onwards, making them well placed to publicise the potential for embryo research to facilitate detection and control of genetic disease.

Thus, before 1978, limited references to the concept that we have termed the genetic embryo were eclipsed by fears that IVF would cause, rather than prevent, abnormalities. However, the notion of the genetic embryo took shape in medico-scientific rhetoric from 1978 onwards, and was used by the MRC to justify a radical policy change on human embryo research. In this way, the fear of elusive IVF abnormalities was transformed into a desire to pursue, rather than impede, research on genetic abnormalities in IVF embryos.

The genetic embryo and the Warnock Committee

In July 1982, the Department of Health and Social Security (DHSS) formed a Committee of Inquiry to investigate 'the social, ethical and legal implications'

85 NA3.
86 NA8.
87 Anon. 'Research related to human fertilisation and embryology. Statement by the Medical Research Council', *Br Med J (Clin Res Ed)*, 285 (1982): 1480.
88 Angell, R. R., Aitken, I., van Look, F., Lumsden, A. A. and Templeton, A. A., 'Chromosome abnormalities in human embryos after in vitro fertilization', *Nature*, 303 (1983): 336–8.
89 Ibid.
90 MRC. 1983/84. Annual Report.

of 'recent and potential developments in medicine and science related to human fertilisation and embryology',[91] chaired by Dame (now Baroness) Mary Warnock. A Government circular was issued in late 1982 by Jenny Croft, one of the Committee's two Secretaries, calling for submission of evidence by numerous medical, scientific, religious, charity and lobby groups.[92] The circular requested evidence specifically on the '*therapeutic . . . scientific . . . legal . . . social . . . moral and ethical*' implications of 'recent and potential developments' in human fertilisation and embryology, and identified the 'therapeutic aspects' as involving 'the treatment of infertility and the prevention of inherited disease'.[93] An explanatory note was also attached, which outlined the technological basis of assisted reproduction, and discussed the potential for research on embryo genetics involving trans-species fertilisation, sexing, genetic manipulation and cloning 'to investigate the chromosome normality'.[94] As such, the genetic embryo was framed as an important player, although not yet the main protagonist, in this circular, which may have influenced the focus of the evidence submitted subsequently. Jeremy Metters, the Committee's other Joint Secretary, may have contributed to this framing, as he was an observer at the 1979 and 1982 MRC meetings on policy review,[95] and so may have been influenced by the MRC's increasing focus on the genetic embryo.

We have reviewed the evidence submitted by six major medico-scientific bodies, including the MRC,[96] the BMA,[97] the Royal College of Obstetricians and Gynaecologists (RCOG),[98] the Royal Society,[99] the Royal College of General Practitioners (RCGP)[100] and the Council for Science and Society (CSS).[101] With the exception of the RCGP, all were broadly pro-research. However, they differed somewhat in focus, with the reports of the MRC and the Royal Society devoted entirely to the practicalities and wider implications of embryo research, while the evidence by the BMA and the RCGP was focused more on the ethics and provision of infertility treatment. Nonetheless, almost all of these bodies identified the control of genetic disease as one of the main potential benefits of research, alongside infertility treatment. Alternative approaches to PGD were

91 Warnock Report.
92 NA9.
93 Ibid.
94 Ibid.
95 NA7 and 8.
96 Anon., 'Research related to human fertilisation and embryology'.
97 Anon., 'Supplementary annual report of Council, 1982–1983. Appendix VI: Interim report on human in vitro fertilisation and embryo replacement and transfer', *Br Med J (Clin Res Ed)*, 286(6377) (1983): 1594–5.
98 RCOG, *Report of the RCOG Ethics Committee on in vitro Fertilisation and Embryo Replacement or Transfer*, London: Chameleon Press, 1983.
99 Royal Society, *Human Fertilization and Embryology: Submission by the Royal Society to the Department of Health and Social Security Committee of Inquiry into Human Fertilization and Embryology*, London: Royal Society, 1983.
100 RCOG, *Report of the RCOG Ethics Committee.*
101 CSS, *Human Procreation: Ethical Aspects of the New Techniques: Report of a Working Party, Council for Science and Society*, Oxford: Oxford University Press, 1984.

discussed, such as 'the removal of cells from the very early embryo',[102] or 'embryo division',[103] and the reports advised that intact embryos could be frozen for later transfer, while the cells or 'cloned' embryos could be sexed to exclude sex-linked disease, or tested using 'DNA probes'.[104] Significantly, these suggestions preceded the technological developments, such as PCR, which facilitated research progress on human PGD from 1986 onwards.[105]

It was proposed that such methods were 'more acceptable than amniocentesis with a view to mid-trimester termination',[106] and that, while IVF treatment would 'be of help only to that small percentage of parents who are ever likely to use the IVF procedure', a 'better understanding of inherited disease . . . could be of immense benefit to . . . vast numbers of individuals'.[107] Furthermore, these medico-scientific bodies either condemned ethically challenging aspects of research on embryo genetics, such as sexing for non-medical reasons,[108] or else downplayed these aspects. In a presentation to the Warnock Committee, the MRC stressed that genetic manipulation of embryos was not 'a simple or even desirable method of preventing genetic disease',[109] while the CSS insisted that 'Aldous Huxley's literary fantasy' of reproductive cloning was 'very far indeed from realization'.[110] As such, the pro-research rhetoric, identified by Mulkay[111] as being pivotal to the passage of the HFE Act 1990, featured already in the evidence of a handful of major medico-scientific bodies in 1982/3. In addition, several individuals involved in producing this evidence subsequently participated heavily in pro-research lobbying, such as Anne McLaren and M. C. Macnaughton, and so were well placed to re-emphasise such rhetoric. Thus, the genetic embryo was emerging as a political tool significantly earlier than Mulkay suggests.

Considering that the Committee's call for evidence[112] referred extensively to embryo research, and framed the genetic embryo as an important player, it is somewhat surprising that the Warnock Report itself focused almost entirely on infertility treatment. Only three chapters dealt explicitly with the issue of research, the possible future developments, and the wider application of IVF technology, amounting to 22 of 79 pages. Where embryo genetics and genetic disease were discussed, the Report was distinctly hesitant. Detection of abnormalities by embryo biopsy was considered 'unlikely' to become feasible 'for some considerable time', due to the 'relatively low success rates for pregnancy

102 Royal Society, *Human Fertilization and Embryology*.
103 RCOG, *Report of the RCOG Ethics Committee*.
104 Ibid.
105 Theodosiou and Johnson, 'Politics of human embryo research'.
106 RCOG, *Report of the RCOG Ethics Committee*.
107 CSS, *Human Procreation*, at p. 53.
108 Ibid., at pp. 55–6.
109 NA10.
110 CSS, *Human Procreation*, at p. 10.
111 Ibid., at pp. 62–6, 132–3.
112 NA9.

following IVF'.[113] In addition, the insertion of 'a replacement gene' to 'prevent certain genetic diseases' was described as 'purely speculative', and likely to be 'precluded' due to 'public anxiety' about the 'overtones of selective breeding'.[114] Pre-implantation sex selection to avoid sex-linked disease was approved as an alternative to the 'psychological and physical trauma' of amniocentesis and late abortion, although 'wide scale' social sexing was described as 'dubious'.[115] This hesitation is all the more curious considering that Anne McLaren, later a strong supporter of embryo research, was responsible for writing 'the strictly scientific, biological part'.[116]

The genetic embryo and the parliamentary debate on embryo research

The Warnock Report's recommendations that licensed research on human embryos be allowed was met by intense parliamentary opposition when debated in October and November 1984,[117] with the majority of anti-research MPs drawing largely on the rhetoric of anti-abortion moral arguments.[118] That December, Conservative MP Enoch Powell tabled a private member's bill to ban all production and use of human embryos, except to help an infertile woman achieve pregnancy. In response, a small group of scientists and pro-abortionists, including Peter Braude, James Gowans, Martin Johnson, M. C. Macnaughton, David Whittingham and Robert Winston, as well as Joanna Chambers of the British Birth Control Campaign, began lobbying in favour of embryo research.[119] They organised an 'all party discussion on embryo research in the House of Commons',[120] and distributed materials to members of the public, encouraging them to write to their MPs.[121] Some of these materials framed the genetic embryo as a key player. Indeed, a factsheet disseminated by the MRC in January 1985 described the 'detection and prevention of congenital and hereditary disorders' as the 'greatest long-term benefit' of research for many.[122] In addition, both James Gowans, Secretary of the MRC, and Edinburgh geneticist John Evans sent MP Peter Thurnham briefs[123] challenging Jerome Lejeune, the pro-life geneticist who had publicly rejected claims that embryo research could facilitate understanding or prevention of genetic disease. Lejeune in turn briefed anti-research MPs, and his views were widely cited by anti-

113 Warnock Report, at p. 73.
114 Ibid., at p. 74.
115 Ibid., at p. 51.
116 Unpublished interview with Mary Warnock, 2008 (now deposited in the British Library Oral History Archive).
117 Hansard 1984a, b.
118 Mulkay, *Embryo Research Debate*, at p. 22.
119 Theodosiou and Johnson, 'Politics of human embryo research'.
120 LSE1.
121 LSE2.
122 CC1.
123 LSE3.

research speakers in the debates on the Powell Bill,[124] indicating that the genetic embryo featured in both pro-research and anti-research political rhetoric as early as 1985.

Mulkay suggests that 'in the early debates, reference to control of genetic disease had been a minor feature', and that only 'during later pro-research speeches' did it become 'the central topic'.[125] However, in response to the briefs received, ten out of eleven pro-research Commons MPs in the February debate on the Powell Bill, and all but three of thirteen anti-research MPs, referred to the potential for embryo research to prevent genetic disease.[126] Pro-research MPs defended the principle of intervening to prevent disability, and even asserted that 'society clearly does not want handicapped children', as evinced by the 'many thousands' of such children awaiting adoption.[127] MPs Peter Thurnham and Dafydd Wigley contributed a powerful personal dimension, as the former had recently adopted a handicapped child, while the latter had lost a son to genetic disease only six weeks previously. Crucially, pro-research speakers made a moral distinction between embryos, foetuses and children, stressing that 'the future well-being of all children . . . should take precedence over the protection of individual embryos',[128] and that embryo destruction was surely preferable to either late abortion or genetic handicap.

Despite initial pro-research lobby efforts, however, the Bill received an anti-research Commons majority of 238:66 in February 1985.[129] This powerful opposition stimulated the organisation of a larger and more organised pro-research lobby. An increasing number of parliamentarians were given 'briefs to the new clauses' introduced in the Committee and Report stages of the Powell Bill,[130] and were encouraged to 'raise as many amendments as possible' in order to 'delay the Bill'.[131] In March 1985, the MRC and RCOG established the Voluntary Licensing Authority (VLA), and that July, Joanna Chambers 'put forward . . . a proposal that an umbrella organisation be formed to campaign for embryo research'.[132] The campaign group Progress was launched that November, and was given almost immediate credit for the fact that MPs seemed 'to have moderated their views' by the end of 1985.[133] Over the next five years, Progress increasingly emphasised the potential for 'prevention of infertility, miscarriage and congenital handicap',[134] and recruited support from numerous disability charities, including Mind, Sense and Mencap,[135] framing

124 Hansard, 1985.
125 Mulkay, *Embryo Research Debate*, at p. 63.
126 Hansard, 1985.
127 Thurnham: Hansard, 1985.
128 Richardson: Hansard, 1985.
129 Hansard, 1985.
130 LSE5.
131 LSE4.
132 LSE6.
133 Clarke, M. 'Embryo research: chances of legislation fade', *Nature*, 318(6043) (1985): 197.
134 LSE7.
135 LSE8.

the genetic embryo as central to the pro-research case. In January 1988, Progress issued a brief to all parliamentarians on the 'effect of banning pre-embryo research', devoting only five lines to IVF treatment, but 28 lines to 'preventing handicap'.[136] They even arranged for 200 families affected by genetic disorders to visit Parliament.[137]

The pro-research lobby efforts shifted the focus of the debate, such that by the 1989 Lords debate, 75% of pro-research speakers made significant reference to the regulation of genetic disease, compared with only 50% emphasising the possible contribution to infertility treatment.[138] Patterns of word usage provide further evidence of the geneticisation of rhetoric in the embryo research debates (see Table 3.3). Indeed, both pro-research and anti-research MPs referred more frequently to genetic abnormalities and handicaps than to non-genetic deformities and malformations in the 1980s' embryo research debates (Table 3.3a), and also more frequently than in the 1960s' abortion debates (Table 3.3c).

The increased focus on genetics and genetic disease was not, however, seen in the 1980s' debates on abortion, in which parliamentarians considered whether to reduce the time limit of legal termination from 28 weeks to 18, 20, 22, 24 or 26 weeks (Table 3.3b). These parallel debates on abortion, however, did reinforce the political focus on genetic disease in the embryo research debates, as the undesirability of late terminations following amniocentesis was highlighted by both sides. Pro-research speakers insisted that embryo research 'holds out the promise of fewer abortions through the possible new technique of pre-implantation diagnosis'.[139] Crucially, this claim was used to attack the moral basis of the anti-research case, which was based largely on anti-abortion arguments, such that the pro-research speakers accused their opponents of being 'anti-life' rather than 'pro-life'.[140]

There is evidence that this tactic proved effective even amongst some openly anti-abortion speakers, such as the Archbishop of York, who 'spoke up vigorously in favour' of embryo research, but later sided 'with those whom [he had] then opposed', by refusing to support a permissive amendment to the Abortion Act 1967.[141] He reconciled his views by stating that 'the development of human life is a process from almost imperceptible beginnings, when it makes little sense . . . to ascribe full human value to an embryo which has just been conceived, right up to the stage when we begin to acknowledge the independent existence of a new person'.[142] Thus, the gradualist view on the moral status of the embryo and the foetus facilitated acceptance of the genetic embryo as a political tool.

There is substantial evidence that pro-research lobbying between 1985 and 1990 was highly effective. By the late 1980s, Members felt that 'the onus' on

136 LSE8.
137 Mulkay, *Embryo Research Debate*, at p. 63.
138 Ibid., at p. 187.
139 Thurnham: Hansard, 1988b.
140 Jackson: Hansard, 1985.
141 Hansard, 1990d.
142 Ibid.

Table 3.3 Total usage of key words (1965–90); absolute values cannot be compared between Tables (a), (b) and (c), as different debates were studied for each; however, the relative order of key word usage can be compared

(a) 19 debates on embryo research (1980–90)

Tag	*Key words*	*Total usage*
Gene	gene(s); genetic(s)	828
Handicap	handicap(s); handicapped; handicapping	288
Abnorm	abnormal; abnormality; abnormalities	169
Defect	defect(s); defective	167
Disab	disability; disabilities; disabled; disabling	130
Congenital	congenital	122
Chromos	chromosome(s); chromosomal	97
Risk	risk	78
Hered/herit	hereditary; heritable; inherited; inheritance	77
Diagnos	diagnose(s); diagnosis; diagnostic	67
Deform	deformity/ies; deformed; deformation(s); deforming	15
Malform	malformation(s); malformed; malforming	14

(b) 11 debates on abortion (1980–90)

Tag	*Total usage*
Handicap	305
Disab	173
Abnorm	166
Diagnos	55
Risk	40
Deform	28
Defect	19
Gene	18
Congenital	10
Chromos	8
Malform	8
Hered/herit	2

(c) 14 debates on abortion (1965–7)

Tag	*Total usage (D1–14)*
Risk	356
Handicap	219
Abnorm	177
Deform	167
Defect	76
Diagnos	42
Malform	40
Gene	17
Hered/herit	13
Disab	12
Chromos	6
Congenital	5

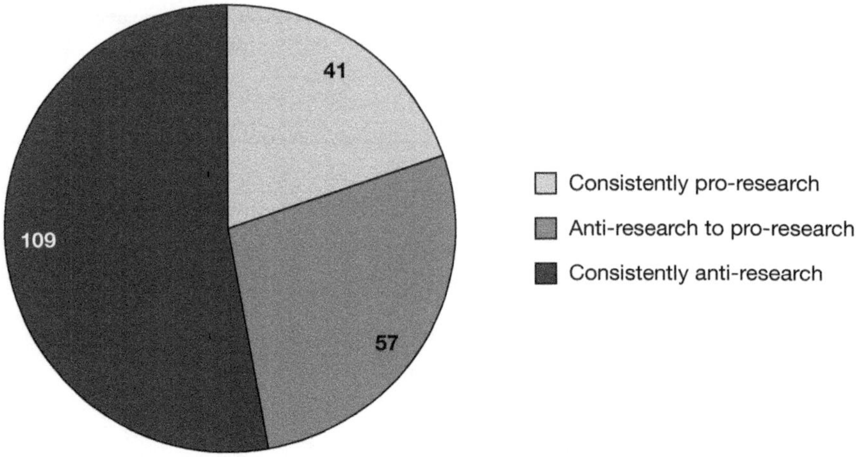

Figure 3.1 Voting patterns of 207 MPs who voted on both the 1984 Unborn Child (Protection) Bill and later, the embryo research clause of the 1990 HFE Bill. Data labels indicate number of votes

the scientist had been 'discharged', shifting the 'burden' to the opposition 'to explain why we should be deprived of the benefits of research',[143] including infertility treatment and the control of genetic disease. Of the 207 MPs who voted on both the Powell and HFE Bills, 57 opposed research in 1985 but supported research in 1990 (see Figure 3.1), while no Members switched from a pro-research to an anti-research vote, such that only a minority of 193:364 voted against research in 1990. In 1988, David Alton's Abortion (Amendment) Bill gained a majority vote in favour of prohibiting abortion beyond 18 weeks,[144] even in most cases of congenital abnormality, although this Bill eventually ran out of time and so was not passed. The majority of Commons MPs who voted on both the Alton and HFE Bills sided in favour of embryo research and against Alton's restrictive Bill, or vice versa (see Figure 3.2). Interestingly, 92 MPs voted to allow embryo research, but to restrictively amend abortion legislation (see Figure 3.2), which may represent those MPs who viewed embryo research and PGD as morally distinct from and preferable to prenatal testing and abortion. For instance, Robert Key justified his stance by balancing the 'benefits and losses' of allowing embryo research in order to 'provide couples with the opportunity to have a healthy baby'.[145]

Thus, the genetic embryo featured in the evidence to the Warnock Committee and in the Parliamentary briefs by a handful of pro-research scientists between 1982 and 1985, but subsequently became the focal point of a strategic campaign by a powerful and effective pro-research lobby between 1985 and

143 Lord Meston: Hansard, 1989.
144 Hansard, 1988a.
145 Hansard, 1990c.

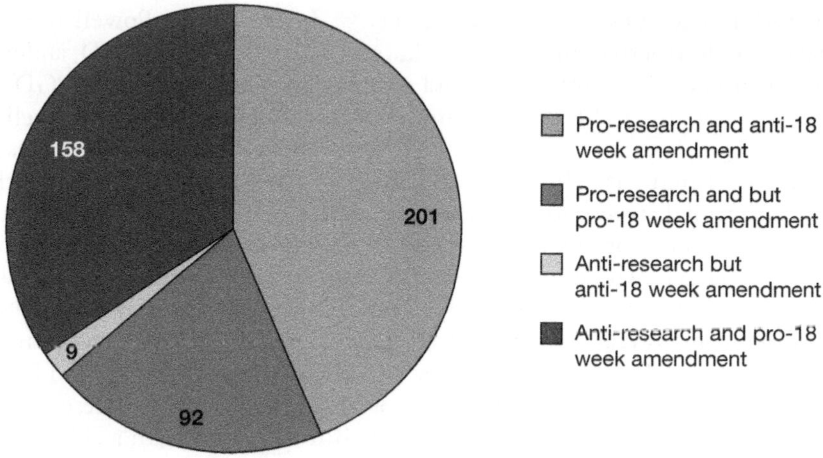

Figure 3.2 Voting patterns of 460 MPs who voted on both the 1988 Alton Bill and later, the embryo research clause of the 1990 HFE Bill. Data labels indicate number of votes

1990. Why then did the pro-research lobby choose this strategic focus, and how robust was the genetic embryo as a political tool?

The value of the genetic embryo as a political tool

As we have seen, the suffering of families affected by genetic and non-genetic diseases was emphasised by both the pro-abortion lobby in the 1960s and by a handful of medico-scientific bodies in the early 1980s in the hopes of securing permissive legislation and research policies. In the same way, we argue that the pro-research focus on genetic disease seen in the embryo research debate between 1985 and 1990 was politically driven.

We have provided evidence previously that the immediate stimulus to adopting the genetic embryo as a focal point of the pro-research case was the large anti-embryo-research majority vote on the Powell Bill, as well as the attitudes of the anti-research MPs to the issue of PGD in particular.[146] Anti-research speakers took subtly different stances on PGD, introducing inconsistencies in their case. For instance, only some argued that intervention in pregnancy to prevent handicap was morally wrong,[147] while others accepted the principle of handicap prevention, but objected to the need for destructive embryo research.[148] Others were concerned less with the prevention of disease than with fears of genetic engineering and positive selection for characteristics,[149] while still others insisted that PGD and genetic engineering could never be

146 Theodosiou and Johnson, 'Politics of human embryo research'.
147 Beith: Hansard, 1985.
148 Winterton: Hansard, 1985.
149 Campbell-Savours: Hansard, 1985.

achieved and so research was unnecessary.[150] Interestingly, Powell himself objected to destructive embryo research, but endorsed IVF and PGD, and was keen to emphasise in both public and private communications that PGD by 'embryonic biopsy could continue' under his Bill.[151] This stance cost Powell at least some pro-life support, and alerted pro-research lobbyists to a weakness in the anti-research case. Indeed, the Order of Christian Unity[152] and the Association of Lawyers for the Defence of the Unborn[153] withdrew their approval of his Bill on the grounds of Powell's lenient stance. In contrast, the public was largely sympathetic to research aimed at preventing genetic disease, which likely further encouraged the pro-research focus. As early as April 1985, a Marplan poll revealed that 'half of the opponents [of embryo research] changed their mind when asked if they would favour research if it would help eliminate genetic diseases', giving a total of 51% in support of such research.[154]

Evidence that the debates on the Powell Bill coincided with a substantial increase in the pro-research focus on genetic disease supports our claim that this focus was politically driven.[155] In July 1984, McLaren submitted a six-page review article on PGD, which was published in the January/February 1985 edition of *Prenatal Diagnosis*. McLaren was markedly hesitant, just as in her chapters in the Warnock Report, concluding that PGD could 'only be considered as a last resort' as it would further decrease the already very low success rate of IVF, and that CVS 'would seem to offer better prospects'.[156] Then, only one month after the majority Commons vote on the Powell Bill, Evans and McLaren published a commentary in *Nature*, insisting that 'attempts to circumvent the production and transfer of severely genetically abnormal embryos' were 'almost within the grasp of medical science', but would be prevented by the Bill.[157] Building on arguments introduced in the evidence to the Warnock Committee and in the Commons debate,[158] they cast the genetic embryo as the central figure, challenging Lejeune's views,[159] promising a 'concomitant reduction in the requirement of abortions', and assuring readers that genetic manipulation was 'not only clearly undesirable, but also unnecessary' due to the approach of PGD.[160] Thus, Evans – who in 1971 had criticised Edwards and Steptoe's proposed research on IVF and PGD[161] – and

150 Braine: Hansard, 1985.
151 CC2.
152 CC3.
153 CC4.
154 Clarke, M., 'UK embryo research: government stops Powell bill', *Nature*, 314 (1985): 573.
155 Theodosiou and Johnson, 'Politics of human embryo research'.
156 McLaren, A., 'Prenatal diagnosis before implantation: opportunities and problems', *Prenat. Diagn*, 5 (1985): 85–90.
157 Evans, H. J. and McLaren, A., 'Unborn children (protection) bill', *Nature*, 314 (1985): 127–8.
158 Hansard, 1985.
159 Lejeune *et al.*, 'Étude'.
160 McLaren and Evans, 'Unborn children (protection) bill'.
161 Johnson *et al.*, 'Why the Medical Research Council refused Robert Edwards and Patrick Steptoe'.

McLaren seem to have proved strategically malleable in the face of political pressure. Similarly, the medico-scientific community, which had criticised the Warnock Report's proposed legislation in late 1984 as an 'extremely retrograde step' that would cause 'insurmountable difficulties' in the field of embryo research,[162] quickly endorsed the Warnock recommendations, and promised to make them 'immediately effective' under the VLA, when faced with the far more restrictive alternative of Powell's ban.[163]

Several scientists, who were later to be involved in pro-research lobbying, began discussing and researching approaches to achieving PGD in humans, suggesting that their efforts were stimulated by the political status PGD had acquired.[164] In late 1986, both the Ciba Foundation[165] and the European Society for Human Reproduction and Embryology (ESHRE)[166] held meetings to discuss the prospects for PGD. Soon afterwards, Marilyn Monk's team at University College London and Robert Winston's Hammersmith team developed a mouse model for PGD,[167] and sexing of human IVF embryos by Y-chromosome PCR was reported in 1989,[168] with pregnancy resulting from transfer of such embryos following a year later.[169]

Thus, it seems that the pro-research lobby's focus on genetic disease, and even the ensuing research on PGD, was stimulated by political pressure, implying that the genetic embryo was a political tool crafted to further the pro-research case.

The validity of the genetic embryo as a political tool?

We suggest that the use of the genetic embryo in this way was founded, at least in part, on scientific ambiguities and exaggerated claims. Thus, it is often unclear whether pro-research parliamentarians and lobbyists were arguing that embryo research could facilitate the prevention, cure or eradication of genetic disease, or could simply further understanding of normal and abnormal embryo

162 NA11.
163 CC5.
164 Theodosiou and Johnson, 'Politics of human embryo research'.
165 Whittingham, D. G. and Penketh, R., 'Prenatal diagnosis in the human pre-implantation period: meeting held at the Ciba Foundation on 13 November', *Hum. Reprod*, 2 (1987): 267–70.
166 Brambati, B., 'Preimplantation and early post-implantation diagnosis: report of the first meeting of the ESHRE Working Group, held on 16 December 1986 in Strasbourg, France', *Hum. Reprod.*, 2 (1987): 399.
167 Monk, M., Handyside, A., Hardy, K. and Whittingham, D., 'Preimplantation diagnosis of deficiency of hypoxanthine phosphoribosyl transferase in a mouse model for Lesch–Nyhan syndrome', *Lancet*, 2(8556) (1987): 423–5.
168 Handyside, A. H., Pattinson, J. K, Penketh, R. J., Delhanty, J. D., Winston, R. M. and Tuddenham, E. G., 'Biopsy of human preimplantation embryos and sexing by DNA amplification', *Lancet*, 1(8634) (1989): 347–9.
169 Handyside, A. H., Kontogianni, E. H., Hardy, K. and Winston, R. M., 'Pregnancies from biopsied human preimplantation embryos sexed by Y-specific DNA amplification', *Nature*, 344 (1990): 768–70.

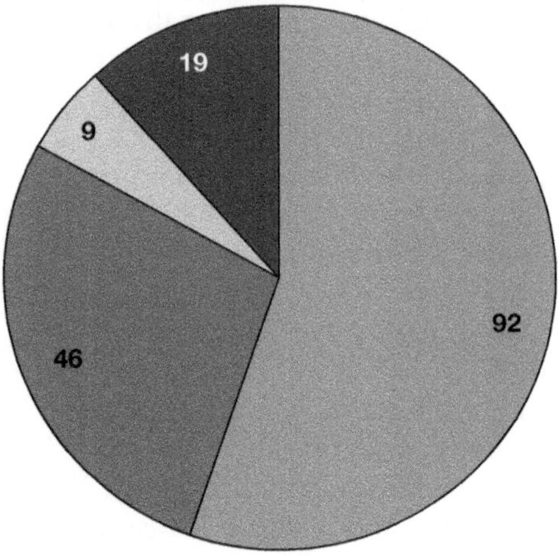

Figure 3.3 Grounds for abortion in a sample of 166 terminations at 20 weeks or more-92: central nervous system defects; 46: chromosomal defects; 9: single gene defects; 19: other non-genetic defects. Source: based on Alberman *et al.*, 'Congenital abnormalities in legal abortions at 20 weeks' gestation or later', *Lancet*, 1(8388) (1984): 1226–8.

genetics. A widely disseminated MRC factsheet insisted that research would 'progressively . . . eliminate many serious inherited diseases', and so '*reduce* the need for abortions',[170] while MP Robert Jackson promised that such research would allow abnormalities to be 'corrected or prevented in the womb'.[171] It was also not made clear whether techniques such as PGD would be applicable to all couples, to all couples at risk of genetic disease, or simply to those couples for whom prenatal testing followed by abortion was unacceptable. Indeed, some pro-research speakers claimed that the Powell Bill would be a 'disaster . . . to the one couple in 50 who are at risk of giving birth to a handicapped child', and to the '1.25 million people with mental handicap in Britain',[172] while allowing such research 'could reduce the annual number of abortions by about 1,500 . . . as a result of the detection of abnormalities at up to 16 weeks'.[173] However, these statistics grouped genetic and non-genetic abnormalities together, obscuring the fact that embryo research and PGD were primarily concerned with the former. Indeed, a study by the RCOG[174] revealed that only about one-third of late terminations on grounds of foetal abnormality were performed to avoid genetic or chromosomal defects, while over half were due to central nervous system defects such as spina bifida, and the rest to other non-genetic defects (Figure 3.3).

170 CC1.
171 Hansard, 1985.
172 Baroness Faithfull; Hansard, 1986a.
173 Morrison; Hansard, 1990b.
174 Alberman, E., Kani, W. and Stanwell-Smith, R., 'Congenital abnormalities in legal abortions at 20 weeks' gestation or later', *Lancet*, 1(8388) (1984): 1226–8.

Clinical experience over the past 20 years further suggests that pro-research claims were unduly optimistic about the clinical scope of PGD, and pessimistic about IVF. Since 1990, only 4,091 PGD pregnancies have been recorded in Europe, and only 1,542 of these were to prevent transmission of genetic disease in 'at risk' couples,[175] while three million IVF babies had been born worldwide by 2006.[176] Contrary to pro-research promises, the annual termination rate for diagnosed abnormality increased between 1985 and 2000, and, by 1995, '80% of UK maternity units offered an anomaly scan to all expectant mothers',[177] while only a very small minority of patients were offered PGD.

A minority of anti-research individuals, including Powell, seemed aware of both the changing tactics and the potential flaws in the pro-research case. John McLean, Professor of Embryology and Anatomy at the University of Manchester and a frequent correspondent of Powell's, called attention to McLaren's pessimistic earlier appraisal of PGD,[178] and insisted that the eradication of genetic disease would prove 'impossible to achieve', as the incidence of such disorders remained 'unchanged despite several years of antenatal screening by amniocentesis'.[179] Even if the 'impracticable' technique of embryo biopsy were perfected, thousands of at risk, yet fertile, couples would have to 'relinquish their procreative role to the IVF laboratories'.[180] In addition, Lord Harvington,[181] who was not a clinician or a scientist, suggested that 'parents who have handicapped children have been misled by the experimentation lobby', citing a Progress leaflet which described the suffering of a mentally disabled child with 'no speech, a club foot, partial vision and epilepsy'. He pointed out that it was 'most unlikely' that the child's condition was 'a genetic one', and so would not be detectable by 'embryo biopsy'.[182] However, almost all anti-research lobbyists focused their case on the moral status of the embryo, and so largely neglected the weaknesses in pro-research argumentation, thus facilitating the acceptance of the genetic embryo in the absence of robust scientific justification.

Despite lobby claims that embryo research would help to eradicate genetic disease, the medico-scientific community rarely publicised what experiments were under way, or what future projects were planned to achieve this aim. A small number of anti-research lobbyists expressed concern that scientists were withholding their intentions, or even conducting secret experiments, and publicly demanded 'evidence . . . rather than vague conjectures', particularly

175 Goossens, V., Harton, G., Moutou, C., Traeger-Synodinos, J., Van Rij, M. and Harper, J. C., 'ESHRE PGD Consortium data collection IX: cycles from January to December 2006 with pregnancy follow-up to October 2007', *Hum Reprod*, 24(8) (2009): 1786–810.

176 Horsey, K. 'Three million IVF babies born worldwide', *BioNews (online)*, 364 (2006), www.bionews.org.uk/page_12772.asp (accessed May 2010).

177 Richmond, S. and Atkins, J., 'A population-based study of the prenatal diagnosis of congenital malformation over 16 years', *BJOG*, 112(10) (2005): 1349–57.

178 CC6.

179 CC7.

180 Ibid.

181 Hansard, 1990a.

182 Ibid.

of projects 'relating to genetic diseases'.[183] Throughout 1985, Powell searched actively for research projects or proposals that he felt would be outside the terms of his Bill, and even paid a visit to Edwards and Steptoe's clinic. However, when he found no evidence of such projects, he began 'to suspect' that this was 'quite generally the case'.[184] At a rally of the Society for the Protection of the Unborn Child (SPUC) in July 1985, he demanded that 'the Government and the professions must come clean with [the] public', and accused the parents of handicapped children of being gullible and emotional, having displayed 'their private griefs in lieu of logical argument'.[185] The lack of publicised research progress and proposals was due to the fact that, before 1987, very little research on PGD was in fact in progress.[186] However, as early as 1985, supporters of embryo research insisted that PGD was 'just around the corner',[187] but dismissed the 'science fiction nightmares' of 'human–hamster hybrids, carbon copy cloning . . . or wanton torture of living foetuses' as 'pure research myths which can never happen'.[188] Lejeune's testimony was undermined by accusations that opponents of research were 'picking and choosing', and reminders that many 'respectable and eminent people' took the 'opposite view',[189] despite the fact that examples of such people or their research projects were largely absent until the late 1980s. As a result, the pro-research lobby relied heavily on an 'extended temporal perspective' that centred on 'imaginative claims about the future'.[190] Interestingly, although the anti-research lobby presented a future fraught with the socially disruptive, rather than clinically beneficial, consequences of embryo research, supporters of such research dismissed these claims as lacking the 'authority of science'.[191]

As clinical experience with PGD was non-existent before 1990, pro-research lobbyists cited evidence obtained from animal models to maintain their scientific authority. Significantly, they assured Parliament and the public that embryo biopsy to achieve PGD was 'known to be safe in animals'[192] and would 'not necessarily prejudice further development'.[193] Evans and McLaren[194] even claimed that viability had 'already been shown' for human embryos following blastomere loss, although they supported this claim by citing the effects of freezing and thawing,[195] rather than biopsy. However, at the 1986 ESHRE

183 CC8.
184 CC9.
185 CC10.
186 Theodosiou and Johnson, 'Politics of human embryo research'.
187 McLaren and Evans, 'Unborn children (protection) bill'.
188 Meacher: Hansard, 1985.
189 Clarke: Hansard, 1985.
190 Mulkay, *Embryo Research Debate*, at pp. 129–30.
191 Ibid., at pp. 113–15.
192 CC11.
193 Dobson: CC2.
194 McLaren and Evans, 'Unborn children (protection) bill'.
195 Trounson, A. and Mohr, L., 'Human pregnancy following cryopreservation, thawing and transfer of an eight-cell embryo', *Nature*, 305 (1983): 707–9.

meeting on PGD, Nijs and Van Steirteghem[196] discussed their experience with mouse embryo biopsy, revealing that 'all isolation procedures had a negative impact on the growth patterns of the isolated blastomeres', including 'loss of viability and subsequent in-vitro development of dissociated two-cell embryos into normal and abnormal embryos'.[197] Moreover, they found that this was 'in agreement' with at least six other studies, including those by scientists McLaren, Tarkowski and Willadsen. However, none of the participants at the ESHRE meeting suggested that PGD biopsies were unsafe or unfeasible, or that it would be unethical to proceed without further experimental or clinical data.

Conclusion

In this chapter, we draw on our previous work to develop the concept of the 'genetic embryo' as a 'political tool'. We find this concept both useful and justifiable when trying to understand how PGD came to occupy such a central role in the parliamentary debates, providing a unifying conceptual framework that encompasses the normal and aberrant genetics of human embryos in relation to diagnosis, prevention or cure of genetic disease. The origins of the genetic embryo are traced to the post-war period during which the disciplines of genetics and embryology were moving into cellular and molecular territory. Both of these disciplines came together critically in the studies of Robert Edwards, who had begun his career in research as a developmental geneticist, and who foresaw already by 1965 the opportunities and difficulties that the genetics of the human embryo would pose.[198] To a considerable extent, this chapter charts the extended playing out of Edwards' 1965 vision. However, the realisation of that vision does not in itself provide sufficient explanation for the rise of the genetic embryo as a political tool. We suggest that this rise required the interest in the genetics of the early human embryo to converge with the abortion debates. These two threads initially ran in parallel, the medical debates about foetal abnormality and abortion being the more prominent, and informing the embryo debate negatively through the fear that IVF would lead to foetal deformities. The critical convergence of the two threads, and the increasing influence of the early embryo within the political debates, came only after IVF babies were born and were apparently healthy. The dominant tone was then reset by the MRC's decision to focus on the essential role that human

196 Nijs, M. and Van Steirteghem, A. C., 'Assessment of different isolation procedures for blastomeres from two-cell mouse embryos', *Hum Reprod.*, 2 (1987): 421–4.

197 Ibid.

198 Edwards, R. G., 'Maturation in vitro of human ovarian oocytes', *Lancet*, 2(7419) (1965): 926–9; Edwards, R. G., 'Fertilization of human eggs in vitro: morals, ethics and the law', *Q Rev Biol*, 49 (1974): 3–26; Edwards, R. G. and Sharpe, D. J., 'Social values and research in human embryology', *Nature*, 231 (1971): 87–91; Johnson, M. H., 'Robert Edwards: the path to IVF', *Reprod BioMed Online*, 23 (2011): 245–62; Johnson, 'Robert Edwards'.

embryo research might play in gaining an understanding of the origins of foetal abnormality, and how the incidence of this abnormality might be reduced or avoided – both *in vivo* and *in vitro*.

Importantly, this convergence of scientific interests was accompanied by the coalition of scientific campaigners with pro-choice campaigners, both groups forming a united front. This broad-based alliance was thrown together hastily in response to Enoch Powell's Bill, and led to the later recruitment of the medical charities concerned with handicap. This shotgun working relationship proved enduring and highly effective. Thus, Powell's political move proved ultimately to be counter-productive to his aims, and it is arguable that without the stimulus of the Powell Bill, such an effective interdisciplinary lobby group would not have formed – indeed, there is little evidence of such a strong and broadly based political campaigning group in other jurisdictions.

Given Powell's catalytic role, it is interesting to speculate why he took on the anti-embryo-research cause, especially given the evidence of his approval of PGD as a way of reducing foetal and neonatal disease, a stance that ultimately contributed to his defeat politically.[199] We have found no useful clues to his motivation on either question in his papers. However, in an unpublished 2008 interview with Roy L. Cunningham (now deposited with the British Library Oral History Archive), the senior civil servant at the Department of Health with whom Powell dealt, Cunningham claimed:

> Enoch Powell won second place in the annual lottery for Private Members Bills and he chose to introduce a Private Members' Bill, the Unborn Children Protection Bill. Quite why he chose that, I've never been terribly sure. I suspect that a bit of it was to see if he could [succeed], because he was a great Parliamentarian, and he was fascinated by and extremely knowledgeable about Parliamentary procedure. And I think part of it was to test the procedure to destruction really. And he established the fact that it couldn't deal with a highly controversial topic . . . It would be unfair to say, I'm sure, that he . . . just chose it for that reason alone. I'm quite sure . . . he cared about the topic. But I think certainly a bit of it was around that.

Cunningham continues by describing one of Powell's strategies, which also suggests that the process was as important to him as the argument.

> [P]art of his approach to maximising the chance, which I'm sure in his mind he would never have expected it would have got through . . . [was that] he had to restrain some of his more enthusiastic supporters because if any of them spoke, they used up more and more . . . of the very limited amount of time that was available. And . . . you could see him absolutely furiously looking at one or two of them that couldn't stop yabbering.

199 Theodosiou and Johnson, 'Politics of human embryo research'.

Finally, when asked directly whether Powell truly was able to square intellectually his support for PGD with forbidding embryo research, Cunningham says: 'It can't be squared and I think he had to accept it, because the technique would inevitably have meant that there was some embryos which could perish. There's no getting around that.' Indeed Powell himself privately acknowledged that his decision 'not to interfere with any existing fertility procedures' was based more on strategy than personal beliefs as the 'basis [on] which the Bill received its majority'.[200] If, as seems likely, Cunningham is correct, Powell's heart may not have been fully engaged in the cause of anti-embryo research, but more in pursuing the fight itself.

There is also the pertinent question of why Powell supported PGD while opposing the embryo research required for its development. Again, direct information is lacking, but might the explanation lie in the scarring experience he had as Minister of Health from 1960–3? According to Harold Evans,[201] Powell was responsible for the NHS when it was telling doctors that it was safe to prescribe thalidomide, but he subsequently refused any help for affected families.

> He had received a delegation of affected parents in January 1963 and rejected their every request. No to a public inquiry on the origins of the disaster. No to immediately setting up a drug-testing centre – 'anyone who takes an aspirin puts himself at risk'. No to a public warning against using any of the thalidomide pills that might still be in medicine cabinets – 'a scaremonger publicity stunt'. No to giving a statement after the meeting – 'no need to bring the press into this'. And 'no to his setting eyes on a thalidomide child'.[202]

Is it possible that this collision with congenital abnormality decisively influenced his later positive approach to PGD? On both these conjectural explanations, we lack firm evidence.

The outcome of Powell's pro-PGD stance, however, was an increasingly fractured anti-embryo-research campaign confronting a cohesive broad-based pro-embryo-research campaign. A final conundrum then is why the anti-research campaign failed to effectively target some of the misleading claims being made by the opposition, and indeed, why the opposition felt it necessary to make such claims? The latter cannot be simply ascribed to MPs misunderstanding their briefs, because there is evidence of scientists themselves overstating their case. Perhaps Powell's crafty use of a range of parliamentary tactics stimulated a similarly low craftiness in the opposition. The fact remains that however distorted the political tool of the genetic embryo might have become, it was wielded with an effectiveness that went unchallenged.

200 CC12.
201 *My Paper Chase*, London: Little, Brown, 2009.
202 Ibid.

Acknowledgements

We thank Lizzy Minty for her preliminary scoping of the Powell papers, Katrina Dean for access to uncatalogued McLaren papers at the British Library, Sue Donnelly for access to uncatalogued Braude papers at the LSE Archive and Marilyn Monk for access to her private papers. We also thank Reproductive BioMedicine Online for permission to use extracts from Theodosiou and Johnson (2011) at various places in this chapter. This work was supported by grants from the Wellcome Trust (084418 and 088708), which otherwise had no involvement in the research or its publication.

Archival references

BL1, 1971; Some thoughts on the ethics of reproductive technology (Kennedy Symposium, Washington): Anne McLaren papers 83833.

CC1, *c.*1985; Summary fact-sheet, Medical Research Council 'Research on human fertilisation and embryology': Papers of Enoch Powell 3/2/1/51.

CC2, 1985; Parliamentary proceedings. Standing Committee D. 13 March: Papers of Enoch Powell 3/2/1/46.

CC3, 1985; Letter Lady Watherston (Order of Christian Unity) to Enoch Powell. 12 Feb.: Papers of Enoch Powell 3/2/1/50.

CC4, 1985; Letter David Poole to Enoch Powell. 20 April: Papers of Enoch Powell 3/2/1/51.

CC5, 1985: Letter Dame Mary Donaldson (VLA) to all MPs. 3 June: Papers of Enoch Powell 3/2/1/47.

CC6, 1985; Letter John McLean to Enoch Powell. 4 Sep.: Papers of Enoch Powell 3/2/1/47.

CC7, 1985; Letter John McLean to the editor of *The Times.* 3 June: Papers of Enoch Powell 3/2/1/47.

CC8, 1985; Letter Bernard Braine, MP, Ann Winterton, MP and James White, MP to the editor of *The Times*. 20 March: Papers of Enoch Powell 3/2/1/50.

CC9, 1985; Letter Enoch Powell to Roy Cunningham. 4 April: Papers of Enoch Powell 3/2/1/45.

CC10, 1985; Statement Enoch Powell to all MPs. Human embryo research: the government and the professions must come clean with the public. 15 July: Papers of Enoch Powell 3/2/1/54.

CC11, 1985; Martin Bobrow *Sunday Times*' article 'It's a matter of life and life'. 28 July: Papers of Enoch Powell 3/2/1/52.

CC12, 1985; Letter Enoch Powell to Hugh Rossi, MP. 2 March: Papers of Enoch Powell 3/2/1/48.

LSE1, 1985; Letter Peter Braude to Leo Abse, MP. 11 Jan.: Braude papers.

LSE2, 1985; Information sheet Joanna Chambers to members and supporters of the Birth Control Campaign. 30 Jan.: Braude papers.

LSE3, 1985; Letters James Gowans and John Evans to Peter Thurnham, MP. 13 and 25 Feb.: Progress papers Box 44.

LSE4, 1985; Letter Joanna Chambers to Keith Gibson. 23 April: Progress papers Box 16.

LSE5, 1985; Letter Peter Braude to M.C. Macnaughton. 25 Feb.: Braude papers.

LSE6, 1985; Minutes Meeting of the Warnock Legislation Group. 23 July: Progress papers Box 7.
LSE7, 1985. Letter Joanna Chambers to Peter Braude. 25 Sep.: Braude papers.
LSE8, 1988; Progress briefing for the House of Lords Debate on 15 Jan.: Progress papers Box 7.
NA1, 1978; Statement. Ramaswamy, S. 28 July: FD10/161.
NA2, 1971; Grant application Edwards, R. G., Steptoe, P. C. 10 Feb.: FD10/161.
NA3, 1971; Referees' reports. Short, R. V., Evans, H. J. Mar.: FD10/161.
NA4, 1978; Minutes MRC Advisory Group. 4 Oct.: FD13/242.
NA5, 1978; Letter Roger Short to Saroja Ramaswamy. 12 June: FD 13/242.
NA6, 1978; Letter Anne McLaren to Barbara Rashbass. 3 July: FD 13/242.
NA7, 1979; Minutes Meeting of the advisory group to review policy on research on *in vitro* fertilisation and embryo transfer in humans. 6 Mar.: FD 7/2307.
NA8, 1982; Minutes Meeting of the advisory group to review policy on research on *in vitro* fertilisation and embryo transfer in humans. 13 May: FD 7/2307.
NA9, 1982; Circular Jenny Croft. 14 Dec.: FD 7/2307.
NA10, 1982; Presentation transcript John Evans 'Genetic aspects'. 9 Dec.: FD 7/2307.
NA11, Circa 1984; Statement David Whittingham 'Comments on Warnock Committee Report'. FD 7/2332.

Hansard references

Hansard, 1965. Abortion Bill [HL] HL Deb. 30 November 1965, vol. 270, cc1139–241.
Hansard, 1966. Medical Termination Of Pregnancy Bill. HC Deb. 22 July 1966, vol. 732, cc1067–165.
Hansard, 1967a. Clause 1 (Medical Termination of Pregnancy.) HC Deb. 29 June 1967, vol. 749, cc895–1102.
Hansard, 1967b. Medical Termination Of Pregnancy Bill. HL Deb. 26 July 1967, vol. 285, cc981–1103.
Hansard, 1984a. Human Fertilisation: Warnock Report. HL Deb. 31 October 1984, vol. 456, cc535–93.
Hansard, 1984b. Human Fertilisation and Embryology (Warnock Report). HC Deb. 23 November 1984, vol. 68, cc528–44 and 547–90.
Hansard, 1985. Unborn Children (Protection) Bill. HC Deb. 15 February 1985, vol. 73, cc637–702.
Hansard, 1986a. Disability: Prevention. HL Deb. 14 May 1986, vol. 474, cc1169–91.
Hansard, 1986b. Unborn Children (Protection) (No. 2) Bill. HC Deb. 21 October 1986, vol. 102, cc971–7.
Hansard, 1987. Infant Life (Preservation) Bill [HL]. HL Deb. 28 January 1987, vol. 483, cc1406–51.
Hansard, 1988a. Abortion (Amendment) Bill. HC Deb. 22 January 1988, vol. 125, cc1228–96.
Hansard, 1988b. Human Fertilisation and Embryology. HC Deb. 4 February 1988, vol. 126, cc1198–256.
Hansard, 1989. Human Fertilisation and Embryology Bill [HL]. HL Deb. 7 December 1989, vol. 513, cc1002–114.

Hansard, 1990a. Human Fertilisation and Embryology Bill [HL]. HL Deb. 8 February 1990, vol. 515, cc950–1000 and 1006–20.
Hansard, 1990b. Human Fertilisation and Embryology Bill [HL]. HC Deb. 2 April 1990, vol. 170, cc914–85.
Hansard, 1990c. Licences for Treatment, Storage and Research. HC Deb. 23 April 1990, vol. 171, cc31–133
Hansard, 1990d. As an Amendment to Commons Amendment No. 20. HL Deb. 18 October 1990, vol. 522, cc1043–87.

4 Statutory regulation of PGD in the UK: unintended consequences and future challenges

Emily Jackson

Until 2009, pre-implantation genetic diagnosis (PGD) in the UK was regulated by the Human Fertilisation and Embryology Authority (HFEA), through its Code of Practice and its licensing and inspection regime. The statute which set up the HFEA and lays out the circumstances in which fertility treatment, carried out under licence, is lawful in the UK – the Human Fertilisation and Embryology Act 1990 – did not mention PGD, although it was assumed that it was nevertheless a licensable treatment. In part as a result of its absence from the statutory scheme, the scope of the HFEA's powers was subject to a legal challenge which culminated in the House of Lords confirming that the 1990 Act gave the Authority very broad discretion when formulating guidance on the circumstances in which PGD could be provided. The 2008 amendments to the 1990 Act, which came into force on 1 October 2009, now set out, on the face of the statute, the criteria which the HFEA must use when deciding whether to vary a clinic's licence to allow it to provide PGD for a particular condition. Since the statutory criteria are broadly similar to the most recent pre-2009 HFEA guidance, it could be argued that this is a change of form, rather than substance. This chapter will argue, to the contrary, that far from simply being a procedural technicality, the decision to codify the regulation of PGD has had and will continue to have some potentially far-reaching consequences.

A very brief history of the regulation of PGD in the UK

Although the pioneers of *in vitro* fertilisation (IVF) had realised that it might be possible to biopsy cells from embryos as early as the late 1960s, the first successful cycle of PGD did not take place until 1989, at the Hammersmith Hospital in London. The Warnock Committee, which was appointed in 1982 to consider IVF and embryo research and to make recommendations, did not devote much space to PGD in its report, believing its clinical application to be some way off. The Warnock Report, published in 1984, described the use of embryo biopsy for detecting abnormalities before implantation as a potentially useful technique, particularly since it could 'avoid . . . the difficult decision for the parents of whether to seek a termination where abnormality is detected'.[1] However, its conclusion was that, 'given the present relatively low success rates for pregnancy following IVF, it is unlikely that embryonic biopsy will become a feasible method of detecting abnormal embryos for some considerable time'.[2]

Although the 1990 Act itself does not mention PGD, for two reasons it has generally been assumed that Parliament's intention in 1990 *was* to allow PGD to be carried out under the licensing regime introduced by the Human Fertilisation and Embryology Act. First, when the Human Fertilisation and Embryology Bill was introduced, in the 1989/90 session, the fact that IVF might be used not only to help infertile couples to have children, but also to prevent serious disease is believed to have been a factor which greatly assisted its passage through Parliament.[3] The pictures of smiling pregnant women, whose embryos had been sexed in order to ensure that they did not give birth to boys who might have inherited the X-linked diseases which ran in their families, is widely credited with giving a significant boost to the legislation.[4]

Second, one of the specified research purposes under the Act for which a licence to carry out embryo research may be issued was to 'improve methods of detecting genetic and chromosomal abnormalities in embryos'.[5] If research to improve PGD techniques can be licensable, it would be extraordinary if the technique itself was a criminal offence (as anything done to an embryo without a licence is under the legislation).[6] The statute's silence on the circumstances in which PGD could be carried out, coupled with the assumption that licensing it fell within the HFEA's statutory powers, meant that it was left to the HFEA to devise its own rules through successive editions of its Code of Practice.

In the first ten years of the HFEA's existence, licensing PGD to enable couples to avoid passing on very serious genetic conditions to their offspring proved to be relatively uncontroversial. It was only when a new use for PGD techniques emerged at the start of the twenty-first century that the scope of the HFEA's licensing powers was challenged. Tissue or HLA (human leukocyte antigen) typing involves taking a cell from an early embryo, in the same way as in ordinary PGD, and testing it to see if the resulting child would be a good tissue match for a sick sibling in need of a bone marrow transplant. If the selected embryo is a good tissue match, when the baby is born, blood taken from her umbilical cord can be used to treat the older sibling.

When it first considered the issue in 2001, the HFEA initially decided that tissue-typing could be legitimate in certain circumstances; in particular, the child to be born had to be at risk of suffering from the same genetic condition

1 *Report of the Committee of Inquiry into Human Embryology and Fertilisation* (Warnock Report), London: Stationery Office, 1984, Cmnd 9314, at para. 12.13.
2 Ibid.
3 For further discussion, see Chapter 3 in this volume.
4 Mulkay, M., *The Embryo Research Debate*, Cambridge: Cambridge University Press, 1997.
5 Human Fertilisation and Embryology Act 1990, Schedule 2, para. 3 (2)(e).
6 Ibid., section 41.

as its older sibling.[7] In the extensive media coverage that this issue attracted, a distinction was then drawn between two couples, each of whom wished to use PGD with HLA-typing in order to treat their seriously ill son.[8] The Hashmis' son Zain was suffering from beta-thalassaemia major, and any future child they might have might also be at risk of suffering from the same condition. This meant that the Hashmis might legitimately use PGD without tissue-typing, in order to avoid having a child with the same condition as Zain, and according to the HFEA, carrying out an additional test on the biopsied cell – in order to find out whether the embryo would be a good tissue match for Zain – would be acceptable. In contrast, the Whitakers' son Charlie suffered from Diamond–Blackfan anaemia, which is not an inherited condition. Given the HFEA's requirement that HLA-typing could only be carried out if the couple could also legitimately access PGD to screen out the older child's condition, the Whitakers were not able to access tissue-typing in the UK. They therefore decided to have treatment in Chicago, and subsequently gave birth to a son who proved to be a good tissue match for Charlie.

The reason for drawing this distinction between the Hashmis and the Whitakers was said to be that – in the case of Zain – embryo biopsy would be carried out to benefit the child to be born as well as to benefit his or her older brother, whereas in the case of Charlie Whitaker, the embryo biopsy would be done solely to benefit him, and not to benefit the child to be born. In practice, however, because PGD does not *treat* the inherited genetic condition, the only way it 'benefits' the future child is by enabling the latter to be selected and hence born, and of course this 'benefit' would exist for both Zain and Charlie's younger sibling. Subsequently, and in my view rightly, the HFEA abandoned this rather dubious distinction, and permitted PGD with HLA-typing for both inherited and non-inherited conditions, including Diamond–Blackfan anaemia.[9]

Following the HFEA's 2001 decision to allow PGD accompanied by HLA-typing, its power to do so was challenged by a 'pro-life' pressure group, Comment on Reproductive Ethics (CORE). Schedule 2 of the 1990 Act specified that a licence 'cannot authorise any activity unless it appears to the Authority to be necessary or desirable for the purpose of providing treatment services'. 'Treatment services' were defined in section 2 as 'medical, surgical or obstetric services' provided 'for the purpose of assisting women to carry children'. CORE argued that since PGD and HLA-typing were not done *in order to help women to conceive*, they did not fall within section 2's definition of treatment services, and hence could not be licensed by the Authority. At first instance, Maurice Kay J. agreed with CORE: since HLA-typing was not

7 HFEA, 'HFEA to allow tissue typing in conjunction with preimplantation genetic diagnosis', press release, 13 December 2001.
8 Boseley, S., 'A tale of two families whose desperate plight fuelled debate', *The Guardian*, 22 July 2004.
9 'HFEA agrees to extend policy on tissue typing' (HFEA press release, 21 July 2004).

necessary in order to help a woman to bear a child, it did not fall within the statutory definition of treatment services, and could not therefore be licensed by the HFEA. Of course, this is also true for ordinary PGD: it is not necessary in order for women to conceive, and hence if this decision had not been successfully appealed, it would have prevented the HFEA not only from licensing HLA-typing, but also from licensing *any* PGD treatment. On appeal, the Court of Appeal unanimously reversed his decision, taking a much more purposive interpretative approach, and its decision was upheld, again unanimously, by the House of Lords.[10]

The House of Lords drew attention to Schedule 2 of the Act, which listed a number of activities that fell within the definition of 'services provided for the purpose of assisting women to carry children'; in particular paragraph 1(1)(d) referred to 'practices designed to secure that embryos are in a suitable condition to be placed in a woman or to determine whether embryos are suitable for that purpose'. The House of Lords found that the licensing power of the Authority was 'defined in broad terms', and it was therefore entitled to construe the concept of suitability broadly, to include whether the embryos were suitable 'for the purposes of the particular mother'. This could include 'determining the genetic characteristics of the embryo by way of PGD or HLA typing', and the Authority was 'entitled to take the view' that PGD or HLA-typing was 'necessary or desirable' for the purpose of providing such treatment services.[11]

There was a gradual evolution of the HFEA's criteria for licensing PGD from the First to the Seventh Code of Practice. For example, the Code used to specifically equate PGD with 'current practice in the use of (post-implantation) prenatal diagnosis (PND)'.[12] The intention was to equate the circumstances in which it is acceptable to carry out PGD with the 'foetal abnormality' ground for abortion in the Abortion Act 1967, namely that abortion is lawful where there is 'a substantial risk that, if the child were born, it would suffer from such physical or mental abnormalities as to be seriously handicapped'.[13] Translating this to apply to PGD, the Sixth Code specified that PGD 'will be available only where there is a significant risk of a serious genetic condition'.[14]

The abortion model was imperfect for a number of reasons, however. First, it was not entirely clear whether the Code was equating PGD with the circumstances in which *prenatal diagnosis* can be carried out or whether it was equating it with the *criteria for the lawful termination of pregnancy*. The Code appeared to elide the two, but they are not the same thing. The decision to carry out PND is a matter of clinical discretion, whereas termination of

10 *Quintavalle (Comment on Reproductive Ethics)* v. *Human Fertilisation and Embryology Authority* [2005] UKHL 28.
11 Ibid., at para. 24, per Lord Hoffmann.
12 HFEA 6th Code of Practice, at para. 14.21.
13 Abortion Act 1967, s. 1 (1)(d).
14 HFEA 6th Code of Practice, para. 14.22.

pregnancy can lawfully be carried out only for one of the four statutory grounds in the Abortion Act 1967. Ultrasound – while commonly regarded as the first chance to see one's baby – is a prenatal diagnostic technique, and although practice varies, it is not uncommon for pregnant women having the standard 20-week anomaly scan to be told the sex of their baby. Since sex selection, other than for medical reasons, was not permitted by the HFEA, its intention in the Sixth Code of Practice was plainly not to equate current practice in the use of ultrasonography with PGD.

Second, it is possible for a woman to be denied access to abortion under the foetal abnormality ground if two doctors, acting in good faith, believe that the foetus's abnormality is insufficiently serious. A woman can, in theory at least, be forced to carry a pregnancy to term if the foetus's condition is not serious and she cannot avail herself of one of the other statutory grounds. It is, however, hard to see how a woman could be forced to have an embryo transferred. In short, in relation to PND, there are no formal limits on testing; rather the restrictions relate to the criteria which must be satisfied in order to lawfully terminate an established pregnancy. In contrast, in relation to PGD, the HFEA did not intend to restrict the woman's right to refuse embryo transfer, but rather to restrict what tests could be carried out in the first place.

In addition to the target of the restrictions being different in each case, there was already some internal inconsistency in the HFEA's rules. Tissue-typing is not done to avoid a serious genetic condition in the embryo, and hence fell outside the wording in the Sixth Code. Given these multiple pressures on the abortion analogy, it was abandoned in the Seventh Code, which instead set out specific criteria to cover both standard PGD and tissue-typing.

The non-PND linked criteria in the Seventh Code concentrated on the need for the child to be born to be at substantial risk of suffering from a serious genetic condition, or, in the case of tissue-typing, for the affected sibling's condition to be serious. Sex selection would be permitted only where there was a risk of a serious sex-linked disease. In all three cases then, PGD could be licensed only if the relevant genetic condition was judged to be 'serious', making it important to have a clear definition of what seriousness means.

Many genetic conditions self-evidently meet any threshold level of seriousness. If a child is born with Tay–Sachs disease, for example, her nervous system will start to degenerate during her first year of life, and she will die within three or four years. Tay–Sachs is undoubtedly a serious condition, and it is readily understandable why parents who are at risk of having a child with Tay–Sachs disease – many of whom will have already had a child with this condition – would want to use PGD to try to ensure that their future children do not die in infancy. At other times, however, drawing a line between serious and non-serious conditions may be more difficult. In particular, is seriousness an objective clinical fact, or does it depend upon the subjective views and experience of the individual family? The HFEA, through its Eighth Code of Practice, has taken a mixed approach: some of the criteria – such as 'the availability of effective therapy' and 'the speed of degeneration in progressive disorders' – can be judged objectively, whereas others – such as 'the views of the people seeking treatment in relation to the condition to be avoided, including their previous reproductive experience' and their 'family circumstances' – are family-specific and hence variable.[15] And it is clear that this mixed approach reflects the reality of PGD in clinical practice, where the previous reproductive experience of the people seeking treatment – usually of having an existing child with the condition – is commonly what prompts interest in PGD and this will, in addition to more objective consideration of the condition's seriousness, be taken very seriously by clinic staff when deciding whether PGD is appropriate.[16] This comes across very clearly in Scott *et al.*'s interviews with healthcare professionals working in licensed centres.

> I saw a couple last week who came for Cystic Fibrosis, a fertile, intelligent couple, who have a Cystic Fibrosis child. And I said, 'What are you doing this for? Why don't you just have another pregnancy?' And they couldn't consider terminating a Cystic child because, firstly they said, '[W]e do not want to have another child that we have to watch die or be very ill. But on the other hand, if we kind of [terminate the] pregnancy it's like terminating [our existing child] . . . And we feel we can't do that. And we want some other way of approaching this.'[17]

Of course, it should be remembered that the rules contained in the HFEA's Code of Practice are directed towards *clinics*, rather than the HFEA itself. It might then be argued that the criteria contained in the successive editions of the Code were simply instructing centres when *they* could legitimately offer PGD to a particular couple. However, given that the statute itself did not set out when the HFEA could legitimately issue a licence for PGD, the HFEA had decided to use the criteria set out in the Code itself when determining whether a licence should be varied to permit PGD. Hence, the criteria in the Code were, in practice, applied twice: first by the HFEA when deciding whether to vary a clinic's licence to include PGD for a particular condition, and then by the clinic, when determining whether PGD was appropriate for a particular couple.

In sum, then, before the 2008 reforms to the 1990 Act, the HFEA had reserved to itself the power to decide when a clinic could obtain a licence to carry out PGD – which it did via a mixed objective–subjective 'seriousness' test – and its broad discretion to do so had received the unanimous support of the House of Lords.

15 8th Code of Practice, para. 10.7

16 Scott, R., Williams, C., Ehrich, K. and Farsides, B., 'The appropriate extent of preimplantation genetic diagnosis: health professionals' and scientists' view on the requirement for a significant risk of a serious genetic condition', *Medical Law Review*, 15 (2007): 320–56.

17 Ibid.

Background to the 2008 reforms

The process of reforming the 1990 Act began with the House of Commons Science and Technology Select Committee's decision to embark on a review of the 1990 Act, in the light of technological changes and shifts in ethical and social attitudes. Its report, *Human Reproductive Technologies and the Law*, was published in 2005. In relation to PGD, the Committee found that:

> [t]he HFEA's room for manoeuvre can be seen as both its major strength and its biggest weakness. We have seen that by giving the HFEA jurisdiction over what is a 'suitable condition' for an embryo to be transferred, it has been able to license PGD despite legal challenge. Professor Kenyon Mason told the committee that 'the very real problem is that there is too much in this act that is not in the act but is in the Code of Practice'.[18]

The then Chair of the Authority, Suzi Leather, agreed that greater clarity was desirable, and told the Committee that she would like to see the permitted uses of PGD set out in legislation, in a similar way to the research purposes which set out a strictly limited set of purposes for which the HFEA is permitted to issue licences to use embryos in research.

The Science and Technology Committee concluded that it had 'concerns about the criteria imposed by the HFEA'.[19] Given the inherent limitations of PGD – in particular that 'it cannot be used to create 'designer babies' – the Committee saw 'no reason why a regulator should seek to determine which disorders can be screened out using PGD'.[20] At first sight, this looks like a call for the deregulation of PGD, in which decisions would simply be devolved to doctors' clinical discretion, but the Committee went on to say that these decisions 'should operate within clear boundaries set by Parliament and informed by ethical judgements'. The Science and Technology Committee's judgement that 'the regulation of preimplantation testing is highly unsatisfactory'[21] was grounded in their view that the HFEA should not 'regulate its use beyond ensuring that it is performed to the highest standards within statutory boundaries'.[22] Of course, at the time there were no formal statutory boundaries, and so removal of the HFEA's powers to control the use of PGD, absent legislative reform to *insert* statutory boundaries, would in practice amount to deregulation.

In its response to the Science and Technology Committee's report, the government did 'not accept that the development of the HFEA's policy on

18 Science and Technology Committee, Fifth Report of Session 2004–5, para. 315.
19 Ibid., Recommendation 27.
20 Ibid., para. 124.
21 Ibid., Recommendation 60.
22 Ibid., para. 24.

PGD has been "highly unsatisfactory"'.[23] It drew attention to its consultative and 'cautious approach' to licensing PGD. However the government agreed 'with the Committee that it would be preferable if the parameters for PGD were more clearly set out in law'. It therefore decided to 'seek wider public views on the boundaries of acceptable uses of preimplantation genetic diagnosis and preimplantation tissue typing, and on the appropriate scope and nature of regulatory intervention'.[24]

The 2008 reforms

When the 2008 amending Act was drafted, there was no intention to alter the criteria set down by the HFEA for when PGD could be licensed; rather the intention was to clarify and make these explicit on the face of the legislation. This was in part to give Parliament 'ownership' of the parameters within which PGD is acceptable: the Science and Technology Committee, in particular, was keen to ensure that Parliament, rather than the HFEA, should be responsible for setting the boundaries within which PGD could lawfully be provided. In addition, it was thought desirable to shield the HFEA from future legal challenges to its powers to make licensing decisions in relation to PGD. The original Act's failure to mention PGD had undoubtedly left the Authority vulnerable to challenges like the one mounted by CORE, and the government was keen to ensure that the HFEA did not have to spend more time and money defending the scope of its powers in the courts.

When introducing the Bill into the House of Lords, Lord Darzi explained that '[t]he Bill will . . . make explicit the basic parameters for screening and selecting embryos. Again, the intention is that this should be undertaken only on the grounds of avoiding serious disease.'[25] It could then be argued that 2008 Act reforms to the 1990 Act simply put the criteria which justify PGD on a statutory footing. Under Schedule 2 1ZA (2) a licence cannot authorise the testing of an embryo unless the Authority is satisfied 'that there is a significant risk that a person with the abnormality will have or develop a serious physical or mental disability, a serious illness or any other serious medical condition'. Also in line with previous HFEA policy, non-medical sex selection is ruled out, and HLA-typing is acceptable only if the older sibling 'suffers from a serious medical condition which could be treated by umbilical cord blood stem cells, bone marrow or other tissue of any resulting child'.[26]

When the embryo-testing provisions were debated in Parliament, there was considerable interest in HLA-typing and the creation of what had become known as 'saviour siblings'. In contrast, the criteria for 'regular' PGD were

23 *Government Response to the Report from the House of Commons Science and Technology Committee: Human Reproductive Technologies and the Law*, London: Department of Health, 2005, para. 44.
24 Ibid.
25 Hansard 19 Nov. 2007: Column 666.
26 Schedule 2, para. 1ZA (1).

treated as unproblematic and discussion on them was limited. The only time that PGD – as opposed to tissue-typing or sex selection – was discussed at any length in Parliament was when the statute's use of the word 'serious' was debated in the House of Lords. Baroness Royall explained why 'serious' had not been further defined on the face of the Act.

> [T]here is no definition of 'serious' in the legislation. A definition was not included in the Bill in order to allow the HFEA and clinicians appropriate levels of flexibility within which to make licensing decisions, while ensuring that it would be allowed only for medical conditions that are considered to be serious. The HFEA would continue to provide guidance on embryo testing and on the criteria that it would take account of when making decisions about such testing. It would be expected that part of the guidance would include consideration of words such as 'serious' in the legislation.[27]

In the same exchange, Baroness Royall also made the point that the Act – by putting the permissible uses of PGD on its face – in fact limited the HFEA's previous discretion in relation to PGD.

> There is currently no reference to embryo testing in the 1990 Act. Therefore, by including in the Bill the purposes for which embryos can be tested, we are introducing more stringent requirements than are currently in place. Because of the regulatory oversight from the HFEA and further guidance relating to embryo testing in the code of practice, we do not consider a definition of 'serious' to be necessary in the Bill.[28]

At no point in the debates in either House was consideration given to any potential downsides from placing the criteria for PGD on the face of the Act. The Science and Technology Committee did draw attention to one possible drawback – namely that primary legislation is inevitably slower to respond to changing circumstances than a regularly updated Code of Practice might be – but it also came down firmly in favour of giving Parliament more control.

> We have heard that the HFE Act's longevity is attributable to the degree of flexibility it allows the HFEA. We have recommended that the scrutiny of Parliament is sufficiently important to reduce that freedom. In our view, Parliament's ability to revisit contentious issues relating to the creation of new life and the permissible uses of human embryos is vital. We recommend that new legislation is more explicit and provides Parliament with greater powers to debate and amend legislation.[29]

27 Hansard 21 Jan. 2008: Column 30.
28 Ibid.
29 See n. 18 above, para. 315.

So, although the Science and Technology Committee acknowledged that putting greater detail on the face of the Act could slow down future reform, it did not consider that it might have any *substantive* disadvantages. I turn now to consider whether the prevailing assumption that codification was not only unproblematic but straightforwardly desirable should have been questioned, and whether more thought should have been given to its possible consequences, both intended and unintended.

The consequences of codification

No more 'family-specific' applications

Under the 'old' system, the HFEA had instituted a number of measures to streamline the licensing of PGD in order to try to eliminate or reduce unnecessary bureaucracy. In particular, it had set up a licensing system which enabled experienced PGD centres to carry out PGD for conditions which had already been approved, without the need for a cumbersome application and separate consideration by the Licence Committee. In practice, this meant that a clinic which wished to perform PGD for an entirely new condition would have to make a specific application, on behalf of a family, which would then be considered by the HFEA's Licence Committee. If the Licence Committee agreed to vary this centre's licence to include this condition, then other clinics with well-established PGD programmes and experienced embryo biopsy practitioners would be able to perform PGD for the same condition by simply notifying the HFEA that they intended to do so. Their licence would then be varied to include this new condition, thus eliminating a whole layer of bureaucracy, and enabling them to offer PGD to other couples without delay. This more streamlined procedure acknowledged the reality that, having agreed on one occasion that Tay–Sachs disease, say, satisfies the 'substantial risk of a serious condition' criterion, it would be hard to imagine circumstances in which the Licence Committee might decide, on another occasion and in relation to a different family, that it did not.

There was, however, an anomaly in this approach: the first time a decision was taken to license a particular condition, the decision was 'family-specific'. The Licence Committee would have before it anonymised information about the particular family's circumstances and their reasons for seeking PGD for the condition in question. This was because the Code of Practice – which as we saw earlier was assumed to apply both to individual clinics *and* to the HFEA's Licence Committee – acknowledged that judgements as to seriousness will, in addition to consideration of objective clinical facts about the condition, also sometimes involve a degree of subjectivity and depend in part upon the particular family's circumstances. So – when licensing a condition for the first time – the Licence Committee would essentially be making a mixed objective–subjective judgement about the condition's seriousness *in the context of this particular family's situation*. Subsequently, however, licence variation to include this condition on another's centre's licence would effectively be automatic, suggesting that the condition had been judged to be objectively and universally sufficiently serious in all other cases.

To be coherent, either the condition is being judged as objectively serious for all families, in which case there should be no need for family-specific information when licensing it for the first time, or, alternatively, seriousness is always to be judged on a case-by-case basis, looking at the particular family's circumstances, in which case there could be no justification for automatically varying licences to include the previously licensed condition, and the Licence Committee should consider each family's application separately. In short, the middle ground of a family-specific initial application, followed by automatic licence variation to cover all future cases, may have reduced bureaucracy but it did not make much sense.

The proposed solution to this problem, to be implemented at the same time as the new Act, was to ensure that decisions as to the seriousness of the condition, made by the HFEA, according to the statutory criteria on the face of the legislation, are objective and not influenced by subjective and variable factors, such as the couple's views of the condition and their previous reproductive experience. The Act charges the HFEA with judging whether *the condition* is serious, objectively speaking, and it is only once this decision is taken by the Authority that the subjective and variable criteria in the Code come into play; that is, when the *clinic* decides whether a particular couple should have access to PGD. Whereas under the 'old' system, the understanding that seriousness can be subjective applied to both clinics when offering treatment, and the HFEA when varying a licence, now the HFEA is bound by the Act, and must make objective condition-specific, as opposed to subjective family-specific, decisions. Clinics, in contrast, are bound by the Code, and so clinic staff (but not the HFEA) must use the subjective family-specific criteria in the Code to decide whether to offer PGD in a particular case, and the HFEA will, on its inspections, monitor compliance with this. (An exception to this model is PGD with HLA-typing, which continues to be licensed on a family-specific case-by-case basis, even though it could be argued that, having decided once that Diamond–Blackfan anaemia, say, is serious enough to warrant tissue-typing, it is hard to imagine why it would not be sufficiently serious on another occasion.)

One consequence of the move towards licensing PGD for conditions, rather than families, is that there is no need for a clinic which wants to be able to carry out PGD for a particular condition even to have a specific family in mind. As a result, there was initially a significant surge in the number of applications for new conditions. The clinic does not now need to have any would-be patients seeking to screen out the condition, meaning that it could apply to have a number of conditions added to its licence so that it could publicise the fact that it is licensed to carry out PGD for a long list of conditions, even if it never does so. Of course, in practice, most clinics normally will only be prompted to apply to carry out PGD for a new condition if asked to do so by a particular couple, but this is not required by the legislation. The reformed Act instead enables the licensing of conditions for which no one, in fact, wishes to undergo PGD.

The new process has also formalised the existence of a list of conditions which have been licensed for PGD in the UK. Only where a condition does not appear on the list is an application to the HFEA necessary. Of course, it could be argued that a de facto list emerges whenever the previous licensing of a condition is treated as a sufficient reason for PGD to be licensed for use by a new couple. However, now that there is no need to apply for any variation to a licence in order to carry out PGD for the first time for a condition that appears on the list, the list does not just offer a summary of previous decisions, but also represents the definitive source of decisions as to whether named conditions meet the statutory tests.

Of course, it is imperative that 'the list' is a living document. As more is understood about variations in seriousness *within* different conditions, it may be necessary to qualify a condition's inclusion on the list. Cystic fibrosis, for example, can be a life-threatening condition, but there are now thought to be milder versions that only manifest themselves much later in life and which may have few adverse consequences for the sufferer. As it becomes possible to distinguish between different forms of the same condition, it may be necessary to specify that only certain variations of a condition meet the statutory criteria. It is also possible that treatment may become available for a condition that was previously untreatable, and, if this is simple and effective, it may affect whether the condition should remain on the list.

It should be noted that this newly formalised 'list' is unpopular with some disability rights activists, who believe that it is offensive to people living with conditions that appear on it, believing that it sends a powerful message to them that society regards their condition as so bad that it justifies preventing the birth of a child who would suffer from it.[30] This is a familiar example of what is sometimes called the 'expressivist' objection to PGD, namely that the decision to carry out PGD for a condition *expresses a view* about the value of the lives led by people who have that condition. There are, however, a number of problems with the expressivist objection to PGD. First, as Colin Gavaghan has pointed out, one rather obvious solution to objections to PGD grounded in the 'message' it sends would, in fact, be to allow PGD for any reason at all, thus 'avoid[ing] the imposition by the state of a single, simplistic view of what constitutes "normality" and "disability"'.[31] Yet few people who object to the list of conditions for which PGD may be carried out would prefer there to be no restrictions at all. Their objection – in reality – is to PGD as a technique to screen out disease, rather than to whether the conditions for

30 See, for example, the contributions to Parens, E. and Asch, A. (eds), *Prenatal Testing and Disability Rights*, Washington, DC: Georgetown University Press, 2000.

31 Gavaghan, C., 'Right problem wrong solution: a pro-choice response to "expressivist" concerns about preimplantation genetic diagnosis', *Cambridge Quarterly of Healthcare Ethics*, 16 (2007): 20–34.

which it is used are included on a list, or lie within the would-be parents' discretion.

Second, and of more practical importance, we do not generally believe that taking steps to eliminate diseases, like cancer, sends a negative message about the worth of the lives of people living with cancer. People who undergo PGD have usually already had at least one child suffering from the condition for which they now seek PGD, or they may have suffered repeated miscarriages as a result of it. A desire that one's next child does not die in the womb or in infancy, or is not very seriously ill throughout her childhood, does not 'say' anything about the love one feels for one's affected children. Children who die in early childhood from Tay–Sachs disease are loved just as much as children who survive to adulthood, but it is understandable that parents who know that they are both carriers of the gene that causes Tay–Sachs would wish to take steps to ensure that their next child does not inherit a double dose from them and die before the age of five. Of course, not all genetic conditions for which PGD is carried out are fatal in early childhood, but the point is simply that parents of sick children love those sick children as profoundly as they would love a healthy child. Where one is able to exercise a choice over whether or not one's next child is likely to have a life marked by ill-health and discomfort, choosing to have a healthy child is unquestionably not to abandon or disvalue one's sick child.

The need for the Authority to 'be satisfied'

Before the 2008 Act came into force, the HFEA consulted upon the Eighth edition of its Code of Practice, which was due to come into force at the same time as the new Act. During the consultation period, it was suggested that the bureaucracy associated with the licensing of PGD could be further streamlined by leaving it up to clinics to determine whether to offer PGD to a particular couple, and for the clinic – or more precisely the responsible clinician – to be charged with judging compliance with the statutory criteria. This would lighten the regulatory burden on clinics, but importantly it would not be a 'free-for-all': clinics could not carry out PGD for any condition at all, under cover of their discretion to judge seriousness for themselves. Rather, the HFEA would use its inspection regime to monitor the centre's compliance with both the Act and the Code (as it already does), and it could invoke sanctions – including the removal of a clinic's licence – in the event of non-compliance.

This simpler and cheaper system would remove the need for time-consuming licence applications, which inevitably delay treatment for the first couple to seek PGD for a new condition. The clinic would be left to determine whether the condition for which the couple was seeking testing was a serious condition, but it would have to notify the HFEA of its decisions and its reasoning, which would then be monitored by the HFEA to ensure compliance with both the statutory criteria and the Code.

Legal advice was sought to discover whether a move to regulating access to PGD through inspections, rather than through decisions of the HFEA's Licence Committee, would be possible under the new Act, and the advice was that it would not.[32] The old system – which, as we saw earlier, gave the Authority a 'broad discretion' over the licensing of PGD – would have permitted a radical reorganisation of PGD licensing along these lines. The 2008 amendments were clear, however, that the Authority itself has to *be satisfied* that there is a substantial risk of a serious condition *before a licence can be issued*. This means that the decision has to be taken by the Authority in advance of patients embarking on a cycle of PGD. Under the newly configured Act, it was simply impossible to devolve decision-making to clinicians, with post-hoc monitoring of their judgements as to seriousness, given teeth by the HFEA's use of sanctions (including the possibility of licence revocation) if necessary. It is perhaps ironic that the Science and Technology Committee's recommendation that control over the circumstances in which PGD would be acceptable *should be removed from the HFEA* and devolved to clinicians, within statutory boundaries, was *the opposite* of what was, in fact, achieved by the 2008 amendments, which instead set up the HFEA as the only possible arbiter of seriousness.

Variations in seriousness

The statutory criteria for PGD appear to rest on the assumption that the question of whether a condition is serious is a simple binary one – it either is or it is not – and because it is now the condition that is licensed, rather than the individual family, the Act presumes that a prospective condition-wide and definitive judgement as to seriousness is possible. The reality is often much more complicated. For many genetic conditions, it is not possible to say anything other than that it *might* be serious.

Of course, it is sometimes possible to subdivide conditions into more serious and less serious variations. The system for recording all known Mendelian disorders is known as OMIM (Online Mendelian Inheritance in Man), and for many disorders, OMIM records a number of genetic variations, each with their own separate OMIM number. An example might be Niemann–Pick disease, which is separated into Types A, B and C. Niemann–Pick Type A and B are caused by an enzyme deficiency, which leads to a build-up of toxic materials in the body's cells. Niemann–Pick Type A occurs very quickly, and an affected child will usually die before reaching three years of age. In contrast, Niemann–Pick Type B does not affect the brain and, although growth may be slow, those affected will survive into adolescence or early adulthood, with many being able to lead a full and normal life. Niemann–Pick Type C is not caused by an enzyme deficiency, but the end result is the same: an accumulation of materials (cholesterol and other fatty acids) in the body's cells. In Niemann–Pick Type

32 HFEA, 'Licensing of embryo testing', paper considered in March 2009, www.hfea.gov.uk/docs/AM_Item_12_March09.pdf.pdf (accessed 10/01/2012).

C, the brain and other organs are affected, leading to progressive intellectual decline, loss of motor skills, seizures and dementia. In relation to 'Niemann–Pick disease', it is not the overarching condition which has been licensed. Rather, while both Niemann–Pick Type A and Type C do appear on the 'list' of conditions for which PGD may be carried out, Type B has not been licensed.

This example might suggest that where there are different versions of the same disease, it is each individual variation that should be licensed. But if this were the general rule, it would lead to a different sort of problem in other cases. For example, there are a large number of different gene mutations, each with their own OMIM number, which lead to Leigh's disease, a fatal and untreatable childhood disorder of the brain and nervous system. Children usually develop Leigh's disease before the age of two and death is likely within a year of diagnosis. Regardless of which gene mutation is involved, however, the phenotype of the disease will be the same: that is, it is always fatal. This means that requiring each different mutation to be separately licensed would be overly bureaucratic, not to mention a huge waste of time. Leigh's disease's seriousness does not vary between mutations, and so, in this case, it would be pointless for the HFEA to require each variation to be represented by a different OMIM number to receive separate consideration and separate licensing.

When deciding whether each OMIM mutation must receive a separate licence, the answer is more complicated than 'yes or no'. For some conditions, such as Leigh's disease, the overarching disease can receive a licence which covers all known mutations, but for others, like Niemann–Pick disease, each separate OMIM mutation requires a fresh licence. More complicated still, of course, are cases where the phenotype of the disease varies, but we do not understand why or how. If the HFEA must license the condition – in cases where it is sometimes serious and sometimes not serious – should it base its judgement on the most serious possible manifestation of the condition (which might be over-inclusive, in terms of the statutory criteria) or the least serious (which could be under-inclusive)?

Tissue-typing and the perils of statutory drafting

In contrast to the relative lack of debate in Parliament on the 2008 Act's inclusion of PGD, the inclusion in the Bill of the circumstances in which it would be acceptable to carry out HLA-typing in order to ensure that the child that is born is a good tissue match for a sick older sibling was much more controversial. Again, however, this was not because of the decision to codify the previous HFEA rules, but because there was significant opposition both inside and outside Parliament to this sort of treatment. In the end, there was a free vote in the House of Commons, and the decision to allow the creation of 'saviour siblings' was supported by a majority of 179 votes.

As this provision provoked particular controversy – with concerns being expressed over the tissue-matched child being treated as a source of 'spare parts' throughout his or her life – an amendment was introduced in the House of

Lords which was intended to specify that that the 'other tissue' which might be taken from the resulting child should not include whole organs.[33] While this was plainly the intention behind the amendment, which was accepted, it is not clear that this is actually what the wording of the statute achieves. What the relevant part of the Act says is that tissue-typing is acceptable where a sibling 'suffers from a serious medical condition *which could be treated by* umbilical cord blood stem cells, bone marrow or other tissue of any resulting child';[34] and it further specifies that 'the reference to "other tissue" of the resulting child does not include a reference to any whole organ of the child'.[35]

If read literally, I would suggest that this has two possible meanings, neither of which captures what Parliament was intending to accomplish through this amendment. First, it could mean that tissue-typing would not meet the statutory criteria where the sick older sibling has a condition *which could be treated by an organ transplant*. Remember that the section does not say that there must be no intention to take a whole organ, but rather that the medical condition must not be *treatable* by organ transplantation. It is, therefore, possible to conceive of a situation in which the sick older sibling has a condition which *could*, in theory, be treated by organ transplantation, but where the intention is only to use the umbilical cord's stem cells. On a literal reading of this provision, tissue-typing in such circumstances would not fit within the statutory criteria.

Second, it could be argued that the use of 'or' here means that the three types of tissue which could be used to treat the sick older sibling are separable: the sibling must be treatable by *either* umbilical cord blood *or* bone marrow *or* other tissue, which does not include whole organs. On this reading, then, provided the sick older sibling is treatable by cord blood, tissue-typing is acceptable, regardless of whether he or she *also* happens to be treatable by bone marrow or organ transplantation. This would then mean that tissue-typing would be lawful provided the older sibling *could* be treated by any one of those three groups of tissue (umbilical cord blood stem cells, bone marrow or other non-organ tissue). So, on this reading, provided the sibling *could* in theory be treated by a bone marrow transplant, it would not matter if organ transplantation would be the optimum treatment. Indeed, if read literally, it would not matter if organ transplantation would be the preferred first-line treatment, provided that the sibling's condition is theoretically also treatable by a bone marrow transplant.

Of more practical importance than either of these readings of this oddly drafted provision (if the intention was to say that there should be no *intention* to take a whole organ, it is hard to see why this was not stated plainly), this is a redundant and essentially meaningless provision. Neither the HFEA nor the clinics which carry out PGD exercise any control over subsequent decisions

33 Schedule 2, para. 1ZA(4).
34 Schedule 2, para. 1ZA (1); emphasis added.
35 Ibid.

about the medical treatment of children born following licensed treatment. Such decisions are governed instead by the ordinary law relating to the treatment of children, and, as Lord Hoffmann explained in his judgment in the House of Lords' decision discussed earlier, 'the authority is . . . entitled to assume that a child conceived pursuant to its licence will, after birth, receive the full protection of the law'.[36] There is no doubt that a court would have to consider any case in which it was proposed to take an organ from a non-*Gillick*[37] competent minor, or even a *Gillick* competent one. No such cases have arisen in the UK, but it is possible that a court could decide that donating a kidney to a dying sibling *was* in a child's best interests, especially if they were *Gillick* competent and had expressed a clear desire to donate the organ. Of course once they reach adulthood, if a tissue-typed person decides that they *want* to donate their kidney to their older sibling, this would be a matter for the independent assessors at the Human Tissue Authority (or whatever replaces it if is abolished under the powers granted to the Secretary of State by the Public Bodies Act 2011). The Human Fertilisation and Embryology Act 1990's Schedule 1ZA could have no impact upon the decision of the donor and its evaluation by the regulator.

Conclusion

Those who argued for greater clarity from Parliament on the circumstances in which PGD is acceptable were undoubtedly driven by the best of intentions. The 2008 reforms of the Human Fertilisation and Embryology Act 1990 put the criteria governing the licensing of PGD on a statutory footing, giving them democratic legitimacy and insulating the HFEA from further legal challenges to the scope of its powers to license PGD in the UK. My purpose in this chapter has been to suggest that there are reasons to question this move which go beyond the obvious fact that where detailed rules are laid down in primary legislation, they are more difficult and time-consuming to change in the light of shifting scientific and clinical developments than a regularly updated Code of Practice. By setting in stone the need for the Authority to be satisfied – objectively and in advance – that a condition is serious, the Act pre-empts attempts to think creatively about what a streamlined and proportionate regulatory system might look like in relation to PGD. Perhaps more importantly, the Act rests upon the assumption that genetic conditions can be neatly labelled as either serious or not serious, when the reality of many genetic diseases is often much more complicated.

Finally, although a judicial review application grounded in whether the HFEA has any power at all to license PGD or HLA-typing would now be impossible, might other sorts of legal challenge be *more* likely as a result of codification? Under the 'old' system, seriousness – as laid out in the Code and

36 See n. 10 above.
37 *Gillick* v. *West Norfolk and Wisbech AHA* [1984] QB 581.

applied by the HFEA in its Licence Committee's decisions – was acknowledged to vary between families. If all of a woman's female relatives have died before the age of 40 as a result of a particularly aggressive strain of breast cancer, it is easy to see why she might have a different view of genetic susceptibility to breast cancer than someone with no family history of the condition. Now, while clinics themselves can make family-specific decisions about offering PGD to individual couples, the HFEA's condition-by-condition approach is meant to *exclude* subjective considerations. Might this narrowing of the criteria which the HFEA can legitimately take into account, and the restrictions on its discretion to make family-specific decisions, potentially leave it *more* open to challenge by people who disagree with its judgements?

It is too early to know what the long-term implications of codification will be, but my contention is that more thought should have been given to the possible consequences, both intended and unintended, of solidifying the rules governing something as complex and variable as genetic disease into what looks like a simple binary seriousness test. Moreover, given the emphasis placed in recent years on 'better' (for which generally read more proportionate) regulation, it is perhaps odd that the 2008 reforms set in stone a regulatory system based upon the HFEA's prior approval of PGD, on a condition-by-condition basis, when before the Act even came into force, it had to be acknowledged that there might be an alternative, and perhaps more proportionate, way to regulate access to PGD which has now been ruled out by codification.

Given that it regulated an extraordinarily fast moving area of scientific and clinical practice, the 1990 Act stood the test of time remarkably well. Only time will tell if the same is true of the 2008 reforms, and, in particular, the decision to put so much more detail on the face of the Act. The Science and Technology Committee and the UK Government assumed that greater clarity from Parliament about the appropriate parameters for PGD would have only beneficial consequences, but it is at least possible that it may turn out to be a case study in the importance of being careful with regards to what one wishes for.

5 The welfare of the child principle and the use of PGD: selecting for disability

Sarah Elliston

Introduction

Campbell and Cabrera argue in this volume 'that prospective parents should be free to take such steps as they think fit to have what they regard as healthy and capable children', adding the caveat 'provided this does not cause undeniable harm, to these children or to other people, which is sufficiently serious to outweigh the presumptive case for reproductive freedom'.[1] Notions of parental freedom and harms to children will be explored in a more specific context in this chapter: that of preventing the use of embryos for treatment based on their genetic make-up.

The enactment of the Human Fertilisation and Embryology Act 2008 (HFEA 2008) may be viewed as enhancing the scope for choice of those who wish to become parents through assisted reproduction in the UK, largely due to its provisions concerning the possibility of founding families outside the two parent heterosexual model and its minor revision of the welfare principle.[2] The approach taken by the HFEA 2008 was to a considerable extent based on the House of Commons Select Committee on Science and Technology (HCSTC) report: *Human Reproductive Technologies and the Law*.[3] This report had been criticised by some members of the Committee for having taken an 'extreme libertarian approach', their dissenting views being reflected in a special report issued at the same time as the substantive report.[4] However, in one area the HFEA 2008 has taken a uniquely restrictive step. For the first time in the UK, legislation has sought to make it impermissible, at least in certain circumstances, to choose to try to have children that are known to have particular genetic constitutions. Testing of gamete donors may enable these kinds of decisions to be made before embryos are created and restrictions are imposed on preferential selection of donors where there is a significant risk of

1 See Chapter 2.
2 Part 2 of the HFEA 2008, and s. 14(2), amending s. 13(5) of the HFEA 1990.
3 Fifth Report of Session 2004–5, *Human Reproductive Technologies and the Law*, vol. 1, HC 7–1, London: Stationery Office, 24 March 2005.
4 HC 491, 24 March 2005.

genetic abnormalities being passed on to children.[5] However, the principal technique under consideration here will be prenatal genetic diagnosis (PGD), involving genetic testing of embryos.[6] The idea that a state would involve itself through legal regulation in decisions about the genetic makeup of children and intrude on the reproductive choices of potential parents in this way raises troubling questions, despite the apparently beneficent motive of preventing children being born with potentially devastating genetic conditions. While concerns about the appropriate weight to be given to the welfare of children born through assisted reproductive technology were clearly prominent during the reviews of existing legislation and practice that led to the passage of the HFEA 2008, there was also a perceived need for clarity concerning when techniques such as PGD should be deemed to be acceptable and legally permissible.[7] It will be argued here that if achieving clarity was a principal aim of the new legislative provisions, they may in fact fall short of achieving this goal. It will be suggested that they may provide some scope for interpretation that would allow potential parents who wished to do so to attempt to select embryos for disability, despite the legislative intent to the contrary. Even so, the retention of the general welfare principle in the amended HFEA 1990 may still render such attempts null and void, highlighting the need to consider the appropriateness of a child welfare test in this context. It also raises the issue of whether the new provisions serve any practical purpose, if the end result could have been achieved through use of the welfare principle. It will be concluded that their real effect is most likely to be in the message they may be perceived to send about the undesirability of having children with genetic disorders.

The HFEA 2008 amends in many significant ways the original statute regulating particular methods of medically assisting reproduction: The Human Fertilisation and Embryology Act 1990 (HFEA 1990). Hereafter they will be referred to collectively as the HFE Acts,[8] save when reference to a specific Act is necessary. The HFE Acts prohibit certain activities absolutely.[9] Other specified activities can only be carried out with a licence issued by the Authority. The type of licence relevant to this discussion concerns activities in the course of providing treatment services.[10] Performing such activities without a licence is a criminal offence carrying penalties of imprisonment up to ten years or a fine or both.[11]

5 Section 13 (9) of the HFEA 1990, as amended.
6 The history of the development of PGD and the current methods of performing it are discussed elsewhere in this volume.
7 See, for example, HCSTC, Fifth Report of Session 2004–5, *Human Reproductive Technologies and the Law*.
8 For a comparison of the HFE Acts, see Birk, D. *Human Fertilisation and Embryology: The New Law*, Bristol: Jordan, 2009.
9 Section 41 HFEA 1990, as amended, lists offences and penalties.
10 Section 11 (1)(a) and Schedule 2 HFEA 1990, as amended.
11 Sections 4 and 41 (2) HFEA 1990, as amended.

Schedule 2 of the amended HFEA 1990, specifies the kinds of activities that may be authorised under licence. Those critical to PGD are the following:

(a) bringing about the creation of embryos *in vitro*,
(b) procuring, keeping, testing or processing or distributing embryos, . . .
(d) other practices designed to secure that embryos are in a suitable condition to be placed in a woman,
(e) placing any permitted embryo in a woman.

The procedures undertaken in PGD are hence covered here: from the initial creation of *in vitro* embryos, to testing them and finally transferring them to a woman as part of treatment.

Section 14 of the HFEA 2008 modifies the conditions of licences for treatment contained in s. 13 of the HFEA 1990 to include that:

(9) [p]ersons or embryos that are known to have a gene, chromosome or mitochondrion abnormality involving a significant risk that a person with the abnormality will have or develop—

(a) a serious physical or mental disability,
(b) a serious illness, or
(c) any other serious medical condition,

must not be preferred to those that are not known to have such an abnormality.

Similar restrictions are placed where testing involves gender-related genetic disorders.[12] These will not be discussed separately.

On an initial reading, these provisions may seem to allow for no discretion in the use of embryos found to have an abnormality or to carry a risk of illness or disability, once a condition has passed the requirement of sufficient seriousness, and this threshold must be passed to allow PGD to take place at all.[13]

In addition to these provisions, it is also important to note the general 'child welfare' principle which forms part of licence conditions. This must be considered in all treatment decisions governed by the HFE Acts:

13(5) HFEA 1990, as amended

A woman shall not be provided with treatment services unless account has been taken of the welfare of any child who may be born as a result of the treatment (including the need of that child for supportive parenting), and of any other child who may be affected by the birth.

12 Sections 13 (10) and (11), HFEA 1990 as amended.
13 Schedule 2 1ZA (2).

A failure to comply with the requirements of s. 13 is not itself a criminal offence,[14] unlike certain other practices prohibited by the HFE Acts, such as placing an embryo in a woman other than a permitted embryo.[15] Nevertheless, although a breach of the standard licensing conditions in itself would not lead to prosecution, it could result in the HFEA taking proceedings to suspend or revoke a clinic's licence, so they are very likely to be observed.[16] Effectively, the licensing conditions act as a legislative restriction on the choices of couples seeking treatment services governed by the HFE Acts by limiting the freedom of providers to offer such services. The HFEA's regulatory role has been reinforced by the introduction of a specific statutory duty upon it to promote compliance with the requirements of the HFE 1990 and with the Code of Practice it issues under section 25 of the HFE Acts.[17] Its duties also now include maintaining a statement of the general principles which it considers should be followed in carrying out its activities under the Act and its functions in relation to such activities.[18] It has been suggested that 'the Authority has always defined its general role by reference to its statutory remit. This new requirement is likely to produce a more detailed breakdown of its role in respect of particular and specific activities and functions.'[19]

In order to examine the potential impact of the new s. 13 restrictions on treatment following embryo testing, it is useful to consider examples of how they might be applied. For the sake of simplicity, it will be assumed that both gamete providers are intending to parent any child born as a result of the assisted reproduction service.

The application of the new embryo-testing provisions

PGD results in a possible choice within a batch of embryos – couple does not wish to use an affected embryo

In this example, the couple has a number of embryos in storage and is seeking to avoid a specific disorder which comes within the terms of being a condition that can be tested for using PGD. All of the embryos are tested, and the results show that only one of these embryos is affected. The couple chooses to avoid using the affected embryo.

This is the most likely scenario to arise in practice. The vast majority of people who seek to use PGD will do so precisely to avoid particular genetic disorders due to a family history of a condition or increased risk of disorders, such as those associated with conception of children by older gamete providers. Should such a condition be detected in a particular embryo following PGD,

14 Section 25 (6) HFEA 1990, as amended.
15 Section 3 (2) HFEA 1990, as amended.
16 Sections 18, 19 and 25 HFEA 1990, as amended.
17 Section 8 (1)(9cb) HFEA 1990, as amended.
18 Section 8 (1)(ca) HFEA 1990, as amended.
19 Birk, *Human Fertilisation and Embryology*, para. 4.19.

their conclusion will almost inevitably be to reject this embryo for implantation in favour of one that does not have this condition. In such situations, there is no need to bring into play any of the new section 13 restrictions, as the potential parents' preference is in line with them.

However, matters may not be entirely simple even here. Schedule 2 of the HFEA 1990 as amended contains further provisions concerning activities which may be licensed, and added in embryo testing as one of these activities.[20] Embryo testing can only be carried out for one or more specified purposes. These include establishing parenthood and tissue-typing where a sibling suffers from a serious medical condition to enable selection of an embryo that could be a match for potential donation to the sibling. The purposes that are relevant here, however, are the provisions relating to testing for genetic abnormality.[21]

> Schedule 2 S1ZA
>
> (1)
>
> (a) establishing whether the embryo has a gene, chromosome or mitochondrion abnormality that may affect its capacity to result in a live birth,
> (b) in a case where there is a particular risk that the embryo may have any gene, chromosome or mitochondrion abnormality, establishing whether it has that abnormality or any other gene, chromosome or mitochondrion abnormality.

In addition, Schedule 2 1ZA (2) provides that a licence cannot be issued for embryo testing unless the Authority is satisfied 'that there is a significant risk that a person with the abnormality will have or develop a serious physical or mental disability, a serious illness or any other serious medical condition'. Difficulties in the interpretation and application of condition-based criteria are discussed by Jackson in this volume.[22]

Nevertheless, once a condition has been authorised by the HFEA as one that can be tested for, it would seem to follow that a decision can be legitimately taken to choose not to implant any tested embryo. Of course it is the case that a woman could not be forced to accept the implantation of any embryo due to the extreme violation of respect for her autonomy and bodily integrity that this would entail, and either gamete provider could withdraw consent to the use of embryos created with their gametes before treatment was provided.[23] However, the point is that the couple could *prefer* to use unaffected embryos to those that

20 As amended by Schedule 2 of the HFEA 2008.
21 Sex-related disorders are dealt with in Schedule 2 S1ZA (1)(c), HFEA 1990, as amended.
22 See Chapter 4.
23 Schedule 3, para. 4 of the HFEA 1990, as amended. Although withdrawal of consent is now subject to a 12-month 'cooling-off' period, the effective right of veto of the use of embryos by a gamete provider is maintained.

are known to have a genetic condition disclosed by PGD. That choice is consistent with the approach taken by the new s. 13 provisions which seek to avoid such embryos being used for treatment.

It is also possible that if one condition is tested for, but the embryo is found to have other abnormalities, the couple could decide not to use it. Once the criteria for permitting PGD to take place have been satisfied, the detection of any other disorder meeting the criteria of sufficient seriousness would seem to permit it to be discarded in preference to other embryos. This would also be consistent with s. 13, which refers to 'embryos that are known to have a gene, chromosome or mitochondrion abnormality', rather than being restricted to considering them only in respect of the condition that was originally being tested for. Section 13 prohibits their use in preference to embryos not known to have such an abnormality. The implications of this will be explored later, but it must follow that to discard such embryos in favour of others that are not known to be affected is a choice that lawfully can be made by a couple.

PGD results in a possible choice within a batch of embryos all of which are tested – couple wishes to use an embryo that may be affected by a genetic disorder

Of course, the obvious question might be why a couple would wish to use an affected embryo when they have others that could be used instead? Although it might be supposed that most potential parents would seek to avoid passing on genetic disorders, there are occasional examples of people seeking to make such reproductive choices. The scenario that has caused most discussion is where a couple deliberately seeks to have a child with a genetic condition for social reasons. The classic example is congenital deafness, illustrated by a deaf lesbian couple in the United States of America, although they did not actually use PGD. Ms Duchesneau and Ms McCullough sought to increase the chance of having a child who would be deaf by using a deaf friend as a sperm donor. Their decision has provoked considerable academic debate on the merits or otherwise of 'choosing for disability'.[24] The couple contended that deafness is a culture, not a disability, and that rather than deafness reducing the child's capacity, being able to hear would constitute a lack of capability in their child since a hearing child would be prevented from full participation in deaf culture.[25] Using PGD to select an affected embryo could make the difference between increasing the chances of having a deaf child to making this a certainty. Another example can be found in the condition of achondroplasia. Its most

24 Mundy, L., 'A world of their own', *Washington Post*, 31 March 2002, W22; Sprigg, M., 'Lesbian couple create a child who is deaf like them', *Journal of Medical Ethics*, 28 (2002): 283; Levy, N., 'Deafness, culture and choice', *Journal of Medical Ethics*, 28 (2002): 284–5; Anstey, K. W. (2002) 'Are attempts to have impaired children justifiable?', *Journal of Medical Ethics*, 28 (2002): 286–8; Savulescu, J., 'Deaf lesbians, "designer disability" and the future of medicine', *British Medical Journal*, 325 (2002): 771–3.

25 Darshak, M. and Sanghavi, M. D., 'Wanting babies like themselves, some parents choose genetic defects', *New York Times*, 5 December 2006.

obvious feature is that it is the commonest cause of disproportionately short stature, or dwarfism, although it may be associated with other medical complications.[26] Achondroplasia is an FGFR3 gene mutation which shows autosomal dominance in inheritance. Where both partners carry the mutation, in natural conception there is a 25 per cent chance of an unaffected pregnancy, a 50 per cent chance of an affected pregnancy, and a 25 per cent chance of a pregnancy where the child carries two copies of the mutation, which is usually fatal shortly after birth. It has been suggested that a couple with achondroplasia might seek not only to avoid the possibility of conceiving a child with the lethal combination of genes but to have a child with achondroplasia, rather than one without.[27] Again the reasons for this would be parental preference for a child like themselves, or practical issues in caring for the child.[28]

Although the circumstances in which there might be a deliberate attempt to use PGD to conceive a child with a particular genetic disorder are likely to be rare in practice, there is evidence that they have been made. Baruch *et al.* surveyed American clinics offering PGD and found that 3 per cent of respondents reported having intentionally used PGD 'to select an embryo for the presence of a disability'.[29] It is exactly this kind of choice that s. 13 of the amended HFEA 1990 is directed against. Indeed this is made crystal clear in the explanatory note that accompanied a draft of the Human Tissues and Embryos Bill published in 2007. Following a description of the intention to make it a condition of treatment licences that embryos tested and known to have specified abnormalities were not to be preferred in treatment services to those which did not, and that this prohibition would also extend to the selection of persons as gamete or embryo donors, it went on to say:

> [t]here have been reported cases outside the UK involving the positive selection of deaf donors in order deliberately to result in a deaf child. The new section [as numbered] would prevent this.[30]

It follows that, in this scenario, a deliberate choice to select an affected embryo in preference to others that were unaffected would be prevented. This may pose

26 Horton, W. A., Hall, J. G. and Hecht, J. T., 'Achondroplasia', *Lancet*, 370(9582) (2007): 162–9; Stratbucker, W.B., Serwint, J.R., 'In brief: achondroplasia', *Pediatrics in Review*, 30 (2009): 114–15.

27 Kolthoff, M., 'Assisted reproduction and *primum non nocere*', *Virtual Mentor*, 9(9) (2007): 605–10.

28 The HCSTC used the example of achondroplasia in its online consultation launched 22 January 2004. In it, a fictional couple gave as the reason for wishing to use PGD to select for achondroplasia that a child of normal height would cause practical problems in their home.

29 Baruch, S., Kaufman, D. J. and Hudson, K. L, 'Genetic testing of embryos: practices and perspectives of US IVF clinics', *Fertility and Sterility*, 89 (2008): 1053–8; Baruch, S., Kaufman, D. J. and Hudson, K. L., 'Preimplantation genetic screening: a survey of in vitro fertilization clinics', *Genetics in Medicine*, 10 (2008): 685–90.

30 Department of Health, Human Tissue and Embryos (Draft) Bill, May 2007, Cm 7087, para. 66.

particular problems for couples with conditions such as achondroplasia, where one possibility is that an embryo will have a combination of genes incompatible with survival. Although amniocentesis or chorionic villus sampling can be performed during pregnancy to detect double dominant mutations, the use of PGD would enable decisions to be made without having to consider abortion where this variation is found to exist. However, there may be couples with achondroplasia who, while they might not prefer to have a child who also has a single copy of the mutation and who is affected by the condition, would be content with this. The same of course may be true for other genetic conditions, but unless they have variants which are likely to be fatal or cause additional problems for the child, couples who have no preference would be unlikely to opt for PGD.[31] If a woman had undergone screening during pregnancy, there would be no question of forcing her to undergo a termination of pregnancy, whether the foetus had a single or even double copy of the mutated gene. However, if PGD were undertaken to avoid the fatal mutation, then could a decision be made to use an embryo with the single mutation? According to the new provisions, it would appear not, at least if they had other embryos that were free from the mutation.[32] While wishing to avoid a fatal condition, and the consequent decision that might arise as to whether to abort a pregnancy, it appears that women using PGD who might have chosen to carry an embryo with achondroplasia could be denied that opportunity under the new provisions.

However, it may be argued that the legislation was not intended to achieve this outcome and that there are means of interpretation that would avoid it. One possible solution might be to focus on the wording of the legislative provisions, which are couched in terms of 'preference'. It could be suggested that if a couple were willing to have either a child with achondroplasia or one without, that they are not in fact expressing a preference for a child with a genetic disorder. If this were accepted, then they could be permitted to use an embryo chosen at random from the embryos that do not have the fatal genetic combination, but which may include embryos with and without the non-fatal mutation. This would appear to satisfy the intention of the provisions to prohibit deliberately using affected embryos for treatment but allow some room for manoeuvre for potential parental choice to run the risk of a child having what is likely to be regarded as a disabling medical condition. The potential parents in such a situation are not 'preferring' an embryo with such a condition, nor seeking to select one on this basis; they are merely accepting the possibility.

31 See, for example, a survey of children of deaf adults where more than 70 per cent stated no preference for a hearing or deaf child, and believed that genetic selection for and against deafness was not appropriate. Mand, C., *et al.* 'Genetic selection for deafness: the views of hearing children of deaf adults', *Journal of Medical Ethics*, 35 (2009): 722–8.

32 The issue of the comparator group to which an affected embryo is being preferred will be considered in more detail later.

There are some grounds to suggest that the provisions might bear such an interpretation since, despite the clear intention behind them, it does not necessarily follow that even where there is a known risk that an embryo may have a genetic abnormality or be of a sex giving rise to the risk of a resulting child having a serious physical or mental disability, serious illness or serious medical condition, it cannot be implanted. This is apparent from the guidance given in the HFEA's 8th Code of Practice in relation to embryo testing.[33] There is no absolute prohibition on implanting such embryos. In addition, although the Code of Practice omits to refer to the preferential selection of embryos here, the wording of the statute does appear to make 'preference' a necessary criterion for the restrictions on embryo selection to apply. Furthermore, there is no requirement that couples submit their embryos to PGD. Rather, the expectation is the opposite: that PGD is currently seen as requiring justification in defined circumstances and is not to be used as routine practice. There is no statutory requirement that a couple with a known inheritable disorder, or where there is a clear risk of a genetic abnormality in an embryo, have to agree to PGD on embryos created with their gametes before they can use them in treatment. Similarly, donors who are known to have such disorders or be at risk for them are not prevented from providing gametes under s. 13 (9); it is only preferentially selecting them that is prevented. In fact, it is possible that limitations on providing treatment to couples or using donor gametes might be placed where there is a known risk of embryos having genetic disorders, but these would need to rest on a different provision – that of the general welfare of a resulting child, contained in s. 13 (5). This will be explored further in due course. For the moment, I will turn to an even more contentious possibility – that the prohibitions on embryo selection may not prevent a deliberate attempt to select for an embryo with a genetic disorder.

PGD undertaken on one embryo at a time – couple wishes to use an affected embryo

Here the couple chooses not to undertake PGD on a batch of embryos, but rather only one embryo at a time is created and tested. For the sake of argument, the first embryo tested has a genetic disorder that is contained in the HFEA's authorised list of conditions for testing, but the couple wishes to use it for treatment.

My contention would be that the conditions set out in ss. 13 (9–11) may not prevent them from making this choice. This is because of the wording of these provisions which is expressed in terms of 'preference' in selection, comparing the affected embryo with others that are 'not known' to have the abnormality or carry the risk.

33 HFEA, 8th Code of Practice, London: Stationery Office, 2009, 10C.

This is reinforced by the guidance given in the HFEA's 8th Code of Practice on the interpretation of the restrictions on selecting embryos for treatment in s. 13 of the HFEA 1990, as amended.

> The law prohibits the selection of an embryo for treatment if it is known to:
>
> (a) have a gene, chromosome or mitochondrial abnormality involving a significant risk that the person with the abnormality will develop a serious physical or mental disability, a serious illness, or a serious medical condition, or
> (b) be of a sex that carries a particular risk that any resulting child will have or develop a gender-related serious physical or mental disability, serious illness, or serious medical condition
>
> *This applies only where there is at least one other embryo suitable for transfer that is not known to have the characteristics. Where there is no other embryo suitable for transfer, an embryo with these characteristics may be transferred.* [at 10C, my italics]

The issue then becomes what the comparator group for the affected embryo is. There are a number of possible options here. These could include all *in vitro* embryos; embryos donated for other people's treatment; or embryos created using the couple's gametes. Another factor would relate to whether these other embryos would need to currently exist or whether the possibility that they could be created would be relevant. Presumably some territorial restriction would operate so that only *in vitro* embryos coming under the remit of the HFE Acts would be contemplated. Which comparator group the affected embryo is being 'preferred' to will determine whether or not these restrictions bite.

It should be said at the outset that there is a difference between embryos 'known not' to be affected, and those 'not known' to be affected. The former suggests that there has been a positive test to determine the genetic makeup of the embryo, the latter does not. So, for example, if the requirement against preference was that embryos known to be affected could not be preferred to those known not to be affected, the scope for selecting affected embryos might be increased by simply not testing all of the embryos at the same time. There would then be no other embryos which were *known* not to have the condition and hence the prohibition on selection would not come into effect. While there might still be room for doubt here, since the comparator group of embryos would remain to be determined, requiring the comparator group to have been tested and found not to have the condition would make it more likely that the couple could avoid the restriction since there is no general requirement to conduct PGD.

However, this is not what the provisions say. They require a preference to be expressed in comparison with embryos that are not known to be affected. This still would seem to permit a wide or a narrow scope for such a comparison to be made. There are strong arguments against the idea of a very widely drawn category of comparator embryos. It may be contended that there should be a realistic possibility of the couple being able to access and use an alternative embryo. For example, the fact that other people have embryos stored for their own treatment that are not known to be affected by genetic disorder would not allow the couple with the affected embryo to seek to use them. It would therefore be absurd to suggest that in seeking to use their own embryo, they are 'preferring' to do so rather than use these other embryos. This is not a choice that is open to them. This supports immediately narrowing the category of comparator embryos to those that could be available to the couple to use, which leaves only embryos that are donated for other people's treatment and other embryos of the couple.

The next issue is whether the other embryos must actually be in existence at the time that the comparison is being made or whether the possibility of future unaffected embryos that they could use can be brought into consideration. The response to this is less obvious, since there is no guidance as to the timeframe in which the comparison need be made. Again, however, it can plausibly be argued that the preference which the couple expresses should be directed to options that are currently available to them, not predicated on some, as yet uncertain, prospect of being able to secure donated embryos or successful creation of embryos from their own gametes that are not known to have disorders. This would suggest that the comparator group that the s. 13 provisions are concerned with are other embryos that the couple has available to use at the time when decisions about the affected embryo are being made. This seems to be implied from the HFEA guidance which refers to 'no other embryos being suitable for transfer', which suggests that the comparator embryos must be available for transfer at the time that the decision is being made.[34]

If this is accepted, and it is fair to say that this remains a speculative approach, then it would seem to follow that if the couple do not have any other embryos in existence, they would not fall foul of the ss. 13 (9–11) of the treatment provisions by seeking to use the affected embryo. As noted earlier, these do not provide a blanket prohibition on the use of embryos that have been tested and found to have particular genetic conditions; only upon preferring to use them to those that are not known to have such conditions if there 'is at least one other embryo suitable for transfer that is not known to have the characteristics'.[35] For a couple determined to seek to have a child with a particular genetic makeup, the route might accordingly be to ask to have embryos created and tested serially and to consent to the disposal of embryos found not to have the condition until one is found to have it. Consent could be withdrawn for an unaffected embryo's continued storage; it could be donated for treatment of

34 Ibid., at 10C.
35 Ibid.

others, training purposes or for research. Any of these options would render it unavailable for a couple's own treatment.[36] Embarking on this route would rest on the feasibility of having gametes available to use to create embryos in this way. It is likely to involve egg freezing which, as the HFEA notes, 'is still a relatively new and experimental technique' and has a low success rate in maintaining viable gametes.[37] Although additional methods such as vitrification are becoming available which appear to improve the chances of eggs surviving the freezing and thawing processes:

> [r]ecords show that up to 31/12/2008, around 6388 eggs have been stored in the UK for the patient's own use. To date around 88 embryos from stored eggs have been created. These embryos were transferred to women in around 32 cycles, which resulted in around 3 live births. These figures are for both eggs which have been stored using slow freezing and vitrification methods.[38]

This would also require the willingness of clinics to participate in what would clearly be an attempt to circumvent the statutory provisions. Nevertheless, such circumvention would not appear to be unlawful nor to directly contravene current HFEA policy. The HFEA's 8th Code of Practice, having allowed for the possibility that embryos known to have genetic abnormalities can be implanted, goes on to say:

> 10.17
> The use of an embryo known to have an abnormality as described above [in 10C] should be subject to consideration of the welfare of any resulting child and should normally have approval from a clinical ethics committee.
>
> 10.18
> If a centre decides that it is appropriate to provide treatment services to a woman using an embryo known to have an abnormality as described above, it should document the reason for the use of that embryo.
>
> NOTE: An example of an embryo not suitable for transfer in this context is one that has no realistic prospect of resulting in a live birth.

Therefore, even if the specific statutory restrictions on selecting affected embryos can be avoided, it is entirely possible that such a practice would still be caught by the more general restrictions of the HFEA 1990, if the implantation of an affected embryo was thought to sufficiently risk any resulting child's

36 HFEA 1990 s. 12 (1), s. 14 (12), s. 15 (4) and Schedule 3, as amended.
37 HFEA website, 'Freezing and storing eggs', www.hfea.gov.uk/46.html (accessed 11/11/2011).
38 Ibid.

welfare. There is, therefore, a two-stage process in considering whether embryos can be implanted where PGD is involved: first, the embryo-testing provisions in ss. 13 (9–11), and, second; the welfare provisions in s. 13 (5).

It has been asserted that the underlying justification for limiting the use of embryos found to have genetic abnormalities is based on the welfare of the child principle. The basis for this assertion will be considered in more detail, before turning to two fundamental issues that deserve closer examination: to what extent is the concept of the welfare of the child really appropriate in this context, whether it is the reason behind those sections related solely to PGD or in the overarching conditions for treatment in s. 13 (5); and how should it be balanced against respect for the wishes of the potential parents to select an embryo known to have genetic abnormalities?

The welfare of the child principle as a basis for embryo-testing provisions

The welfare of the child and ss. 13 (9–11) of the embryo-testing provisions

The development of the techniques of PGD was based on apparently beneficent grounds: to improve the success rates for assisted reproduction by not commencing a pregnancy with an embryo that has a serious disorder that might result in miscarriage; to avoid a choice having to be made as to whether to abort a foetus with a serious disorder identified during pregnancy; and, underlying this, concerns about the welfare of children.[39] The development of the role of the HFEA in regulating PGD has been discussed elsewhere in this volume and so will not be repeated here.[40] However, questions about the use of PGD to select for disability have been asked in a number of public consultations and reviews. For example, in 1999 a public consultation exercise was carried out by a joint working party of the HFEA and the Advisory Committee on Genetic Testing.[41] After outlining the potential choices that could be made to test embryos and act on the results, including seeking to use an affected embryo, it asked respondents 'Can the principle of the Welfare of the Child ever be compatible with the decision to begin a pregnancy knowing that a child will be born with a genetic disorder?' The responses were as follows:

> 47% acknowledged that there might be situations in which the replacement of an affected embryo would be compatible with the principle of the

39 See, for example, the *Report of the Committee of Inquiry into Human Fertilisation and Embryology* (Warnock Report), London: Stationery Office, 1984, para. 12.13.

40 See, for example, Jackson's contribution (Chapter 4).

41 Human Fertilisation and Embryology Authority and Advisory Committee on Genetic Testing, *Consultation Document on Preimplantation Genetic Diagnosis*, London: Stationery Office, 1999.

> welfare of the child. 31% argued that this should be a decision left to the parents. 22% argued that starting such a pregnancy could never be compatible with this principle.[42]

Although the number of responses was small (98), and hence the weight that can be placed on them is limited, they revealed a range of factors that were thought to be relevant:

> The majority of these responses qualified their answers by stating that this might only be appropriate in certain circumstances, depending on severity of the condition, family situation and other similar considerations. In addition, most of the 'yes' responses concerned only the question of affected embryos where there were no unaffected ones for transfer, but rejected PGD as a method of choosing an affected embryo for social or other reasons.
>
> It should also be noted that many respondents were unfamiliar with the terminology of 'welfare of the child' and some respondents questioned its meaning, range or relevance.[43]

It is interesting to see some doubts being expressed about the meaning of the welfare of the child principle and how it might apply in this situation.

On the specific issue of selecting for disability, the HCSTC in its report entitled *Human Reproductive Technologies and the Law* was ambivalent and did not reach a final conclusion on whether embryos with, as it termed them, 'undesirable characteristics' should be able to be used in treatment. On this issue it said:

> We can imagine that many clinicians would baulk at the idea of selecting, for example, a deaf child using PGD, but we do not feel that the creation of a child with reduced life opportunities is sufficient grounds for regulatory intervention, else we might logically deny poor people IVF. Professor Tom Shakespeare told us that PGD should not be allowed to select out 'minor or trivial' conditions such as restricted growth or deafness. [Ev 363] On this basis, it is difficult to argue that they should not be selected rather than deselected. A more challenging but unlikely scenario would be the desire to select a child who would suffer obvious discomfort (rather than disadvantage), or worse. In this area there needs to be further debate.[44]

It was therefore not at the behest of the HCSTC that ss. 13 (9–11) of the provisions on embryo selection were included in the legislation, nor was any

42 Human Genetics Commission and the Human Fertilisation and Embryology Authority, *Outcome of the Public Consultation on Preimplantation Genetic Diagnosis*, London: Stationery Office, November 2001, paras 30–3.

43 Ibid.

44 Para. 145.

suggestion of this raised in the government response to this report.[45] However, a further consultation exercise undertaken by the Department of Health appears to have provided the basis for their inclusion in subsequent legislative proposals. This consultation specifically asked whether there should be a prohibition on deliberately screening in, or selecting for, impairments or disabilities as opposed to screening out, or selecting embryos free from impairments or disabilities.[46] Responses to the consultation were published in March 2006. There was no attempt in this document to draw conclusions, and it was noted that on the issue of screening in or selecting for impairments the responses demonstrated a range of perspectives.[47] Nevertheless, it appears likely that the impetus for including legislative provisions on this subject came from the HFEA's response, which sought parliamentary guidance. Following this consultation, proposals for legislation appeared in a White Paper issued in December 2006. Despite the lack of any clear consensus or recommendation for this approach in the prior consultative processes, it was stated that '[d]eliberately screening-in a disease or disorder will be prohibited'.[48] While the sections in which this issue was addressed changed at different stages of the drafting of the Bill and its passage through Parliament, the fundamental principle of prohibiting a preference for affected embryos to those not known to be affected remained consistent.[49]

As well as seeking to improve success rates in terms of live births in assisted reproduction, and in order to try to avoid the issue of abortion arising, as it might if abnormalities were discovered only during pregnancy, the inclusion of these provisions seems, therefore, to be rooted in some notion of the concept of child welfare.

The welfare of the child principle and child law

The need to take account of the welfare of children born as a result of treatment services governed by the HFE Acts may seem at first to be an uncontroversial proposition.[50] Concern to protect children is at the heart of international declarations such as the United Nations Convention on the Rights of the Child,

45 *Human Reproductive Technologies and the Law: Government Response to the Report of the HCSTC*, London: Stationery Office, Cm 6641, August 2005.

46 Department of Health, *Review of the Human Fertilisation and Embryology Act: A Public Consultation*, London: Stationery Office, August 2005, para. 5.20.

47 Department of Health, *Report on the Review of the Human Fertilisation and Embryology Act: A Public Consultation*, London: Stationery Office, March 2006, para. 5.3.

48 Department of Health, *Review of the Human Fertilisation and Embryology Act 1990: Proposals for Revised Legislation (Including Establishment of the Regulatory Authority for Tissues and Embryos)*, London: Stationery Office, December 2006, Cm 6989.

49 See, for example, Draft Human Tissue and Embryology Bill published for pre-legislative scrutiny. May 2007, s. 21(4).

50 I have explored the issues arising from the use of the welfare–best interests test in more detail in Elliston, S., *The Best Interests of the Child in Healthcare*, Abingdon: Routledge-Cavendish, 2007, esp. ch. 1. Some parts of this discussion are taken from it.

which is the most widely ratified international convention in existence.[51] This Convention states in Article 3 that:

> [i]n all actions concerning children, whether undertaken by public or private social welfare institutions, courts of law, administrative authorities or legislative bodies, *the best interests of the child shall be a primary consideration.* [my italics]

In the UK this approach may be seen to be reflected in the general legal principles that govern decisions about children. In England and Wales these are set out in the Children Act 1989, which provides that when hearing cases under the Act, the courts are required to have the welfare of the child as their paramount consideration. There are similar provisions under the equivalent statute in Scotland, the Children (Scotland) Act 1995. In England and Wales there is also the inherent jurisdiction which is usually exercised in wardship proceedings, although it may be used independently. Here, the principle is that judicial decisions must be made in the child's best interests.[52] It can be argued that there are differences between the expressions set out in statute and at common law; however, largely for practical reasons, the courts have sought to minimise them so that the terms 'welfare' and 'best interests' are used interchangeably.

However, equating the two terms is not unproblematic. It can be suggested that a welfare approach is less protective of children than a best interests approach, since, as has on occasion been recognised by the courts, if we are speaking of what is in a child's best interests, then logically there can be only one answer.[53] This presents a number of difficulties – first in the actual prediction of what the outcome will be of a particular choice. Breen has suggested that this requires the decision-maker to have shaman-like qualities for the prediction of future events.[54] It also implicitly involves a value judgement: what factors are relevant to a person's interests and how are these factors to be weighed? Although it has been held that best interests encompass medical, emotional and all other welfare issues,[55] there may well remain ample scope for disagreement over what outcomes, to the extent that they can be predicted, are best for a child. Evidence to support this can be found in the numerous treatment decisions brought before the courts in England and Wales,

51 The United Nations Convention on the Rights of the Child, adopted and opened for signature, ratification and accession by General Assembly Res. 44/25 of 20 November 1989. It came into force in the UK on 16 December 1991.

52 For the use of wardship, see, for example, *Re J (a minor) (medical treatment)* [1992] 3 WLR 507 CA; *R* v. *Portsmouth NHS Trust, ex part Glass* [1999] 2 FLR 905 CA.

53 *Re SL (adult patient) (medical treatment)* [2000] 2 FCR 452 CA, *per* Dame Elizabeth Butler-Sloss P., at p. 464.

54 Breen, C., *The Standard of the Best Interests of the Child: A Western Tradition in International and Comparative Law, International Studies in Human Rights Vol.72*, The Hague: Martinus Nijhoff, 2002.

55 *Re A (medical treatment: male sterilisation)* [2000] 1 FCR 193 CA, *per* Dame Butler-Sloss P., at p. 200.

notably in the context of withholding or withdrawing treatment from severely ill children who have profoundly disabling conditions.[56]

A welfare test by contrast can be suggested to be more flexible and less dogmatic, since it does not claim that there is one answer that is best, merely that a decision promotes or safeguards, or is at least not harmful to, the interests of the child. Of course, the problems of ascertaining and predicting the outcome of alternatives on child welfare will remain. A range of different outcomes for the child may be viewed as being in the child's interests, depending on the values and priorities given to particular aspects of child welfare and development. In fact, in the main, such decisions are devolved to parents to make, with relatively limited scope for intervention, unless it seems likely to result in what is regarded as serious harm. Indeed this can be considered to be part of a social contract.

> It is a hallmark of a democratic society that while parents have the primary responsibility to look after their children, they are free to bring them up in the manner in which they deem best for the children's welfare.[57]

Parents have the legal responsibility to safeguard and promote the child's health, development and welfare.[58] Nevertheless, the circumstances in which their decisions are open to challenge are relatively limited and it can be suggested that they generally hinge on a threshold of a significant risk of serious, avoidable harm being reached.

A further problem lies in deciding what weight the welfare of a child should be given. As we have seen, the United Nations Convention on the Rights of the Child states that 'the best interests of the child shall be a primary consideration' when decisions are taken by outside agencies, including courts.[59] This followed considerable debate over the wording to be used.[60] However, it is not the expression used in the Children Acts, which is that the child's welfare is the *paramount* consideration. At first glance, then, the Children Acts appear to apply a less protective standard of decision-making than the UN Convention, since they refer to child welfare rather than a child's best interests, but this factor is then given overriding importance, being *the paramount* consideration rather than *a primary* consideration. The test under the inherent jurisdiction of the courts in England and Wales is that the child's best interests are the prime

56 See, for example, *Re C (a minor) (withdrawal of lifesaving treatment)* (1997) 40 BMLR 31; *Re T (a minor) (wardship: medical treatment)* [1997] 1 WLR 242, [1997] 1 All ER 906, 35 BMLR 63 CA; *Wyatt* v. *Portsmouth Hospitals NHS Trust* [2005] EWCA Civ 1181 CA.

57 Thomson, J., *Family Law in Scotland*, 5th edn, Glasgow: Tottel, 2006, at p. 257.

58 This is explicit in the Children (Scotland) Act 1995, s. 1 (1)(a) and implicit in the Children Act 1989, s. 3.

59 Article 3 (1).

60 Breen, C., *The Standard of the Best Interests of the Child: A Western Tradition in International and Comparative Law, International Studies in Human Rights Vol.72*, The Hague: Martinus Nijhoff, 2002, at pp. 78–84.

and paramount concern.[61] However, as noted, the courts have sought to avoid imposing different standards when making decisions about children, whatever the procedure taken to bring a case before them. Effectively, therefore, the standard adopted is that the best interests of the child are the paramount concern of the court.

However, no legally enforceable rights attach to embryos as they are not regarded as legal persons, so decisions affecting them cannot be made on the basis of child welfare[62] and it would effectively alter the provision of assisted reproductive treatment beyond recognition were this to be contemplated. Family law statutes such as the Children Act 1989 and the Children (Scotland) Act 1995 only apply to children after birth. Furthermore, the UK, upon its ratification of the United Nations Convention on the Rights of the Child, declared that it interpreted the Convention as applicable only following a live birth.[63] Nevertheless, consideration of these instruments highlights the potential for disagreement over the standard of child protection that ought to apply in decisions concerning children, the weight that it should be given and the difficulties in interpreting deceptively simple statements, even in the context of children who have legally recognised and protected interests. This also raises the issue of the legitimate role of the state in displacing the views of parents about what is in their children's interests and when their decisions can be regarded as so detrimental to child welfare that steps may be taken to protect children from them.

It should be said that some have questioned the continuing adherence to the central place of a principle of child welfare or best interests of the child in the era of human rights, and it has been contended that:

> [i]t will no longer do, it seems, to frame issues of child welfare in terms of making traditional 'best interests' judgments: at the very least, concern for a child's welfare should be conceptualised as a matter of the child's rights-protected interests.[64]

While there is merit in this, welfare is the terminology used in domestic legislation and the content of such evaluations may be unlikely to differ in practice. For this reason, discussion in this chapter has concentrated on this concept.

61 See, for example, *Re J (a minor) (wardship: medical treatment)* [1990] 3 All ER 145, CA.

62 *Paton* v. *BPAS* [1979] 1 QB 276, considered by the European Court of Human Rights (EctHR) in *Paton* v. *United Kingdom* (1981) 3 EHRR 408 (ECHR); *Kelly* v. *Kelly* 1997 SLT 896 CS (IH). The likely impact of a decision upon the welfare of a foetus or resulting child can only be considered indirectly in so far as it may affect the best interests of a pregnant woman who lacks capacity to make treatment decisions for herself: *St George's Healthcare NHS Trust* v. *S (No. 2)* [1998] 3 All ER 673 CA; *Re F (in utero)* [1988] FCR 529; [1988] Fam 122 (CA).

63 The UK Reservation and Declarations, CRC/C/2/Rev 4, at para. 32, 16 December 1991.

64 Brownsword, R., 'Happy families, consenting couples, and children with dignity: sex selection and saviour siblings', *Child and Family Law Quarterly*, 17(4) (2005): 435–73, at p. 435.

The development and retention of s. 13 (5) welfare of the child principle within the HFE Acts

The difficulties in applying a welfare standard multiply when what is at stake is not parental decision-making concerning children they already have, but rather whether to allow the couple to seek to have children using assisted reproductive technologies. The restrictions on selection of embryos for treatment following PGD do not make any direct reference to the welfare concept, although as has been demonstrated, this is undoubtedly the justification for them; this is explicit in s. 13 (5). The standard of child protection that is set out in this section is couched in the language of welfare rather than best interests. However, in respect of the weight to be given to it in deciding whether or not treatment services should be provided, this section does not prioritise the welfare of the child. It must be 'taken into account' but it is not the paramount, or even a primary, consideration on the face of the statute. This notwithstanding, it appears to be a provision that may assume considerable importance in determining whether specific embryos can be used in treatment services.

In the development of a legislative approach to reproductive technologies, concern to safeguard the interests of children who might be born as a result of assisted reproduction can be traced back at least to the Warnock Committee Report, and references are made to this issue in various contexts throughout it.[65] It is interesting to see, however, that, even then, there was disagreement about the extent to which such concerns should be a governing factor.

> Our emphasis on the arguments may make it appear that there was a uniformity of approach and moral feeling in the Inquiry. The reality however has been that our personal feelings and reactions have been as diverse as those presented in the evidence. Some members have a clear perception of the family and its role within society; in considering the various techniques before us their focus has been on the primacy of the interests of the child, and on upholding family values. Other members have felt equally strongly about the rights of the individual within society.[66]

In fact, when the White Paper introducing what came to be the HFEA 1990 was issued, it contained no specific reference to a child welfare principle, nor did the Bill itself. It came into consideration almost by chance in the course of debates about whether access to treatment should be confined to married couples and it was in this context that concerns about child welfare led to amendments to the Bill. Nevertheless, once the principle had been put forward, it commanded unstinting support. As Jackson, writing in 2002, notes:

65 Warnock Report.
66 Ibid., para. 3.

> [i]n the Parliamentary debates leading up to the passage of the Human Fertilisation and Embryology Act in 1990, the inclusion of a welfare principle was neither challenged nor defended. Instead, it was simply assumed to be self-evidently true that their future children's welfare ought to be taken into account before a couple is offered assistance with conception, and this assumption undoubtedly persists today.[67]

Indeed, it came to be considered that one of the 'most important principles' underlying the HFEA 1990 was the welfare of any children born.[68] However, a more critical appraisal of the welfare principle appeared in the Report of the HCSTC, where Recommendation 24 stated that:

> [t]he welfare of the child provision discriminates against the infertile and some sections of society, is impossible to implement and is of questionable practical value in protecting the interests of children born as a result of assisted reproduction . . . The welfare of the child provision has enabled the HFEA and clinics to make judgements that are more properly made by patients in consultation with their doctor. It should be abolished in its current form. The minimum threshold principle should apply but should specify that this threshold should be the risk of unpreventable and significant harm. Doctors should minimize the risks to any child conceived from treatment within the constraints of available knowledge but this should be encouraged through the promotion of good medical practice not legislation.[69]

It is worth noting, however, that the HCSTC expressed most concern in respect of judgements being made about the prospective parenting environment. No issue was taken with the general idea of protecting children from harm, although the suggested threshold for any legislative provision was a relatively high one. While recommending that good medical practice should be sufficient to minimise risks of harm, this does, of course, raise the question of the proper extent of clinical discretion and whether it might be amenable to challenge, for example, through human rights principles.[70] Nevertheless, it might be expected that justification for the exercise of discretion in a particular case would be required.

However, in response to the HCSTC recommendations, the government only recognised 'that attempting to frame these matters in national

67 Jackson, E., 'Conception and the irrelevance of the welfare principle', *Modern Law Review*, 65 (2002): 176–203, at p. 177.
68 *Evans* v. *Amicus Healthcare Ltd; Hadley* v. *Midland Fertility Services Ltd* [2004] 1 FLR 67 CA para. 37, *per* Wall, J.
69 Para. 107.
70 Human Rights Act 1998. See for example, Bell, L., 'Is the Human Fertilisation and Embryology Act 2008 compatible with the Universal Declaration of Human Rights (UDHR)?', *Web JCLI*, 1 [2009], http://webjcli.ncl.ac.uk/2009/issue1/bell1.html (accessed 09/02/2012).

legislation and guidance which pays due regard both to individual circumstances and to the need for objectivity and fairness is extremely difficult' and undertook to 'seek wider public views on how the welfare of children born as a result of assisted reproduction may best be secured'.[71] This it did in 2005 in the Department of Health public consultation previously referred to.[72] The questions asked included whether the welfare of the child principle should be retained and if so, whether this should be a matter of 'good medical practice' as recommended by the HCSTC, or overseen by the HFEA. It also asked whether welfare should be restricted to consideration of the child's medical circumstances and whether it should be specified that risk assessment should relate to 'serious' or 'significant' harm. As with the questions asked about embryo testing, responses were mixed and no conclusions were drawn in the report on the consultation.[73] In the end, the government rejected abolition of the welfare of the child provision, or even a major revision, opting instead to address only the assessment of future parental support for a resulting child. This principle therefore operates on two levels: as both a general condition for offering any assisted reproduction governed by the HFE Acts and now, in addition, as an implicit justification for the specific provisions concerning treatment involving PGD. As it stands, the provisions in the HFE Acts provide no guidance on how the welfare principle should be interpreted. This is provided instead by the HFEA in its Code of Practice.

The welfare principle and the HFEA Code of Practice

Concerns about the application of the welfare principle to treatment decisions resulted in the HFEA conducting its own review of this issue at the same time as the HCSTC was conducting its more wide-ranging review of the HFEA 1990 and the role of the HFEA.[74]

As a result, the HFEA introduced a number of changes that it claimed would lead to a 'better system for protecting the welfare of children born as a result of fertility treatment'.[75] It went on to summarise some of the key changes as follows:

> A clear focus on areas of serious harm, with vague and subjective social questions removed from the assessment.
>
> That clinics should assume they will provide treatment unless there is evidence that the child is likely to be at risk of serious harm. This will

71 *Human Reproductive Technologies and the Law*, paras. 39 and 40.

72 *Review of the Human Fertilisation and Embryology Act*, s. 3.

73 Department of Health, *Report on the Review of the Human Fertilisation and Embryology Act*, ch. 3.

74 HFEA, *Tomorrow's Children: A Consultation on Guidance to Licensed Fertility Clinics on Taking in Account the Welfare of Children to be Born of Assisted Conception Treatment*, London: Stationery Office, January 2005.

75 HFEA press release 'Improved welfare checks system will be better, fairer and clearer for fertility patients, GPs and clinics', 2 November 2005.

> enable treatment for the majority of patients to go ahead with the minimum of disruption.
>
> Clinicians should use their professional judgement to decide which cases warrant further investigation rather than being obliged to contact a patient's GP in each and every case.[76]

What is interesting to observe here is the concentration on a risk-based assessment and, in particular, the emphasis on medical conditions that might affect a child resulting from treatment regulated by the HFEA.

The current guidance at the time of writing is the 8th Code of Practice which was produced to take account of the HFEA 2008. It includes the following provisions:

> The centre should assess each patient and their partner (if they have one) before providing any treatment, and should use this assessment to decide whether there is a risk of significant harm or neglect to any child.[77]

While some of the factors concern the criteria of 'supportive parenting', there is a specific consideration of the likely health of the child at 8.10.

> (b) (iii) medical history, where the medical history indicates that any child who may be born is likely to suffer from a serious medical condition . . .
> and more generally,
> (iv) circumstances that the centre considers likely to cause serious harm to any child mentioned above.
>
> The Code of Practice states that the centre should refuse treatment if it:
>
> (a) concludes that any child who may be born or any existing child of the family is likely to be at risk of significant harm or neglect,
> or
> (b) cannot obtain enough information to conclude that there is no significant risk.[78]

Despite offering such guidance, the statutory responsibility for making the assessment required by s. 13 (5) remains that of the treatment centre, which must decide how to apply the welfare principle in an individual case. For procedures involving PGD, this would be the provision that would finally determine whether treatment could be provided if the hurdle

76 Ibid.
77 At 8.3.
78 Ibid., para 8.15.

of avoiding restrictions on using embryos at risk of or known to have genetic abnormalities can be overcome in any of the ways outlined earlier. However, where the question arises of using an embryo which has been tested and found to have abnormalities arises, the approval of a clinical ethics committee is also expected by the HFEA, adding another layer of scrutiny in this situation.[79]

Applying the welfare principle to assisted reproduction

Notwithstanding the retention of the welfare principle, the importing of a familiar concept in child law to assisted reproduction has, as has already been indicated, provoked a range of criticism.[80] Much of it stemmed from the application of this concept to the potential parenting environment that a child might be born into, especially related to the original version of s. 13 (5) which required the 'need of the child for a father' to be taken into account. With the replacement of this wording with the 'need for supportive parenting' by the 2008 Act some of these concerns may have been addressed, although they do not disappear. However, there are more fundamental objections to the use of the principle at all when deciding whether reproductive treatment services should be offered.

The usual way of looking at a welfare of the child assessment is to attempt to weigh the relative burdens and benefits that would accrue to a child depending on the decision that is taken. A 'balance sheet' approach has been advocated in cases involving medical treatment, for example, where the provision of treatment to severely ill or disabled young children is under consideration.[81] While this is a far from straightforward approach even in these circumstances, it might seem an initially attractive way of evaluating the consequences of any impairment that a child might have if it were born. There is, however, a difficulty with this when making decisions about embryos and that is that the alternatives for this embryo are either for it to become a child with the abnormality and all that this would entail, or not to be born at all. This is what has become known as the non-identity problem and has generated particular interest in the field of bioethics as a result of the work of Parfit.[82] If

79 HFEA, 8th Code of Practice, at 10.17.

80 See, for example, Douglas, G., 'Assisted reproduction and the welfare of the child', *Current Legal Problems*, 46 (1993): 53–74; Jackson, 'Conception and the irrelevance of the welfare principle'; Harris, J., 'Rights and reproductive choice', in Harris, J. and Holm, S. (eds.), *The Future of Human Reproduction: Ethics, Choice, and Regulation*, Oxford: Clarendon, 1998, pp. 5–37.

81 See, for example, *Wyatt* v. *Portsmouth Hospital NHS Trust* [2005] EWCA Civ 1181 CA, at paras 87 and 90.

82 Parfit, D., *Reasons and Persons*, Oxford: Oxford University Press, 1984, ch. 16. For authors drawing on this work, see, for example, Gavaghan, C., 'Designer donors'? Tissue-typing and the regulation of pre-implantation, genetic diagnosis', *Web Journal of Current Legal Issues*, 3 (2004), http://webjcli.ncl.ac.uk/2004/issue3/gavaghan3.html (accessed 09/02/2012); Kavka, G., 'The paradox of future individuals', *Philosophy and Public Affairs*,

the decision had been taken to use another embryo than an affected one, a different child – with a different identity – would be born. Viewed in such terms, it might appear that considering the welfare of the child would require an assessment of the benefits of existence (with the anticipated level of resulting disability) against non-existence.

Comparisons of existence with non-existence have been considered to be inherently problematic as may be seen by looking at wrongful life claims. In such claims, as with the case of embryo selection, it is not alleged that wrongful conduct caused the disability, rather, that it caused a child with disability to be born due to opportunities to prevent this not having been offered to the parent(s). In such cases, it is the child that is the claimant, not the parents.[83] This kind of claim was considered in the case of *McKay* v. *Essex Area Health Authority* (1982) which concerned a child whose mother had contracted rubella during pregnancy and had not been advised about the possible consequences for the foetus nor given the opportunity to consider an abortion. For Ackner, LJ no comparison was possible between existence and non-existence. As he put it: '[H]ow can a court begin to evaluate non-existence. "the undiscovered country from whose bourn no traveller returns"?'.[84] By contrast, for Stephenson, LJ such a comparison was possible, but existence with disability was almost always preferable to non-existence.[85] Despite this difference of approach, none of the judges had any real trouble in holding that wrongful life actions were inadmissible. Jackson suggests that Stephenson LJ's judgment may be preferable 'because it is . . . plainly not true that the courts are *incapable* of deciding that non-existence would be preferable to (or at least no worse than) existence, since this is precisely the assessment that has sometimes been made when authorising the non-treatment of very severely disabled neonates'.[86] However, the courts have generally sought to avoid the philosophical conundrum of weighing the respective benefits of existence and non-existence by claiming that they are seeking to evaluate the burdens and benefits of treatment. In other words, they do not overtly conclude that a patient 'would be better off dead' since one of the consequences of doing so would be to invite the prospect of increased challenges to the current legal position that prevents active steps being taken with the primary intention of ending life, but allows doctors in some circumstances to fail to save or prolong life.[87] So for

11 (1981): 93–112; Roberts, M. and Wasserman, D. (eds), *Harming Future Persons: Ethics, Genetics and the Nonidentity Problem*, Dordrecht: Springer, 2009.

83 This is in contrast to cases for wrongful conception or wrongful birth which are brought on behalf of parents and where the child may or may not have disabilities. See for example *McFarlane* v. *Tayside Health Board* [1999] 3 WLR 1301HL; *Parkinson* v. *St James and Seacroft University Hospital NHS Trust* [2001] 3 All ER 97 CA.

84 *McKay* v. *Essex Area Health Authority* [1982] QB 1166 CA, at p. 1189.

85 Ibid., at p. 1182.

86 Jackson, 'Conception and the irrelevance of the welfare principle', at p. 196; original emphasis.

87 See, for example, *Airedale NHS Trust* v. *Bland* [1993] 1 All ER 821, Fam D, CA and HL. emphasis

example in the case of *Bland*, involving an adult in a persistent vegetative state and where the best interests of the patient were considered to be the guiding principle, it was said by Lord Goff that:

> the question is not whether it is in the best interests of the patient that he should die. The question is whether it is in the best interests of the patient that his life should be prolonged by the continuance of this form of medical treatment or care.[88]

Similarly in the case of *Re A (conjoined twins)* (2000), involving the proposed surgical separation of twin girls Mary and Jodie. Ward LJ, representing the majority of the court, considered Mary's profound disabilities and incapacity to survive independently in this way.

> Given the international Conventions protecting the 'right to life' . . . I conclude that it is impermissible to deny that every life has an equal inherent value. Life is worthwhile in itself whatever the diminution in one's capacity to enjoy it . . . Mary's life, desperate as it is, still has its own ineliminable value and dignity.[89]

Despite such seemingly strong support for the merits of existence, whatever its condition, the court concluded that the separation could be performed. The situation of conjoined twins poses special difficulties, due to the need to consider the effect of the same treatment upon the best interests of two children, and the impossibility of both of their interests being regarded as paramount if they are in conflict. The judicial reasoning employed to arrive at the court's conclusion has been criticised on a number of cogent grounds.[90] However, it highlights the fact that deeming non-existence preferable to existence is not an approach that has been explicitly endorsed as an appropriate guiding principle for the judiciary, although it is hard not to see this kind of calculation as playing at least some part in assessments in fact.

Section 13(5) requires that an assessment of the welfare of an as yet unconceived child must take place, by asking treatment centres to consider the possible future for a child resulting from treatment. One option would be for them, like Ackner, LJ in *McKay*, to conclude that a comparison of existence with non-existence is simply not possible. If this were the extent of the consideration that a centre was bound to give, it would appear to follow that no harm to the resulting child could be demonstrated and

88 Ibid., *per* Keith LJ, at p. 869.

89 *Re A (children) (conjoined twins: surgical separation)* [2000] 4 All ER 961 CA, at p. 1002.

90 See, for example, Clucas, B. and O'Donnell, K., 'Conjoined twins: the cutting edge', *Web JCLI* 5, (2002); Harris, J., 'Human beings, persons and conjoined twins: an ethical analysis of the judgment in *Re A*', *Medical Law Review*, 9(3) (2001): 221–36; Huxatable, R., 'Logical separation? Conjoined twins, slippery slopes and resource allocation', *Journal of Social Welfare and Family Law*, 23(4) (2001): 459–71.

treatment could never be refused on this basis.[91] As Gavaghan points out, 'since it is presumably unlikely that parliamentary intent was that such a consideration should have no bearing on the decision whether to provide treatment, it seems obvious that the intention was that certain welfare considerations would lead to the refusal of treatment'.[92] As he goes on to explain, 'it was contemplated that in certain circumstances, it is foreseeably in the potential interests of a future child to be spared existence', or that the balance of harms and benefits in its life are such that 'its life would constitute a harm "on balance"'.[93]

In other words, what appears to be intended by s. 13 (5), at least where the medical condition of the child is concerned, is an approach that is more akin to Stephenson, LJ in *McKay*, taking the view that there are some conditions in which life would be thought to provide such little opportunity for enjoyment of any interests that it would be preferable to avoid the foreseeable suffering of a child, in this case by avoiding its conception.[94] Furthermore, despite the courts' evident reluctance to enter into such assessments in wrongful life claims, their approach has been suggested to be somewhat disingenuous when compared with other areas of judicial consideration, for example in relation to claims involving wrongful death, where it is equally impossible to embark by personal experience on an assessment of the value of existence against non-existence.[95] It also echoes the thinking in cases concerning withholding or withdrawing treatment, that existence is not always a sufficient benefit to outweigh all circumstances, although again, an explicit determination that a child or adult would be better off not existing is not the reason given for judgments.[96] However, the threshold for restricting access to treatment under the HFE Acts has the potential to be set rather lower than would be expected where decisions concern the treatment of living patients, as illustrated by the examples of congenital deafness and the single copy gene mutation for achondroplasia. These are conditions that meet the criteria for seriousness that would permit testing using PGD, and hence engage the provisions prohibiting preferential selection, but that might be thought to fall short of the kinds of expectations of extreme suffering and lack of opportunity for positive experiences that have formed the basis of consideration in the treatment of

91 Authors differ on whether a child in such circumstances can be described as being harmed or wronged. See, for example, Feinberg, J., *Harm to Others*, Oxford: Oxford University Press, 1984, at pp. 97–104; Feinburg, J., 'Wrongful life and the counterfactual element in harming', *Social Philosophy and Policy*, 4(1) (1986): 145–78; Harris J., 'The wrong of wrongful life', *Journal of Law and Society*, 17 (1990): 90–105.

92 Gavaghan, C., *Defending the Genetic Supermarket*, Abingdon: Routledge, 2007, at p. 97.

93 Ibid.

94 Of course, s. 13 (5) is not limited to welfare concerns relating to conditions likely to have health implications for the child. It extends to factors such as parenting environment, which creates additional difficulties in determining in what circumstances assisted reproduction treatment should be denied.

95 Gavaghan, *Defending the Genetic Supermarket*, at p. 97.

96 Jackson, 'Conception and the irrelevance of the welfare principle'.

seriously ill or disabled children. Here, although the criteria of the child's life being 'intolerable' or that it would be 'demonstrably so awful' that continued treatment should not be provided have been dismissed as being separate from the test of best interests, such notions are still regarded as 'a valuable guide in the search for best interests in this kind of case'.[97] By contrast, the guidance offered on interpreting the welfare test offered by the HFEA in respect of health implications for a child suggests only that clinics should consider whether 'any child who may be born is likely to suffer from a serious medical condition' or 'circumstances that the centre considers likely to cause serious harm to any child'.[98]

The difficulty for parents seeking to use affected embryos is that if the genetic abnormalities the embryos have are the ones which PGD was undertaken to detect, then the condition must already have passed a threshold of seriousness, as there are restrictions on what kinds of condition can be tested for. As Jackson discusses elsewhere in this volume,[99] there is a two-tier consideration of whether PGD can be offered to a couple. First, the HFEA must consider whether the condition itself meets the test of 'seriousness': it has to be satisfied that there is a substantial risk of a serious condition before a licence for testing of this condition can be issued.[100] This criterion must be judged by objective, non-family-specific criteria. By contrast, treatment centres, before offering PGD to a couple, must apply individualised criteria to decide whether testing for this condition for this particular couple is appropriate. This is dealt with in the HFEA Code of Practice.[101] These criteria include the following:

> 10.5 When deciding if it is appropriate to provide PGD in particular cases, the centre should consider the circumstances of those seeking treatment rather than the particular heritable condition.
>
> 10.6 The use of PGD should be considered only where there is a significant risk of a serious genetic condition being present in the embryo. When deciding if it is appropriate to provide PGD in particular cases, the seriousness of the condition in that case should be discussed between the people seeking treatment and the clinical team. The perception of the level of risk for those seeking treatment will also be an important factor for the centre to consider.
>
> 10.7 The centre should consider the following factors when deciding if PGD is appropriate in particular cases:

97 *Portsmouth Hospital NHS Trust* v. *Wyatt* [2004] EWCA 2247 Fam D, *per* Hedley J., at para. 24.
98 HFEA, 8th Code of Practice.
99 See Chapter 4.
100 Schedule 2 1ZA (2) HFEA 1990, as amended.
101 HFEA, 8th Code of Practice, at 10.5–7.

(a) the views of the people seeking treatment in relation to the condition to be avoided, including their previous reproductive experience
(b) the likely degree of suffering associated with the condition
(c) the availability of effective therapy, now and in the future
(d) the speed of degeneration in progressive disorders
(e) the extent of any intellectual impairment
(f) the social support available, and
(g) the family circumstances of the people seeking treatment.

However, the attention paid to the views of the couple and their particular circumstances is not repeated in the Code of Practice where what is at issue is making a decision as to whether to use an affected embryo. The guidance here is couched solely in terms of reference to the welfare of the child provision.[102] Presumably, however, the couple's circumstances and reasons for seeking to use an affected embryo would be significant factors and, as will be discussed further, the welfare of the child criterion is not determinative under s. 13 (5) of the HFEA 1990, hence permitting other factors, such as these, to be taken into account. Once again it is critical to note that the prohibitions in the legislation under ss. 13 (9–11) of the HFEA 1990 rest on 'preferential' selection of affected embryos. As a result, the restrictions on the use of affected embryos are less clear-cut than they might at first appear. As I have outlined, there is the possibility that a couple could be in the position where no unaffected embryos are available, either because all embryos in a batch are affected or, more controversially, where embryos have been created and tested serially so that the couple has chosen to be in a position of only having an affected embryo. If these provisions are based on welfare of the child considerations, it could be argued that the restriction on using affected embryos should not depend on the presence or absence of other embryos that the couple could use. The condition of a child born using an affected embryo would be the same regardless of whether the couple could potentially have another child using a different embryo. However, that is not the approach that has been taken, and no discretion is permitted to allow a couple who prefer to use an affected embryo to do so where an unaffected embryo is available.[103] Welfare of the child concerns here appears definitively to trump any consideration of the views or circumstances of intending parents. They do not where the only embryo that a couple can use is one affected by a genetic disorder. Whether this is an appropriate response depends very much on the perception of the role of parental views on the kinds of children the couple feels willing and able to parent and the context in which such parental views are formed.[104] As such, it

102 HFEA, 8th Code of Practice, at 10.17–18.
103 Sections 13(9–11) HFEA 1990, as amended.
104 See, for example, Krahn, T. M., 'Regulating preimplantation genetic diagnosis: the case of Down's syndrome', *Medical Law Review*, 19(2) (2011): 157–91; Gilbar, R. 'Between unconditional acceptance and responsibility: should family ethics limit the scope of reproductive autonomy?', *Child and Family Law Quarterly*, 21(3) (2009): 309–35.

engages questions of reproductive decision-making, which will be considered in the next section.

Nevertheless, whether a treatment centre would obtain the approval of a clinical ethics committee and be prepared to exercise its discretion to enable affected embryos to be used in an individual case remains a matter of conjecture.

Reproductive choice

In Western societies, autonomy and privacy have been recognised as fundamental ethical principles and are given significant legal protection, although not, it must be said, to the exclusion of all others. Nevertheless, generally included as part of this recognition is the area of reproductive decision-making, so that as a broad proposition it can be suggested that there is an expectation that matters concerning when and whether to have children are largely regarded as matters of individual choice. As Jackson notes, people who can conceive children without medical assistance can do so 'without any external scrutiny of the merit or otherwise of their decision'.[105]

However, although we may live in a time in which the notion of individual rights is pervasive, the extent to which reproductive rights exist and may be enforced is by no means uncontentious. As Brazier suggests:

> Few might dissent from a rhetorical assertion that men and women have a right to found a family. Begin to debate what that right entails and who enjoys it and dispute resurfaces.[106]

The reasons that have been put forward for claiming that there is a presumption of non-interference in decisions about founding a family are various.[107] Robertson, for example, has described it as follows:

> The moral right to reproduce is respected because of the centrality of reproduction to personal identity, meaning and dignity . . . Because of this importance the right to reproduce is widely recognised as a prima facie moral right that cannot be limited except for very good reason.[108]

For others, such as Jackson, this right is grounded more specifically on two different aspects of privacy:

105 Jackson, 'Conception and the irrelevance of the welfare principle', at p. 177. Even so, they may not be exclusively matters for the individual so that, for example, the criminal law has a role to play in matters such as abortion, incest and the legal age of consent to sexual intercourse.

106 Brazier, M., 'Regulating the reproductive business?', *Medical Law Review*, 7 (1999): 166–93, at p. 168.

107 For more detailed discussion, see, for example, N. Priaulx, 'Rethinking progenitive conflict: why reproductive autonomy matters', *Medical Law Review*, 16(2) (2008): 169–200.

108 Robertson, J., *Children of Choice*, Princeton, NJ: Princeton University Press, 1994, at p. 30.

> First, that interfering with a particular individual's decision to conceive a child would usually involve violating their bodily integrity and sexual privacy. The second and I would argue equally important reason for respecting people's conception choices is that the freedom to decide for oneself whether or not to reproduce is integral to a person's sense of being, in some important sense, the author of their own life plan.[109]

Authors such as Laing and Oderberg on the other hand suggest that autonomy and decisional privacy should not be regarded as trump cards where reproductive decisions are concerned. They argue that:

> [A] proper evaluation of AR [assisted reproduction] and of the relevance of welfare will be sensitive not only to the rights of 'commissioning parties' to AR but also to public policy considerations. We argue that AR has implications for the common good, by involving matters of human reproduction, kinship, race, parenthood and identity.[110]

The thrust of their argument is directed at the use of assisted reproduction in itself as a means of creating children and suggests a number of grounds to support restrictions on individual choice, welfare of resulting children being one of them. However, even they concede that '[t]here are legitimate general principles against state interference in reproductive decision-making; these derive both from anti-eugenicist considerations' and from human rights principles.[111]

The importance of reproductive decision-making may seem to be protected by the human rights principles contained in the European Convention on Human Rights and Fundamental Freedoms (ECHR), particularly in Article 12, the *right to marry and to found a family* and Article 8, the *right to respect for private and family life*, although as UK case law, such as *Evans* and *Briody* demonstrate, these rights are by no means absolute.[112]

It can be suggested that what is really being protected by the ECHR is a negative right, a liberty, to seek to found a family without outside interference, but that it does not go so far as to accord a positive right: a right to assistance. This kind of thinking was clearly evident in the judgment of Hale, LJ in the case of *Briody*, concerning whether there could be an award of damages to enable a surrogacy arrangement to be undertaken.

109 Jackson, 'Conception and the irrelevance of the welfare principle', at p. 177.

110 Laing, J. A. and Oderberg, D. S., 'Artificial reproduction, the "welfare principle", and the common good', *Medical Law Review*, 13(3) (2005): 328–56, at p. 328.

111 Ibid., at p. 330.

112 *Evans* v. *Amicus Healthcare* [2004] EWCA Civ 727, [2004] 2 All ER 309 (HL), *Briody* v. *St Helens and Knowsley Area Health Authority* (Claim for Damages and Costs) (2001) 62 BMLR 1 CA.

> While everyone has the right to try to have their own children by natural means, no-one has the right to be provided with a child.[113]

The reasons for regarding reproductive choice as only a liberty are diverse but, along with the kinds of public interest and human dignity concerns referred to by Laing and Oderberg, include the recognition that to do otherwise might be to commit the state to furnishing the means of reproduction if they were not available otherwise to the individual or couple: a commitment that could not be fulfilled without significant material, technical and financial resources. Nevertheless, even if this more limited approach is adopted, there remains the question of whether the regulation of an available means of founding a family, such as assisted reproduction, can be seen as an acceptable restriction on the liberty of individuals. After all, it could be argued that the restrictions on the provision of treatment services in the HFE Acts interfere with the possible choices of the medically infertile, those whose social circumstances lead them to seek to use assisted reproductive techniques, or those who for medical reasons wish to use IVF and embryo testing in order to make certain choices regarding the genetic makeup of any child they will have. As such, this may in itself be regarded as a restriction on reproductive liberty.[114]

So far the approach that has been taken both by British courts and by the European Court of Human Rights has been to allow such restrictions to be imposed in principle without much comment, although the nature of particular restrictions may still need to be justified. So in the case of *Briody*, it was said in relation to the Article 12 right in the European Convention on Human Rights and Fundamental Freedoms that:

> [t]he right to marry and found a family are freedoms which should not be arbitrarily restricted, for example by preventing prisoners from marrying; this may well preclude placing arbitrary or disproportionate restrictions upon access to the reproductive services which are generally available. But that is quite different from having a right to be supplied with a child (or a spouse).[115]

Similarly, in the European Court of Human Rights in the case of *Dickson*, restrictions imposed by the Secretary of State on access to assisted reproduction by a prisoner and his wife were said to be disproportionate to the legitimate aims of the state when dealing with offenders.[116] Although specifically

113 *Briody* v. *St Helens and Knowsley Area Health Authority* (Claim for Damages and Costs) (2001) 62 BMLR 1 CA, para. 26.

114 Discussed in Jackson, 'Conception and the irrelevance of the welfare principle', at pp. 184–5.

115 *Briody* v. *St Helens & Knowsley AHA* (Claim for Damages and Costs) (2001) 62 BMLR 1 CA, *per* LJ Hale, para. 26.

116 *Dickson* v. *UK* (ECHR 2007) (Application no. 44362/04).

concerned with the right to access IVF treatment during imprisonment, the case contains some interesting comments on the extent to which restrictions may be imposed. It was held by the majority of the European Court of Human Rights that Article 8 of the European Convention on Human Rights and Fundamental Freedoms was engaged, in that the complainants' right to respect for their private and family lives incorporated rights to respect for their decision to become genetic parents. Prisoners retained Convention rights on imprisonment and any restrictions must be justified in each case; such justification could not be based solely on what would offend public opinion. However, in respect of welfare of the child concerns it was said that:

> [t]he Court is prepared to accept as legitimate, for the purposes of the second paragraph of Article 8, that the authorities, when developing and applying the Policy, should concern themselves, as a matter of principle, with the welfare of any child: conception of a child was the very object of the exercise. Moreover, the State has a positive obligation to ensure the effective protection of children.[117]

However, it went on to say that the state could not go so far as to prevent parents from conceiving a child in these circumstances. UK policy was held to have placed an inordinately high burden on the complainants to demonstrate that deprivation of the opportunity to undertake assisted reproduction might prevent conception altogether, and that their circumstances were 'exceptional'. That did not allow a balancing of competing individual and public interests, nor a proportionality test to be applied, as required by the Convention. The policy was not embodied in primary legislation, competing interests had never been weighed, and the issues of proportionality had never been assessed by Parliament.[118] In the absence of such an assessment, the policy was seen as falling outside any acceptable margin of appreciation. The complainants were awarded €5,000 by way of damages for frustration and distress.

Nevertheless, the general principle that a regulatory framework may be imposed on assisted reproduction services has so not far been successfully challenged in the EctHR, and there are those who have doubts about the utility of human rights principles as a means of protecting people's choices in assisted reproduction.[119] Furthermore, whether people should have a right not only to choose to try to have children, but to attempt to determine the characteristics of their children, adds another dimension to the meaning and scope of decisions concerning reproduction. As Robertson puts it:

117 Ibid., para. 76.
118 Ibid., paras 77–85.
119 See, for example, Eijkholt, M., 'The right to found a family as a stillborn right to procreate?', *Medical Law Review*, 18(2) (2010): 127–51.

> Choices about who may conceive, bear or rear a child are distinct from choices about the conduct that occurs in the process of conceiving, bearing and rearing. In other words, arguably, the freedom *to* procreate is [would be] distinct from the freedom *in* procreation.[120]

As has been made clear, one of the principal grounds for refusing treatment using embryos tested and discovered to have specific genetic conditions is the welfare of the child. It is implicit in the HFEA 1990, ss. 13 (9–11) conditions and it appears to have been given overriding importance where what is at issue is the preferential selection of an affected embryo. However, somewhat paradoxically, where the child welfare principle is explicitly set out, in s. 13 (5), it is not stated to be of paramount importance: it is a matter only that must be taken into account by treatment centres. While one of the major factors to be considered in the welfare assessment is undoubtedly the medical condition of a child resulting from treatment covered by the HFE Acts, the approach taken by s. 13 (5) does allow other factors, such as the views and circumstances of couples, and more broadly, their reproductive freedom, to be weighed against it.

One possible argument suggests that depriving people of the ability to choose to have children with genetic abnormalities is permissible as this is simply not the kind of reproductive choice that *should* be protected. For example, Harris has stated that 'it is wrong to bring avoidable suffering into the world'.[121] Two widely accepted ethical principles are those of beneficence (to do good) and non-maleficence (to avoid causing harm). In the 1970s, Beauchamp and Childress popularised an approach combining these with respect for autonomy and justice, which went on to strongly influence healthcare ethics.[122] While the 'four principles' approach they championed has been subjected increasingly to a more critical evaluation,[123] nevertheless the importance of a desire to do good and avoid harm as general touchstones for ethical behaviour must surely remain. Difficulties inevitably arise, however, in the application of such principles in practice, such as in making decisions about the kinds of children one should seek to have.

In the context of human reproduction, Savulescu has described a principle of 'procreative beneficence' as follows: '[C]ouples . . . should select the child, of the possible children they could have, who is expected to have the best life,

120 Robertson, J. A., 'Procreative liberty and the control of conception, pregnancy, and childbirth', *Virginia Law Review*, 69 (1983): 405–65, at p. 410; original emphasis.

121 Harris, J., 'Is there a coherent social concept of disability?', *Journal of Medical Ethics*, 26 (2000): 95–100, at 96.

122 Beauchamp, T. L. and Childress, J. F., *Principles of Biomedical Ethics*, 6th edn, New York: Oxford University Press, 2008. See, for example, Gillon, R., 'Medical ethics: four principles plus attention to scope', *British Medical Journal*, 309(6948) (1994): 184–8.

123 See, for example, Campbell, A., 'The virtues (and vices) of the four principles', *Journal of Medical Ethics*, 29 (2003): 292–6; Walker, T., 'What principlism misses', *Journal of Medical Ethics*, 35 (2009): 229–31.

or at least as good a life as the others'.[124] While making some concessions to the degree of prediction that is possible, he concludes: 'Even if we cannot know the value of a whole life, we can know that conditions are good or bad, and this provides a reason to prefer to bring children into existence without those conditions.'[125] Nevertheless, he also makes a substantial limitation on his argument, saying: 'If, in the end, couples wish to select a child who will have a lower chance of having the best life, they should be free to make such a choice.'[126] He therefore ultimately places a higher priority on respecting the wishes of prospective parents in respect of their reproductive choices than on protecting the welfare of the child that might be born. He distinguishes between what might be a virtuous argument and what should be a legal restriction. This is an important distinction. In a similar vein, the HCSTC considered that '[e]ven strong ethical arguments that there should be constraints on reproductive choice do not necessarily mean that legislation should provide that check' and quoted with approval a line from a contributor to their online consultation which read that 'there is an important difference between disapproving and disallowing'.[127]

There may be some conditions for which it is difficult to argue that positive experiences for a child outweigh negative ones. One frequently used example is that of Tay–Sachs, a genetic disorder which causes death in early childhood, preceded by increasingly debilitating and distressing physical and mental decline, and for which there is no cure.[128] Other conditions, however, will inevitably be much more contentious. As Scott explains:

> [A]s we move away from the extreme and rare case, judging seriousness is very difficult. It is made more complex by the potentially competing perspectives – parental, medical and those of the impaired – on this issue.[129]

She goes on to say:

> In some cases, although a possible child may have the prospect of a reasonable quality of life, his impairments may still implicate his parents' interests in reproduction in serious ways; he might have a significant

124 Savulescu, J., 'Procreative beneficence: why we should select the best children', *Bioethics*, 15 (2001): 413–26, at p. 415.

125 Savulescu, J., 'In defence of procreative beneficence', *Journal of Medical Ethics*, 33 (2007): 284–8, at 284.

126 Savulescu, 'Procreative beneficence', at p. 425.

127 HCSTC, Fifth Report of Session 2004–5, *Human Reproductive Technologies and the Law*, vol. 1, para. 112

128 National Institute of Neurological Disorders and Stroke (NINDS), Tay–Sachs disease information page, www.ninds.nih.gov/disorders/taysachs/taysachs.htm (accessed 11/11/2011).

129 Scott, R., 'Choosing between possible lives: legal and ethical issues in preimplantation genetic diagnosis', *Oxford Journal of Legal Studies*, 26(1) (2006): 153–78, at p. 164.

mental impairment or serious health problems requiring repeated hospitalisation with an uncertain future.[130]

Her discussion concerns whether parents should be able to seek PGD, in terms of the assessment of a condition being serious enough to merit testing and the consequent rejection of embryos found to have it. However, it is also applicable to the situation where a couple seeks to use embryos that have been tested and found to have genetic disorders or to be at risk of developing particular medical conditions. Here too the rights and interests of the couple are engaged along with those of a future child. Balancing these potentially competing considerations raises profound questions about legitimate boundaries upon reproductive decision making. Scott's conclusion is that 'in cases of reasonable disagreement about seriousness, parental views and interests should carry the most weight'.[131] Of course the immediate difficulties return – what is a 'reasonable quality of life' or 'reasonable disagreement about seriousness'? In cases where agreement cannot be reached between couples and treatment providers over the proposed use of affected embryos, resort may be had to the courts in an attempt to resolve them. The likelihood of success for couples may, however, be limited.[132] The issue remains, however, that no concession is made to considerations of reproductive autonomy for a couple that wishes to use an affected embryo rather than an unaffected one, where the couple has both available.

Conclusion

Questions have been raised about the suitability and applicability of a welfare of the child standard where what is under consideration is the possible conception of a child rather than the welfare of a child who has been born. Although there are some circumstances in which it might be argued that a future child's life would have so few redeeming features that it might be considered better to avoid this by not seeking to implant an affected embryo, the extent to which this would be true in many cases is a matter about which opinions may differ sharply. Where certain conditions, such as congenital deafness or achondroplasia are concerned the scope for interference with potential parental choice becomes particularly troubling. The application of the welfare principle to the selection of embryos is undoubtedly problematic, but interpreting it in the only way that is practicable still leaves room to suggest that overriding the views of potential parents on the basis of child

130 Ibid.

131 Ibid. This argument is made in more detail in Scott, R., 'Prenatal screening, autonomy and reasons: the relationship between the law of abortion and wrongful life', *Medical Law Review*, 11(3) (2003): 265–325.

132 See, for example, the discussion in Bell, 'Human Fertilisation and Embryology Act 2008', *Web JCLI*, 1 [2009], http://webjcli.ncl.ac.uk/2009/issue1/bell1.html (accessed 09/02/2012).

welfare, where they wish to proceed with treatment using affected embryos, should be undertaken with extreme caution.

The clear intention of the amendment of the treatment licensing provisions of the HFEA 1990 was to prevent potential parents from exercising a choice to select for disability. As a result, there is now no discretion to allow a couple to choose to use an affected embryo where there is at least one unaffected embryo available. Despite this, there is in fact no absolute prohibition on using an affected embryo for treatment if there is no unaffected embryo that could be used instead. This may apply even where a couple has deliberately sought to engineer the situation by serial creation and testing of embryos, so as to circumvent the provisions on preferential selection in ss. 13 (9–11) of the HFEA 1990. However, the use of any embryo for treatment remains subject to the overarching principle of child welfare set out in s. 13 (5) HFEA 1990, as amended. Given that this is the case, there are reasons to doubt whether the inclusion of the embryo selection restrictions was strictly necessary if, as seems, clear the justification for the more specific provisions is also child welfare. Simply relying on s. 13 (5) would have allowed discretion to be exercised in respect of the use of a particular embryo, regardless of the availability of other embryos that the couple could use. That would in many ways appear to be a more logical approach to have taken, since the welfare of a particular child, judged on its genetic condition, is not usually dependent on the absence or presence of alternative children that a couple could have.[133] Welfare decisions could therefore have been made on a case-by-case basis where any couple sought to use an embryo which had a genetic condition placing it at risk of, or with a certainty of developing, a serious medical condition. Such decisions might well have remained contentious and the application of the welfare principle no easier a task. Nevertheless, as it stands, discretion to allow the use of embryos has been curtailed absolutely in some situations.

As such it may be concluded that the real effect of the new provisions is in the signals that it sends about the kind of decisions people should make where there is a possibility of having certain kinds of children. In fact, the aims of the legislation go further and deem certain choices unacceptable and hence prohibited. This brings into play what may be termed 'expressivist objections'. The most common arguments based on expressivist grounds concern choices to select against disability. Here it has been contended that selection for reproductive purposes to *avoid* the conception or birth of people with disabling medical conditions can cause 'offence and hurt to people currently living with the kinds of conditions screened for'.[134] A frequent counter to such objections to

133 An exception might be where a child has a genetic condition for which PGD might be used to create a 'saviour sibling' to provide material for donation. This, however, concerns the welfare of a born child rather than the welfare of the yet-to-be conceived child, which is at issue here.

134 Edwards, S. D. 'Disability, identity and the "expressivist objection"', *Journal of Medical Ethics* 30 (2004): 418–20, at p. 418.

PGD is that allowing people to have the choice to avoid having children with disabilities does not necessarily devalue people who have such disabilities.[135] However, legislating that choices to have particular children are unacceptable, based on their predicted medical condition, may have more force in engendering these kinds of objections. A couple may wish to avoid having a child with physical or mental illness for many reasons, which do not necessarily imply a value judgement about people who have such conditions.[136] However, for the law to provide that couples should not be able to choose to create a child with genetic abnormalities in some circumstances seems to come rather closer to a state-endorsed view that certain kinds of lives are not worth living by mandating that the creation of such lives should be avoided, at least where other lives that would be considered to have greater opportunities could be brought into being. In doing so, it restricts reproductive freedom with the purported aim of child protection. If it is accepted that there are family circumstances which permit a couple legitimately to be permitted to seek to avoid having children with disabilities, it may be arguable that in some cases at least, having children with specific conditions that may be regarded as disabling would be a legitimate choice for the couple concerned. Notwithstanding the approach of the new legislation, there may be some scope for such preferences to be achieved, but the interpretation of child welfare based provisions, through the HFEA, treatment centres and clinical ethics committees, will be critical. The likelihood of such cases arising in practice may be small, but nevertheless they raise significant issues.

135 See, for example, Gavaghan, C., 'Right problem wrong solution: a pro-choice response to "expressivist" concerns about preimplantation genetic diagnosis', *Cambridge Quarterly of Healthcare Ethics*, 16 (2007): 20–34; Edwards, 'Disability, identity'.

136 For a discussion of this issue see Gavaghan, *Defending the Genetic Supermarket*, at pp. 110–14.

6 Regulating abortion and pre-implantation genetic diagnosis in the Australian states of New South Wales, Victoria and Western Australia: comparing and contrasting regulative approaches

Kerry Petersen

Introduction

In Australia, the state governments have residual powers over criminal and health matters such as abortion, pre-implantation genetic screening (PGS) and pre-implantation genetic diagnosis (PGD)[1] and the laws concerned with abortion and PGD vary from state to state. In the nineteenth century, abortion was regulated in all the States and Territories by criminal legislation which was based on the English Offences Against the Person Act 1861. Since then, abortion laws have been modified by the common law as well as legislation. Nevertheless 'unlawful' abortion remains a criminal offence in all States except Victoria. In contrast, PGD does not have a criminal law background, but belongs to the so-called 'reproductive revolution' of the late twentieth century and is a product of scientific advances in assisted reproductive technologies (ARTs). PGD is regulated in some States by ART statutes and in others by the National Health and Medical Research Council (NHMRC) Ethical Guidelines.[2] These Guidelines deal with social and ethical questions rather than clinical

1 The term 'pre-implantation genetic diagnosis' (PGD) covers diagnostic procedures performed because of a known risk of transmitting a genetic abnormality or disease; the term 'pre-implantation genetic screening' (PGS) is used when the purpose of the procedure is to screen for aneuploidy (abnormal number of chromosomes) and to select embryos for implantation in order to reduce the risk of miscarriage and improve the chances of carrying the foetus to term. For the sake of simplicity the term PGD will be used to include PGS in this chapter.

2 NHMRC, *Ethical Guidelines on the Use of Assisted Reproductive Technology in Clinical Practice and Research*, Canberra: Australian Government, 2007, www.nhmrc.gov.au/publications/synopses/e78syn.htm (accessed 28/01/2011).

practice[3] and non-compliance can lead to the loss of accreditation, the loss of a clinic's licence and de-registration.[4] Nevertheless, in *YZ* v. *Infertility Treatment Authority*[5] Justice Morris emphasised that the NHMRC Guidelines are *not* legally enforceable.[6]

In the case of abortion, a woman chooses to terminate a pregnancy for a range of personal, medical or social reasons, or to avoid having a child with disabilities after an adverse prenatal test. In the case of PGD a woman chooses to undergo *in vitro* fertilisation and a diagnostic procedure in order to enhance her chances of having a healthy child. Abortion and PGD are both controversial medical procedures concerned with sanctity of life principles and reproductive autonomy rights. The subject of decision-making in both procedures is an embryo/foetus; that is, a human entity without any independent legal rights as it is not defined as a legal person prior to live birth.[7] Abortion is concerned with a human entity which develops *in utero* over a period of 36–40 weeks' gestation. PGD involves the genetic testing of embryonic cells which have been removed from an eight-cell IVF embryo for specific defects.

The embryo/foetus is not a rights bearer in a legal sense, but most agree that it is entitled to some respect from the point of fertilisation, and to an increasing degree of respect as it becomes a foetus and gradually grows and develops towards live birth. This gradualist approach which was specifically articulated in the Warnock Report[8] has been adopted by courts in Australia and the United Kingdom.[9] Two decades after the Warnock Report was published, the UK House of Commons Science and Technology Committee endorsed this approach and described it 'as the most ethically sound and pragmatic solution'[10] to classifying the status and interests of the embryo/foetus. Nevertheless, as McLean points out, even though an embryo/foetus is not as morally relevant as a child or adult 'whatever status we concede to the [embryo or] foetus is directly relevant to the status which we accord to the woman carrying it'[11] and has the potential to trump 'the interests of others, most notably the pregnant woman'.[12]

3 The Reproductive Technology Accreditation Committee (RTAC) Code of Practice deals mainly with clinical practice. See: Reproductive Technology Accreditation Committee, Fertility Society of Australia Code of Practice for Assisted Reproductive Technology Units (revised October 2010).

4 NHMRC, *Ethical Guidelines* (2007), 1.2; Fertility Society of Australia, RTAC Committee, *Code of Practice for Assisted Reproductive Technology Units* (revised 2010).

5 [2005] VCAT 2655, at p. 2668.

6 Ibid., at p. 68, *per* Morris J.

7 *Re MB* [1997] 8 Med LR 217; *In the Marriage of F* (1989) 13 Fam LR 189; *Attorney-General (Qld) (ex rel Kerr)* v. *T* (1983) 46 ALR 275; *Paton* v. *BPAS* [1979] 1 QB 276.

8 Report of the Committee of Inquiry into Human Fertilisation and Embryology (Warnock Report), Cmnd 9314, London: Stationery Office, 1984.

9 *Re MB* [1997] 8 Med LR 217; *In the Marriage of F* (1989) 13 Fam LR 189; *Attorney-General (Qld) (ex rel Kerr)* v. *T* (1983) 46 ALR 275; *Paton* v. *BPAS* [1979] 1 QB 276.

10 United Kingdom, House of Commons, Science and Technology Committee, *Human Reproductive Technologies and the Law*, Report of Sessions 2004–5, London: Stationery Office, 2004, Recommendation 1.

11 McLean, S. A. M., *Old Law New Medicine*, London: Pandora, 1993, at p. 50.

12 Ibid.

Reproductive autonomy is classified as a negative right – the liberty or freedom to exercise reproductive choice without unjustified interference. In the case of *Secretary, Department of Health and Community Services* v. *JWB and SMB*[13] the majority of the High Court held that there is no fundamental right to reproduce and warned that it is impossible 'to spell out all the implications which may flow from saying there is a right to reproduce, expressed in absolute terms and independent from a right to personal inviolability'.[14]

The reproductive autonomy of a pregnant woman to make reproductive choices is recognised in abortion laws in Victoria[15] and to a lesser degree in Western Australia[16] under the mantle of health legislation. However, in New South Wales, abortion statute law and case law is not based on reproductive autonomy but on the criminal defence of necessity which requires a medical practitioner to decide in good faith whether or not an abortion is necessary to safeguard the woman from the dangers of proceeding with a pregnancy.

Reproductive freedoms and the legal status of the foetus have influenced courts presiding over 'paternity' cases in Australia and the United Kingdom where biological fathers have applied for injunctions to prevent a pregnant woman from terminating a pregnancy.[17] In the High Court case, *Attorney-General (Qld) (ex rel Kerr)* v. *T*, the court refused the putative father of a foetus the right to prevent a woman from having an abortion.[18] Gibbs CJ held: 'There are limits to the extent to which the law should intrude upon personal liberty and personal privacy.'[19] In the Australian Family Court case, *In the Marriage of F* the court refused a husband's application for an injunction to prevent his wife from having an abortion.[20] Lindenmayer J. emphasised the physical proximity between the pregnant woman and her foetus. He said:

> The fact that the foetus must grow within the wife's body, not the husband's cannot in my opinion be overlooked. To grant the injunction would be to compel the wife to do something in relation to her own body which she does not wish to do. That would be an interference with her freedom to decide her own destiny. Whilst it may be said that to refuse the injunction will permit the wife to interfere with the destiny of the intended child, I have already held that the unborn child has no legal rights to be born which this court can protect.[21]

13 (1992) 175 CLR 218 (Marion's Case).
14 Ibid., at p. 254.
15 Abortion Law Reform Act 2008 (Vic.).
16 Health Act 1911 (WA).
17 *Paton* v. *British Pregnancy Advisory Service* [1979] 1 QB 276; *Attorney-General (Qld) (ex re Kerr)* v. *T* (1983) 46 ALR 275; *In the Marriage of F* (1989) 13 Fam LR 189.
18 (1983) 46 ALR 275.
19 *Attorney-General (Qld) (ex re Kerr)* v. *T* (1983) 46 ALR 275, at pp. 277–8.
20 *In the Marriage of F* (1989) 13 Fam LR 189.
21 Ibid., at p. 198.

Reproductive autonomy rights in the context of abortion have long been significant for those concerned with abortion laws and policies and more recently in the context of technologies such as PGD. The autonomy rights of a woman wishing to become pregnant with the assistance of PGD do not fit absolutely into the traditional concepts expressed in these 'paternity cases', in part because the woman consents to IVF taking place outside her body and the selection of a healthy embryo in order to give birth to a child. In the (UK) *Quintavalle* case,[22] the House of Lords held that the Human Fertilisation and Embryology Authority (HFEA) has the authority to grant PGD licences because PGD is a treatment service provided for the purpose of 'assisting women to carry children'. The judgments delivered by the House of Lords in *Quintavalle* were essentially supportive of autonomy rights being respected in reproductive decision-making, at least in this area.[23]

As access to reproductive technologies and PGD has become more socially and ethically acceptable, it is also becoming increasingly clear that the concept of reproductive freedom is broad enough to include PGD where the technology is chosen to avoid a child being born with a genetic disorder or to reduce the risk of miscarriage. PGD has become a means of enabling a woman to have children in cases where otherwise she may not have embarked on a pregnancy. In these circumstances, refusing a woman this opportunity would interfere with her right to reproductive autonomy and her destiny in the same way as compelling a woman to continue with an unwanted pregnancy interferes with her freedom.

This chapter compares abortion and PGD regulation in the three states of New South Wales Victoria and Western Australia in order to throw some light on the role of women's reproductive autonomy rights in regulatory frameworks dealing with abortion and the use of PGD. These states represent three models regulating abortion and PGD in Australia. The main concern in this chapter is to assess and compare the scope and limits of a woman's reproductive autonomy in the patchwork of abortion and PGD laws and policies. It is argued that abortion and PGD represent two sides of the reproductive autonomy coin and even though there are differences between the reasons for the two procedures, they are both concerned with the scope of reproductive liberty and the legitimate degree of state intervention in reproductive decision-making.

Abortion: context

In Australia, abortion is a common, safe and publicly subsidised medical procedure and although there is no national reporting system, the number of

22 *R (on the application of Quintavalle)* v. *Human Fertilisation and Embryology Authority* [2005] 2 All ER 555.

23 For further discussion on this point see, Sheldon, S., 'Saviour siblings and the discretionary power of the HFEA' (commentary), *Medical Law Review*, 13 (Autumn 2005): 403–11, at p. 408.

abortions has been estimated to be 80,000–85,000 per annum.[24] The majority of abortions are surgical first-trimester procedures.[25] In Western Australia, Victoria and New South Wales, abortions are available from private clinics and there is limited availability in public hospitals.[26] When compared to nine other developed countries, Australia has the third highest rate of abortion after the United States and New Zealand.[27]

On the question of general community attitudes in the highly polarised abortion debate, the Victorian Law Reform Commission (VLRC) recently concluded that:

- A majority of Australians support a woman's right to choose to have an abortion.
- A subset of those supporters regard the rights as capable of limitation, with restriction of choice based on factors such as gestational age and women's reasons for seeking the abortion. However, there is insufficient evidence to estimate the size of that subset.
- Several socio-demographic characteristics are associated with positive (and negative) views of abortion. For example, there is less support for abortion among persons with religious beliefs than among persons without religious beliefs; nonetheless, even among persons with religious beliefs, supporters remain in the majority.[28]

In another study of community attitudes, De Crespigny *et al.* found that 'Australians are supportive of both access to abortion, including later abortion in many circumstances, and liberal law reform.'[29]

It is a routine aspect of prenatal care in Australia (as in most Western countries) for health professionals to offer women screening and testing for complications which could affect the pregnant woman's health or that of the foetus, with the option of abortion when permitted by law. The Royal Australian and New Zealand College of Obstetricians and Gynaecologists (RANZCOG) advises that '[a]ll women, irrespective of their geographical location, resources or chosen model of antenatal care, are entitled to informed prenatal screening and diagnostic testing for fetal abnormalities or genetic conditions that may impact on the future life and health of their baby.'[30] RANZCOG further advises: 'In the event of the diagnosis of an anomaly, the woman and her partner

24 VLRC, *Law of Abortion: Final Report*, Melbourne: VLRC, 2008, at p. 32.
25 Chan, A. and Sage, L. C., 'Estimating Australia's abortion rates 1985–2003', *Medical Journal of Australia*, 182(9) (2005): 447–52.
26 Children by Choice, Australian *Abortion Law and Practice*, www.childrenbychoice.org.au/nwww/campabortlaw.htm (accessed 26/01/2011).
27 Chan and Sage, 'Estimating Australia's Abortion Rates 1985–2003'.
28 VLRC, *Law of Abortion: Final Report*, at p. 68.
29 De Crespigny, L. J., Wilkinson, T. D., Textor, M. and Savulescu, J., 'Australian attitudes to early and late abortion', *Medical Journal of Australia*, 193(1) (2010): 9–12.
30 RANZCOG, College Statement C-Obs 35 (March 2010).

may choose to terminate or continue with the pregnancy.'[31] Medical developments have expanded the options for reproductive choice, and have also influenced abortion debates because advances such as ultrasound technology, 'visualise' or 'personify' the pregnancy and present the foetus as separate physical identity – that is, separate from the pregnant woman.[32] Available investigations may also include chromosomal tests and scans which provide information about foetal abnormalities later in a pregnancy.[33]

Abortion: legal frameworks

Women have sought abortion since time immemorial and it is usually a safe and simple procedure today, due to advances in medicine. The abortion debate is based on arguments about reproductive autonomy rights, the duty to protect the interests of the embryo/foetus, and the conflict between the right of the woman to control her body and the interests of the foetus to continued life. Absolutist pro-choice advocates prioritise the woman's interests over foetal interests until live birth; and absolutist anti-choice advocates prioritise foetal interests over woman's interests from fertilisation. However, a third way – which appeals to the majority – is to balance the interests of the unwillingly pregnant woman with the interests of the foetus in the context of the woman's health, the woman's personal and social circumstances, and the gestational age and health of the foetus. This approach is followed in most legal regimes. As already noted, Australian abortion laws vary between jurisdictions. It can be added that many of these laws are outdated and confusing.[34] This section of the chapter examines the scope and limits of reproductive autonomy in a criminal model and two reform or 'health' models of abortion law in Australia. It commences with legal developments in New South Wales, and is followed by Western Australia and Victoria. In general, parliamentarians avoid legislating in areas such as abortion because it is usually a conscience vote and the constituents they represent will have diverse views. However, in Western Australia and Victoria, liberal reform statutes have been passed after much public debate and with sufficient 'political will' to succeed.

New South Wales

Sections 82, 83 and 84 of the Crimes Act 1900 (NSW) are essentially the same as the three offences set out in the Offences Against the Person Act 1861 (Eng.).

31 Ibid.
32 Savell, K., 'Life and death before birth: 4DUltrasound and the shifting frontiers of the abortion debate', *Journal of Law and Medicine*, 15 (2007): 103–16.
33 De Crespigny, L. J. and Savulescu, J., 'Pregnant women with fetal abnormalities: the forgotten women in the abortion debate', *Medical Journal of Australia* 188(2) (2008): 100–2.
34 Douglas, H. A., 'Abortion reform: a state crime or a woman's right to choose?', *Criminal Law Journal*, 33 (2009): 74–86, at p. 74.

> Section 82. Whosoever, being a woman with child, unlawfully administers to herself any drug or noxious thing; or unlawfully uses any instrument to procure her miscarriage, shall be liable to penal servitude for ten years.
>
> Section 83. Whosoever unlawfully administers to, or causes to be taken by, any woman, whether with child or not, any drug or noxious thing; or unlawfully uses any instrument or other means, with intent in such cases to procure her miscarriage, shall be liable to penal servitude for ten years.
>
> Section 84. Whosoever unlawfully supplies or procures any drug or noxious thing, or any instrument or thing whatsoever, knowing that the same is intended to be unlawfully used with intent to procure the miscarriage of any woman whether with child or not, shall be liable to penal servitude for life.

In New South Wales sections 82, 83 and 84 of the Crimes Act 1900 make it an offence for a woman to have an 'unlawful' abortion, for a person to 'unlawfully' perform an abortion and for a person to 'unlawfully' supply the means for an abortion. The legislation does not clarify when an abortion is unlawful. The original abortion statute has not been amended, reformed or repealed, unlike all of the other Australian States. Furthermore, as New South Wales is a common law State, the courts have played an instrumental role in legal developments and changes in abortion law have taken place within a criminal law framework without any express recognition of women's reproductive autonomy rights.

In *CES* v. *Superclinics (Australia) Pty Ltd*,[35] the Court of Appeal accepted that *R* v. *Wald*[36] represents the law on abortion in New South Wales. The *Wald* case,[37] involved a trial of five medical practitioners who were charged under section 83 of the Crimes Act 1900. In his ruling, Judge Levine drew on the earlier Victorian case of *R* v. *Davidson*[38] in formulating the test of unlawfulness but expanded the reasons justifying abortion to include economic and social factors. Levine CH.QS stated:

> [F]or the operation to have been lawful in this case the accused must have had an honest belief on reasonable grounds that what they did was necessary to preserve the women involved from serious danger to their life or physical or mental health, which the continuance of the pregnancy would entail, not merely the normal dangers of pregnancy and childbirth; and that in the circumstances the danger of the operation was not out of proportion to the danger intended to be averted. The Crown of course bears the onus of establishing that the operation was unlawful.[39]

35 (1995) 38 NSWLR 47.
36 (1971) 3 DCR (NSW) 25.
37 Ibid.
38 [1969] VR 667.
39 (1971) 3 DCR (NSW) 25, at p. 29.

This test of unlawfulness contains two limbs: the first being an honest belief on reasonable grounds that the operation was necessary for the woman's life and health and the second concerning proportionality. It has been widely accepted that in the *Davidson* case both limbs are framed as subjective tests, meaning that the Crown must prove beyond reasonable doubt that the accused did not hold an honest belief on reasonable grounds, but the ruling in the more recent *R* v. *Sood* (Ruling No. 3)[40] suggests that the proportionality test is subjective.

In *R* v. *Sood* (Ruling No. 3),[41] Dr Sood was charged with two offences under section 83 of the Crimes Act 1900 (NSW). Dr Sood had been consulted by a young woman aged 20 who was nearly 24 weeks pregnant and desperate to have an abortion. It was found that Dr Sood had agreed to perform the procedure without carrying out a physical examination, discussing any alternatives to a termination or discussing the reasons for her patient seeking a late-term abortion. Dr Sood gave the woman some medication but as a result of 'mismanagement', the woman delivered a live baby in a toilet bowl at home, and the newborn baby died shortly after the delivery. The jury found that Dr Sood did not act in good faith because she failed to form the requisite honest beliefs about necessity and proportionality for the abortion to be lawful. Justice Simpson pointed to a discrepancy between the rulings in *Davidson* and *Wald*. She said that the *Wald* ruling might 'fairly be read as imposing a subjective test in respect of the first limb – that is focussing on the actual belief said to have been held by the accused person',[42] whereas, the second test of proportionality may be read as framing an objective test which does not incorporate the subjective belief of the accused person.[43] This would mean that the assessment as to whether or not the danger of an abortion was, or was not, out of proportion to the danger of continuing the pregnancy, could be based on a reasonable grounds test rather than an honest belief test. However, Justice Simpson ruled that whether or not the second limb should be approached as a subjective or objective test must be decided according to principle, not solely upon the authority of either *Wald* or *Davidson*.

Dr Sood was convicted of performing an unlawful abortion, given a two-year behaviour bond and was de-registered by the New South Wales medical board. The *Sood* decision is a significant development in New South Wales abortion law, because although Justice Simpson did not hold that the appropriate test for the second limb was subjective, she did not rule that it was objective. If a future court in New South Wales were to apply an objective test to the second limb, the prosecution would have to prove that a reasonable person would not have honestly believed that the risk of continuing the pregnancy exceeded the risk abortion in the circumstances. Currently, abortion services continue to be available in private clinics in Sydney as well as some regional cities under the

40 [2006] NSWSC 762.
41 Ibid.
42 Ibid., at para. 32.
43 Ibid.

common law *Wald* ruling with few restrictions being imposed on medical practice.[44]

Victoria: abortion

The Abortion Law Reform Act 2008 (Vic.) decriminalised abortion in Victoria. The main purposes of the Act are: to reform the law relating to abortion, to regulate health practitioners, to repeal the provisions relating to abortion in the Crimes Act (Vic.) 1958, to abolish common law offences relating to abortion and amend the definition of serious injury to include the destruction of a foetus in the Crimes Act (Vic.) 1958.[45] The Act clearly establishes that abortion is prima facie lawful, albeit subject to gestational limits. Under section 4 of the Act 'a registered medical practitioner may perform an abortion on a woman who is not more than 24 weeks pregnant'. The Act provides women with a *negative* right based on reproductive choice principles which excludes State interference with the decision-making process between a patient and doctor during the prescribed gestational time period.[46] Apart from the two medical opinions needed for late-term abortions, the Act does not impose any special conditions concerning places where abortions can be performed, nor consent or counselling requirements.[47] It is an offence under the Crimes Act 1958 (Vic.) for an unqualified person to perform an abortion, but a woman who consents to an abortion in these circumstances is not guilty of an offence.[48]

If a woman is more than 24 weeks pregnant, a registered medical practitioner may decide that an abortion is appropriate after consulting with another registered medical practitioner and considering all relevant medical circumstances as well as the woman's current and future physical, psychological and social circumstances.[49] This provision permits a medical practitioner to consider a wide range of circumstances when deciding whether or not to perform a late abortion. There is no specific reference to a foetus, but the Act does not exclude the relevant medical circumstances of the foetus and therefore can be interpreted as including cases of foetal abnormality. Cases where the woman's psychological health is endangered by the prospect of giving birth to a child with disabilities would also appear to come within the range of permitted circumstances.[50] However, while there is legislation specifying

44 Children by Choice, *Australian Abortion Law and Practice.*

45 Abortion Law Reform Act (Vic.) 2008, s. 1; Crimes Act (Vic.) 1958 s. 65.

46 For a discussion about the impact of the Charter of Human Rights and Responsibilities Act 2006 (Vic.) and the Abortion Law Reform Act 2008 (Vic.), see: Oreb, N., 'Worth the wait? A critique of the Abortion Act 2008 (Vic.)', *Journal of Law and Medicine*, 17 (2009): 261–9, at p. 262.

47 Section 4.

48 Section 65.

49 Section 5.

50 See, *Royal Women's Hospital* v. *Medical Practitioner's Board of Victoria* [2006] VSCA 85 (20 April 2006).

reasons for abortion, there will also be different interpretations of statutory terminology which can lead to uncertainty.

The current Victorian abortion law protects and strengthens the reproductive interests of the pregnant woman and restricts clinical freedom by closing the door on a well-trodden medical escape route whereby doctors who refuse to assist women have also refused to refer them to a pro-choice doctor or a facility where abortion services are available. The Act requires registered health practitioners who have a conscientious objection to abortion to inform the woman about their views and to refer her to another 'registered practitioner in the same regulated health profession who the practitioner knows does not have a conscientious objection to abortion'.[51] This new provision should reduce the delays experienced by women dealing with antagonistic doctors. Furthermore in an emergency, where an abortion is necessary to preserve the life of pregnant women, a registered medical practitioner is required to perform an abortion and a registered nurse has a duty to assist the medical practitioner in performing it.[52]

The Abortion Law Reform Act 2008 was passed after the VLRC conducted an inquiry and published a report addressing the law of abortion in Victoria. The new law is based on Model B – one of the three models recommended by the VLRC[53] and it is founded on the right to reproductive autonomy, within limits. However, if the Parliament had chosen Model C, a repeal model which regulates abortion in the same way as other medical procedures (an approach which has been followed in the Australian Capital Territory (ACT)), the decision-making responsibility would have been placed with the woman and the clinicians in *all* cases of an unwanted pregnancy. In practice, hospital policies and the attitudes of medical practitioners continue to influence the provision of abortion services, particularly post first trimester abortions in the public sector, because this is a matter which continues to be politically sensitive.

Western Australia

In Western Australia, Dr Victor Chan and Dr Hoh Peng were charged with procuring an unlawful abortion in February 1998.[54] The prosecution of the doctors led to a very heated public debate in Western Australia and throughout the country. All abortion services in Western Australia were suspended and women were forced 'to continue with unwanted pregnancies, fly interstate to access medical procedures or perform abortions on themselves'.[55] In this troubled atmosphere the Western Australian Parliamentarian Cheryl Davenport introduced a private member's Bill for the purpose of decriminalising abortion

51 Section 8 (1).
52 Section 8 (3) and (4).
53 VLRC, *Law of Abortion: Final Report*, at pp. 6–7.
54 Western Australia, Parliamentary Debates, Legislative Council, 10 March 1998, at p. 16 (Cheryl Davenport).
55 Teasdale, L., 'Confronting the fear of being "caught": discourses on abortion in Western Australia', *University of New South Wales Law Journal*, 22(1) (1999): 60–99, at p. 63.

in that state. After much debate and compromise on both sides of the debate, the Acts Amendment (Abortion) Act 1998 (WA) was passed and abortion law in Western Australia at that time were the most liberal in Australia. The charges against the two doctors were not pursued.

As a result of these reforms, the state continues to control aspects of abortion practice but the law is based on reproductive autonomy principles and the meaning of 'unlawful' is clearly set out in the statute. A woman can no longer be prosecuted for having an unlawful abortion in Western Australia. However, it is a criminal offence for a medical practitioner to perform an abortion unlawfully,[56] or for a person who is not a medical practitioner to perform an abortion unless he or she acted in good faith and with reasonable care and skill to save the woman's life.[57] An abortion is lawful under section 199 of the Criminal Code Act Compilation Act 1913 (WA) if it is performed by a registered medical practitioner in good faith with reasonable care and skill *and* is justified. The grounds for justification have been transferred to the Health Act 1911 (WA) and essentially 'informed consent' is the only requirement for pregnancies under 20 weeks.[58] The consent is 'informed' when it is given freely after a medical practitioner who does not perform the abortion[59] has:

- advised the woman about the medical risk of abortion and the risk of carrying a pregnancy to term;
- offered to refer her to counselling for other matters, and
- informed her of appropriate counselling if she terminates the pregnancy or carries the pregnancy to term.[60]

A woman under 16 who is supported by her custodial parent(s) is defined as a dependent minor and is not regarded as having the capacity to give informed consent. Informed consent in these circumstances can only be given if a custodial parent has been informed that an abortion is being considered and has had the opportunity to participate in the consultation and counselling process, or if the Children's Court has made an order to the effect that the custodial parent should not be informed or involved in this process.[61] The Act is silent on the capacity of a woman under 16 who is not supported by her custodial parents and presumably this would depend on the capacity of the

56 Criminal Code Act Compilation Act 1913 (WA) s.199 (1–2).

57 Ibid., ss.199 (3), 259.

58 Health Act 1911 (WA) s. 334 (3) (a). In addition paras (b), (c) and (d) and ss. 4, permit a woman to have an abortion on social, physical or mental health grounds. If she seeks an abortion on these grounds she must still give informed consent as defined by the legislation unless it is impracticable due to the serious danger to her physical and mental health if the abortion is not performed, or to the serious danger the pregnancy is causing to her physical and mental health.

59 Health Act 1911 (WA) s. 334 (6) (a) and (b) provides that the second medical practitioner must not perform the abortion or assist in the performance of the abortion.

60 Ibid., s. 334 (5).

61 Ibid., s. 334 (8).

young woman to understand and weigh up the risks associated with having an abortion or carrying the foetus to term.

Limits are imposed upon the availability of all abortions once a pregnancy reaches 20 weeks' gestation. However, the legislation does not specify an upper limit for late terminations. After 20 weeks of a woman's pregnancy an abortion must be performed in an approved facility but only if two medical practitioners, who are members of a government-appointed panel of at least six medical practitioners, have agreed that 'the mother of the unborn child has a severe medical condition' which justifies the procedure.[62] The decision-making process operates in a structured manner with the woman (and her partner if appropriate) undergoing specific counselling by health professionals. The counselling includes information about the termination procedure and the available alternatives.[63] There is no right of appeal when a request is refused. The overwhelming majority of abortions take place in the private sector and during the first trimester.[64] There are very few late-term abortions performed in Western Australia[65] and abortions performed after '20 weeks account for 0.5 per cent of all abortions'.[66] Even though the number of late abortions is very small there is anecdotal information suggesting that women resent not being permitted to make their own decisions about later terminations.[67]

Unlike most other jurisdictions in Australia, where the abortion decision is technically the doctor's decision, in Western Australia, a woman who is less than 20 weeks pregnant and has given informed consent has the legal authority to make the decision herself. Nevertheless, given that lawful abortion has been redefined as a health rather than a criminal matter, the requirement that the woman consult a second medical practitioner continues to distinguish abortion from other medical procedures and perpetuates the shadow historically associated with abortion. In addition, the gestational restrictions are a reminder of the limited rights that women have to reproductive autonomy, as most applications for abortion after 20 weeks will be made after prenatal tests which can take place late in the pregnancy. On the other hand, Western Australia has made a major shift towards moving abortion from the province of criminal to health law, and in doing so has expanded the scope of reproductive autonomy in that State. As Teasdale says: '[T]he fact that a woman's consent is primary is of great symbolic value for all Western Australian women and goes some way towards redressing the power imbalance women have experienced between

62 Ibid., s. 344 (7).

63 Dickenson, J. E., 'Late pregnancy termination within a legislated medical environment', *Australian and New Zealand Journal of Obstetrics and Gynaecology*, 44(4) (2004): 337–41, at p. 341.

64 WA, Department of Health, *Induced Abortion in Western Australia 1999–2005 Report of the WA Abortion Notification System*, East Perth, WA: Department of Health, 2006, at p. 12.

65 Ibid.

66 Ibid.

67 Dickenson, 'Late Pregnancy Termination', at p. 340.

their reproductive choices and the policies and decisions of medical and legal institutions.'[68]

Pre-implantation genetic diagnosis: context

PGD is a relatively new technology, without a criminal law history, which directly affects a small group of people. It has been available since the early 1990s in Australia. The main indication is for unsuccessful infertility treatment where there is no identifiable cause in the male or female partner and for 'fertile couples at genetic risk of conceiving a child with a serious genetic condition such as cystic fibrosis'.[69] PGD is also an alternative to prenatal diagnosis and 'couples who choose this option usually have a strong objection to termination of pregnancy or have had one or more terminations in the past'.[70] In rare 'saviour sibling' cases, PGD is used for embryo tissue-typing and selection to identify a tissue match for an existing person, usually a sibling who is suffering from a serious medical condition. PGD can also be used to select embryos to prevent the transmission of sex-linked disease, but is not permitted where the reasons for sex selection are social ones. The ban on non-medical sex selection was introduced by NHMRC Guidelines (2004),[71] although previously there were clinics in New South Wales which offered this service.[72]

The incidence of PGD is very low compared to abortion, and there has only been a gradual increase in the success rates over the last decade.[73] The use of PGD triggers public apprehension about the future of human reproduction, the future of the family and the freedom of people to choose the qualities of their children. The debate is influenced by the tension between the capacity of PGD to 'assist in the avoidance of specific genetic disorders and its potential to address a broader range of parental objectives'.[74] A major consideration is compassion for those who are infertile, those who are afflicted with genetic diseases and those caring for children with deadly and devastating conditions. Nevertheless, there are concerns about the reasons for creating embryos for selection and possible rejection and destruction. It is argued that the social effects of accepting PGD as an 'alternative to natural reproduction will include

68 Teasdale, 'Confronting the fear of being "caught"', at p. 73.

69 Cram, D. S. and Pope, A., 'Preimplantation genetic diagnosis: current and future perspectives', *Journal of Law and Medicine*, 15 (2007): 36–44, at pp. 3–37.

70 Ibid.

71 NHMRC, *Ethical Guidelines on the Use of Assisted Reproductive Technology in Clinical Practice and Research*, Canberra: Australian Government, 2004.

72 Petersen, K., Baker, H. W. G., Pitts, M. and Thorpe, R., 'Assisted reproductive technologies: professional and legal restrictions in Australian clinics', *Journal of Law and Medicine*, 12 (2005): 373–85, at p. 383.

73 ITA *Annual Report* (2000) table 10, p. 28; VARTA *Annual Report* (2010) tables 6.1 and 6.2, p. 34.

74 VLRC, *Assisted Reproductive Technology & Adoption: Final Report*, Melbourne: VLRC, 2007, at p. 69.

a diminished tolerance for difference'.[75] It is also argued that PGD amounts to a form of eugenics because it has 'negative implications for those people in the community who live with the disability'.[76] However, there appears to be no empirical evidence to support the claim that PGD has led to negative implications for disabled people.[77] Other concerns about the 'slippery slope' and broader applications would also seem to have been exaggerated. The (UK) Human Genetics Commission has pointed out:

> The anxiety that PGD lies at the top of the slippery slope leading to the possibility of a wide range of potential enhancements, such as intelligence and beauty is misplaced. While we are still far from a full understanding of how such characteristics are transmitted to children, it is clear that very many genes are likely to be involved and there will be complex interactions between these and other developmental factors. Even if all the genes to be involved were identified, prediction of the required characteristics would remain uncertain and the limited supply of embryos available for selection would make the finding of particular gene variant combinations very unlikely.[78]

The use of PGD to choose the sex of a child according to personal preference is highly controversial because it is argued that the choice is made to gratify the parental wishes, not for the benefit of the future child. Opponents of non-medical sex selection also argue that 'it elevates the status of gender in society and contributes to sex discrimination'.[79] However, views are less 'black and white' when sex selection is sought for family balancing. For example, the UK House of Commons, Science and Technology Committee found on balance that there is 'no adequate justification for prohibiting the use of sex selection for family balancing'.[80] The VLRC reported that, of the small number of the submissions it received in favour of sex selection, most of them argued that it was appropriate for family balancing.[81] Those who agree that the scope of

75 NHMRC, *Ethical Guidelines* (2007), Appendix C, 'Issues for further community discussion', C2.

76 VLRC, *Assisted Reproductive Technology & Adoption*, at p. 69.

77 *Choosing Genes for Future Children: Regulating Preimplantation Diagnosis/Human Genome Research Project*, University of Otago: Dunedin, NZ: Human Genome Research Project, 2006, at p. 8.

78 UK, Human Genetics Commission, *Making Babies: Reproductive Decisions and Genetic Technologies*, London: Stationery Office, 2006, at para. 31.

79 VLRC, *Assisted Reproduction and Technology & Adoption*, at p. 82. See also: President's Council of Bioethics, Staff Working Paper (2003), http://bioethics.georgetown.edu/pcbe/background/sex_control.html (accessed 05/01/2012); Ethics Committee of the American Society of Reproductive Medicine, 'Sex selection and preimplantation genetic diagnosis', *Fertility and Sterility*, 72(4) (October 1999): 595–8.

80 UK, House of Commons, Science and Technology Committee, *Human Reproductive Technologies and the Law*, vol. 1, at para. 142.

81 VLRC, *Assisted Reproductive Technology & Adoption*, at p. 80. See also: Dahl, E., 'Preconception sex selection demand and preference in the United States', *Fertility and Sterility*, 85(2)

reproductive liberty extends to non-medical sex selection regard it as a matter for a woman (or couple) to decide in consultation with her doctor on the grounds that the state should only interfere with reproductive decisions in order to prevent harm to others. As there is no evidence that 'children born following a sex selection procedure for non-medical reasons had been harmed as a result of their parents' choice',[82] the justification for the ban appears to be more precautionary than rational.

Pre-implantation genetic diagnosis: legal frameworks

The Parliaments in New South Wales, Western Australia and Victoria have all passed specific ART statutes, but their approaches to regulating PGD are quite different. Furthermore, the NHMRC 'Ethical Guidelines on the Use of Assisted Reproductive Technology in Clinical Practice and Research' (NHMRC Guidelines) apply to any aspect of PGD which is not covered by State laws and policies.[83] This section of the chapter examines the scope and limits of reproductive autonomy reflected in PGD regulation in New South Wales where the NHMRC Guidelines apply, Western Australia which has a statutory model and Victoria where people seeking PGD have to satisfy the eligibility requirements for treatment as set out in the Assisted Reproductive Treatment Act 2008 (Vic.) together with the NHMRC Guidelines. This section commences with a discussion about the NHMRC Guidelines as they are the default position, in the absence of specific provisions, in every State.

The NHMRC Guidelines recognise that the welfare of people who may be born as a result of the use of ART is paramount,[84] but the Australian Health Ethics Committee (AHEC) has also taken into account the autonomy and long-term welfare of both men and women who wish to have access to PGD.[85] In contrast, ART statutes in Western Australia and Victoria include statements of principle addressing the paramount interests of the future child, but do *not* specifically address the *autonomy rights* of people seeking ART treatment.

> The NHMRC Guidelines prohibit the use of PGD for:
>
> prevention of conditions that do not seriously harm the person to be born;
> selection of the sex of an embryo except to reduce the risk of transmission of a serious genetic condition; or
> selection of an embryo in favour of a genetic defect or disability in the person to be born.[86]

(2006): 468–73; Dahl, E., *et al.*, 'Preconception sex selection for non-medical reasons: a representative survey from Germany', *Human Reproduction*, 18(10) (2003): 2231–4.

82 VLRC, *Assisted Reproductive Technology & Adoption*, at p. 80.

83 NHMRC, *Ethical Guidelines* (2007).

84 Ibid., 2.5.

85 Ibid., 2.6.

86 Ibid., 12.2.

On the other hand the NHMRC Guidelines recognise that 'PGD is currently used to detect serious genetic conditions, to improve ART outcomes and in rare circumstances to select an embryo with compatible tissue'.[87]

The Guidelines do not define *serious* genetic conditions and treat this aspect of decision-making as part of the clinical assessment. However, they include general provisions which deal with the information to be given to patients, counselling and consent requirements.[88] In addition, when PGD is being considered, clinics have to provide patients with access to clinical geneticists and genetic counsellors.[89] In dealing with specific situations, the Guidelines encourage clinical staff to discuss a range of factors with patients, including medical information and 'social' information (such as information about the experiences of families living with the condition and the availability of social support).[90]

Overall, the Guidelines leave a considerable amount of discretion to the clinics and don't include monitoring and reporting requirements.[91] However, they do control the use of PGD for compatible tissue-typing which is only permitted where a sibling has a life-threatening condition.[92] In these 'saviour sibling' cases, advice must be sought from the clinical ethics committee or a relevant state committee. The committee should ascertain that:

- the use of PGD will not adversely affect the welfare and interests of the child who may be born;
- the medical condition of the sibling to be treated is life-threatening;
- other means to manage the medical condition are not available; and
- the wish of the parents is to have another child as an addition to their family and not merely as a source of tissue.[93]

New South Wales: PGD

The Assisted Reproductive Technology Act 2007 was the first ART statute to be passed in New South Wales. It came into operation on 1 January 2010. The Act provides a 'light touch' approach towards regulating ART and complements professional guidelines, such as the revised NHMRC Ethical Guidelines 2007. The Act does not refer to PGD even though the AHEC, the body which revised and developed the 2007 Guidelines, strongly recommended that legislation regulating ART should be enacted in *all* states and territories on the grounds that pre-implantation genetic diagnosis and other procedures were as much

87 Ibid. [12.1].
88 Ibid. [9].
89 Ibid. [12.4].
90 Ibid. [12.5].
91 Smith, M., 'Reviewing regulation of assisted reproductive technology in New South Wales', *Journal of Law and Medicine*, 16(2) (2008): 120–31, at p. 130.
92 NHMRC, *Ethical Guidelines* (2007), [12.3].
93 Ibid. [12.3.1].

'social and political issues as they were ethical issues'.[94] The New South Wales Act is the least prescriptive ART statute in Australia and does not establish a regulatory authority or impose eligibility requirements for people seeking ART. As the Act does not refer to PGD, the NHMRC Ethical Guidelines regulate PGD practice in that State.[95] One commentator who is critical of the way that PGD is regulated in New South Wales, describes the NHMRC Guidelines as a mere set of 'minimum ethical standards'.[96] However, the New South Wales Parliament by its omission obviously took the view that the NHMRC Guidelines 2007 were adequate for controlling the use of PGD.

Victoria: PGD

The Assisted Reproductive Treatment Act 2008 repealed the Infertility Treatment Act 1995 and came into operation in Victoria on 1 January 2010.[97] Breach of the Act is a criminal offence. Under the 1995 Act, the former Infertility Treatment Authority (ITA) established a PGD[98] policy, in consultation with geneticists, which consisted of a three-tier notification and approval system for accredited clinics offering PGD procedures.[99] The current regulator, the Victorian Assisted Reproductive Treatment Authority (VARTA), does not have the power to develop a PGD policy. However, VARTA continues to monitor PGD, and compliance with this requirement is a condition of registration.[100] The NHMRC Guidelines 2007 would cover any gaps in the Act.

In Victoria, the gateway to PGD, as in Western Australia, is the IVF programme and the five guiding principles in the Assisted Reproductive Treatment Act 2008 Act must be followed by clinicians and other health professionals providing ART services. The interests of a future child who is not yet conceived are paramount in Victoria and take priority over an existing woman undergoing treatment. This is reflected in the following two guiding principles most relevant to these procedures.

> The welfare and interests of persons born or to be born as a result of treatment procedures are paramount[101] and;
> The health and well-being of persons undergoing treatment procedures must be protected at all times.[102]

94 Ibid. [1.3].
95 The Reproductive Technology Accreditation, Committee (RTAC) Code of Practice deals mainly with clinical practice rather than regulatory issues. See: RTAC, Fertility Society of Australia Code of Practice for Assisted Reproductive Technology Units (revised October 2010).
96 Smith, 'Reviewing regulation', at p. 131.
97 This first ART statute, the Infertility (Medical Procedures) Act 1984, was followed by the Infertility Treatment Act 1995.
98 See n. 1 above.
99 Petersen, K., 'Regulating preimplantation diagnosis: a criminal model versus a professional model', *Journal of Law and Medicine*, 17 (2009): 456–7, at p. 452.
100 Assisted Reproductive Treatment Act 2008 (Vic.) s. 100 (1) (iii); s. 75 (1).
101 Ibid., s. 5 (a).
102 Ibid., s. 5 (d).

The Assisted Reproductive Treatment Act 2008 provides that a woman and her partner (if any) will be eligible for PGD if a doctor is satisfied on reasonable grounds that:

> the woman is unlikely to be able to carry a pregnancy or give birth to a child without a treatment procedure; or
> the woman is at risk of transmitting a genetic abnormality or genetic disease to a child born as a result of a pregnancy conceived other than by a treatment procedure, including a genetic abnormality or genetic disease for which the woman's partner is the carrier; and
> a presumption against treatment does not apply to the woman.[103]

In addition, section 10 (3) requires that a doctor may be satisfied that the woman is at risk of transmitting a genetic abnormality or genetic disease only after obtaining a second opinion confirming the risk from another doctor with specialist qualifications in human genetics or a geneticist.[104] The Act does not specify that the genetic condition or harm must be serious, nor the risk significant, and this assessment is a matter for clinical discretion.

The Act bans sex selection except where it is necessary for the future child to be of a particular sex to avoid the risk of transmitting a genetic abnormality or genetic disease.[105] However, the newly established Patient Review Panel (PRP) has the authority to consider applications for sex selection on social grounds. It is not clear what grounds would qualify under this new provision as a PRP approval of this kind has not yet been reported.

The Act has removed previous discriminatory eligibility rules and now single women and lesbian couples are eligible for ART treatment, including PGD. However, Parliament has introduced an eligibility barrier which requires all people seeking ART, including intending PGD participants, to satisfy the newly created statutory presumption against treatment. This provision was passed without a proper debate in the Parliament justifying this intrusion on reproductive rights and without any evidence demonstrating that 'children born from ART procedures were more likely to be at risk than the general population; or that people seeking to undergo ART were more likely to have a history of violent or sex crimes'.[106] As a result, both the woman and her partner (if any) must undergo a criminal records check and a child protection order check to be eligible for PGD treatment. The statutory presumption against treatment will apply if a criminal records search reveals that charges have been proved against a woman or her partner for a sexual offence or the woman or her partner have been convicted of a violent

103 Ibid., s. 10 (2) (a) (ii), (iii) and (b).
104 Ibid., s. 10 (3).
105 Ibid., s. 28 (1) and (2) (a).
106 Thorpe, R., Petersen, K., Pitts, M. K. and Baker , H. W. G., 'New assisted reproductive technology laws in Victoria: a genuine overhaul or just a cut and paste', *Journal of Law and Medicine*, 18 (2011): 835–50, at p. 845.

offence;[107] or if a child protection order check reveals that a child protection order has been made which removed a child from the custody or guardianship of the woman or her partner.[108] In these circumstances, it is a criminal offence for an ART provider to provide treatment.[109]

When a presumption against treatment arises, an application can be made to the PRP for a review and, if unsuccessful, a further application can be made to the Victorian Civil and Administrative Tribunal (VCAT) for a review of the PRP's decision.[110] *ABY, ABZ* v. *Patient Review Panel* (*Health & Privacy*)[111] is the only VCAT decision dealing with this new barrier to treatment. In this case, a presumption against treatment arose because ABY, a teacher's aide, had been convicted in January 2009 on three counts of sexual penetration of a 16-year-old student under his care. His partner, ABZ was seeking IVF treatment. The central issue was whether or not ABZ could be permitted to undergo IVF treatment and, if so, would this be 'consistent with the best interests of a child who would be born as a result of a treatment procedure'.[112] The focus of the Tribunal was on the risks of ABY, a convicted sex offender, being permitted to parent a child rather than on exacting retribution for ABY's past conduct. On balance, the Tribunal found that the positive aspects of ABY's character outweighed the negative aspects and the barrier to treatment was lifted. This VCAT decision is a victory for reproductive autonomy (at least for the time being) and would appear to override the concern of Parliament about the possible harm of allowing a person with a sexual conviction to be a good parent. An appeal, filed on 25 August 2011 was heard by the Court of Appeal on 16 July 2012 and at the time of writing the Judgment was still reserved.

The regulation of PGD in Victoria since the Assisted Reproductive Treatment Act 2008 (Vic.) was passed is more flexible than under the previous legislation.[113] However, if a woman or her partner (if any) fail to satisfy the criminal records or child protection order checks and their review applications are rejected, their future children could be afflicted with a genetic disease or disorder, a situation that could have been avoided.

Western Australia: PGD

In Western Australia, the use of PGD was prohibited prior to 2004. However, currently it is permitted and highly regulated. The Human Reproductive

107 Assisted Reproductive Treatment Act 2008 (Vic.) s. 14 (1) (a); see also Sentencing Act 1991(Vic.), Clause 1 of Schedule 1 (sexual offences); Clause 2 of Schedule 1 (violent offences).
108 Assisted Reproductive Treatment Act 2008 (Vic.) s. 14 (1) (b).
109 Ibid., s. 14 (2).
110 Ibid., ss. 85 (b) and 96 (a).
111 [2011] VCAT 1382 (29 July) 2011.
112 Section 15 (3) (b)(ii).
113 VARTA is the current ART regulator in Victoria.

Technology Act 1991 (WA) sets out the legal framework for ART practice, and the Reproductive Technology Council has published a 'Policy of Approval of Diagnostic Procedures involving Embryos' (PGD Policy) which defines the boundaries of PGD practice.[114] The PGD Policy requires either a general or specific approval from the Council for all diagnostic procedures carried out on a fertilised egg or an embryo in Western Australia. Non-compliance with the PGD Policy is a criminal offence and an offender is liable to imprisonment for five years.[115]

The gateway to PGD is the IVF programme. Heterosexual couples, single women and women in a same-sex relationship are eligible if there is a significant risk of transmitting a genetic abnormality or disease to a future child.[116] In all cases, consideration must be given to the welfare and interests of the participants and the child likely to be born as a result of the procedure.[117] Under section 14 (2b) of the Human Reproductive Technology Act 1991(WA), the Council must not approve any diagnostic procedure on a human embryo in these circumstances unless the embryo is intended for use in the reproductive treatment of a woman and the Council is satisfied on the basis of existing scientific and medical knowledge that:

(i) the diagnostic procedure is unlikely to leave the embryo unfit to be implanted in the body of a woman; and
(ii) where the diagnostic procedure is for the genetic testing of the embryo, there is a significant risk of a serious genetic abnormality or disease being present in the embryo.[118]

The PGD Policy provides a general authorisation for PGS screening,[119] for:

- women over 35 years of age providing eggs; or
- women with >2 miscarriages; or
- women with >2 failed IVF attempts where embryos have been transferred; or
- women referred by a clinical geneticist with a family history of aneuploidy not caused by translocations or other chromosomal rearrangements.[120]

114 Reproductive Technology Council, Policy on Approval of Diagnostic Procedures Involving Embryos, March 2008, www.rtc.org.au/. . ./Approval_for_Diagnostic_Testing_of_Embryos_ Advice_ to_Clinics.pdf (accessed 18/01/2011).
115 Human Reproductive Technology Act 1991 s. 7.
116 Ibid., s. 23; Acts Amendment (Lesbian and Gay Reform) Act 2002 (WA).
117 Human Reproductive Technology Act 1991 (WA) s. 23 (1) (e).
118 Ibid., s. 14 (2) (b).
119 See n. 1 above.
120 Reproductive Technology Council, Policy on Approval of Diagnostic Procedures, at para. 2 (www.rtc.org.au/clinics/docs/Approval_for_Diagnostic_Testing_of_Embryos_ Advice_to_Clinics.pdf) (accessed 28/05/2012).

The PGD Policy also provides for case-by-case approval for diagnostic procedures where a pre-existing diagnosis has indicated that an embryo is at a *significant risk* of being affected by a *serious genetic condition*.[121] There is no list of genetic conditions, and each application has to be considered on its own merits. The Council must be satisfied that the genetic condition will have serious implications for a future child. The application for approval is made by the clinic, with a supporting report from a clinical geneticist. The report *must* address factors such as the seriousness of the genetic condition, the experience and attitude of the family, the likely level of impairment and the expected impact on the potential person's life. Geneticists should also provide information concerning the prospects of new and longer term treatment, the level of support for the future child that would be required and the capacity of the family to support a child with the condition. The Council's approval will generally be subject to a preliminary feasibility study confirming that the genetic condition is able to be tested for by PGD and the other key factors for regulators are the severity of the condition and the risk of the potential child inheriting the condition. On the question of non-medical sex selection, the Act makes it clear that the use of an embryo diagnostic procedure for sex selection alone would not be permitted and NHMRC Guidelines prohibit sex selection for non-medical purposes.[122]

Conclusion

This chapter has examined the regulation of abortion and PGD in the Australian States of New South Wales, Victoria and Western Australia and it has been shown that the gradualist approach underpins abortion regulation with varying restrictions and prohibitions after the first trimester of pregnancy. None of the abortion regimes include a separate ground for foetal abnormality. In New South Wales, a lawful abortion is framed as a clinical decision made by a doctor acting *bona fides* if the danger of continuing a pregnancy exceeds the risks of having an abortion. Statistically this legal 'formula' can justify abortion for most of the gestation period. In Victoria, a woman has a *negative* right to abortion up to 24 weeks' gestation, but after this stage of gestation, the availability of an abortion is subject to two medical assessments of her physical, psychological and social circumstances. In Western Australia, a woman is entitled to have an abortion prior to 20 weeks' gestation once she gives her informed consent as defined by section 334 of the Health Act 1913 (WA). After this stage of the pregnancy more restrictions are imposed and an abortion will only be lawful if two medical practitioners on a therapeutic abortion panel agree that she has a severe medical condition.

Reproductive autonomy is less visible in the controls over the use of PGD as the best interests of the potential child are paramount in the three states and the emphasis is on the risk posed by the genetic condition to the

121 Ibid.
122 NHMRC, *Ethical Guidelines* (2007), at para. 11.1.

potential child. Each state permits the use of PGD to improve ART outcomes in cases of infertility. However, the indications for genetic testing are less consistent. In New South Wales, access to PGD is a clinical decision and a woman is eligible if the purpose is to detect a *serious* genetic condition. The medical practitioner has the authority to decide if the seriousness of the genetic condition justifies the PGD procedure. In Victoria a woman can have access to PGD if the presumption against treatment does not apply and two doctors agree that there is a risk of genetic abnormality or disease. In Western Australia there is a number of requirements for PGD including the approval of the Council when there is a significant risk of a serious genetic condition.

Comparing the regulation of prenatal testing and later terminations highlights the incongruence underpinning abortion and PGD laws in these three states. There is far less state intervention under the criminal law and abortion statutes laws when abortions are performed before 12–14 weeks' gestation compared to later abortions. Pregnant women are routinely offered prenatal screening, and if the tests reveal evidence of foetal abnormality or a genetic disorder which will affect a woman's physical or psychological health, the availability of lawful abortion will depend on the medical assessment of the condition and gestational stage. Even though a woman at risk of having a child with a genetic disorder may prefer to maximise her chances of having a healthy child using PGD, this option may not be available to her if she is not eligible for PGD – for whatever reasons. It is difficult to find a convincing justification for laws which deny a woman the opportunity to avoid conceiving a child with a heritable abnormality or disease, but permit her to terminate a later pregnancy after an adverse prenatal test result. This incoherence is unacceptable, and may be the result of regulatory compartmentalisation as much as it reflects more concerns about the potential of PGD and social harm than any harm associated with terminating a 'defective' foetus.

Those who oppose any use of genetic technologies associated with ART commonly support their case by arguing that the use of genetic technologies implies that 'admission to life' is no longer unconditional. This is a highly unrealistic approach in the twenty-first century. People in most Western countries have become used to the benefits of medical progress expanding reproductive horizons and allowing them to make choices about infertility, fertility, family size, health and abortion. As a consequence, the expectation of a woman having reproduction control has greatly increased and it is implausible to claim that admission to life is otherwise unconditional, particularly given the availability of pregnancy termination.

In conclusion, this examination of reproductive regulation in three Australian states suggests that the physical proximity between the woman and the foetus has made the woman's interests highly visible in abortion regulation; whereas the contingent physical proximity and concerns about the interests of a future child in the case of PGD, have been instrumental in subjugating women's interests, even though women carry the embryo/foetus and give birth to these children.

7 Regulatory legitimacy: the case for controlling and restricting access to PGD for sex-selection purposes

Don Chalmers

Pre-implantation genetic diagnosis embryo screening and assisted reproductive technology

Thirty years after the first birth using *in vitro* fertilisation (IVF), the assisted reproductive technology (ART) debates have continued, raising issues concerning embryo experimentation, including the use of pre-implantation genetic diagnosis (PGD) to screen embryos for genetic characteristics and conditions.

PGD is used to screen embryos to assist in deciding which may be judged suitable for implantation. Those not deemed suitable are generally discarded, although they may be used for research purposes, given that any required consent has been obtained. This chapter examines the regulatory regime for PGD in Australia which can be found principally in the National Health and Medical Research Council's (NHMRC) *Ethical Guidelines on the Use of Assisted Reproductive Technology and Clinical Practice and Research* (2007). Where PGD is used in embryo research, the regulatory regime established by the Research Involving Human Embryos Act 2002 applies. An Australian government committee[1] reviewed this regime, which resulted in revisions to the NHMRC guidelines and to the legislation. This chapter focuses on PGD embryo screening and the regulatory justifications for controlling and restricting access to PGD in ART clinical procedures, with specific reference to its use in sex selection for non-medical reasons.

Towards liberalisation in ART regulation

Following the first ART births at the end of the 1970s, enquiries were established (early examples were Waller[2] in Victoria and Warnock[3] in the UK)

1 Australian Government (2005) Legislation Review Committee, *Prohibition of Human Cloning Act 2002* and *Research Involving Human Embryos Act 2002*, reports, Canberra, December 2005 (hereafter Lockhart Reports).

2 Committee to Consider the Social, Ethical and Legal Issues arising from in Vitro-Fertilisation, *Report on Donor Gametes in IVF*, State of Victoria 1983 (Chair, Professor Louis Waller, the Victorian Law Reform Commissioner, issued two other reports: *Interim Report* and *Report on the Disposition of Embryos produced by In Vitro Fertilisation*).

3 *Report of the Committee of Enquiry into Human Fertilisation and Embryology*, Cmnd 9312 (Warnock Report), London: Stationery Office, 1984.

and regulation was introduced. From the outset, there was a community tolerance of ART procedures, but the regulation introduced had a restrictive tilt,[4] with carefully regulated licensing authorities such as those in Australia,[5] the United Kingdom[6] and Canada.[7] There are parallels between the predominantly public healthcare systems in these three countries and their legislative ART schemes, with licensing regulatory authorities and regulated standards of clinical practice.[8] At the other extreme, the free market United States relies on professional self-regulation,[9] has little regulation beyond the federal Fertility Clinics Success Rates and Certification Act 1992 and has been described as a 'patchwork, with authority divided among numerous sources of oversight'.[10] However, ART is regulated in most countries by a system of licensing or professional codes of practice, with regulation covering:

- ART clinic licensing (or professional accreditation)
- clinic requirements to follow prescribed clinical and professional standards of treatment, patient care and record keeping
- written consents from the parties involved, including, if required, gamete donors and their spouses
- clinic requirements to maintain records, including consent forms and the outcome of the procedures (pregnancies, births, miscarriages)[11]
- counselling to be available
- certain procedures are excluded, such as cloning, mixing of gametes, research on embryos, or sex selection, except for medical reasons to avoid a genetic disease.

It should be noted that, even in those countries which have a national health service, the provision of assisted reproductive services is often left to the private sector, and there are real questions about the public interest, cost and appropriateness of rigid legislative models of regulation in a largely privatised

4 Brownsword, R., 'Regulating human genetics: new dilemmas for a new millennium', *Med. L R*, 12 (2004): 14–39, notes that countries which have legislation for ART often include procedures that have a 'restrictive-tilt' rather than being permissive.

5 Assisted Reproductive Treatment Act 2008 (Vic.), which introduced the world's first legislative scheme; Assisted Reproductive Treatment Act 1988 (SA); Assisted Reproductive Technology Act2007 (NSW); and, Human Reproductive Technology Act 1991 (WA).

6 Human Fertilisation and Embryology Authority Act 1990 UK (HFEA).

7 There is a useful summary of international regulation of ART on the Health Canada website: www.hc-sc.gc.ca/hl-vs/reprod/hc-sc/general/international-eng.php (accessed 31/08/2011).

8 Nelson, E., 'Comparative perspectives in the regulation of assisted reproductive technologies in the United Kingdom and Canada', *Alberta Law Review*, 43 (2006): 1023–48.

9 Storrow, R., 'The bioethics of prospective parenthood: in pursuit of the proper standards for gatekeeping in fertility clinics', *Cardozo Law Review*, 28 (2007): 2283–320.

10 See Robertson, J., 'Reproductive technology in Germany and the United States: an essay in comparative law and bioethics', *Columbia Journal of Transnational Law*, 43 (2004): 189–203.

11 The provision of statistical information to the HFEA is a requirement for licensed ART clinics in the UK. In Australia, the FSA requires data on reproductive technology pregnancies and births to be provided to the National Perinatal Statistics Unit.

area of clinical practice.[12] Debates on the regulation of ARTs are compounded both by this and by the international trade in these services, with the capacity to avoid national prohibitions or restrictions by crossing borders and using services in less regulated jurisdictions. In addition to legislation, the development of Codes of Clinical Practice and Standards is a significant aspect of the regulation of ART clinics.[13] For example, in Japan, ART is regulated under guidelines developed by the National Society of Obstetricians and Gynaecologists.[14]

The trend in recent years has been from restrictive to more permissive[15] regulation and this continues as ART has become established as essentially a standard infertility treatment, accounting for an estimated 2–3 per cent of annual births in developed countries. Indeed, there are some who question whether this area should have been regulated at all.[16] In the United Kingdom, the House of Commons Science and Technology Committee in 2005 proposed a balance between individual freedom in reproductive choices and the legitimate interests of the state, but argued that any intervention into reproductive choice must have a sound ethical basis and also take into account evidence of harm to children or to society.[17] A more recent Victorian Law Reform Commission Report concluded that 'our consultations revealed that almost everyone believes the promotion of the best interests of the child should remain the primary concern in the regulation and provision of ART services, even if they differ on precisely how a child's interests should be protected in the context of access to ART'.[18] The qualifying last words recognise the general importance given to the 'best interests of the child'[19] test, but also raise the possibility of the importation of judgemental tests for parenthood potential.[20]

12 See Johnson, M. and Peterson, K., 'Public interest or public meddling? Towards an objective framework for the regulation of assisted reproduction technologies', *Human Reproduction*, 23 (2008): 716–28.
13 See Haagen, E. *et al.*, 'Sub fertility guidelines in Europe: quantity and quality of intrauterine insemination guidelines', *Human Reproduction*, 21(8) (2006): 2013–109.
14 Takeshita, N. *et al.*, 'Regulating assisted reproductive technologies in Japan', *Journal of Assisted Reproduction and Genetics,* 20(7) (2003): 260–4.
15 McGleenan, T., 'Reproductive technology and the slippery slope argument: a message in blood', in Hildt, E. and Graumann, S. (eds), *Genetics and Human Reproduction*, Aldershot: Ashgate, 1999, at pp. 273–83.
16 Skene, L., 'Why legislate on assisted reproduction?', in Freckelton, I. and Petersen, K. (eds), *Controversies in Health Law*, Leichhardt: NSW: Federation Press, ch. 14.
17 House of Commons Science and Technology Committee, *Human Reproductive Technologies and the Law Fifth Report of Session 2004–5*, vol. 1, London: Stationery Office, 2005, p. 169. The recommendations were generally supported in *Government Response to the Report from the House of Commons Science and Technology Committee: Human Reproductive Technologies and the Law* Cm 6641, London: Stationery Office, 2005.
18 Victorian Law Reform Commission Report, *Assisted Reproductive Technology and Adoption*, Final Report 2007, ch. 3, 'Regulation', at p. 47 (hereafter VLRC Report (2007)).
19 Ibid., pp. 46–7, for a good summary of the controversies on the best interests of the child.
20 See, for example, Jackson, E., 'Conception and the irrelevance of the welfare principle', *Modern Law Review*, 65 (2002): 176–203.

Whatever the tests applied for suitability of access to ART, arguably a less restrictive and more liberalised approach to ART regulation can be seen, at least in those areas considered in the following sections.

Status of children

Internationally, regulations have consistently removed legal doubts about the status of children born as a result of ART procedures where donor gametes were used.[21]

Access to programmes

At the outset, ART was often restricted to married couples and still may be in some countries.[22] For example, in Japan, guidelines restrict the availability of ART to married couples.[23] There are similar restrictions in a number of other countries,[24] and this restrictive access regime extends in general to South American nations, Muslim nations and much of Africa.[25] Gradually, however, access has been extended in other jurisdictions, particularly after legal challenges in the courts, often on the basis of discrimination. Such challenges have come from same-sex couples[26] and single would-be parents.[27] As an example of a more liberal approach in these cases, the Canadian Royal Commission on New Reproductive Technologies stated: '[E]xcluding single women or lesbians from DI programmes not only contravenes their equality rights it also puts their health at risk . . . if a service is to be available, women should be treated equally, unless there is good evidence that the best interests of the child will suffer.'[28] More strongly, the Canadian Commission recommended that access to treatment be 'determined on the basis of legitimate medical criteria without discrimination on the basis of factors such as marital status, sexual orientation or economic status'.[29]

21 See Lee, R. and Morgan, D., *Human Fertilisation and Embryology: Regulating the Reproductive Revolution*, London, Blackstone, 2001, ch. 9; see also Warnock, M., 'The artificial family', in *Moral Dilemmas in Modern Medicine*, Oxford: Oxford University Press, pp. 138–54.
22 Chakravarty, B., 'Legislation and regulations regarding the practice of assisted reproduction in India', *Journal of Assisted Reproduction and Genetics*, 18 (2001), at p. 11.
23 Takeshita, N. *et al.*, 'Regulating assisted reproductive technologies in Japan', *Journal of Assisted Reproduction and Genetics*, 20 (2003): 260–4, at p. 261.
24 Schenker, J., 'Assisted reproduction practice in Europe: legal and ethical aspects', *Human Reproduction Update*, 3 (1997): 174–6.
25 See Wardle, L,. 'Global perspective on procreation and parentage by assisted reproduction', *Capitol University Law Review*, 35 (2007): 413–63 and appendices at pp. 427–31.
26 See *JM* v. *QFG, GK* and *State of Queensland* [1997] Qld SC 206.
27 See *MW, DD, PA* and *AB* v. *Royal Women's Freemasons Hospital and State of Victoria* [1997] HREOCA 6. See also *Pearce* v. *South Australian Health Commission and others* (1996) 66 SASR 486 and *McBain* v. *State of Victoria* 2000 FCA 1009.
28 Royal Commission on New Reproductive Technologies, *Proceed with Care: Final Report of the Royal Commission on New Reproductive Technologies*, Ottawa: Minister of Government Services Canada, 1993, vol. 1, at p. 457.
29 Ibid., at p. 554, Rec. 1.21.

Donor anonymity

Donor anonymity in ART was originally assured in many regulatory schemes. There have again been significant shifts over the decades towards abolition of anonymity for gamete donors. This abolition first occurred in Sweden in 1988,[30] with a considerable initial impact on the recruitment of donors to ART programmes. The pioneering ART legislation in Victoria established a comprehensive scheme for access to donor information in an ART procedure for the child.[31] Similar access rights to donor-identifying information have been introduced in New Zealand.[32] In many jurisdictions, children are given the right to obtain access to non-identifying information about the donor. However, a number of countries, particularly the largely unregulated United States, still allow anonymity. The regulation of donor anonymity can be a decisive factor in reproductive tourism choices.

Research on human embryos: liberalisation with a restrictive tilt

The liberalising trend in ART regulatory schemes[33] has been reflected to a degree in embryo research, albeit more slowly and cautiously. Research and experimentation[34] on embryos was and remains controversial, particularly because of religious and philosophical differences of opinion about the moral status of the embryo.[35] In Australia, there was a generally strict regulatory approach to embryo research,[36] before a national regulatory scheme was introduced in 2002 permitting embryo research.[37]

30 Act (1988: 711) on fertilisation outside the body (SFS 1988: 711). This was later supplemented with a 1991 Act Concerning Measures for Research or Treatment Involving Fertilised Human Ova.

31 Assisted Reproductive Treatment Act 2008 (Vic.), ss. 59–60, replacing the Infertility Treatment Act 1995. See also Assisted Reproductive Treatment Act 1988 (SA); Assisted Reproductive Technology Act 2007 (NSW); and Human Reproductive Technology Act 1991 (WA). Donovan, K., 'What shall we tell the children? Reflections on children's perspectives and the reproduction revolution', in Lee, R. and Morgan, D. (eds.), *Birthrights: Law and Ethics in the Beginning of Life*, London: Routledge, 1989, at p. 96.

32 Section 50 of the New Zealand, Human Assisted Reproductive Technology Act, 2004 allows the offspring of a donor conception access to both non-identifying and identifying information that is relevant for medical purposes.

33 The diversity of approaches can be gauged from a WHO report: Vayena, E., Rowe, P. and Griffin, P., *Current Practices and Controversies in Assisted Reproduction*, Geneva: WHO Geneva Report of a meeting on Medical, Ethical and Social Aspects of Assisted Reproduction, 2001.

34 See Lee and Morgan, *Human Fertilisation and Embryology*, ch. 3; NBCC, *Human Embryo Experimentation*, a background paper and select bibliography, Commonwealth of Australia, November 1990.

35 See Lockwood, M., 'The Warnock Report: a philosophical appraisal', in *Moral Dilemmas in Modern Medicine*; Andrews, L., 'The legal status of the embryo', *Loyola LR*, 32 (1986): 357–408.

36 Senate Select Committee on the Human Embryo Experimentation Bill 1985 *Human Embryo Experimentation in Australia*, September 1986, AGPS Canberra 1986.

37 Chalmers, D. and Nicol, D., 'Embryonic stem cell research: ethical and economic values (part 1)', *Law and the Human Genome Review*, 18 (2003): 43–53 and (part 2) 19: 91–108; on

The Legislation Review Committee in Australia[38] (the Lockhart Reports) considered whether non-transferred PGD embryos could be classified as 'excess' embryos and able to be available for non-medical treatment purposes with the consent of the gamete donors. The Lockhart Reports made a recommendation that embryos identified by PGD as carrying genetic diseases or other abnormalities and which would normally be discarded should be available for research, training and improvements in clinical practice.[39] Originally only stored frozen embryos were able to be used in research but recommendations were made on the use of fresh ART embryos.[40] However, the use of unfrozen, fresh embryos was recommended but required the prior development, by a group of experts, of an objective and revised biological definition of 'human embryo' for use in determining whether the embryo is unsuitable for implantation.[41] The definition was to take account of emerging technologies in reproductive science rather than legal, moral, religious or social views,[42] with the caveat that 'it is important that the definition does not become so wide as to encompass human cells or cellular structures that traditionally have not been previously considered to be embryos'.[43] The expert group settled on a revised definition that was later published.[44]

embryo research, Research Involving Human Embryos Act, 2002 and cloning, Prohibition of Human Cloning Act, 2002 administered by the NHMRC Embryo Research Licensing Committee. See also Assisted Reproductive Treatment Act 2008 (Vic.), s. 30.

38 Lockhart Reports.

39 Ibid., Rec. 22, at p. 169.

40 Ibid., Rec. 21. Fresh ART embryos that are unsuitable for implantation, as defined by the objective criteria, should be permitted to be used, under licence, for research, training and improvements in clinical practice.

41 Ibid., ch. 8, where a discussion paper, 'Human embryo – a biological definition' (NHMRC, 2005) was considered extensively by the Lockhart Committee.

42 Ibid., at p. v, 'Introduction'. The following questions were listed:

- When does human life begin?
- How far should society allow research involving human embryos?
- How should 'human embryo' be defined?
- What safeguards should be provided to protect the rights of women?
- Can common ground be found between the widely varying, indeed divergent, views of morality held by members of our society?
- What are the limits of the use of in vitro fertilisation (IVF) and related methods (or ART) and human embryo research?
- Should excess ART embryos continue to be available for research, with permission under licence?
- Should the creation of human embryos for research be permitted?

43 Findlay, J., 'Human embryo: a biological definition', *Hum Reprod*, 22 (2007): 905–11, at p. 908.

44 Ibid. The definition proposed was that a human embryo is a discrete entity that has arisen from either:

(a) the first mitotic division when fertilisation of a human oocyte by a human sperm is complete; or
(b) any other process that initiates organised development of a biological entity with a human nuclear genome or altered human nuclear genome that has the potential to develop up to, or beyond, the stage at which the primitive streak appears; and has not yet reached eight weeks of development since the first mitotic division.

The Lockhart Reports were silent on the timing for consent for a PGD embryo to be declared 'excess' and therefore available for use in research. The 'proper consent' requirements under the NHMRC *Ethical Guidelines* (2007) normally require a two-week cooling-off period after consent was given for specific research.[45] Such a two-week cooling-off period would, however, render the fresh PGD embryo unusable in research. Professor Agnes Bankier submitted to the Review Committee that couples undertaking PGD should receive genetic counselling and that it should be discussed with them what would happen to their embryos in the event of an adverse diagnosis. Therefore, in her view, 'consent obtained before the PGD procedure would not need the cooling-off period'.[46] The Research Involving Human Embryos Act 2002 was amended and the Licensing Committee developed a shorter consent cooling-off period for PGD couples.[47]

Australia is now in the company of countries such as the UK, Finland, Greece, Israel,[48] the Netherlands, Singapore, Sweden and South Korea and the American states of California and New Jersey[49] that have moved to approve embryo and embryonic stem (ES) cell research with a system of statutory licensing of the research on excess (surplus)[50] ART embryos. Some other countries have permitted restricted research on surplus embryos but have done so by guidelines rather than legislation (for example, Japan).[51]

The legislation and guidelines in these countries include broadly similar provisions, permitting embryo research but in defined conditions, including:

- only surplus ART embryos allowed may be used (except in the UK);
- consent of the parties creating the embryos is required at two stages – consent that the embryos are no longer required for ART treatment and consent to research;
- the purposes of the research are restricted and must be explained and justified;
- the research purposes must be approved by ethics review committees;
- the research is generally required to be reported and research results published; and

45 Guideline 17.19.

46 Ibid., at p. 120; Professor Bankier is a distinguished geneticist with Genetic Health Services, Victoria.

47 NHMRC Licensing Committee, *Guidance on Consent*.

48 Schenker, J., 'Legal aspects of ART practice in Israel', *Journal of Assisted Reproduction and Genetics*, 20 (2003): 7.

49 See also Isasi, R. *et al.*, 'Legal and ethical approaches to stem cell and cloning research: a comparative analysis of policies in Latin America, Asia and Africa', *J of LME*, 32 (2004): 626–40.

50 Halliday, S., 'A comparative approach to the regulation of human embryonic stem cell research in Europe', *Med L R*, 12 (2004): 40–69, suggests that there are different models, but essentially there are bans or licensing.

51 Japan has a mixed system with legislation banning cloning (Law for the Prohibition of Reproductive Cloning, 2000) and regulation for stem cells (Guidelines for the Derivation and Utilisation of Human Embryonic Stem Cells, 2001).

- national committees must license or approve the research and, in the case of licensing, have the power to impose conditions in the licence.

In addition, it is also common in the legislation and guidelines to include restrictive tilt conditions in relation to the *purposes* of the embryo research. In Australia, for example, the research licence applicant must demonstrate that there is a 'likelihood of significant advancement of knowledge or improvement in technologies for treatment'.[52] In the UK, acceptable research purposes were originally restricted to understanding of the causes of infertility, miscarriages, congenital diseases, contraception and chromosome abnormalities but were later expanded to include research for the purposes of understanding the development of embryos, increasing knowledge of serious disease and the treatment of those diseases.[53]

So, like ART regulation, the trend in embryo research regulation has been towards liberalisation, albeit with a distinctly restrictive tilt. However, it must be noted that some countries have maintained strict bans on human embryo research, such as Austria, Ireland, Canada, the Philippines and Germany.

Pre-implantation genetic diagnosis and the reasons for its use

Within ART programmes, techniques have been developed enabling the genetic analysis and diagnosis of embryos before transfer and implantation (*pre-implantation* genetic diagnosis or, PGD, for short).[54] These PGD techniques were preceded by the introduction of two post-fertilisation *prenatal* diagnostic procedures in the latter half of the twentieth century, namely, amniocentesis and chorionic villus sampling.[55] These procedures may be used during pregnancy to diagnose the health of the child *in utero* with the possible consequential, and often controversial, choice of abortion if a serious genetic condition is identified. As is now the case with PGD, these procedures were subject to early criticisms over their potential use for sex selection.[56] The American College of Obstetricians and Gynecologists

52 Research Involving Human Embryos Act 2002, s. 21 (4)(b).

53 Human Fertilisation and Embryology Act (Research Purposes) Regulations 2001 (UK).

54 See Petersen, K., 'Genetic technologies and ART: ethical values, legal regulation and informal regulation', in Freckelton, I. and Petersen, K., *Disputes and Dilemmas in Health Law*, Sydney: Federation Press, 2006, ch. 11, pp. 217–36; Johnson, G. *et al.*, *British Journal of Human Reproduction*, 8 (1993): 1733.

55 Oladapo, O. T., 'Amniocentesis and chorionic villus sampling for prenatal diagnosis: RHL commentary' (last revised: 1 April 2009). *WHO Reproductive Health Library*, Geneva: World Health Organization; Alfirevic, Z., Mujezinovic, F. and Sundberg, K., 'Amniocentesis and chorionic villus sampling for prenatal diagnosis', *Cochrane Database of Systematic Reviews*, 3 (2003), art. no.: CD003252. DOI: 10.1002/14651858.CD003252.

56 Wertz, D. and Fletcher, J., 'Fatal knowledge? Pre-natal diagnosis and sex selection', *Hastings Center Report*, 19 (1989): 26.

(ACOG) accepted these procedures as ethically permissible to prevent the birth of children with serious genetic disorders,[57] but there was less unanimity on how test results were dealt with, principally in terms of the possibility of abortion.[58]

PGD offers an alternative to *prenatal* diagnostic procedures for those concerned about genetic conditions.[59] It enables clinicians to screen and to identify embryos that may be considered unsuitable for transfer and implantation because the diagnostic test results on the embryo indicate adverse genetic conditions.[60] Arguably, PGD is more acceptable than using prenatal amniocentesis or chorionic villus sampling as PGD[61] can avoid the use of selective abortion where a genetic disorder is identified during the pregnancy. Decisions to terminate a planned and wanted pregnancy are inevitably more traumatic than a decision not to transfer an embryo initially.[62] The Legislation Review Committee Reports in Australia[63] made a number of specific comments about the technological development of PGD within ART and stated that it was generally used 'to help couples with a specific genetic disease to have a baby free of the disease',[64] but cautioned that, '[s]tudies indicate that the technique is efficient and safe, but PGD requires removing a sample of the embryo, and the long-term effects of decreasing the mass of an embryo by removing cells at the cleavage stage are unknown'.[65] The potential applications of PGD are likely to increase as more genes associated with serious genetic conditions are identified. There are some indications that this is in fact already the case.[66]

57 See, 'ACOG committee opinion sex selection', *International Journal of Obstetrics and Gynecology*, 56 (1997): 99–202. (Now the American Congress of Obstetricians and Gynecologists.)

58 See, for example, French National Consultative Ethics Committee for Health and Life Sciences, *Opinion No. 5 and Problems raised by Prenatal and Perinatal Diagnosis*, 13 May 1985.

59 For a full discussion, see Chapter 1 in this volume.

60 Gleicher, N., Weghofer, A. and Barad, D., 'Preimplantation genetic screening "ready" for prime time?', *Fertility and Sterility*, 89 (2008): 780–8. (I acknowledge the valuable advice on PGD in Australia received from Dr S. Junk.)

61 Pre-implantation genetic screening (PGS) aims to improve the chances of a successful pregnancy in women of advanced maternal age or women with histories of miscarriages where there is a high risk of miscarriage or complications in the pregnancy undergoing *in vitro* fertilisation (IVF). Generally, there are poor chances of a successful pregnancy and live birth for these women. PGS is used to screen for cleavage-stage embryos with abnormal chromosome formations (aneuploidies). Those normal embryos are transferred in the hope of improving the chances of a successful birth. Mastenbroek, M. *et al.* '*In vitro* fertilization and preimplantation genetic screening', *N Engl J Med*, 357 (2007): 9–17.

62 See comments of Bennett, B., 'Prenatal diagnosis, genetics and reproductive decision making', *Journal of Law and Medicine*, 9(28) (2001), at p. 38.

63 Lockhart Reports.

64 Ibid., at p. 25.

65 Ibid., at p. 27.

66 See *Policy in Relation to the Use of PGD for Genetic Testing*, Infertility Treatment Authority Victoria, 2004, cited in Petersen, K., 'Genetic technologies and ART: ethical values, legal regulation and informal regulation', in Freckelton *et al.*, *Disputes and Dilemmas in Health Law*, ch. 11, at p. 219.

PGD for medical indications

PGD is employed where there are medical indications for its use and there is general ethical agreement that PGD is acceptable in these circumstances. Medical reasons provide the primary motivation for couples requesting sex selection. Clinical ethical guidelines in Australia support the use of PGD for medical reasons to reduce the risk of transmission of a *serious* genetic condition.

PGD is currently used to detect serious genetic conditions, to improve ART outcomes and, in rare circumstances, to select an embryo with compatible tissue for a sibling. These uses have profound ethical significance consequent of:

- what counts as a serious genetic condition is controversial; and
- the procedures involve the disposal of some healthy embryos.

Clinics must ensure careful evaluation of these and all other relevant issues before the use of PGD.[67]

Regulations regarding the use of PGD vary from country to country but are generally consistent with the Australian stance that PGD is only permitted for medical reasons and indications. This is the position in Germany,[68] Italy,[69] Turkey,[70] New Zealand[71] and Canada[72] where PGD is permitted for medical reasons, including the prevention, diagnosis or treatment of sex-linked diseases or disorders. PGD is not permitted for non-medical sex selection. The pattern of genetic inheritance means that some such conditions are sex linked. For example, hydrocephalus – an abnormal accumulation of cerebrospinal fluid in the skull – is an inherited condition, which is likely caused by a faulty neural adhesion gene on the X chromosome. The trait is X-linked recessive, which can be passed on to boys who inherit the chromosome with the flawed allele from their mother. Similarly, for a couple at risk of having children affected by the X-linked recessive condition of haemophilia, identifying that their embryo has an X chromosome may be critical, as the disorder causes symptoms in males whereas females are, save in unusual circumstances, only carriers of the genetic condition. Such genetic conditions may be serious, debilitating and even life-threatening and diagnosis by PGD is likely, after counselling, to lead to a decision not to transfer the embryo. But other conditions may be arguably wrongly classified as 'serious' or even undesirable. Such a case of controversy

67 *Ethical Guidelines on the Use of Assisted Reproductive Technology in Clinical Practice and Research*, Australia: NHMRC, 2007, Guideline 12.1.
68 Embryo Protection Act 1990, s. 3.
69 Law 40 Legge 19 February 2004, no. 40 'Norme in material di procreasionemedicalmenteassistita', art. 13(3)(b).
70 Kalaca, C. and Akin, A., 'The issue of sex selection in Turkey', *Hum Reprod*, 10 (1995): 1631–2.
71 Human Assisted Reproductive Technology Act 2004, s. 11.
72 Assisted Human Reproduction Act 2004, c. 2, s. 5 (1) (e).

involves Down syndrome,[73] and there has been concern that the use of PGD to identify the condition may serve to 'reinforce prejudices, stigmas and unjust social discrimination' against persons living with the condition.[74] It has, for example, been argued that the intellectual and social impairments associated with the syndrome have been arguably exaggerated and fail to take account of the fact that the disadvantages associated with the syndrome can be 'significantly alleviated by way of changes to family circumstances, the provision of social supports, and various forms of societal reform'.[75] There is a clear need to be more precise about what is a serious and non-serious genetic condition when PGD is used to determine the fate of embryos.

Pre-implantation genetic diagnosis for non-medical reasons: sex selection

ART programmes experienced early criticisms over prenatal procedures and their potential for sex selection.[76] In the development of ART, PGD remains ethically contentious given its potential use for non-medical sex-selection purposes. A controversial line is drawn where couples are not seeking PGD for medical reasons but to select a particular sex for their child.[77] Sex selection can be achieved through PGD, with a high degree of reliability.

Broadly speaking, there seems to have been general acceptance of the need to regulate to prevent the use of PGD for sex selection for non-medical reasons in most Western countries. The Victorian Parliament introduced the world's first legislation on reproductive technology,[78] and its latest legislation bans the procedure except for medical indications for serious genetic conditions 'to avoid the risk of transmission of a genetic abnormality or a genetic disease to the child'.[79] Guidelines in Australia, as in many other countries, prevent the use of PGD for non-medical sex selection. These guidelines are recognised by the Fertility Society of Australia in their professional codes of practice and must be complied with. The NHMRC *Ethical Guidelines* (2007), state as follows:

> 11.1 Sex selection is an ethically controversial issue. The Australian Health Ethics Committee believes that admission to life should not be conditional upon a child being a particular sex. Therefore,

73 Krahn, T., 'Regulating preimplantation genetic diagnosis: the case of Down's syndrome', *Medical Law Review*, 19 (2011): 157–91

74 Ibid., at p. 158.

75 Ibid., at p. 190.

76 Chappell, T., 'Sex selection for non-medical reasons', *Journal of Medical Ethics* 23 (1997): 120.

77 Pennings, G., 'Personal desires of patients and social obligations of geneticists: applying preimplantation genetic diagnosis for non-medical sex selection', *Prenatal Diagnosis*, 22 (2002): 1123.

78 Infertility (Medical Procedures) Act 1984, replaced by the Infertility Treatment Act 1995 and then the Assisted Reproductive Treatment Act 2008 (Vic.).

79 Assisted Reproductive Treatment Act 2008 (Vic.), s. 28.

pending further community discussion, sex selection (by whatever means) must not be undertaken except to reduce the risk of transmission of a serious genetic condition.

[. . .]

12.2 Pending further community discussion . . . PGD must not be used for:

prevention of conditions that do not seriously harm the person to be born;

selection of the sex of an embryo except to reduce the risk of transmission of a serious genetic condition; or

selection in favour of a genetic defect or disability in the person to be born.[80]

These NHMRC guidelines operate nationally and are the principal source of regulation in the states and territories that have not introduced specific legislation. These guidelines have been approved and recognised by the Reproductive Technology Accreditation Committee (RTAC) of the Fertility Society of Australia,[81] which can remove accreditation of clinics for breach of these guidelines.[82] However, a decision[83] of the Victorian Civil and Administrative Tribunal considered these guidelines and cast some doubt on the generally accepted view that they are considered mandatory by the ART clinics. The decision[84] of the VCAT concerned the transfer of sperm from a deceased husband from a Victorian to a New South Wales clinic to be used by the deceased's wife to conceive a child. While the Victorian legislation prohibited the export and use of a deceased person's sperm, except to places with similar procedures, the transfer was permitted under the NHMRC guidelines. The consent provisions in the Victorian Act and in the NHMRC guidelines were accepted as essentially equivalent. In his decision, the President of the VCAT stated that the 'NHMRC guidelines . . . do not have the same status as a statute; and should not be interpreted or applied like a statute. The guidelines are intended to be just that – guidelines'.[85]

Objections to non-medical sex selection often centre on concerns that a distinct preference for one sex (usually male) over the other will result in problematic demographic outcomes and reinforce sex-based discrimination. In some countries, however, there is evidence of bias and discrimination

80 NHMRC, *Ethical Guidelines* (2007), Guidelines 11.1 (sex selection) and 12.2 (restriction of use of PGD).

81 See general discussion in ch. 3, 'Regulation', VLRC Report (2007).

82 The Fertility Society of Australia develops guidelines for the operation and accreditation of clinics on a regular cycle. The RTAC adopted the NHMRC *Ethical Guidelines* as a component of its accreditation requirements.

83 *YZ* v. *Infertility Authority* [2005] VCAT 2655 (dealing with the 2004 version of NMHRC, *Ethical Guidelines*).

84 Ibid.

85 Ibid., at para. 68, at pp. 19–20.

against women,[86] with a significantly higher ratio of male births to female births in Bangladesh, Pakistan, South Korea, China and India[87] where sex-selection techniques are available and used. The problem arises that sex selection may lead to an imbalance in the sex ratio with the consequent social problem of individuals without marriage partners. This has been recorded in China[88] with its widening sex imbalance, which may not be sustained, however, into the future.[89] Equally, while this may be a plausible outcome in some countries, where the preference for male children is culturally embedded, there is less reason for concern in the liberal Western democracies. In fact, there is evidence from surveys in the USA and Germany that, rather than there being a distinct preference for one sex over the other, in fact, interest in non-medical sex selection, while rare,[90] is generally related to family balancing.[91] In addition, a UK survey demonstrated that there was no overall preference for either sex.[92] There is, finally, evidence based on the findings of other surveys which supports the view that the sex ratio would not be altered significantly were sex selection for non-clinical indications permitted, at least in Western countries.[93]

Historically, sex selection by parents could be achieved by resort to the grizzly practice of infanticide. Other folkloric sex-selection techniques are supplemented by various quasi-scientific methods, such as altering the pH balance of the vagina before intercourse, timing intercourse to coincide exactly with ovulation and even special positioning of the couple during coitus. In the late 1990s, an Anglo–French company marketed a sex-selection technique which claimed to be nearly 99 per cent successful. The system had a quasi-scientific spin, suggesting the Y chromosomes carried a positive charge whereas X chromosomes carry a negative charge,[94] but never appeared in any peer-reviewed journal. However, aside from this unproved claim, the X and Y chromosomes are the pathway to the technique of sex selection by sperm sorting. In sperm selection, the male sperm are separated into Y-chromosome

86 The President's Council on Bioethics (USA) (whose commission expired in 2009) Staff Working Paper (2003), cited in VLRC Report (2007), p. 82.

87 United Nations Population Fund, *The Promise of Equality: Gender Equity, Reproductive Health and the Millennium Development Goals, State of the World Population*, New York, 2005, p. 67.

88 Hull, T., 'Recent trends in sex ratios at birth in China', *Population and Development Review*, 16(1) (1990): 63–83, male live births exceed female births by a significant number (114: 100) and there is even evidence in some rural areas of ratios which are much higher (130/140: 100).

89 Tuljapurkar, S. *et al.*, 'High sex ratios in China's future', *Science*, 267 (1995): 874.

90 VLRC Report (2007), ch. 7, 'Sex selection', at pp. 80–2.

91 Dahl, E. *et al.*, 'Preconception sex selection demand and preference in the United States', *Fertility and Sterility*, 85 (2006): 468; Dahl, E. *et al.*, 'Preconception sex selection for non-medical reasons: a representative survey from Germany', *Hum Reprod*, 18 (2003): 2231.

92 A survey of some 2,300 pregnant women, Statham, H. *et al.*, 'Choice of baby's sex', *Lancet*, 341 (1993): 564–5, discussed in Liu, P. and Rose, G., 'Sex selection the right way forward', *Hum Reprod* 11 (1996): 2343.

93 Lilford, R., 'Sex selection – ethical issues', *Hum Reprod*, 10 (1995): 762–4.

94 Abbasi, K., 'The spin on sperm', *British Medical Journal*, 315 (1997): 1386.

sperm, which produce male conceptuses, or X-chromosome sperm, which produces females. The mother is then inseminated, or IVF conducted, using the chosen sperm to produce the desired sex of the child, although the results are not assured.[95]

Pre-implantation genetic diagnosis for sex selection: the legitimacy of a continuing ban

ART regulation, and now PGD, has proved controversial over the last 30 years.[96] The NHMRC guideline on restricting PGD for sex selection accepts that the procedure is an 'ethically controversial issue' and should not be undertaken. The issue of sex selection for non-medical reasons is not, however, closed and a range of arguments will be relevant to any future discussion of the issue of further liberalisation of access to PGD. Discussion will, for example, involve a consideration of whether there is general community acceptance of the continued ban. Community acceptance of such restrictions or their liberalisation can result in what has been described as 'regulatory legitimacy'.[97] Even if we accept that ART medical practice generally, and PGD in particular, will remain regulated in various ways, the issue of 'regulatory legitimacy' should focus on the *nature and extent* of the regulation and whether that regulation is 'driven by clear, outcome-based objectives'.[98] Equally, future discussion should involve consideration of the following relevant principles.

Autonomy

The liberal premise of democratic societies[99] places value on the ability of citizens to exercise personal autonomy, provided that their choices and actions do not cause undue harm to others.[100] The commitment to respect for autonomy has been a recurrent theme in ART regulation, and can be extended to include PGD. This principle was addressed in the Victorian Law Reform Commission enquiry on ART, which noted:

95 See Gillis, A., 'Finding the right sperm for the job', *Bio Science*, 45 (1995): 525. The technique of sorting the X and Y sperm is unreliable with 80 per cent accuracy, and estimates as low as 52/48 per cent accuracy. Sperm sorting is not available in Australia.
96 See Chalmers, D., 'Professional self-regulation and guidelines in ART', *Journal of Law and Medicine*, 9 (2002): 414–28; English, V., 'Autonomy versus protection – who benefits from the regulation of IVF?', *Human Reproduction*, 21 (2006): 3044–9.
97 Brownsword, R., 'Regulating human genetics: new dilemmas for a new millennium', *Med L R*, 12 (2004): 14–39.
98 Johnson, M., 'The art of regulation and the regulation of ART: the impact of regulation on research and clinical practice', *Journal of Law and Medicine*, 9 (2002): 399, at p. 413.
99 Dworkin, R., ch. 10, 'Liberty and moralism', in *Taking Rights Seriously*, London: Duckworth, 1977; see also Charlesworth, M., *Bioethics in a Liberal Society*, New York: Cambridge University Press, 1993, at pp. 10–29.
100 Warnock, M., 'Morality and the law: some programmes', *Cambrian LR* 18 (1987): 14–24.

> [s]ome people think ART is simply a medical procedure which should not be regulated differently from any other treatment . . . the principles of individual autonomy and reproductive freedom should prevail and decisions should be made by the treating doctor and the patient . . . [also] because there is no consensus in the community about what ethical principles should apply to reproductive choices, moral and ethical decisions should be made by the individuals concerned and not imposed by the state.[101]

Arguments, based on autonomy are often framed in terms of human rights, referenced, in some cases, to express constitutional rights.[102] In the United States, for example, the argument may be raised in relation to the implication of a constitutional procreative right.[103] Such arguments may also be framed with reference to the United Nations Universal Declaration of Human Rights 1948 and the basic human right to establish a family.[104]

However, two qualifications arise in relation to this personal autonomy approach. First, it is essential to distinguish between *positive* and *negative* rights. There is a distinction between the exercise of liberties free from restrictions from other parties and an exercise that involves others. The liberty to create the child, free from interference by others, is not the same as the right to choose the sex of a child by PGD, which requires the *intervention of professional third parties* to carry out the procedure. Of course, third-party intervention is required in *all* cases of ART. Perhaps more importantly, a couple can procreate *without* restriction by law but cannot *positively* require the state to provide PGD sex-selection services.[105] Second, the liberal premise of personal autonomy is qualified by the principle that the exercise of such freedom should not cause undue harm to others. Some harms, however, may occur and some will be allowable. The presumption in favour of liberty was expressed by John Stuart Mill in the following way:

> [T]he only purpose for which power can rightfully be exercised over any member of a civilised community against his will is to prevent harm to others. His own good, either physical or moral is not a sufficient warrant. He cannot rightfully be compelled to do or to forbear because it will be better for him to do so, because it will make him happier, because in the opinion of others, to do so would be wise or even right.[106]

This argument was mentioned in the Victorian Law Reform Commission Report:

101 See VLRC Report (2007), ch. 3, 'Regulation', at p. 45.
102 On the Canadian Charter and rights, see Boetzkes, E., 'Sex selection and the Charter', *Canadian Journal of Law and Jurisprudence*, 7 (1984): 173–4.
103 Robertson, J., 'Liberty, identity and human cloning', *Texas Law Review*, 76 (1998): 6.
104 Article 16.
105 This is equally applicable to ART in general.
106 Mill, J. S., *On Liberty*, New York: Knopf, 1859, at p. 72.

> Supporters of sex selection argue that choosing the sex of a child is a matter of reproductive autonomy to be determined by individuals in consultation with their doctors. Drawing on libertarian principles, they argue each person is entitled to live as they choose as long as they do not infringe upon the rights of others. The state may only interfere with these choices to prevent harm to others. Supporters of non-medical sex selection argue that without evidence of harm there is no valid justification for banning the procedure . . . By its very nature, sex selection establishes children's gender as a critical part of their identity.[107]

The case for harm resulting from PGD sex selection for non-medical reasons is by no means clear. Opponents of the prohibition of sex selection for non-medical reasons can argue that there is no evidence of harm and that there are no long-term studies showing that sex selection for non-medical reasons has 'harmed' any child.[108] Opponents also argue that there is no likelihood that parents will be harmed by sex selection for non-medical reasons, which fulfils their wishes and is more likely to promote their happiness. Finally, opponents reject any argument by analogy between adoption and donated gametes. Harm was established in adoption where some adopted children who were unable to trace their biological parents suffered psychological distress, later described as 'genealogical bewilderment'.[109] There is no such bewilderment in PGD sex selection as the parents' own gametes will be generally used. However, the use of PGD techniques has consequences that may affect not only the intending parents and future children, but may also involve symbolically important social values. Regulation may be justified in cases where there is an 'ethically controversial issue'. However, many of the objections to PGD in general, and PGD for sex selection in particular, focus on the important question of the welfare of the child to be born.

The welfare of the child

Regulation can be justified not just for the protection of citizens from undue harm but also to promote their welfare. It is the generally accepted principle in the family law of most countries that the welfare of any child is of paramount importance. This principle is accepted as a fundamental principle in the resolution of disputes about a child. The welfare of the child is a specific instance of the more general function of the law to protect those, such as the young or the mentally challenged, who cannot protect themselves.

The paramountcy of the welfare and interests of the child to be born rather than the wishes of the parents was affirmed in an important decision of the

107 VLRC Report (2007), ch. 7, 'Sex selection', at pp. 81–2.

108 Harris, J., 'Sex selection and regulated hatred', *Journal of Medical Ethics*, 31 (2005): 291; Savulescu, J., 'Sex selection: the case for', *Medical Journal of Australia*, 171 (1999): 373.

109 Triseliotis, J., *In Search of Origins: The Experience of Adopted People*, London: Routledge and Kegan Paul, 1973.

VCAT. Some Australian states have legislation dealing with ART,[110] but only Victoria has specific legislation on PGD.[111] Under the Victorian legislation, PGD must not be used 'with the purpose or a purpose of producing or attempting to produce a child of a particular sex' unless it is to 'avoid the risk of transmission of a genetic abnormality or a genetic disease'.[112] Applications for PGD and other applications under the Act are referable to a Patient Review Panel. The VCAT has the power to review administratively any decision of a Patient Review Panel, established under the Assisted Reproductive Treatment Act 2008 (Vic.). A couple had applied to the Patient Review Panel to approve a PGD procedure for non-medical reasons but this was refused. In a preliminary hearing, an application to the Patient Review Panel for PGD approval that was refused was held, in principle, to be reviewable by the VCAT.[113] At the later VCAT review hearing,[114] the facts surrounding the application for review were presented. The applicant couple had lost a child as a result of complications at birth. The circumstances were traumatic. Both partners were diagnosed as suffering from post-traumatic stress disorder (PTSD). The wife was under psychiatric care and wanted PGD to ensure that she could have a child of the same sex as the baby she had lost. The VCAT review received psychiatric evidence. Critically psychiatric opinion was presented that there was a 'small chance that . . . a child of a particular sex may assist . . . a person in coming to terms with a previous loss . . . [However] [t]here is little chance that it would have any direct beneficial impact on recovery from . . . PTSD.'[115]

The VCAT dismissed the application to review. The VCAT stressed the paramountcy of the best interests of the child to be born and quoted the

110 Assisted Reproductive Treatment Act 1988 (SA) (replacing Reproductive Technology Act 1988 (SA)); Assisted Reproductive Treatment Act 2008 (Vic.) (replacing Infertility Treatment Act 1995 (Vic.)); Assisted Reproductive Treatment Act 2007 (NSW) and Human Reproductive Technology Act 1991 (WA).

111 Ludlow, K., 'What about me? How far do we go in the best interest of the child in assisted reproductive technology?', *Queensland University of Technology Law and Justice Journal*, 6 (2006): 214.

112 Assisted Reproductive Treatment Act 2008 (Vic.), s. 28:

> 28 (1) A person carrying out a treatment procedure must not use gametes or an embryo, or perform the procedure in a particular way, with the purpose or a purpose of producing or attempting to produce a child of a particular sex.
>
> Penalty: 240 penalty units or 2 years imprisonment or both.
>
> (2) Subsection (1) does not apply if–
>
> (a) it is necessary for the child to be of a particular sex so as to avoid the risk of transmission of a genetic abnormality or a genetic disease to the child; or
>
> (b) the Patient Review Panel has otherwise approved the use of the gametes or embryo for the purpose or a purpose of producing or attempting to produce a child of a particular sex.

113 *JS & LS* v. *Patient Review Panel* (*Health and Privacy*) [2010] VCAT 1813.

114 *JS & LS* v. *Patient Review Panel* (*Health and Privacy*) [2011] VCAT 856 (8 April 2011).

115 Ibid., at p. 10.

conclusions of the Victorian Law Reform Commission (VLRC) Report on sex selection that:

> [t]he commission believes that the current legislative ban on sex selection for non-medical reasons should remain in place. Under the guiding principles recommended by the commission, the health and wellbeing of a child must be given priority. It is difficult to identify ways in which the best interests of the child are served by permitting sex selection for a non-medical reason. In the absence of available evidence about the likely effects on a child of having been selected for their sex, the commission has adopted a cautionary approach. The commission did not receive submissions to indicate that there is substantial community support for repealing the ban on non-medical sex selection. Moreover, the submissions that the commission did receive focused on the rights of parents, and not the health and wellbeing of the child to be born. The commission believes there should be significantly more community discussion and debate about sex selection for non-medical reasons before the ban could be repealed. This view is consistent with NHMRC guidelines and the UK government position.[116]

The VCAT concluded that this review application involved neither a case of sex selection to avoid the risk of transmission of a serious genetic disorder nor a saviour sibling case within the NHMRC guidelines[117] and stated:

> As sad and cruel as the loss of their child was . . . and as strong as their desire is to have a child of the same sex, we do not consider it is in the interests and welfare of a child to be born . . . In our view, the evidence was concerned predominantly with *the welfare and interests of the parents* . . . allowing them to sex select would . . . benefit their emotional wellbeing, allow them to move on, and so make them happier and better parents for all their children . . . are, in truth, arguments about the welfare and interests of the parents, not of a child to be born . . . We do not consider 'replacement' of a child who dies . . . gives *paramountcy to the interests or welfare of a child to be born*. It is again, when analysed, an argument, which requires a child to be born to have a particular characteristic, which serves a purpose or purposes of the parents . . . addition, we must consider the need to protect, at all times, the health and wellbeing of [the mother] . . . If there is a conflict between the welfare and interests of a child to be born, and the health and wellbeing of the person undergoing an ART procedure, then, given the paramountcy of the welfare and interests of the child to be born under s 5(a), the conflict must be resolved in favour of the child's welfare and interests. For these reasons we are not satisfied it would be in

116 VLRC Report (2007), at p. 82.
117 NHMRC, *Ethical Guidelines* (2007), Guidelines 11.1 and 12.1 respectively.

> the best interests of a child to be born to permit the use of an embryo which has been sex selected for the purpose of producing or attempting to produce a child of the desired sex. The application for review of the decision of the PRP is dismissed.[118]

Regulation of PGD sex selection represents one aspect of the role of the state in the regulation of family relationships. However, despite this VCAT decision, arguments about the welfare and best interests of the child can often be inconclusive. In the family law of most countries, the welfare of any child is of paramount importance; however, it is not clear how this principle is breached, if at all, by the selection of a child's sex by the parents. This is a unique case, but it does bear on the argument – sometimes raised by opponents of regulation – that the best interests of the child principle should generally be an irrelevant consideration in ART cases.[119]

Instrumentalism: means to an end

The principle of respect for persons requires in its application that people should not use other people solely as a means to their own ends.[120] Respect for persons requires that people should not be exploited. To treat others solely as means to an end, regardless of the desirability of the ends, must generally be considered morally objectionable.[121] In this regard, the VLRC mentioned that 'opponents of non-medical sex selection also say that entry to life should not be conditional upon being a particular sex, as each human has an inherent dignity that should be respected . . . Proponents argue that sex selection is incompatible with the belief that the parent–child relationship involves unconditional acceptance. Instead, sex selection for non-medical reasons places a burden on a child to fulfill a particular role.'[122]

Those who support the current ban on using PGD for non-medical sex selection may argue that using PGD in this way uses the future child for selfish parental ends. One commentator has gone so far as to say 'one may form the impression that these reasons [for seeking sex selection] assume a certain *light-heartened mindedness or frivolity* – a lack of depth in our thinking about what makes people matter, which is a symptom of consumer capitalism's tendency to make a marketable commodity out of whatever it can, even gender'.[123]

118 Ibid., at paras. 80–1, 84, 88–9; italics added.
119 Jackson, 'Conception'; Laing, J. and Oderberg, D., 'Artificial reproduction, the "welfare principle", and the common good', *Medical Law Review*, 13 (2005): 328–56.
120 'Humanity itself is a dignity: for a human being cannot be used merely as a means by any human being . . . but must always be used at the same time as an end' (Kant, I., *The Metaphysics of Morals*, ed. and trans. M. Gregor, Cambridge: Cambridge University Press, 1996, at p. 209).
121 Warnock Report, at p. 46.
122 VLRC Report (2007), at p. 82.
123 Chappell, T., 'Sex selection for non-medical reasons', *Journal of Medical Ethics*, 23 (1997): at p. 121; italics added.

Discrimination

The principles of the equality of all human beings and of non-discrimination are enshrined in the major international declarations on human rights and in the national legislation of many countries.[124] As we have already seen, arguments have been presented against PGD sex selection on the grounds that the practice has a tendency to reinforce discrimination. This was noted by the VLRC report, which noted that, '[o]pponents of the practice of sex selection argue that its use for non-medical reasons elevates the status of gender in society and contributes to sex discrimination'.[125] In a similar vein, the ACOG stated that it 'opposes meeting requests for sex selection that are based on the belief that offspring of a certain sex are inherently more valuable . . . [and that] may ultimately support *sexist practices*'.[126] Along the same lines, it has been proposed that there are threats in sex selection because of the likelihood of 'symbolically repudiating women as moral equals [and being] . . . unintentionally discriminatory'.[127] The danger of sex selection lurks in its tendency to shape and reinforce negative attitudes. This threat has also been expressed in the emotive terms of eugenics, even though sex selection is limited to a selection based on sex alone, and has nothing to do with the eugenic selection of desired genetic or physical attributes on a mass scale.[128]

On the other hand, it has also been argued that the preference for children of the same sex (or one of each) in a family may be reasonable and morally innocent.[129] On the reasoning of virtue-based ethics, motive and intention are significant in judging the moral worth of an action and, as such, sex selection may not be intrinsically sexist; for example, if a couple deliberately choose to have males by sex selection for the express purpose of raising them to oppose sexist social attitudes.[130]

Conclusion

An editorial in *Nature* reflected that, after some 30 years of ART, the evidence so far is that there are no major health problems with the procedures. However,

124 See Universal Declaration of Human Rights, 1948 and European Convention of Human Rights, 1950, Art. 14.

125 VLRC Report (2007), ch. 7, 'Sex selection', at p. 81.

126 See, 'ACOG committee opinion sex selection', *International Journal of Obstetrics and Gynecology*, 56 (1997): at p. 201; italics added.

127 Boetzkes, E., 'Sex selection and the Charter', *Canadian Journal of Law and Jurisprudence*, 7 (1984): 173–92, at p. 174.

128 Marteau, T., 'Sex selection: the rights of man or the thin edge of a eugenic wedge?', *British Medical Journal*, 306 (1993): 1704. Sex selection is very far from some of Galton's extreme comments on eugenics, such as: 'A democracy cannot endure unless it be composed of able citizens; therefore it must in self defence withstand the free introduction of degenerate stock' (Sir Francis Galton FRS, *Memories of My Life*, London: Methuen, 1908, at p. 312).

129 See Overall, C., *Ethics and Human Reproduction: A Feminist Analysis*, London: Unwin Hyman, 1987.

130 Such an intention may, of course, offend the principle of respect for persons by using a person as a means to an end of political change.

few countries require long-term data to be maintained which would allow research on subtle problems that may arise in the health profiles of these children, particularly in later adult life. More relevantly, this editorial also predicted that personalised medicine may promote widespread use of genetic screening in ART programmes, building on the availability of PGD.[131] This may prove to be a rather over-enthusiastic prediction, however, in view of the fact that PGD is only carried out in half a dozen centres in Australia.[132] Moreover, PGD procedures are currently only available in the private sector and no public funding subsidy is available through the Australian national Medicare health rebate scheme. Expanding availability would require a major injection of public funding which, for the foreseeable future at least, seems more than unlikely.

It can safely be concluded that the use of PGD for serious medical conditions is probably relatively uncontroversial. There would also seem to be general agreement that it is ethically acceptable to use PGD for sex selection to avoid X-linked genetic diseases. However, like the established procedures of ART, the newer PGD technique raises significant issues about the importance of 'reproductive freedom' and 'decisional privacy',[133] the argument being that states should not interfere with reproductive choices which are largely characterised as private.[134] The scope of 'reproductive freedom' and 'decisional privacy' is uncertain in the case of the current restrictions on PGD in Western countries. This uncertainty is significantly sharpened where PGD is wanted not for medical reasons but for sex selection. This is controversial on its own, but even more so when coupled with the possible – even probable – outcome of PGD – that is, the discarding and destruction of unselected embryos.[135]

The current NHMRC *Ethical Guidelines* (2007) in relation to PGD are not expressed in definitive terms. There are two important moderating qualifications to the current restriction in Guideline 11.1, which includes the caveats that this is the belief of the 'Australian Health Ethics Committee' and that this position is 'pending further community discussion'.[136] Similarly, Guideline 12.2 contains the caveat that the position may be subject to 'pending further community discussion'. Finally, Guideline 12.5.1 states that people seeking testing should be 'encouraged to consider the following factors when deciding the appropriateness of PGD', including the likelihood of false positive and false negative results; genetic and clinical information about the specific condition;

131 *Nature*, 454 (17 July 2008): 253.
132 One in Queensland; two in WA; one in Melbourne; and two in Sydney (with tests from one sent to Melbourne).
133 Laing and Oderberg, 'Artificial reproduction'; Priaulx, N., 'Rethinking progenitive conflict: why reproductive autonomy matters', *Medical Law Review*, 16 (2008): 169–200.
134 See, as an example, Egozcue, J., 'Sex selection: why not?', *Hum. Reprod.*, 8 (1993): 1777.
135 Scott, R., 'The uncertain scope of reproductive autonomy in preimplantation genetic diagnosis and selective abortion', *Medical Law Review*, 13 (2005): 291–327.
136 NHMRC, *Ethical Guidelines* (2007), Guideline 11.1 (sex selection).

their previous reproductive experience; the distinction between the genotypic and phenotypic expression of the condition; the variable range of effects of the condition, including the likely rate of degeneration in the case of progressive disorders; the experiences of families living with the condition; the likely availability of effective therapy or management now and in the future; and the extent of social support available.

These guidelines are ambivalent and will be reconsidered and possibly revised in Australia in the next review of the NHMRC Ethical Guidelines to be conducted by the Australian Health Ethics Committee, following the statutorily required public consultation on the guidelines. One of the interesting questions will be whether the current, apparently strict, guidelines on PGD for sex selection may be relaxed and liberalised, allowing parents, albeit probably rarely, to choose the sex of their future offspring for personal reasons rather than medical indications. What is certain is that these NHMRC guidelines will continue to be applied in Australia to regulate PGD and thereby purportedly to represent the values of society. The guidelines operate nationally and have been approved and recognised by the RTAC of the Fertility Society of Australia, which can remove accreditation for clinics for breach of these guidelines.[137] Although, as noted, the Victorian legislation is unique in Australia in that it includes criminal penalties for the unapproved use of PGD, none have ever been imposed and the couple and practitioner can apply for an administrative ruling on the procedure from the Patient Review Panel.[138]

Regulation of PGD, like ART services in general, is affected by the internationalised trade in these services and the capacity of those with enough money to cross borders and use services in less regulated jurisdictions. PGD restrictions, like ART restrictions, in one country may be avoided by crossing the border into less or non-regulated states (referred to as 'reproductive tourism').[139] This regulatory cosmopolitanism enables the restrictions of Australia to be avoided by using PGD services in other countries, such as Thailand,[140] which does not prohibit PGD for sex selection. Interestingly, the website of a major ART provider in Australia refers to four Thailand providers.[141] Sex selection for

137 In Australia, the Fertility Society of Australia (FSA) develops guidelines for the operation of the infertility clinics and accredits clinics on an accreditation cycle. The RTAC adopted the NHMRC, *Ethical Guidelines* (2007), as a component of their accreditation requirements, noting the comments of VCAT in *YZ* v. *Infertility Authority* [2005] VCAT 2655.

138 Assisted Reproductive Treatment Act 2008 (Vic.), s. 28.

139 This can also occur within federal systems, like Australia, with different state and territory regulations, Parliament of Australia, Senate, Legal and Constitutional Affairs Reference Committee, *Donor Conception Practices in Australia*, February 2011.

140 See www.health-tourism.com/pgd/asia-7 (accessed 23/01/2012).

141 Genea, formerly Sydney, IVF on their website, on the page, 'Sex selection with PGD', state: 'Meanwhile, we are frequently asked where IVF for sex selection is available outside of Australia. Geographically the clinic that is closest to Australia and which we can recommend is Superior ART in Bangkok, Thailand' (www.genea.com.au/How-we-can-help/Our-Services/Preimplantation-Genetic-Diagnosis—PGD-/Sex-selection-with-PGD/Sex-selection-with-PGD, accessed 31/01/2012).

non-medical reasons, using PGD, is also available in ART programmes in other Asian countries, such as China, the Philippines and India.[142]

Finally, in line with the wider public policy reasons for ART regulation, it can be argued that continuation of some form of PGD regulation is justified on the following grounds:[143] PGD will be delivered within ART programmes, which are licensed, accredited, monitored and audited under legislation and codes of practice to ensure the quality of services provided. Regulation can prohibit the use of a technique but also ensure that the technique is done well, particularly at an early stage in its development. Regulation can ensure quality control, including accurate record keeping to assess the development of PGD supported by evidence. Second, given that ART is a worldwide multi-billion dollar industry, regulation can contribute to ensuring proper market quality of services provided.[144] In this respect, it is desirable that similar, or at least harmonised, international regulations are developed to avoid jurisdiction tourism, but this is unlikely to be achievable. The different cultural and social conditions of societies, particularly those that favour sex selection make such harmonisation unlikely. Most importantly, to a degree, regulation can balance public concerns about PGD with claims for 'reproductive freedom' and effectively promote the state's regulatory purposes.[145]

142 National Guidelines for the Accreditation, Supervision and Regulation of ART Clinics in India, www.icmr.nic.in/art/art_clinics.htm at 64 (accessed 05/04/2011).

143 Also, regulation can protect the clinicians involved from potential malpractice actions as they have the defence of acting within the parameters of legislation.

144 See Deech, R., 'Playing God: who should regulate embryo research?', *Brooklyn Journal of International Law*, 32 (2006): 321–38.

145 Ayres, I. and Braithwaite, J., *Responsive Regulation*, New York/Oxford: Oxford University Press, 1992.

8 Cartwright calamities, Frankenstein monsters and the regulation of PGD in New Zealand

*Jeanne Snelling**

> This is a complex Bill about complex matters affecting the future of humanity . . . We have a potential Cartwright-like calamity on our hands. We have the potential to prevent disease and deformity. We can also venture into Dr Frankenstein-like territory where, as Mary Shelley warned us, in our search to become God we may create monsters.[1]

Introduction

In 1996 Dianne Yates, Labour MP and author of the above quote introduced a private member's bill into the New Zealand Parliament that proposed, for the first time, to establish a specific legislative framework regulating human-assisted reproduction and research. The impetus behind the introduction of the Bill was apparent in Yates's comments that – with the oblique reference to the Cartwright Inquiry – invoked both the potential for unethical medical research and the spectre of future human monstrosities unless there was immediate legislative intervention.[2] The parliamentary process that followed resulted in the enactment of the Human Assisted Reproductive Technology Act 2004 eight years later.

New Zealand was comparatively slow to introduce primary legislation governing assisted human reproduction and research. The approach adopted

* The author would like to gratefully acknowledge the support of the Centre for Law and Policy in Emerging Technologies (Faculty of Law, University of Otago) in preparing this chapter.

1 (23 April 1997) 7 NZPD 1228.

2 The reference to 'Cartwright' is to the Inquiry chaired by (now) Dame Sylvia Cartwright. The Inquiry was appointed to examine the conduct of Professor Herbert Green, a doctor at National Women's Hospital who undertook research into the natural history of carcinoma *in situ* (CIS) or pre-cancerous abnormalities of the cervix. Green, in contrast to what became the prevailing medical opinion and growing medical evidence, considered that CIS did not proceed to invasive cancer. *Inter alia*, he failed to inform patients of cervical abnormalities and that they were being treated conservatively. Some of the women subsequently developed invasive cancer. See *The Report of the Cervical Cancer Inquiry into Allegations Concerning the Treatment of Cervical Cancer at National Women's Hospital and Into other Related Matters* (Auckland, 1988).

by the government during the 1980s and early 1990s was characterised by a preference for minimal state intervention. This was primarily based on the view that a specific legislative framework was unnecessary, given the particular context of New Zealand, but also implicitly upheld the concept of reproductive liberty by averring that state intervention, particularly in the sphere of *private* reproductive decisions, required justification. Arguably this reticence, given New Zealand's track record in matters of reproduction, was uncharacteristic.

A history of reproductive control

The ideologies of pronatalism, social purity and the concept of motherhood as a vocation were characteristic of colonial New Zealand.[3] These views converged in the concomitant reluctance to ascribe to women any kind of control over their own fertility. In the early twentieth century, organised campaigns for access to birth control, so that even *married* couples could space or limit their families to mitigate the effects of uncontrolled fertility, were unsuccessful.[4] Instead while the Māori population grew, the falling white European birth rate sparked concern that burgeoning numbers in Asian countries could overrun 'civilised' society.[5] This led to exhortations for larger families.[6] The threat of war in the 1930s served only to further fuel the call to 'populate or perish' – an anathema given the poverty experienced by families at the time.[7]

In 1936, faced with evidence that the number of women dying from abortion-related complications was increasing significantly, the government

3 Dalziel, R., 'The Colonial Helpmeet', in Binney, J. (ed.), *The Shaping of History*, Wellington: Bridget Williams, 2001 at pp. 185, 191; Bunkle, P., 'The origins of the women's movement in New Zealand: the Women's Christian Temperance Union 1885–1895', in Bunkle, P. and Hughes, B. (eds), *Women in New Zealand Society Auckland*, Auckland: George Allen & Unwin, 1980 at p. 73.

4 Brookes, B., 'Housewives' depression: the debate over abortion and birth control in the 1930s', in Binney, *Shaping of History*, at p. 197.

5 Parkes, C. 'New Zealand Women and Access to Birth Control' in Corey, S. (ed), *Standing in the Sunshine: A History of New Zealand Women Since they Won the Vote*, Auckland: Viking, 1993, at p. 70. Between 1880 and 1920 the average number of children born to European women fell from 6.5 to 2.4. See Van Der Krogt, C., 'Exercising the utmost vigilance: the Catholic campaign against contraception in New Zealand during the 1930s', *Journal of Religious History*, 22 (1998): 320, at p. 322, citing Olssen, E. and Andree, L., 'Towards a history of the European family in New Zealand', in Koopman-Boyden, P. (ed.), *Families in New Zealand Society*, Wellington: Methuen, 1978.

6 Parkes, C. 'New Zealand Women and Access to Birth Control' in Corey, S. (ed), *Standing in the Sunshine: A History of New Zealand Women Since they Won the Vote*, Auckland: Viking, 1993, at p. 70. See also Oliver, W., 'Social policy in New Zealand: an historical overview', in *The Report of the Royal Commission on Social Policy, Te Kōmihana A Te Karauna Mō Ngā Āhuatanga-Ā-Iwi* (April 1988, vol. 1), at p. 23.

7 Dominion Settlement and Population Association, *New Zealand Must Populate or Perish*, cited in Parkes, C. 'New Zealand Women and Access to Birth Control' in Corey, S. (ed), *Standing in the Sunshine: A History of New Zealand Women Since they Won the Vote*, Auckland: Viking, 1993, at p. 71.

appointed a Committee of Inquiry to investigate the issue of abortion.[8] The Inquiry estimated that around 6,000 abortions were performed annually in New Zealand, 4,000 of which were criminal.[9]

Although appointed to consider abortion, the Inquiry became a platform for debate over reproductive control in general. With the decline in family size a major consideration, the Committee recommended that the sale of contraceptives to unmarried people should be illegal, and was opposed to any liberalisation of the abortion law.[10] Ultimately the report appealed:

> to the womanhood of New Zealand, in so far as selfish and unworthy motives have entered into our family life, to consider the grave physical and moral dangers, not to speak of the dangers of race suicide which are involved.[11]

The Committee's report evinced little concern for women's health, fertility or individual autonomy, which were subjugated to the overriding duty to the state to procreate.[12] Similarly, the abortion law reform undertaken in the 1970s reflected an impoverished view of reproductive liberty. This reform, which resulted in what remains New Zealand's current abortion law, is largely a result of the 1975 Royal Commission of Inquiry into contraception, sterilisation and abortion, which reported in 1977.[13]

An event that contributed to the Commission's appointment was the Court of Appeal decision in *R* v. *Woolnough*.[14] Although the Crimes Act 1961 established that abortion was a criminal offence, the legislature had left open what constituted the meaning of 'unlawfully' procuring an abortion.[15] The Court held that (at least in regard to the early stages of pregnancy) a defence to the crime of abortion was not limited to the doctrine of necessity. Consequently a '*bona fide* intention to preserve the health [as distinct from life] of the mother

8 The provisions governing abortion were contained in ss. 220–223 Crimes Act 1908. It was considered that these allowed 'of no interference except to save the *life* of the mother' (italics in original). See Committee of Inquiry into Various Aspects of Abortion in New Zealand, *Report of the Committee of Inquiry into Various Aspects of Abortion in New Zealand* (Wellington, 1937, McMillan, D., chair), at p. 20.

9 Ibid., at p 5.

10 Ibid., at pp. 21, 27.

11 Ibid., at p. 27.

12 Brookes, 'Housewives' depression', at 207.

13 Royal Commission on Contraception, Sterilisation and Abortion, *Report of the Royal Commission of Inquiry: Contraception, Sterilisation and Abortion in New Zealand* (Wellington, 1977, McMullin, D., chair; hereafter *Report* (1977)).

14 [1977] 2 NZLR 508.

15 Crimes Act 1961, s. 183. The Crimes Act 1961 was preceded by the Crimes Act of 1908. The Crimes Act 1908 was preceded by the Criminal Code Act 1883, and before that by the Offences Against the Person Act 1866. All criminalised the *unlawful* administration of a poison/noxious thing or use of an instrument with the intent to procure a miscarriage; or the supply or procurement of a poison or noxious thing or instrument or thing intended to be *unlawfully* used to procure miscarriage.

from serious harm' constituted justification for lawful abortion.[16] The decision extended lawful abortion beyond instances where the woman's life was at risk and briefly clarified the scope of lawful abortion in New Zealand, until recommendations made by the Commission of Inquiry were subsequently implemented by Parliament.

The Commission noted in its Report that the role of women in society had changed over time, and that it was generally accepted that a woman had a right to decide whether she married, whether she had children, and if so how many.[17] However, rights claims in respect of an established pregnancy were considered problematic, because the Commission considered that, from the moment of implantation, the foetus had a status entitling it to preservation and protection. This did not confer an absolute right to life, but rather 'should yield in the face of compelling competing interests'.[18] Consequently it concluded that any rights in relation to an established pregnancy must be 'considered against the status of the unborn child'.[19] But 'status' proved to be a malleable concept for the Commission.

The Commission accepted that abortion should be lawful when the pregnancy posed a 'serious danger' to the life of the mother but it was far less sympathetic when there was no such threat to life.[20] It was suggested that women in the early stages of pregnancy were prone to biologically induced irrationality and that such psychological stress was insufficient to justify abortion, which should only be available if continuance of the pregnancy would pose *serious* danger to physical or mental health.[21] In contrast, the Commission advocated the

16 [1977] 2 NZLR 508, at 517.

17 Royal Commission on Contraception, Sterilisation and Abortion, *Report* (1977), at p. 192. Yet, it was apparent that even this perceived right to control one's fertility was being infringed in practice, with the Commission expressly noting that for a 'large number' of young unmarried women, some doctors were making abortion conditional on sterilisation (at p. 194). While such coerced sterilisations were not subjected to judicial scrutiny, doctors have been prosecuted for sterilising competent women without the woman's knowledge or consent during a Caesarean section in other jurisdictions. See *Winn et al.* v. *Alexander* [1940] 3 DLR 778; [1940] OWN 238; *Murray* v. *McMurchy* [1949] 2 DLR 442; *Kelton* v. *District of Columbia* 413 A2d 919 (DC 1980). See also more recently *A.S.* v. *Hungary* (2007) 45 EHRR SE1.

18 Royal Commission on Contraception, Sterilisation and Abortion, *Report* (1977), at p. 192.

19 Ibid., at p. 194.

20 Ibid., at p. 270.

21 Ibid. 'It is well accepted medically that in the first trimester of pregnancy women undergo biological changes as a result of which some suffer from anxiety, insomnia, and emotional outbursts . . . it would be wrong, on the view which we have taken of the status of the unborn child, to terminate a pregnancy because of some psychological stress which was relatively short in duration or of relatively mild intensity.' Consequently the Crimes Act 1961, s. 187A(1)(a) provides that an abortion under 20 weeks is lawful if 'the continuance of the pregnancy would result in serious danger (*not being danger normally attendant upon childbirth)* to the life, or to the physical or mental health, of the woman or girl' (italics added). When first enacted, it was also required that '*the danger cannot be averted by any other means*', to ensure that abortion on life or health grounds could only be invoked as a last resort. However the additional restriction was repealed by the Crimes Amendment Act 1978, s. 2(1).

availability of prenatal testing if there was substantial risk of foetal abnormality.[22] Significantly, the Commission rejected abortion on the grounds of rape because a rape provision could be the 'subject of abuse' – essentially meaning that some women seeking abortion would lie in order to obtain one.[23] Instead, any claim of rape should merely be 'taken into account' by doctors making the abortion decision, but should not be a ground for abortion in itself.[24]

The Commission expressed a very different view towards incest, as it was considered highly unlikely that 'unjustified' complaints of incest would be made. Ultimately it opined that 'no sanctity can be attached to a pregnancy' which has resulted from incest.[25] Similarly, the pregnancy of a severely subnormal woman or girl had 'little, if any, status' and could constitute a ground for abortion.[26]

Rape, incest and sexual intercourse with a severely subnormal woman or girl were (and still are) criminal offences. Precisely why protected status could attach to a foetus resulting from an alleged rape, but not incest or in the case of a subnormal woman is unclear. A cynical view may be that protected status or sanctity attached only to pregnancies that were considered genetically fit – yet the Commission included non-biological relationships within the incest grounds.[27] It may possibly be inferred that incest appeared to transgress social norms to a greater extent than rape and consequently the pregnancy that resulted from incest (even non-biological) was less worthy of protection than was the pregnancy resulting from rape. What is clear is that, apart from instances where a pregnancy posed *serious* danger to a woman's life or health or

22 Royal Commission on Contraception, Sterilisation and Abortion, *Report* (1977), at p. 211. These grounds were expressed as a 'substantial risk that if a child were born it would suffer from such physical or mental abnormalities as to be seriously handicapped'.

23 This is despite the view expressed by the Commission that: '[M]ost people would regard it as quite unreasonable that a woman should be compelled to bear the child of someone who has made a violent sexual assault upon her against her will. We share that view' (ibid., at p. 212).

24 While rape in general has always been a crime under the Crimes Act 1961, s. 128(3) originally conferred spousal immunity on a husband who raped his wife, unless the couple were legally separated or divorced and no longer living together. Marital rape only became a criminal offence with the enactment of the Crimes Amendment Act 1985.

25 Royal Commission on Contraception, Sterilisation and Abortion, *Report* (1977), at p. 214.

26 Ibid., at p. 215. Section 138(2) of the Crimes Act, as amended by the Crimes Amendment Act 2005, now makes it an offence to have exploitative sexual connection with a person with significant impairment, rather than with a woman or girl who is severely subnormal.

27 The Commission extended this abortion ground to relationships between a man and girl that did not involve blood ties, but where a girl under 21 was living under a man's care and protection. The Crimes Act 1961 made sexual intercourse in such circumstances unlawful. Whereas section 130 of the Crimes Act 1961 limits incest to blood ties, section 131 also made it an offence to have intercourse with a girl living under a man's care and protection. This included a stepdaughter, foster daughter or a ward living with a man as a member of his family; or a girl who is at the time of the intercourse or attempted intercourse living with him as a member of his family and is under his care or protection. Section 7 of the Crimes Amendment Act 2005 substituted section 131, and now makes it an offence to have sexual intercourse with a 'dependent family member', which is defined in s. 131 A.

in the case of foetal abnormality, the Commission only contemplated abortion in circumstances when there was an absence of 'fault' on the part of the woman.

Evidently a right to reproductive liberty did not figure in the Commission's report at all but nor, it seems, did a consistent view of the moral status of the foetus. It was expendable in some circumstances, but not others, which seems to incorporate a questionable judgement as to the moral or social 'worth' of a pregnancy. There was an appreciable lack of concern for the woman carrying the pregnancy, the focus being rather on whether the foetus had 'sanctity' or protected status and on the likelihood of a woman's veracity regarding the circumstances of conception. It was apparent that a major objective was to inculcate, and enforce, certain moral values and virtues, primarily in respect of women and their reproductive choices.[28]

The recommendations were eventually codified in subsequent amendments to the Crimes Act 1961 and currently provide the scope of lawful abortion in New Zealand for pregnancies of not more than 20 weeks' gestation.[29] Despite this, New Zealand's abortion statistics are comparable to Canada and the USA[30] because of physicians' liberal interpretation of what was intended to be very illiberal legislation.[31] The reality is that most New Zealand women have *de facto*, if not *de jure*, access to state-funded abortion. This involves a euphemistic interpretation of abortion on mental health grounds[32] assuring access to legal and safe abortion for many women, despite a seemingly restrictive legislative

28 Paula Abrams argues that States' 'willingness to authorize exemptions from abortion restrictions based on incest, rape, severe birth defects, physical harm to woman, etc., strongly suggests that the legislative goal of protection of potential life is fraught with assumptions about women's behavior as it relates to reproductive function. Exemptions for rape and incest establish a "fault" standard whereby women who involuntarily engage in intercourse are excused. The exemptions for severe birth defects reflect a state conclusion that the protection of potential life does not prevail in all circumstances. An exemption based on physical harm to the woman suggests that a woman's only legitimate interest in not carrying a pregnancy to term must be grounded in physical damage' ('Tradition of reproduction', *Arizona Law Review*, 37 (1995): 453, at 499, citing Siegel, R., 'Reasoning from the body: a historical perspective on abortion regulation and questions of equal protection', *Stan. L Rev*, 44 (1992): 261, at p. 365).

29 See Crimes Amendment Act 1977, s. 6 that inserted s. 187A into the Crimes Act 1961. However not all of the Commission's recommendations were immediately implemented by the government. The Crimes Amendment Act 1978 subsequently inserted the abortion grounds for foetal abnormality (Crimes Act 1961, s. 187A (1)(aa)) the following year. Abortions after 20 weeks are only lawful if necessary to save the life of the woman or to 'prevent serious permanent injury to her physical or mental health' (Crimes Act 196, s. 187A (3)).

30 *Right to Life New Zealand Inc.* v. *Abortion Supervisory Committee* [2008] 2 NZLR 825, para. [3], *per* Miller J.

31 This abortion rate is not as anomalous as it may seem. In the report of the Victorian Law Reform Commission, *Law of Abortion: Final Report* (Melbourne, 2008), at p. 33, it was noted that the restrictiveness or otherwise of legislation is not predictive of abortion rates. It cited a Guttmacher–World Health Organization report that found that 'unrestrictive abortion laws do not predict a high incidence of abortion, and by the same token, highly restrictive abortion laws are not associated with low abortion incidence' (see Sedgh, G. *et al.*, 'Induced abortion: estimated rates and trends worldwide', *The Lancet*, 370 (2007): 1338, at 1343).

32 Cf. *Right to Life New Zealand Inc.* v. *Abortion Supervisory Committee* [2008] 2 NZLR 825.

approach, but this arguably also undermines the integrity of the law and diminishes reproductive rights claims.

Despite the assumed legitimacy of state intervention in citizens' reproductive lives historically, there was less apparent enthusiasm for state involvement in the early years of assisted reproduction.

The history of legislative intervention in human-assisted reproduction and research

The birth of Louise Brown's first IVF peer in New Zealand occurred in 1984. It was accompanied by requests[33] for the appointment of an official body to examine the issues raised by assisted reproduction – as had occurred in similar jurisdictions.[34] However, the response of New Zealand's Labour government, a notably less interventionist government than that which had preceded it, was comparatively muted.[35]

Nevertheless, the Law Reform Division of the Department of Justice released an *Issues Paper* for public consultation in 1985.[36] The tone both of the consultation document and the resulting *Summary of Submissions Received on the Issues Paper* (*Summary*) was that assisted reproduction was a reality in New Zealand; that attention should be focused on the issues raised by this rather than on prohibition; and that different moral views could not diminish the 'deep human need to procreate'.[37] The *Summary* indicated an official view that assisted reproduction was generally considered a primarily private matter and consequently the preference was to take a watching brief and a restrained approach, despite calls for legislative intervention. It was stated unequivocally that:

> the waiting lists for IVF at NW's Hospital suggest very strongly that many New Zealand women do want to take advantage of the new techniques. If this trend is to be reversed, the onus of changing public

33 Members of the Royal Society of New Zealand, the New Zealand Law Society, the Medical Council and the New Zealand Medical Association sought the appointment of a standing committee, while the New Zealand Catholic Bishops called for a parliamentary inquiry into IVF. See Coney, S. and Else, A., 'Assisted reproductive technologies timeline', in Coney, S. and Else, A. (eds), *Protecting Our Future: The Case for Greater Regulation of Assisted Reproductive Technology: A Discussion Document*, Auckland: Women's Health Action Trust, 1999, at p. 3.

34 Waller, L., *Interim Report of the Committee to Consider the Social, Ethical and Legal Issues Arising from In Vitro Fertilisation* (Victoria, 1982); *Report of the Committee of Enquiry into Human Fertilisation and Embryology*, Cmnd 9312 (Warnock Report), London: Stationery Office, 1984.

35 The Lange-led Labour government replaced the National Government led by Prime Minister Robert Muldoon in 1984 instituting what was dubbed 'market philosophy'. Bill Atkin describes the period of government up to the 1990s as: 'affected by a New Right ideology with its minimalist state and market focus' that correspondingly influenced its approach to regulating assisted reproduction ('Assisted human reproduction: New Zealand's "third way" model', in Wardle, L. and Williams, C. (eds), *Family Law: Balancing Interests and Pursuing Priorities*, Buffalo, NY: William S. Hein, 2007, at p. 215).

36 Department of Justice (Law Reform Division), *New Birth Technologies – An Issues Paper on AID, IVF and Surrogate Motherhood* (Wellington, 1985). There were 164 submissions received.

37 Ibid., at p. 8.

> opinion must rest on those who oppose it. The challenge for policy makers – whether in the field or in government – is how best to respond to the facts that the techniques exist, that they are practiced, and that there is a public demand for them.[38]

Around the same time that the United Kingdom introduced the Human Fertilisation and Embryology Act 1990, the New Zealand medical profession assumed a proactive position, undertaking two major initiatives of its own volition. Fertility service providers sought voluntary accreditation from the Reproductive Technology Accreditation Committee (RTAC), which was the accrediting body of the Fertility Society of Australia,[39] a practice that subsequently became a requirement of their professional body (RNZCOG). In addition, the Medical Council of New Zealand (MCNZ) also commissioned a report into issues involving human-assisted reproduction and research from the Bioethics Research Centre of the University of Otago. The resulting report advocated specific legislative measures and the appointment of a licensing authority to oversee assisted reproductive practice and research.[40]

The government subsequently established two new committees in 1993. First, the Minister of Health established an Interim National Ethics Committee on Assisted Reproductive Technologies (INECART) to consider applications for assisted reproductive procedures and research (taking over the role of Regional Ethics Committees). Second, a two-person Ministerial Committee on Assisted Reproductive Technologies (MCART) was appointed by the Minister of Justice to report on options for the future.[41]

The MCART report was notable for several reasons, not least its strong bi-cultural emphasis, as well as the similarly strong theme that simply 'transplanting' a regulatory system from another jurisdiction was not appropriate in the New Zealand context. Also of significance was the formulation of a set of principles not only to guide, but also to justify, any regulatory intervention. These principles included: respect for the dignity of human life; informed

38 See Department of Justice (Law Reform Division), *New Birth Technologies: A Summary of Submission Received on the Issues Paper* (Wellington, 1986), at p. 39.

39 The Reproductive Technology Accreditation Committee (RTAC) imposed extensive professional, ethical and laboratory requirements on fertility service providers through its *Code of Practice*.

40 A Report for the Medical Council of New Zealand by the Bioethics Research Centre Otago, *Biotechnology Revisited: Ethical and Legal Issues in the Application of Biotechnology to Medical Practice* (Wellington: Medical Council of New Zealand, 1991), at p. 2. It recommended legislation ensuring a right for donor-conceived offspring to access donor information, as well as certain prohibitions such as limits on embryo research, prohibiting therapeutic and reproductive cloning, germ-line modification and the creation of human–animal chimera.

41 Ministerial Committee on Assisted Reproductive Technologies, *Assisted Human Reproduction: Navigating Our Future* (Wellington, Department of Justice, 1994), at p. 1. Bill Atkin (a legal academic from Victoria University) and Dr Paparangi-Reid (a medically qualified health researcher of Te Rarawa and Te Aupöuri descent) submitted the report in July of the following year.

consent; a right to know one's genetic origins; the right to individual autonomy; respect for obligations under the Treaty of Waitangi;[42] and the paramount importance of the welfare of any child born.

MCART was neither in favour of introducing specific legislation nor of establishing a licensing body such as the United Kingdom's Human Fertilisation and Embryology Authority (HFEA). The reasons for eschewing a licensing body were strictly pragmatic: New Zealand had only a small number of fertility services and so was in a different position to other jurisdictions such as the UK; a licensing system would merely replicate the accreditation procedures provided by RTAC; it would be difficult to find suitably qualified people to perform licensing functions who were independent of the clinics themselves; and it would be costly to the taxpayer, providers and consumers.[43] However, MCART favoured legislative amendments to the Medical Practitioners Act 1968 to enhance the professional self-regulation of fertility services and also recommended that a national advisory body, the Council on Assisted Human Reproduction, be established.[44]

Ultimately, the Department of Justice did not establish a Council on Assisted Human Reproduction. Instead it recommended that the National Ethics Committee on Assisted Human Reproduction (NECAHR), a body that succeeded INECART, perform some of the roles that MCART envisaged for its proposed Council on Assisted Human Reproduction.[45]

Ultimately, MCART's report established a platform for principled policy-making that relied on professional self-regulation being given greater 'teeth', and oversight by an advisory body rather than legislative intervention, with four exceptions potentially justifying parliamentary scrutiny in the future.[46] It was clearly cognisant of human rights – including autonomy rights and the rights of Māori pursuant to the Treaty of Waitangi – as well as the need for justification of state incursions on reproductive liberty or indigenous culture. Arguably it was a high point in terms of the emphasis it placed on autonomy and rights.

42 Representatives of the British Crown and Māori signed the Treaty of Waitangi in 1840. Although the Treaty is not part of domestic law, it is now generally viewed as part of New Zealand's Constitution alongside the New Zealand Bill of Rights Act 1990 and the Constitution Act 1986.

43 Ministerial Committee on Assisted Reproductive Technologies, *Assisted Human Reproduction*, at p. 43.

44 This would be a non-statutory advisory body that would act as a 'public watchdog'; assist with the formulation of codes and guidelines; advise both the government and the national ethics committee; and liaise with professional agencies involved in assisted reproduction.

45 See Officials Committee, *Assisted Human Reproduction: A Commentary on the Report of the Ministerial Committee on Assisted Reproductive Technologies* (Department of Justice 1995); Daniels, K. and Hargreaves, K., 'The policy and ethics of surrogacy in New Zealand: who is left holding the baby?', *Otago Bioethics Report*, 6 (1997): 1.

46 These were 'matters relating to cloning, animal/human hybrids, implantation of human and animal embryos in the opposite species, and rather more importantly the supply of gametes and embryos for valuable consideration' (Ministerial Committee on Assisted Reproductive Technologies, *Assisted Human Reproduction*, at p. 42). These activities were said to 'breach our principle of respect for human life and dignity'.

At this point there was a clear tension between those advocating immediate and direct legislative action, and the more restrained government approach.[47] The perceived imperative to impose legislative limits on assisted reproductive technology and research resulted in the introduction of Dianne Yates's private member's bill in the mid-1990s.[48] In the debates that followed, references to reproductive liberty, autonomy and indigenous rights became less apparent.

A tale of two bills and a supplementary order paper: enacting the HART Act 2004

When the Yates Bill was debated, the regulatory framework governing assisted reproduction and research consisted of professional self-regulation (which included a requirement that fertility clinics obtain ethical approval prior to performing new or innovative procedures or research and the requirement that NECAHR consider any such proposals) as well as the general medico-legal regime.[49]

The Yates Bill broadly proposed: a licensing scheme facilitated by a statutory licensing authority that was based on the UK Human Fertilisation and Embryology Authority;[50] centralising records to enable access to conception information (codifying an existing, voluntary, practice among clinics); a prohibition on the sale of body parts or babies, and commercial surrogacy arrangements;[51] as well as establishing additional criminal offences, such as in respect of cloning.[52] Sex selection and genetic screening would also be

47 Advocates for legislative intervention characterised and implicitly criticised the reticence of the legislature as taking a 'reactive, rather than a proactive approach' (Daniels and Hargreaves, 'Policy and ethics of surrogacy in New Zealand', at p. 4). See also Caldwell, J. and Daniels, K., 'Assisted reproduction and the law: implications for social policy', in Henaghan, M. and Atkin, B. (eds), *Family Law Policy in New Zealand*, Auckland: Oxford University Press, 1992. See also Coney, S., 'Assisted reproduction technology in New Zealand', *Lancet*, 344 (1994): 674. The Report has been described by one commentator as 'disappointing' because it did not provide ethical or legal guidance regarding specific procedures, such as embryo research or the use of ova from foetuses. See Campbell, A., 'A report from New Zealand: ethics in a bicultural context', *Bioethics*, 9 (1995): 149.

48 Although it seems that the private member's bill, the Human Assisted Reproductive Technology Bill 1996, was first lodged in the ballot before MCART released its report – but was not balloted until 1996. See (17 November 1998) 59 NZPD 13230.

49 NECAHR was established in 1995. Fertility services were not legally required to bring proposals before NECAHR, or to comply with NECAHR's decisions and guidelines. However, its professional body, the Fertility Society of Australia (FSA), required fertility clinics to gain ethical approval as part of the accreditation requirements imposed by the Society's accrediting body, the Reproductive Technology Accreditation Committee.

50 Functions of the Authority included granting licenses to clinics performing activities involving treatment services or research and maintaining a code of practice regarding the proper conduct of activities under a licence [cl. 14]. It was accountable to the Ministers of Justice and Health [cl. 13].

51 Human Assisted Reproductive Technology Bill 1996 (195–1), cl. 9.

52 The prohibitions, set out in clause 19 of the Bill, also included the storage of an embryo after the appearance of the primitive streak; placing a human embryo in an animal;

prohibited. While the Yates Bill incorporated some of MCART's principles,[53] attention to the concept of reproductive liberty was extremely muted.

The private member's bill was unanimously sent to the Justice and Law Reform Committee in 1997, where it remained. A government bill was subsequently introduced to Parliament in the form of the Assisted Human Reproduction Bill in 1998. The Bill covered similar subject matter,[54] but recommended a different structure for decision-making, delegating guideline development and ethical oversight to NECAHR rather than utilising a licensing regime.[55] After its second reading, the Bill was referred to the Health Select Committee in 1998.[56] Somewhat later, the government introduced a Supplementary Order Paper (SOP) in April 2003 that contained substantial amendments to the HART Bill introduced by Dianne Yates. The SOP removed the proposed licensing regime, instituted a different policy-making regime,[57] and declared different purposes and principles. The revised legislative framework was less prescriptive and prohibitive than the Yates Bill.

Effectively faced with a third bill on assisted reproductive technology, the Health Select Committee called for submissions on issues covered by both Bills and the SOP.[58] The Health Select Committee presented its report in August 2004, recommending significant amendments to what was referred to as the Human Assisted Reproductive Technology Bill. PGD, which had not been established as a clinical service in New Zealand at that time, attracted significant attention in the parliamentary debates that followed. The HART Act was enacted in November 2004 after a conscience vote resulting in a majority of 102 votes to 18.[59]

somatic cell nuclear transfer; germ line modification; mandatory genetic screening; and the use of eggs from human foetuses. See Human Assisted Reproductive Technology Bill 1996 (195–1), cl. 19.

53 Human Assisted Reproductive Technology Bill 1996 (195–1), cl. 3.

54 The Bill also introduced provisions regarding access to donor information and contained specific prohibitions regarding cloning, creation of hybrid embryos or implanting a human embryo in an animal or vice versa, and trading in gametes or embryos. It did not specifically ban commercial surrogacy.

55 See Assisted Human Reproduction Bill, cl. 6. This was consistent with the Officials' Committee recommendation to the government following MCART's report three years earlier in 1995.

56 The parliamentary debate that ensued showed a division between some who preferred the more prescriptive Yates Bill, and others who favoured the lower-level approach of the government Bill. (17 November 1998) 59 NZPD 13227.

57 Supplementary Paper 2003 (80) Human Assisted Reproductive Technology Bill 1996 (195–1) (explanatory note), at p. 35.

58 As a result of the lapse of time since submissions were received on the Human Assisted Reproductive Technology Bill (Yates), the Assisted Human Reproduction Bill and the introduction of the Supplementary Order Paper, the Health Committee returned submissions received by previous Health Committees, and invited submitters to resubmit. Seventy-nine submissions and 25 form submissions on the HART Bill and SOP were received.

59 The minority coalition government, consisting of Labour and the Progressive Coalition voted unanimously in favour of the Bill, along with New Zealand First and the Green Party. However, the votes of National, ACT and the United Future party members were split.

The HART Act 2004

The HART Act 2004 contains six specific purposes. The first, and arguably overriding, purpose is to:

> secure the *benefits* of assisted reproductive procedures, established procedures, and human reproductive research for individuals and for society in general by taking appropriate measures for the protection and promotion of the health, safety, dignity, and rights of all individuals, but particularly those of women and children, in the use of these procedures and research.[60]

The remaining purposes are to: prohibit 'unacceptable' assisted reproductive procedures and research – which are not defined, although the following purpose of the Act aims specifically to prohibit 'certain commercial transactions relating to human reproduction'.[61] Another stated purpose is to 'provide a robust and flexible framework for regulating and guiding' assisted reproductive procedures and research.[62] To this end, the Act establishes an Advisory Committee on Assisted Reproductive Technology and Research (ACART) and an Ethics Committee (ECART).[63]

The HART Act 2004 does not deal comprehensively with every aspect of assisted reproductive technology. Apart from creating certain prohibited offences, it delegates authority to ACART to draft guidelines and provide advice to both the Ethics Committee and the Minister of Health.[64] All such policy and advice must be developed in accordance with the Act's guiding principles and stringent statutory consultation requirements.[65] ECART is required to consider applications to perform assisted reproductive procedures, and may only approve those that are consistent with ACART Guidelines.[66]

The Act distinguishes 'assisted reproductive procedures' from 'established procedures' by requiring ethical approval to be obtained prior to the former being performed, but not the latter.[67] Correspondingly, a further purpose of the Act is to prohibit the performance of an assisted reproductive procedure without the approval of the Ethics Committee.[68] The final purpose is to establish an information-keeping regime so that donor-conceived offspring may access information regarding their genetic origins.[69]

60 Section 3(a); italics added. The Health Select Committee recommended the provision to 'clarify' the intent of the Act. It is a modified version of s. 2(b) of the Canadian federal Assisted Human Reproduction Act 2004 (AHR Act 2004).
61 Section 3(b); s. 3(c).
62 Section 3(d).
63 Section 32; s. 27.
64 Section 35.
65 Section 36; s. 39; s. 40; s. 41.
66 Section 29.
67 Section 16.
68 Section 3(e).
69 Section 3(f).

The Act also specifies certain principles that 'all persons exercising powers or performing functions under the Act must be guided by'.[70] The first is that 'the health and well-being of children born as a result of the performance of an assisted reproductive procedure should be an *important* consideration in all decisions about that procedure'.[71] The following two principles are that: 'the health, safety, and dignity of both present and future generations should be preserved and promoted',[72] and that 'while all persons are affected by assisted reproductive procedures and established procedures, women, more than men, are directly and significantly affected by their application, and the health and well-being of women must be protected in the use of these procedures'.[73]

The remaining principles provided that: no assisted reproductive procedure or research should be performed on an individual unless informed consent has been contained;[74] that 'donor offspring should be made aware of their genetic origins and be able to access information about those origins';[75] that 'the needs, values, and beliefs of Māori should be considered and treated with respect';[76] and that 'the different ethical, spiritual, and cultural perspectives in society should be considered and treated with respect'.[77]

The Act establishes three broad categories of assisted reproductive procedures and research: those that are prohibited outright under the Act; those that are regulated by ACART and that can only be performed with ethical approval in accordance with ACART guidelines; and those that are declared, by Order in Council to be 'established'. Established procedures are effectively 'mainstream' medical procedures and may be performed as routine clinical procedures. These procedures are listed in a regulatory instrument: the Human Assisted Reproductive Technology (HART) Order 2005. The Minister of Health may recommend that the Governor-General pass an Order if ACART advises him that an assisted reproductive procedure does not need, or no longer needs, to be regulated and thereby subject to ethical approval.[78]

70 Section 4.

71 Section 4(a); italics added. Although the SOP had originally referred to the welfare of the child being a *paramount* concern, this was amended during the Select Committee process because of a concern that, if premised on the paramountcy principle, procedures might not be approved if they involved any health risks over and above those associated with natural conception. The Select Committee stated: 'We consider it more appropriate that the risks of assisted human reproduction procedures be balanced against the benefits to children, families, and society in general. We intend decisions to be weighted in the best interest of the child, recognizing that there will still be an element of risk' (Report of the Health Committee, Human Assisted Reproductive Technology Bill, 6 August 2004, 195–2, at p. 5).

72 Section 4(b).

73 Section 4(c). This principle was drawn from the Canadian AHR Act 2004. See Cabinet Policy Committee, 'HART SOP: confirmation of framework and proposed changes arising from Select Committee' (21 June 2004) POL 04/147, p. 6.

74 Section 4(d).

75 Section 4(e).

76 Section 4(f).

77 Section 4(g).

78 Section 6. ACART, in tendering such advice, is required to provide the Minister with a report detailing: information about the procedure; an assessment of the known health

The Act specifically prohibits PGD for non-medical sex selection. No robust explanation was given for introducing this prohibition, despite the fact that breach of the provision renders a person liable to a fine of up to $100,000 and/ or imprisonment for up to a year.[79] It was simply stated that, on the basis of submissions received by the Health Committee, there was a 'broad level of support' for adding this prohibition.[80] However, it was likely a pragmatic compromise designed to ensure the passage of the Bill and a concern not to appear more permissive than other countries.[81]

The (minority) Green Party was especially exercised by the prospect of PGD. Not only was PGD perceived to be problematic in general, social sex selection was deemed to be among 'the worst excesses of artificial reproduction'.[82] Other parliamentarians endorsed the prohibition on sex selection, on the basis that it was self-evidently wrong, rather than on the basis of reasoned or rational debate as to exactly why it mandated criminalisation. One conservative MP who considered the Act far too liberal nevertheless said that:

> [o]ne provision shows a great deal of caution about sex selection. There is no particularly rational reason why we cannot have sex selection – if we can select for other things, why can we not select for gender – but deep in our gut we know that it would be wrong to legislate for sex selection. We just know it is wrong – we do not need to have a PhD to know that.[83]

risks and benefits of the procedure drawn from published and peer reviewed research; advice as to whether the health risks fall within a level of risk acceptable in New Zealand; and an ethical analysis of the procedure. Under the interim provisions of the HART Act 2004, the Director-General of Health was deemed to be the advisory committee in the nine months following the introduction of the Act, s. 79. Consequently, it was the Director-General of Health, not ACART, who recommended to the Minister that the HART Order 2005 be passed.

79 Section 11. The prohibition did not appear in the original SOP, which provided that all policy and advice regarding PGD was to be delegated to the Advisory Committee. It was subsequently inserted by the Select Committee and closely resembles the prohibition in s. 5(e) of the Canadian AHR Act 2004.

80 (25 August 2004) 65 NZPD 15059, *per* David Benson-Pope.

81 (10 November 2004) 73 NZPD 16836, *per* David Benson-Pope. 'The most important part of the bill is the clear identification of activities that are simply unacceptable in this country. Such activities include human cloning for reproductive purposes, the implantation of a human embryo into an animal and vice versa, genetically modifying embryos using gametes from foetuses for reproductive purposes, and sex selection for social reasons. These activities are at the extreme end of the spectrum of assisted reproductive technology . . . Prohibiting such activities will place New Zealand on a par with other countries that regulate assisted reproductive technology.' See also Cabinet Policy Committee, 'HART SOP', at p. 3.

82 (25 August 2004) 65 NZPD 15062, *per* Sue Kedgley. See also (25 August 2004) 65 NZPD 15068, *per* Judy Turner (United Future).

83 (10 November 2004) 73 NZPD 16847, *per* Hon Bill English. Earlier reference was made in the debate to a consultation document that stated that the moral status of the embryo was generally not considered sufficient to prohibit PGD for serious conditions, but was significant enough to preclude social sex selection. See (10 November 2004) 73 NPD 16842, *per* Judy Turner.

However, this sentiment fails to demonstrate an appreciation for the fact that the law, particularly when it is reinforced by criminal sanctions, generally requires more than simple disapproval of, or alleged community distaste towards, a particular act.[84] For those individuals wanting to utilise PGD for social sex selection, it is arguably consonant with securing the 'benefits' of assisted reproduction – a stated purpose of the Act. Consequently, for it to be legitimately prohibited there is a need to indicate what harm the resulting individuals or society must be protected from. If, as Bill English asserted, there is no 'rational' objection to sex selection (clearly there might be, but none was raised) the law is obviously enforcing not only a majoritarian moral viewpoint but, contrary to the liberal political tradition, doing so in the absence of evidence of harm.

However, it was not only social sex selection that concerned some members of Parliament. The purported erosion of the rights of persons with disabilities was also claimed to justify narrowly regulating PGD. One MP claimed: 'If we allow the technology to advance slowly but surely to the point where parents are allowed to design their children's genetic inheritance, we threaten those with disabilities and we threaten their right to be born in the future.'[85] Yet the same MP welcomed the use of PGD to prevent serious genetic disorders or diseases such as cystic fibrosis, haemophilia or muscular dystrophy.[86] Yet *if* such a right to be born may be claimed, PGD should surely be banned completely, rather than partially. Instead, the arguments invoked belied the complexity of the disability rights issues that they raise.

Clearly some MPs wished to draw a line between 'acceptable' and 'non-acceptable' choices, although the merits of such an approach are debatable. Even some of the most ardent disability rights activists resist drawing such

84 The prohibition on social sex selection was challenged by the (now disestablished) New Zealand Bioethics Council after it undertook a public deliberative exercise on pre-birth testing in 2007–8. It stated: 'There is [*sic*] insufficient cultural, ethical and spiritual reasons to prohibit the use of preimplantation genetic diagnosis for sex selection for social reasons such as "family balancing"' (Toi Te Taiao: the Bioethics Council, *Who Gets Born? A Report on the Cultural, Ethical and Spiritual Aspects of Pre-Birth Testing by Toi te Taiao: the Bioethics Council* (Wellington, 2008) at p. 51). However, the recommendation was criticised for not reflecting the views of the participants in the deliberative exercise. See Jones, G., King, M. and Whitaker, M., 'Who gets born? How did New Zealand's Bioethics Council arrive at its recommendations?', NZMJ 122 (1294) (2009). Providing further discussion would have greatly enhanced the force of the Council's recommendation and its perceived legitimacy.

85 (25 August 2004) 65 NZPD 15064, *per* Sue Kedgley.

86 See (20 October 2004) 71 NZPD 16360, *per* Sue Kedgely 'the very same technologies that can be used, for example, to cure a child of cystic fibrosis or to avoid such a child being born, can equally be used to threaten human dignity and human rights, to eliminate imperfections, to create perfect persons and a perfect race – in other words, to be used for eugenic purposes . . . where does one draw the line between what is an acceptable and what is an unacceptable use of pre-birth selection; who decides what genetic defects are to be allowed to be eliminated from the human population through embryos selection and preimplantation genetic diagnosis, etc; and where does it stop, given the pressures from consumers?'

(putative) bright lines and indeed challenge the legitimacy of creating a medical–social dichotomy in this context.[87] This is because creating categories of conditions for which PGD is permissible not only potentially 'pathologises' the associated condition, but they argue it devalues those persons actually living with the same conditions when only some selection choices are rendered lawful by the state. Further, there was no apparent appreciation in the debates for the counter-argument that it is prospective parents (who ultimately stand in the closest relationship with the resulting child and assume a responsibility that others simply do not share) who should, in the absence of evidence that such conduct is harmful, be at liberty to make reproductive choices that directly and intimately impact on their lives, including decisions whether to seek to avoid conceiving a child with disabilities.

Slippery-slope arguments were pervasive in the parliamentary debates on the Bill.[88] PGD was frequently referred to, mostly in the context of sex selection, and often conflated with genetic modification.[89] Yet the two are very different things. The amount of 'design' possible in PGD is limited to selection on the basis of genetic characteristics already present in an embryo – whereas genetic modification involves alteration of the genetic code. This kind of modification was to be prohibited in the HART Act 2004.[90] While 'designer baby' terminology was rife, as was the assumption of the legitimacy of state intervention in reproductive lives, any concept of reproductive liberty, or what its scope might be, was generally absent from the debates.[91] Clearly, there was an implicit view that parent(s) could legitimately avoid conceiving a seriously

87 Wasserman, D., 'A choice of evils in prenatal testing', *Florida State University Law Review*, 30 (2003): 295, at p. 300; Asch, A., 'Disability equality and prenatal testing: contradictory or compatible?', *Florida State University Law Review*, 30 (2003): 315, at 339. See also Krahn, T. and Wong, S., 'Preimplantation genetic diagnosis and reproductive autonomy', *Reproductive Biomedicine Online* 19 (2009, Suppl. 2): 34, at p. 38.

88 The Green Party was concerned that the legislation provided scope for the Advisory Committee to 'issue guidelines allowing embryo selection for blue eyes, athleticism, or any other genetic characteristic that may become diagnosable by genetic examination in the future' (Report of the Health Committee, Human Assisted Reproductive Technology Bill (2004), 195–2, at p. 14). See also Park, J., McLauchlan, L. and Frengley, E., 'Normal humanness, change and power in human assisted reproductive technology: an analysis of the written public submissions to the New Zealand Parliamentary Health Committee in 2003', *Research in Anthropology and Linguistics-e*, 2 (2008). The authors note that the epithet 'designer babies' in relation to PGD seems to replicate the use of 'test tube' baby terminology in earlier debates involving IVF.

89 For example: 'We were pleased to see included in this bill provisions that prohibit the genetic engineering of humans, and new provisions that prohibit the sex selection of embryos for any reason other than treating or preventing genetic disease. We did not want to see the growth of a designer baby industry' ((10 November 2004) 73 NZPD 16839, *per* David Benson Pope). See also (6 October 2004) 69 NZPD 15919.

90 See Clause 8, of Schedule 1 of the Act. The Schedule prohibits *implanting* 'into a human being: a genetically modified gamete, a genetically modified human embryo, or a genetically modified hybrid embryo'. However conducting research in relation to these activities, which does not involve human implantation, is not expressly prohibited.

91 With the exception of one vocal member of the ACT party. (6 October 2004) 68 NZPD 15917; 15922.

impaired child utilising PGD, but other matters, either involving less ostensibly serious disease or non-medical selection, were assumed to come within the purview of the state.

Given the assumed legitimacy of the state's authority to determine the limits of reproductive liberty in relation to PGD, what follows examines the parameters that have been established in regard to PGD in New Zealand. This examination highlights not only the considerable ambiguity of current PGD policy, but also the apparent reluctance of the statutory policy-making body to address the issue, as well as the difficulty associated with introducing a revised human leukocyte antigen (HLA) tissue-typing policy. It is suggested that the intervention of the law is misplaced if the appointed policy-making body is unable to react expeditiously and on a principled basis to address legal ambiguity or to progress revised policy. It is also suggested that ultimately these decisions are more appropriately a matter for intending parents and the clinicians involved.

Inconsistencies and anomalies: the permissible limits of PGD

The current regulatory framework for PGD was essentially established prior to the appointment of ACART, which is now statutorily responsible for its monitoring and revision.[92] Before the relevant parts of the HART Act 2004 came into force, PGD was regulated by guidelines formulated by the National Ethics Committee on Assisted Human Reproduction (NECAHR) after the Minister of Health approved the use of PGD in principle in 2003.[93] The *Guidelines* have been partly subsumed by developments since the introduction of the Act. However they are still relevant, primarily in relation to HLA tissue-typing, until such time as ACART replaces them.

As already indicated, the Act prohibits PGD for social sex selection. PGD with preimplantation HLA tissue-typing is a regulated procedure, and may only be performed in the circumstances specified in the *Guidelines* and with prior ethics committee approval. PGD may be performed as an established procedure (that is, without ethical approval) if it is consistent with the applications of PGD described by the Human Assisted Reproductive Technology Order 2005 (HART Order).[94] What follows examines these two latter categories of PGD.

The HART Order 2005: legal limbo

The HART Order essentially restricts PGD to the diagnosis of single gene disorders that are inherited in a Mendelian manner and that may cause a future

92 Section 35. For further discussion, see Chapter 9 in this volume.
93 See NECAHR, *Guidelines on Preimplantation Genetic Diagnosis*, March 2005.
94 See HART Order 2005, clause 6 of part 2 of the Schedule.

individual to be seriously impaired.[95] The Order provides that PGD may be performed routinely if all of the following criteria are met: a familial single gene or familial chromosomal disorder has been identified in the family or *whānau*;[96] there is a 25 per cent or greater risk of an affected pregnancy; and there is evidence that the future individual may be seriously impaired as a result of the disorder.[97] In the case of a familial sex-linked disorder, sex selection may only be utilised if there is no available direct mutation test in order to prevent the elimination of embryos that do not carry the sex-linked mutation.[98]

Despite the intention of policy-makers to restrict PGD to serious Mendelian disorders,[99] it is arguable that the Order nevertheless encompasses PGD for 'susceptibility' or incompletely penetrant conditions.[100] These are conditions to which a person is predisposed because of a particular genetic mutation that they carry, but which may not ever actually manifest in an individual because the gene mutation is not fully 'penetrant' – meaning that the mutation does not always cause the disease to be physically expressed in an individual. Examples of susceptibility conditions include some inherited cancers, such as hereditary breast, ovarian or bowel cancer. Clearly, PGD to diagnose a gene variant conferring susceptibility to a late-onset disease extends beyond traditional PGD performed for serious, fully penetrant disorders that are apparent at birth or develop in early childhood.

There is often considerable rhetoric, particularly in media reports, that accompanies any perceived 'extensions' to PGD. Baroness Mary Warnock, for example, refers to the headline in the UK *Times* newspaper, 'Gene tests to start era of baby-to-order', when it was reported that the United Kingdom's Human

95 In addition, PGD may also be performed as a routine procedure to identify non-familial chromosomal disorders if the woman is of advanced reproductive age or has had recurrent implantation failure or recurrent miscarriage (HART Order 2005, clause 6 of part 2 of the Schedule).

96 *Whānau* signifies the Māori concept of extended family.

97 'Serious' impairment is not defined in the Order although the *Guidelines* provided that it is the responsibility of PGD providers, in collaboration with a geneticist, to determine whether a disorder is likely to be serious in the offspring.

98 Take, for example, haemophilia A and B, both sex-linked heritable disorders that occur as a result of a mutation in the FVIII or FIX genes. Since a test is available to diagnose male embryos with the mutation, performing PGD to select only female embryos is not permitted because it would involve the rejection of *all* male embryos, approximately 50 per cent of which would not have the mutation.

99 The original clause in the draft (NECAHR) Guidelines permitted PGD when there is a *high risk of serious abnormality* and the option of prenatal testing alone is unacceptable to the couple. However, NEHACR reduced the threshold for PGD to evidence that a future individual *may* be seriously impaired because of the difficulty in predicting whether a disorder would be mild or severe and not, it would seem, with the intention of including lower penetrance disorders. The implications of the wording change were not appreciated at the time and the wording was replicated in the HART Order 2005. See Snelling, J., 'Implications for providers and patients: a comment on the regulatory framework for preimplantation genetic diagnosis in New Zealand', *Medical Law International*, 8 (2006): 23, at p. 32.

100 Snelling, J., 'Preimplantation genetic diagnosis for susceptibility conditions: a new frontier or a logical extension?', *JLM*, 16 (2008): 263.

Fertilisation and Embryology Authority had received two applications to perform PGD to diagnose Breast Cancer Gene 1 (BRCA1) and Breast Cancer Gene 2 (BRCA2) mutations.[101] These particular mutations confer a predisposition to developing breast and ovarian cancer in later life and account for around 5 per cent of all breast cancers.[102] In response to the issues raised by such testing, Baroness Warnock states:

> It seems to me beyond doubt that once the new diagnostic tests are available then those families that are at risk have a right to seek the diagnosis, if they are prepared to accept the inherent intrusiveness and relatively low success rate of IVF treatment. They have to weigh these immediate disadvantages against the manifest long term advantages (for the child as well as for themselves) of not having a child who will in all probability die painfully and young. This seems to me no more than the right we all have, if we can afford to exercise it, to seek up-to-date medical treatment. The arguments of those who say that thereby some rejected embryos are denied the right to life are not to be taken seriously.[103]

It is debatable whether or not PGD for susceptibility conditions is comparable with seeking modern diagnostic techniques – or whether this is an oversimplification. As Braude has already alluded to (see Chapter 1 in this volume), PGD is an expensive, highly technical and emotional process with a relatively low success rate, particularly if compared with fertile couples that can conceive naturally. However, it remains the case that it is difficult to justify prohibiting this type of testing when fully informed couples, with a devastating familial history and less-than appealing alternative options for disease prevention, seek it.[104] Arguably, the question as to whether PGD is proportionate to the risk of future offspring developing the disease is ultimately a matter to be resolved by the individuals concerned, and their clinicians, taking into account any surveillance and risk-reducing measures available for those who are genetically predisposed to develop the condition. Risk-reducing measures – such as surgical removal of the breasts and ovaries for BRCA1 or BRCA2 mutation carriers, or gastrectomy in the case of hereditary gastric cancer mutation carriers – are not insignificant measures in themselves.

101 See Warnock, M., 'The limits of rights based discourse', in Spencer, J. and Du Bois-Pedain, A., *Freedom and Responsibility in Reproductive Choice*, Oxford: Hart, 2006, at p. 11, citing Henderson, M., 'Gene test to start era of baby-to-order', *The Times* (UK, 26 June 2004, www.timesonline.co.uk).

102 Noble, R., Bahacur, G., Iqbal, M. and Sanyal, A., 'Pandora's box: ethics of PGD for inherited risk of late-onset disorders', *Reprod Biomed Online*, 3 (2008): 55, at p. 59.

103 Warnock, 'Limits of rights based discourse', at p. 11.

104 Krahn, T., 'Preimplantation genetic diagnosis: does age of onset matter (anymore)?', *Medicine Health Care and Philosophy*, 12 (2009): 187; Braude, P., 'Preimplantation diagnosis for genetic susceptibility', *N Engl J Med*, 355 (2010): 541; Purdy, L., 'Too late to matter? Preventing the birth of infants at risk for adult-onset disease or disability', *Philosophy and Medicine*, 104 (2010): 109.

Despite the original intention to limit the scope of the Order and the otherwise generally conservative approach to PGD, straightforward legal analysis suggests that it encompasses PGD for some susceptibility conditions. Although susceptibility conditions may be considered 'multifactorial' or 'complex' disorders because other factors (such as environmental factors or gene interactions) influence the development of the disease, susceptibility conditions that arise from single gene mutations of major affect are generally accepted as single gene disorders.[105] Further, because conditions such as these heritable cancer syndromes leave behind a trail of intergenerational disease, the first criterion required by the HART Order regarding the existence of a familial single gene disorder that has been identified in the family or *whānau* is met. There is also a 25 per cent or greater risk of an affected pregnancy, *if* it is accepted that this percentage refers to the statistical likelihood of the gene being transmitted, rather than the disease developing.[106] The final criterion requires evidence that the future *individual may* be seriously impaired as a result. Because the Order refers to a future individual, rather than an infant or child, it arguably extends to later-onset conditions. More importantly, the Order does not require that a future individual *will* be seriously impaired, which would limit PGD to fully penetrant conditions; it merely requires evidence that he or she *may* be seriously impaired.

As this extended scope has not occurred on the basis of consideration and consultation, but rather as a result of the terminology adopted when drafting the PGD policy and developments in molecular genetics that have enabled the identification and diagnosis of susceptibility genes, it is uncertain whether PGD may be performed routinely in these circumstances. This is a considerable concern, given that the Act creates a criminal offence for performing a procedure that has not been declared to be an established procedure pursuant to the Order. However, addressing this ambiguity appears to have been accorded a low priority by ACART.[107]

Another application of PGD that is potentially permitted under the Order, although much more equivocally in terms of statutory interpretation, is preimplantation exclusion testing for late-onset autosomal dominant disorders such as Huntington's disease (HD). HD is a serious and non-treatable late-onset neurodegenerative disease that ultimately results in

105 Snelling, 'Preimplantation genetic diagnosis for susceptibility conditions', at p. 264; Wang, C. and Hui, E., 'Ethical, legal and social implications of prenatal and pre-implantation genetic testing for cancer susceptibility', *Reproductive Biomedicine Online*, 19 (2009, Suppl. 2): 23, at p. 24.

106 If the percentage is interpreted as the risk of developing the condition (rather than transmitting the gene), the Order would limit PGD to autosomal dominant susceptibility conditions with a penetrance of 50 per cent or more. See Snelling, 'Preimplantation genetic diagnosis for susceptibility conditions', at p. 277.

107 It is likely that ACART are sympathetic towards this interpretation, which is implicit in advice provided to the former Minister of Health, Hon Steve Chadwick. See *Committee Advice on Preimplantation Genetic Diagnosis* (May 2008), p. 2, www.acart.newhealth.govt.nz (accessed June 2010).

premature death. PGD is generally accepted as justifiable when an individual has the HD mutation. However for many reasons – such as the lack of any effective treatment[108] as well as the emotional, social and financial burdens that some think may result from a positive[109] test – some individuals who are at risk of developing the condition choose not to undertake predictive testing.[110]

As described earlier by Braude, exclusion testing was developed to provide at-risk individuals and their partners, who have determined that they do not want to undertake predictive testing themselves, to eliminate any chance of transmitting the HD mutation to their offspring.[111] Consequently, the embryos are not tested for the HD mutation directly, because a positive test would indicate that the parent is also mutation positive. Instead, the embryos are tested to determine whether they inherited the block of DNA that includes the HD gene from the known-to-be-affected grandparent. If they have, those embryos are not transferred, while embryos with chromosomal DNA originating from the unaffected grandparent are considered low risk and transferrable.

As HD is an autosomal dominant condition, meaning that there is a 50 per cent chance of inheriting it from a parent who has the condition, half of the couples who undertake exclusion testing may be unaffected. PGD in this situation will not be necessary. Similarly, half of the embryos discarded may be mutation free, as only one of the two grandparental alleles will actually carry the HD mutation.

The issue is whether exclusion testing is justifiable to protect a parent's genetic nescience in these circumstances. Clearly, exclusion testing involves potentially unnecessary IVF and PGD, given that approximately half of the couples will not be at risk. It also involves the destruction of potentially mutation-free embryos. Yet if it is accepted that exclusion testing may, in the opinion of those seeking it, promote both the well-being of the at-risk individual as well as the interests of the couple, in conjunction with the ultimate goal to avoid transmitting the putative disorder, it is difficult to see

108 See Walker, F., 'Huntington's disease', *Lancet*, 369 (2007): 218, at p. 220.

109 Braude, P., De Wert, G., Evers-Kiebooms, G., Pettigrew, R. and Geraedts, J., 'Non-disclosure preimplantation genetic diagnosis for Huntington's disease: practical and ethical dilemmas', *Prenatal Diagnosis*, 18 (1998): 1422, at 1423. See Bombard, Y. *et al*., 'Managing Genetic Discrimination: Strategies Used by Individuals Found to Have the Huntington Disease Mutation', *Clin Genet*, 71 (2007): 220.

110 See Snelling, J., 'Preimplantation genetic diagnosis: slipping through the regulatory net', in Human Genome Research Project, *Genes, Society and the Future: Vol. III*, Wellington: Brookers, 2009, at p. 66.

111 Another means of avoiding predictive testing, but ensuring healthy pregnancies is non-disclosure PGD whereby embryos are tested for the HD mutation, but the results are not communicated to the parents. This particular option is not well endorsed. The European Society of Human Reproduction and Embryology (ESHRE) has recommended against it because it is laden with practical and ethical problems. See Sermon, K. *et al*., 'Preimplantation genetic diagnosis for Huntington's disease with exclusion testing', *Europ J Hum Genet*, 10 (2002): 591, at p. 592; Shenfield, F. *et al*., 'Taskforce 5: preimplantation genetic diagnosis', *Human Reproduction*, 18 (2003): 649.

how arguments for prohibition can succeed. Consequently, it is arguable that the risks are not such that a fully informed couple should be prevented from voluntarily undertaking them.[112]

There are good, but not indefeasible, arguments that preimplantation exclusion testing is permitted under the HART Order. Although not expressly defined, the HART Order's description of PGD is broad enough to encapsulate exclusion testing.[113] The HART Order does not expressly limit the scope of PGD to direct mutation analysis.[114] As required by the HART Order, HD will have been identified in the family/*whānau* in this context. As we have seen, because HD is an autosomal dominant condition, there is a 50 per cent risk of an affected pregnancy *if* the parent has the HD mutation. However, if an individual with an affected parent has *not* undergone predictive testing, the risk of transmitting the HD mutation to a future child is 25 per cent. This meets the statistical threshold required by the Order of a '25% or greater risk of an affected pregnancy'. Nevertheless, this is clearly not an indefeasible argument – in fact it may even be claimed to be 'stretching the law', because the risk of an affected pregnancy is zero if the at-risk parent does not have the gene, which could be confirmed if the parent undergoes predictive testing. Finally, as indicated above, the Order does not require that the future individual *will* be seriously impaired; simply that he or she *may* be seriously impaired. This militates towards an interpretation that this type of exclusion testing is permitted as a routine procedure without any necessity for prior ethical approval.

The potential breadth of availability of PGD in these circumstances is clearly an anomaly. It stands in contrast to the otherwise conservative PGD framework that prohibits social sex selection and *only* permits sex selection in the case of sex-linked disorders *if* no specific test for the relevant mutation is available. The regulatory framework clearly intends to prevent the negative selection of

112 Purdy, 'Too late to matter?', at 114. Takala, T., 'The right to genetic ignorance confirmed', *Bioethics*, 13 (1999): 288, at p. 292. Takala states: 'Subjecting oneself to expensive and painful operations just to remain in ignorance might, however, sound foolish to most people, and the foolishness of ignorance is indeed an oft-used argument against genetic ignorance in general. It is felt that there is something wrong in denial and that it is foolish to remain ignorant in crucial matters that have an impact on our future health status. This might well be so. But people are allowed to be foolish in liberal societies, at least in the sense that the mere fact that their behaviour appears to be foolish is not reason enough to deny them the freedom in acting in the way they choose to.'

113 See Part 1 of the Schedule to the HART Order 2005 where it describes PGD as 'a procedure for genetically testing embryos for specific genetic conditions or chromosomal abnormalities prior to embryo transfer and that includes any of the following undertaken for, or in connection with, that procedure: (a) biopsy of embryos to remove 1 or more cells: (b) transportation of the cells to an approved laboratory: (c) analysis of the genetic or chromosomal constitution of cells obtained by biopsy: (d) selection of embryos for transfer on the basis of the results from analysis.'

114 Indeed, not all genetic conditions may be diagnosed by identifying a precise mutation, as specific tests have not yet been developed for many disorders. In the case of certain X-linked conditions, for example, sex selection may be performed to avoid the risk of transmitting a sex-linked disorder when there is no specific test available.

embryos unless they are identified as having specific disease-related mutations. Yet, arguably, permitting exclusion testing for late-onset disorders such as HD is consistent not only with reproductive liberty, but also with the purpose and principles contained in the HART Act 2004.[115] A primary objective of the HART Act is to secure the benefits of assisted reproductive procedures by promoting and protecting the 'dignity and rights of all individuals' in the use of these procedures.[116] Given the interests at stake – specifically not knowing their genetic status and not passing on the disorder – it would seem that preimplantation exclusion testing is at least *prima facie* consistent with promoting the at-risk individual/couple's dignity and rights.

ACART's response to the uncertainty regarding the scope of the HART Order in terms of PGD for late-onset susceptibility conditions and preimplantation exclusion testing for late-onset disorders such as HD is illuminating. There are several options open to ACART in this context. ACART is authorised by the HART Act 2004 to provide advice to the Minister of Health that any established procedure should be modified or should cease to be an established procedure.[117] It may also advise that a moratorium should be imposed on an assisted reproductive procedure, which would allow ACART to consider and consult on the matter and develop appropriate advice or guidelines.[118] ACART may also simply inform the Minister that the potential scope of the Order is ambiguous and provide advice as to whether it officially endorses testing in these contexts. However, when giving 'significant advice' to the Minister, which includes advice on PGD or any issue of significant public interest, ACART is required to provide a discussion paper outlining the proposed advice upon which interested parties and the public may make submissions.[119]

None of these options has been taken, despite the uncertainty of the Order having been raised in direct communication with ACART, in academic commentary and in public submissions to ACART. This is despite the fact that it is a criminal offence under the HART Act 2004 to perform an assisted reproductive procedure, which is not an established procedure, without prior ethical approval.[120] Yet without clarification by ACART, clinics and individuals are not able to determine whether these types of tests are incorporated within the Order and may be performed routinely. If in fact they are not, these procedures may only be performed with the written approval of ECART.

115 Snelling, J., 'Preimplantation genetic diagnosis', at p. 108. See also Asscher, E. and Koops, B., 'The right not to know and preimplantation genetic diagnosis for Huntington's disease', *Journal of Medical Ethics*, 36 (2010): 30.

116 Section 3 (a).

117 Section 35 (1)(iii).

118 Section 35 (1)(iv). The Minister of Health may recommend to the Governor General that an Order in Council be passed declaring these activities to be subject to a moratorium, allowing time for ACART to develop advice or guidelines (s. 24).

119 Section 38 (e), s. 39 (1)(a)(b), s. 39 (2).

120 Section 16. A person who performs an assisted reproductive procedure without ethics committee approval is liable on summary conviction to a fine of up to $50,000.

However, in the absence of ACART guidelines or advice on the matter, ECART is not empowered to approve such applications, in which case these procedures are effectively, if not explicitly, prohibited. Clearly, the value of both reproductive liberty and legal certainty are diminished as a result of this lack of clarity and deliberative deficit on the part of ACART. It is only reasonable that if regulatory control is assumed, efforts are made to ensure that it is clear, unambiguous and justifiable. However, it is apparent that regulating PGD has proven problematic, as the supposedly bright lines drawn between permissible and non-permissible PGD have already become blurred. It is conceivable that responding to these issues is rendered more difficult given the extensive consultation requirements under the Act, but reluctance to engage with these issues does little to enhance ACART's perceived legitimacy and to justify state intervention in these reproductive matters. Leaving aside these procedural issues, the basis on which a liberal democratic state can legitimately claim to justify arbitrating on such matters is questionable once PGD has been accepted in principle, as it clearly has been.

Revision of the pre-implantation tissue-typing policy

In contrast, ACART has been active in its attempts to revise the policy on HLA tissue-typing currently contained in the *Guidelines on Preimplantation Genetic Diagnosis*, although it has not yet been successful. These Guidelines, originally drafted by NECAHR,[121] were designated interim ACART guidelines under the interim provisions of the Act, effective until November 2007.[122] Since their expiry, ACART has ensured that they remain applicable by reissuing them as 'advice to the ethics committee' on the ACART website.

Both the current 2005 *Guidelines*, and ACART's first proposed draft guidelines on HLA tissue-typing published as part of a wider omnibus consultation in July 2007, restrict preimplantation tissue-typing to instances where the sick sibling who is in need of a stem cell transplant suffers from a disease of genetic origin.[123] The 2005 and the 2007 proposed guidelines were flawed in many respects. In particular, the latter consultation failed to provide

121 NECAHR, *Guidelines on Preimplantation Genetic Diagnosis* (March 2005). These guidelines also contain certain prohibitions that remain in effect as long as the guidelines remain in force as 'advice'. These include prohibitions on using PGD to select for a genetic impairment seen in a parent or altering the genetic constitution of an embryo. However, these prohibitions have not been expressly reiterated in the latest draft guidelines. For a discussion of the problematic aspects of these original (and still applicable) guidelines see Snelling, 'Implications for providers and patients'; Snelling, J., Peart, N. and Henaghan, M., 'Preimplantation genetic diagnosis: testing the legal boundaries', in Human Genome Research Project, *Genes, Society and the Future: Vol. I*, Dunedin: Human Genome Research Project, 2007, at p. 53.

122 Under the interim provisions of the Act, the Minister of Health may require the Ethics Committee (ECART) to treat specified provisions in a document as guidelines issued by the Advisory Committee. Section 83 (2)(3).

123 ACART, *Advice on Aspects of Assisted Reproductive Technology: A Consultation on Policy Issues* (Wellington, July 2007).

a full discussion of the issues involved, nor did it explain how the Act's principles applied to the proposed framework. There was also a lack of direction regarding substantive matters, such as the circumstances in which tissue-typing could be performed, other than in reference to the sole parameter of genetic risk to the future offspring.[124]

However, after it undertook a consultation process, ACART altered its position dramatically. It subsequently released a further consultation document in July of 2008, appendixed to which was a summary of submissions on the 2007 consultation.[125] The July 2008 draft Guidelines were extremely brief and generally non-specific, but extended the permissibility of tissue-typing to include circumstances where the condition suffered by the sick sibling was not genetic.

The draft July 2008 Guidelines require that ECART, when considering an application for tissue-typing, must determine that genetic counselling, medical advice and general counselling have been received by the parties.[126] Medical and counselling reports must satisfy ECART that the health and well-being of the resulting child is safeguarded, and that 'the condition for which HLA tissue-typing is undertaken is judged by the clinical team and prospective parents to be of sufficient severity to justify undertaking the procedure'.[127] ECART must also take into account 'all relevant factors' such as whether 'the relationship between parties safeguards the well-being of all parties and especially any resulting child'; and whether counselling covered the implications for all parties (including the possibility that therapy may be unsuccessful) and has been culturally appropriate.[128]

ACART stated in the consultation document that it considered that New Zealand's ethical and legal framework provided adequate protections to prevent the possible exploitation of children born as a result of HLA tissue-typing.[129] There is no specific regulatory framework applicable to tissue or organ donation in New Zealand, which is governed by the general law regarding consent to medical treatment.[130] For incompetent minors, it is highly likely that proxy parental consent would not be 'sufficient' to authorise a solid organ transplant between siblings.[131] However, in the case of donation

124 For a critique of these guidelines, see Snelling, J., 'Embryonic HLA tissue typing and made-to-match siblings: the New Zealand position', *Med Law Int* 9, (2008): 13.

125 ACART, *Consultation on Draft Guidelines for the Use of Preimplantation Genetic Diagnosis with Human Leukocyte Antigen Testing* (Wellington, July 2008).

126 Ibid., at p. 9. However, the relevance of the requirement for genetic counselling is questionable if the condition suffered by the sick sibling is not genetic.

127 Ibid.

128 Ibid., at p. 10.

129 Ibid., at p. 6.

130 Specifically the Care of Children Act 2004 (CoC Act), the Code of Health and Disability Consumers' Rights; and the common law.

131 Section 16(1) of the CoC Act provides that 'the duties, powers, rights, and responsibilities of a guardian of a child include (without limitation) the guardian's . . . (c) determining for or with the child, or helping the child to determine important matters affecting the child'. Section 16 (2)(c) specifies that 'important matters affecting

of regenerative tissue such as bone marrow, donation may be more likely to be deemed to come within the lawful scope of parental authority for incompetent minors, as long as psychosocial benefits accrue to the donor and any harm is *de minimis*.[132]

However it seems some ACART members continued to voice concern in respect of children born following tissue-typing.[133] As a result, ACART sought advice from the Paediatric Society of New Zealand. The response received from the President of the Society reflected the general legal position and was to the effect that while consent to umbilical cord blood collection resides with the parents, '[s]ociety members are agreed that live [solid] organ donation should be limited to donation by individuals over a minimum age of 16 years' and that 'live liver transplantation donation is limited to individuals over the age of 18'.[134] It was also stated that *if* a minor was to donate a solid organ in these circumstances, an independent medical assessment as well as a rigorous psychosocial assessment should be performed as an 'absolute minimum'. In addition, such a donation should be discussed with the Hospital Ethics Committee.

ACART subsequently provided what were slightly revised draft HLA tissue-typing guidelines to the new Minister of Health for consultation in May 2009.[135] Section 41(2) of the Act provides that: '[B]efore the advisory committee issues guidelines to the ethics committee it must *consult* on the proposed guidelines with the Minister.' Somewhat surprisingly, the Minister referred the Guidelines to another Committee, the National Ethics Advisory Committee (NEAC) for consideration, requesting not only a review of the substantive provisions of the Guidelines, but also of the quality of the consultation undertaken by ACART.[136] Whether this indicates a breach of good faith, a lack of Ministerial confidence in ACART or is a legitimate 'second-opinion' process is debatable. Several years later ACART is yet to release revised HLA tissue-typing guidelines.

the child' include medical treatment for the child (if that treatment is not routine in nature). Section 36 (3)(a) provides that, 'if the consent of any other person to any medical, surgical, or dental treatment or procedure (including a blood transfusion) to be carried out on a child is *necessary or sufficient*, consent may be given – (a) by a guardian' (emphasis added).

132 See Snelling *et al.*, 'Preimplantation genetic diagnosis', at p. 67.

133 ACART Paper (Late Paper) Final Draft: *Report to the Minister on Guidelines for the Use of PGD with HLA Tissue Typing* (13 March 2009) A09/04, p. 2. (obtained under Official Information Act 1982 Request).

134 Letter from Dr Rosemary Marks to Professor Sylvia Rumball (ACART chair) regarding donation of cord blood, other tissues, and solid organs (10 February 2009). (Obtained under Official Information Act 1982 Request to the Ministry of Health.)

135 ACART, *Consultation with the Minister of Health on Draft Guidelines for the Use of PGD with HLA Tissue Typing* (Wellington, May 2009), report no.: 20090790. [Request for access to these Guidelines under the Official Information Act 1982 denied by the Ministry of Health pursuant to the Official Information Act 1982, s. 9 (2)(g)(i).]

136 See ACART minutes, 10 July 2009, at p. 5 (viewed 27/7/2012). See www.acart.health.govt.nz (viewed 02/06/2010). NEAC is a statutory body charged with providing advice on 'ethical issues of national significance regarding health and disability research and services'. See www.neac.health.govt.nz (viewed 02/06/2010).

In addition to these significant procedural issues, some substantive problems are apparent. A notable factor in all of the consultations on preimplantation tissue-typing is a lack of explicit discussion as to how the purpose and the principles of the HART Act 2004 apply to this issue. Both the 2007 and 2008 consultations simply rehearse the Act's principles in full as a prelude to introducing proposed policy. Greater attention, it seems, is paid to submissions made on the draft policy.

Yet, it seems imperative that both the purpose of the Act, and the principles contained within it, are demonstrably used to guide and justify policy that is promulgated pursuant to the Act. While it cannot be discounted that this may occur in practice, making it explicit would enable ACART to *demonstrate* its deliberative credentials and would correspondingly strengthen the perceived legitimacy of resulting proposed policy – both to the public and to the Minister. While the general orientation of the guidelines can be supported, given the Act's purposes and principles, this would be greatly enhanced if it were made more explicit.[137]

Conclusion

This chapter has attempted to highlight the ambivalence, both historically and currently, that has been displayed towards reproductive liberty in New Zealand. It has suggested that the value of reproductive liberty has been, and continues to be, subsumed within a flawed assumption of the legitimacy of state intervention in reproduction.

The arguably inherently problematic regulatory framework for PGD has been outlined and critiqued. The HART Order, introduced six years ago, which specifies the criteria necessary before PGD may be performed as a routine clinical procedure, is extremely ambiguous. Despite the issue being raised both by respondents to ACART consultations and by academic commentary, ACART has been (at least publicly) silent on this issue. Yet it is questionable whether there are sufficiently strong reasons to deny either susceptibility testing or preimplantation exclusion testing for certain late-onset conditions such as HD. In this respect, rather than the state justifying regulatory incursion into reproductive liberty by conscientious review of its provisions, it has effectively placed the onus on individuals who might wish to utilise PGD in these circumstances to seek clarification of the law. Arguably, the reverse should be the case. When the law imposes restrictions on ostensibly private conduct, especially when backed by criminal sanctions, that law should lack ambiguity and be based on established principles, such as those provided in the Act. Further, if ACART were to demonstrate a commitment to the principle of reproductive liberty, this would require it to consider the grounds on which access to these types of testing should be denied rather than, as currently seems to be the case, why it should be permitted.

137 See Snelling, 'Embryonic HLA tissue typing and made-to-match siblings'.

It is possible that, just as successive Governments have been content to permit a liberal interpretation of New Zealand's inherently illiberal abortion law, a liberal interpretation of the HART Order may be adopted, such that late-onset susceptibility testing (or even exclusion testing for HD) will be performed by clinics without ACART explicitly endorsing it via the statutory process, but this merely circumvents the real issue at stake, which is the legitimate reach of the law in matters of reproduction and personal morality. Legitimacy, at the very least, requires that there must be good reasons for regulating, and that issues are fully explored rather than simply avoided because they are morally charged.

In addition, the arguably problematic 2005 Guidelines regulating preimplantation HLA tissue-typing remain in force, despite considerable attempts to revise them. This situation appears largely to be the result of political and procedural issues, rather than the actual intent of ACART. However, given that the aim of the HART Act 2004 is to establish a flexible decision-making system that relies on a statutory body to formulate policy and advice based on specified principles, it is difficult to see these principles being expressly applied or flexibility being achieved in practice. The fact that New Zealand has established a regulatory framework for PGD does not presuppose its legitimacy, although arguably the Act provides the tools for principled policy-making.

It is clear that ACART does not have the degree of independence that the HART Act 2004 appears to have intended to establish. While ACART seems to be authorised as a policy-making body given its statutory remit, this does not appear to be the case in practice. Rather it seems that it is the Minister of Health who has authoritative power and that decision-making ultimately remains the prerogative of the Executive. In this sense it is difficult to determine how the HART Act 2004 has changed, or indeed improved upon, the regulatory system that existed prior to its introduction, apart, that is, from adding the force of the criminal law – itself a dubious mechanism in this context. What is more certain is that a rich conception of reproductive liberty does not appear to have informed much of the debate regarding PGD in New Zealand.

9 The state in action: an insider's view of how the state regulates the use of PGD with HLA tissue-typing in New Zealand

Mark Henaghan and Thomas Cleary

Introduction

In New Zealand, the choice by intending parents to use reproductive technology is limited by legislation.[1] This default restriction on the prospective parents' procreative autonomy applies unless the use of the assisted reproductive procedure has been approved[2] on the basis of guidelines or regulations.[3] The task of creating these guidelines falls to a non-governmental advisory committee, the Advisory Committee on Assisted Reproductive Technology (ACART). This advisory committee is supposedly unconstrained by political considerations and, in theory, provides a forum for deliberative discussions on the ethical and social disagreements that surround the use of assisted reproductive technologies.

This chapter provides an analysis, from the perspective of a member of ACART, of how the advisory committee functions in reality. It focuses specifically on the development of guidelines controlling the use of pre-implantation genetic diagnosis (PGD) with human leukocyte antigen (HLA) tissue-typing, more commonly referred to as creating 'saviour siblings'.

Deliberative democracy and the design of ACART

In regulating any ethically controversial issue, society is confronted with two difficulties. The first is how society deals with pluralism and reasonable disagreement on morality. The second problem is ensuring that whatever decision society reaches has legitimacy. These two difficulties have plagued political philosophers for centuries and there have been many suggested responses. One response which has only relatively recently risen to prominence is the concept of 'deliberative democracy'.[4]

1 Human Assisted Reproductive Technology (HART) Act 2004, ss. 8 and 16.
2 The Ethics Committee on Assisted Reproductive Technology has the task of deciding individual applications: HART Act 2004, s. 19 (2).
3 HART Act 2004, ss. 19 (2) and 76.
4 Dryzek, J., *Deliberative Democracy and Beyond*, Oxford: Oxford University Press, 2000, at p. v.

'Deliberative democracy' refers to the idea that in deciding an issue where there is reasonable disagreement, deliberation is the best process for determining a binding outcome, as well as the source of the outcome's legitimacy.[5] It is an 'outcome-oriented process'[6] and provides a synthesis of both the procedural and constitutional democratic theories which had held sway previously. The advantage of deliberative democracy is that it suspends judgement until different viewpoints have been heard and that it provides a strong basis for different viewpoints being heard. It has been selected as a theoretical basis for this chapter because it looks for solutions through a process of open analysis, rather than taking a particular view in advance. Open analysis is essential because:

> For a community to work through potentially deeply divisive issues, it is crucial that an attitude of seeing the concerns of others in their best light is cultivated. This is not the same as giving up one's own values and committing to the values and beliefs that give a particular concern force. Dr Anthony T Kronman has said: Only the person who has surveyed, with sympathetic detachment, the conflicting interpretations that different members of his community offer of its goals is in a position to say whether his own preliminary views should be revised and to make an informed choice among the alternatives before him.[7]

This section will examine the claims of deliberative democracy. First it will consider how deliberative democracy responds to the problems posed by moral disagreement and legitimacy. Next it will examine six deliberative principles proposed by Gutmann and Thompson[8] that provide a framework for how deliberative democracy works. Finally it will assess how the state attempted to create a deliberatively democratic advisory committee.

Sources of reasonable disagreement

John Rawls considered that an unavoidable feature of a liberal, free society – such as New Zealand – is that people will reasonably disagree on moral issues.[9] This was because there are what Rawls terms many 'hazards' that are involved in the conscientious exercise of reason in political life.[10] David Hume's account

5 Ibid.

6 Gutmann, A. and Thompson, D., *Democracy and Disagreement*, Cambridge, MA: Belknap Press of Harvard University Press, 1996, at p. 27.

7 Henaghan, M. and McLean, S., 'Main findings', in Henaghan, M. (ed.), *Choosing Genes for Future Children: Regulating Preimplantation Genetic Diagnosis*, Dunedin, Human Genome Research Project, 2006, at p. 3, quoting Kronman, A., *The Lost Lawyer: Failing Ideals of the Legal Profession*, Cambridge, MA: Belknap Press of Harvard University Press, 1995, at p. 104.

8 Gutmann and Thompson, *Democracy and Disagreement.*

9 Rawls, J., *Political Liberalism*, New York: Columbia University Press, 1993, at p. 58.

10 Rawls, J., 'The domain of the political and overlapping consensus', in Copp, D., Hampton, J. and Roemer, J. (eds), *The Idea of Democracy*, Cambridge: Cambridge University Press, 1993, at p. 248.

of these 'hazards' or sources of moral conflict is that there is a moderate scarcity of resources which, when linked to human nature's limited generosity, causes conflict.[11] However Gutmann and Thompson view this account as incomplete and add two other sources: incompatible values, and incomplete understanding.[12] Moderate scarcity of resources refers to the fact that there are not sufficient resources to sate people's desires. As a result of this, distributing resources is an unavoidable feature of society, and if humans have limited generosity – that is if they act in part for selfish reasons – then one individual's needs will inevitably be prioritised over another's.

While Gutmann and Thompson agree that there are two sources of moral disagreement, they disagree with Hume that if there were sufficient resources and unlimited generosity moral disagreements would cease.[13] This is because the 'problem of moral conflict originates not only between *persons* but also between the moral *values* themselves'.[14] Reasonable people often hold incompatible values that cannot be overcome by simply having sufficient resources. Further, despite each individual's best efforts, there is the problem of incomplete understanding. It is not always possible to see all the relevant perspectives because of a lack of access to facts, and because individual world views can colour the interpretation of ambiguous facts. On this basis, Gutmann and Thompson argue that all four sources of moral disagreement are 'endemic to human politics' and so 'the problem of moral disagreement is a condition with which we must learn to live, not merely an obstacle to be overcome on the way to a just society'.[15]

Dealing with reasonable disagreement

Pluralism in values is something that any proposed method must address. Deliberative democracy responds to different sources of moral disagreement in the following ways. First, deliberative democracy creates a forum where each citizen is 'called upon to weigh interests other than his own and to be guided by some conception of justice and the public good rather than by his own inclinations'.[16] In this forum everyone is required to 'appeal to principles that others can accept'[17] which 'have for their reason of existence the common good'.[18] This is the basis for the principle of reciprocity, which will be elaborated on later. Deliberative democracy seeks to overcome the issue of limited generosity and moderate scarcity of resources by asking participants to stand

11 Gutmann and Thompson, *Democracy and Disagreement*, at p. 22.
12 Ibid.
13 Ibid., at p. 23.
14 Ibid. (emphasis in the original).
15 Ibid., at pp. 25–6.
16 Rawls, J., *A Theory of Justice*, Cambridge, MA: Harvard University Press, 1971, at p. 234.
17 Ibid.
18 Mill, J. S., 'Considerations on representative government', in Robson, J. M. (ed.), *Collected Writings*, vol. 19, Toronto: University of Toronto Press, 1997, at p. 68.

in another individual's metaphorical shoes. Participants are required to try to understand others' interests as well as using arguments others can engage with based on the common good, as distinct from the individual good, which distinguishes 'self-interested claims from public-spirited ones'.[19]

While requiring reasons is no guarantee of reaching agreement, for 'those moral conflicts for which there is no deliberative agreement at present, ongoing deliberation can help citizens better understand the moral seriousness of the views they continue to oppose, and better co-operate with their fellow citizens who hold these views'.[20] Furthermore, simply providing a forum where arguments are heard and listened to rather than ignored is an important part of the political process in both representation and in legitimising the outcome; this is discussed below.[21]

Finally, deliberative democracy helps to temper the problem of incomplete understanding. This is because making people deliberate forces them to 'move beyond the conventional patterns of group politics'[22] and helps to remove the particular perspectives that can colour the facts. Also, as Rawls points out, '[d]iscussion, is a way of combining information and enlarging the range of arguments' and concludes that 'in the course of time, the effects of common deliberation seem bound to improve matters'.[23]

From the above discussion, it is apparent that deliberative democracy addresses sources of moral disagreement by minimising or presenting ways through each problem, rather than ignoring or pretending that each source can be 'overcome'. Unlike other theories of decision-making, this approach respects the inevitability of reasonable disagreement, which is important in respecting minority views. Minority views are accepted and not dismissed as being 'wrong' for the sake of achieving a decision.

Providing legitimacy to the outcome

The second difficulty that any theory must confront is providing legitimacy to a decision. As Gutmann and Thompson state, '[t]he moral authority of collective judgments about policy depends in part on the moral quality of the process by which citizens collectively reach those judgments'.[24] Purely majoritarian decision-making on issues that are binding on society as a whole is generally unsatisfactory, as it does not require a reason for a decision; it only shows that a majority of people wanted a particular outcome.[25] In Gutmann

19 Gutmann and Thompson, *Democracy and Disagreement*, at p. 43.
20 Ibid.
21 Sandel, M. J., *Justice: What's the Right Thing to Do?*, New York: Farrar, Strauss and Giroux, 2010, at p. 268.
22 Gutmann and Thompson, *Democracy and Disagreement*, at p. 43.
23 Ibid., at p. 4.
24 Ibid., at p. 53.
25 Daniels, N., 'Enabling democratic deliberation', in Macedo, S. (ed.), *Deliberative Politics*, New York: Oxford University Press, 1999, at p. 204.

and Thompson's conception, deliberation is the best way for citizens to resolve their moral disagreements about policies and processes, since 'deliberation is not only a means to an end, but also a means for deciding what means are morally required to pursue [society's] common ends'.[26] In order to pursue these ends deliberative democracy sets out a framework which consists of six principles: reciprocity, publicity, accountability, liberty, basic opportunity and fair opportunity. The first three are concerned with how the deliberation and outcome must occur in order to have legitimacy, while the last three are aimed at the outcome and what must be considered. Each principle will be addressed in turn.

'Reciprocity' refers to citizens being required to offer 'reasons that can be accepted by others who are similarly motivated to find reasons that can be accepted by others'.[27] The purpose of requiring these public reasons is that the outcomes of the deliberation 'are mutually binding' and so 'citizens should aspire to a kind of political reasoning that is mutually justifiable'.[28] This idea is borrowed from Rawls who holds that for democratic legitimacy only 'public reasons' (reasons that are publicly accessible to all reasonable people and not based on a higher claim such as the divine) should be used in public decision-making.[29] This idea, however, has been subject to criticism. For example, United States President Barack Obama stated that 'to say that men and women should not inject their "personal morality" into public policy debates is a practical absurdity'.[30] On a theoretical level, Fish argues that it is incoherent to control the contents of arguments in a liberal society.[31] Galston claims that such a limit on the content is highly restrictive, undermines legitimacy, and is contrary to the principle of reciprocity,[32] while others state that such a restriction represents a dominant power structure being imposed, sidelining minorities and their voices.[33] Sandel argues that rather than sidelining these voices and their reasons, society needs to engage with them, and failure to do so can 'provoke backlash and resentment and can make for an impoverished public discourse',[34] which recreates the problem of incomplete understanding that deliberative democracy seeks to address. Therefore there is an inherent tension within this principle of reciprocity of ensuring that everyone can engage in the debate, while at the same time allowing participants to engage with the reasoning behind the decision.

26 Gutmann and Thompson, *Democracy and Disagreement*, at p. 4.
27 Ibid., at p. 53.
28 Ibid.
29 Rawls, J., 'The idea of public reason revisited', *University of Chicago Law Review*, 64 (1997): 765, at p. 766.
30 Obama, B., 'Call to renewal keynote address', Washington, DC, 28 June 2006.
31 Fish, S., 'Mutual respect as a device of exclusion', in Macedo, S. (ed.), *Deliberative Politics*, New York: Oxford University Press, 1999, at pp. 88 and 95.
32 Galston, W. A., 'Diversity, toleration, and deliberative democracy', ibid., at p. 43.
33 Dryzek, J., *Deliberative Democracy and Beyond*, Oxford: Oxford University Press, 2000, at pp. 19, 64–5.
34 Sandel, *Justice*, at p. 268.

Gutmann and Thompson's second principle is that of 'publicity'. This requires that 'the reasons that officials and citizens give to justify their political actions, and the information necessary to assess those reasons, should be public'.[35] This is important in legitimising the outcome as 'only public justifications can secure the consent of citizens, whether it be tacit or explicit'.[36] Providing reasons also helps to create a pattern similar to case law, which improves the decision-making process both internally and externally. This is because '[i]nternally, the requirements lead to more efficient, coherent, and fairer decisions over time' while '[e]xternally, the emerging case law will strengthen broader public deliberation and contribute to the perceived legitimacy of the decision-makers'.[37]

This could be seen as very restrictive. However, while these decisions might create a precedent of sorts, this does not imply past infallibility. Rather it implies 'giving careful consideration to why earlier decision-makers made the choices they did. It involves a form of institutional reflective equilibrium, a commitment to both transparency and coherence.'[38] In a body such as ACART where the membership changes, continuity in the decision-making process is important for the public to accept the decisions made by ACART. At the same time, recognising that past decisions are not set in stone and can be revisited is important to ensure that past guidelines are continually scrutinised to remain coherent with any changes.

Tied into the principle of publicity is the principle of 'accountability'. Accountability is necessary for any public decision that has a binding effect because it means the decision-maker is not disconnected from the decision. While this principle is applied to the representatives making the decision, deliberative democracy 'does not specify a single form of representation'.[39] Instead 'it searches for modes of representation that support the give-and-take of serious and sustained moral argument within legislative bodies, between legislators and the citizens, and among the citizens themselves'.[40] In the case of ACART this representative model is a specialist panel that is intended to represent certain interests of society including ethical, consumer, practitioner, Māori and religious perspectives.[41] The accountability of these representatives is through Parliament and the Minister of Health who can remove representatives without having to give reasons.[42]

However no mode of representation is flawless. The problem with having a non-governmental decision-making body is the danger that representatives

35 Gutmann and Thompson, *Democracy and Disagreement*, at p. 95.
36 Ibid.
37 Daniels, N., 'Enabling democratic deliberation', in Macedo, *Deliberative Politics*, at pp. 204–5.
38 Ibid.
39 Gutmann and Thompson, *Democracy and Disagreement*, at p. 131.
40 Ibid.
41 HART Act 2004, s. 34.
42 Ibid., s. 34(2).

might become specialised deliberators 'while citizens become spectators'.[43] Deliberative democracy requires that the public engage with the deliberation. However, the reverse danger is that of popularism, where policies are adopted, not based on coherent reasons, but because they are generally acceptable policies.[44] Depending on which form of representation is chosen, the principle of accountability is applied differently, which can lead to different outcomes. There is also the related problem of which groups are chosen to have representatives, and how those individuals are selected. Added to this is the extent to which people taking part in public forums can put forward the views of the group they represent, or act as individuals. These issues provide challenges to the principle of accountability and suggest that results will vary depending on who the representatives are.

These three principles mentioned above – reciprocity, publicity and accountability – concern the process and legitimisation of the outcome. The remaining three principles – those of liberty, basic opportunity and fair opportunity – are directed instead at the content of the decisions themselves.

The first of these content principles is 'liberty'. However, this is distinct from a libertarian conception of liberty or autonomy. Under a libertarian conception, autonomy is the paramount value. As John Stuart Mill put it: '[T]he only part of the conduct of anyone, for which he is amenable to society, is that which concerns others. In the part which concerns merely himself, his independence is, of right, absolute.' [45] In the area of assisted reproductive technology, this is the foundation of procreative autonomy. This argument is often used to support few or no restrictions being placed on assisted reproductive technologies, as prospective parents should be able to procreate however they want, unless there would be an objective harm as a result.[46] However, Gutmann and Thompson reject this extreme version of autonomy. Liberty can be tempered by social morality and the harm principle. They argue that failing to temper autonomy would make 'autonomy' a supreme value, which would be contrary to the principle of 'reciprocity'. While the harm principle can be argued to fall within the idea of social morality, it is being used here as a separate consideration because social morality can also include the legitimate intuition that certain things are just wrong.

The second content principle is respecting basic opportunity. This means that the outcome of the deliberation should aim to secure citizens an adequate level of basic goods.[47] This principle is especially important in areas of new technologies where the differences in access to the technologies between the 'haves' and the 'have-nots' can be exacerbated by free market effects. This harks back to Hume's moderate scarcity of resources as a source of moral disagreement.

43 Gutmann and Thompson, *Democracy and Disagreement*, at p. 132.
44 Warnock, M., *An Intelligent Person's Guide to Ethics*, London: Duckworth, 2006, at p. 118.
45 Mill, J. S., *On Liberty*, London: John W. Parker and Son, West Strand, 1859, at p. 22.
46 Ibid.
47 Gutmann and Thompson, *Democracy and Disagreement*, at p. 273.

Deliberative democracy's approach to minimise scarcity of resources is as follows: if something is recognised as a basic good it should be available, as much as possible, to all people, regardless of what resources the individual has. Linked to this principle is the final content principle – fair opportunity. This recognises that access to some resources is not a universal right, as they are not basic goods. However, if the resources are going to be distributed, the distribution should at least be done in a fair manner. This acts as a counter to the previous principle, which can sometimes be seen as egalitarian and so focuses solely on the equality of the outcome, not the process, whereas fair opportunity requires that the process be fair as well. There is an inherent contradiction between the final two principles when expressed in absolute terms. However, the final principle only comes into play where there is not an automatic right to the basic goods. In that sense, the final principle does not undermine the basic opportunity principle.

These six principles provide the foundation for deliberative democracy. However, they are quite vague and flexible. It is only when they are applied that they become more concrete. The next section will examine how these principles have been incorporated into the legislative framework creating the deliberative body that is ACART.

The genesis of ACART

The shape and function of ACART were forged under intense parliamentary scrutiny. The same could be said for the statute that created ACART: the Human Assisted Reproductive Technology (HART) Act 2004. This Act was originally introduced in 1996 and followed a tortuous path until it finally was enacted in a significantly different form eight years later.[48] As first conceived, ACART was modelled on the Human Fertilisation and Embryology Authority (HFEA) in the United Kingdom and designed as a deliberative democracy of representatives that encompassed several areas of society. As originally envisaged, ACART would be autonomous from the legislature, and thus could issue guidelines based on coherent reasons, independent of political pressures.[49]

This context is important because, in 2002, prior to the HART Act 2004, there was considerable debate in the United Kingdom on the autonomy of the HFEA following the approval of a case involving PGD with HLA

48 For the background to the HART Act 2004, see Snelling, J., 'Law and regulation', in Human Genome Research Project, *Choosing Genes for Future Children*, Dunedin: Human Research Project, 2005, at pp. 243–5.

49 Gutmann and Thompson, *Democracy and Disagreement*, at p. 45; Chadwick, S. (25 August 2004) 619 NZPD 15058; under s. 41(2) of the HART Act 2004, ACART is required to only 'consult' with the Minister of Health. Martin argues that this means that the Minister has 'no direct pre-emptive control over the guidelines' and the Minister 'could only take remedial action to hold the Committee to account'. Martin, P., 'HART failure: the power of the Advisory Committee under the Human Assisted Reproductive Technology Act 2004', *Otago Yearbook of Legal Research* [2005]: 48.

tissue-typing.[50] As a result of this, the autonomy of the proposed ACART was the subject of intense Parliamentary debate in New Zealand. Several politicians felt that giving ACART the power to issue guidelines without Parliamentary approval would breach the 'well established Parliamentary principle that matters of policy and substance should be dealt with by Parliament and that only technical issues should be delegated'.[51] However, as Steve Chadwick, the former Deputy Minister of Health under the previous Labour government, pointed out, '[i]f we as politicians needed that amount of detail to get our head around technologies and science in [the HART Bill], we should not expect politicians ever to understand what is behind the making of guidelines that will guide this whole industry,'[52] and thus the autonomous role originally proposed for ACART was retained, albeit in a tempered form, whereby, prior to publishing the guidelines, ACART was required to give the guidelines to the Minister of Health (among others)[53] who subsequently must report on the guidelines to the House of Representatives, as well as the Health Select Committee.[54] This provides some parliamentary supervision of ACART's guidelines, without requiring ACART to seek ministerial approval.[55] However, as a result of the parliamentary debate over whether or not ACART should have autonomy, and because of the need for public acceptance of the guidelines,[56] in practice ACART waits for ministerial approval of its guidelines.[57]

The fear that ACART might have too much power to make public policy that was disconnected from societal values led Parliament to refuse to add more experts to the Advisory Committee, or to make it smaller, as to do so would alter the delicate balance between public policy considerations and technical expertise.[58] In providing this balance, at least half of the members must not be health practitioners, involved in health research, or associated with a provider of assisted reproductive technology.[59] This is one of several statutory constraints of the shape of the Advisory Committee.

50 *Quintavalle* v. *Human Fertilisation & Embryology Authority* [2002] EWHC 3000. This case quotes the House of Commons Select Committee on Science and Technology, Fourth Report, 18 July 2002, which states 'democracy is not served by unelected quangos taking decisions on behalf of Parliament' (para. 18).

51 Kedgley, S. (25 August 2004) 619 NZPD 15063.

52 Chadwick, S. (25 August 2004) 619 NZPD 15058. Also Heather Roy says that most politicians 'would have absolutely no right to be on [ACART], because we do not have the appropriate knowledge' and so 'Parliamentarians should not be involved in that process' ((10 November 2004) 73 NZPD 16844).

53 HART Act 2004, s. 36 (2)(a).

54 Health Committee, 'Human Assisted Reproductive Technology Bill' (6 August 2004), at p. 7.

55 Compare this to Canada where the final guidelines made by the Assisted Human Reproduction Act are subject to Ministerial Approval: Nelson, E., 'Comparative perspectives: regulating preimplantation genetic diagnosis in Canada and the United Kingdom', *Fertility and Sterility*, 85 (2006): 1646–52, at 1649.

56 'We can only regulate insofar as society will accept that regulation' (Szoke, H., 'The nanny state or responsible government?', *Journal of Law and Medicine*, 9(4) (2002): 470–82, at 473).

57 Ryall, T. (16 November 2010) 668 NZPD 35884.

58 Hutchinson, Dr P. (25 August 2004) 619 NZPD 15058.

59 HART Act 2004, s. 34 (6).

Under the HART Act 2004, the Minister of Health is required to appoint between eight and 12 members.[60] The Minister is required to appoint the members based on the 'recipe' specified in s. 34 (4) of the HART Act 2004:

> (a) 1 or more members with expertise in assisted reproductive procedures; and
> (b) 1 or more members with expertise in human reproductive research; and
> (c) 1 or more members with expertise in ethics; and
> (d) 1 or more Māori members with expertise in Māori customary values and practice and the ability to articulate issues from a Māori perspective; and
> (e) 1 or more members with the ability to articulate issues from a consumer perspective; and
> (f) 1 or more members with expertise in relevant areas of the law; and
> (g) 1 or more members with the ability to articulate the interests of children

This membership is a political compromise, and empowers the Minister to stack the committee with one or more members from any particular group. Nonetheless, it attempts to achieve the delicate balance of ensuring technical expertise in the various issues posed by assisted reproductive technologies, while also ensuring that public policy considerations are taken into account. In 2011 there were eight members. The members' expertise often straddles multiple fields in the three fields of ethics, consumer issues, and Māori (the indigenous people of New Zealand) values and traditions, where the membership with specific expertise is more than the statutory minimum. These three areas are not technology based, and indicate that in appointing these members, the Minister of Health placed greater emphasis on the public policy component over technological expertise in representation.

How ACART is designed to decide

Having described the membership of ACART and its relationship to the state, it is necessary to outline how ACART is designed to make decisions. In making any decision the Advisory Committee is required to be 'guided' by several statutory principles set out in s. 4 of the HART Act 2004. Exactly what 'guided' means is not clear. In fact, it has been suggested that 'guided' is too weak a term and provides such a broad discretion that the principles 'may have only little effect on the Committee's decisions'.[61] The principles in s. 4 of the HART Act

60 Ibid., s. 33 (1)(a).
61 Martin, 'HART failure', at p. 38.

2004 that the Committee are to be guided by include that the health and well-being of children born as a result of an assisted reproductive procedure are an important, but not overriding, consideration.[62] The health, safety and dignity of present and future generations are to be preserved and promoted.[63] It is mandatory to protect the health and well-being of women who are acknowledged as being more directly and significantly affected by assisted reproductive procedures than men.[64] Informed consent is required,[65] and the different ethical, spiritual and cultural perspectives – including the needs, values and beliefs of Māori – are to be treated with respect.[66] Donor offspring should be aware of their genetic origins and have access to information about them.[67]

In addition to the statutory principles set out in s. 4, ACART is implicitly required to be transparent in its decision-making process.[68] This implicit requirement is drawn from the statutory requirement to consult. Before issuing any guidelines ACART must first provide a discussion paper on the issue, then provide a reasonable opportunity for interested parties and the public to make submissions, and finally ACART must take all submissions into account.[69] That said, the role of consultation in the drafting of the guidelines is not altogether clear. Indeed the National Ethics Advisory Committee (NEAC), which is set up to provide policy for all ethics committees in New Zealand, and ACART view the role of consultation differently. NEAC views consultation as necessary to 'validate' the guidelines. In contrast, ACART views 'public input [as] an important contribution to developing guidelines' but equally important is the 'knowledge and experience of members'.[70] This difference goes back to the role of deliberation in deliberative democracies. Parliament, in creating ACART and delegating decision-making power, has intentionally set up a forum where the public can enter the discussion, but at the same time the members of ACART are intended to further this discussion and reach a conclusion by acting as a microcosm of society.

Aside from these process-based requirements, as noted earlier, ACART must also provide the Minister of Health with the guidelines before they are issued, to ensure parliamentary supervision. In addition, ACART must publish the agenda and meeting papers of each meeting on the Internet.[71] These requirements, alongside the obligation to consult, form the implicit requirement of transparency in the decision-making process.[72]

62 HART Act 2004, s. 4(a); for a discussion of this, see Martin, 'HART failure', at p. 32.
63 Ibid., s. 4(b).
64 Ibid., s. 4(c).
65 Ibid., s. 4(d).
66 Ibid., s. 4(f) and (g).
67 Ibid., s. 4(e).
68 Atkin, B., 'Regulation of assisted reproduction: the recent New Zealand model in comparison with other systems', *Revue Juridique Polynésienne*, 11 (2005): 81–100, at p. 97.
69 HART Act 2004, s. 36(1).
70 ACART, *Agenda and Meeting Papers*, 13 August 2007, at p. 47.
71 HART Act 2004, s. 33 (3).
72 Atkin, 'Regulation of assisted reproduction', at p. 97.

Once the guidelines are issued, a separate body, the Ethics Committee on Assisted Reproductive Technology (ECART) is tasked with applying the guidelines.[73] This is an improvement upon the position prior to the HART Act 2004 where the National Ethics Committee on Assisted Human Reproduction (NECAHR)[74] was placed in the 'unsatisfactory and often difficult position' of having to create guidelines and also apply them.[75]

The above section has provided an overview of the theory underpinning ACART and the legislative framework upon which it is based. Theoretically ACART follows a deliberative democratic model where reasonable disagreement is respected. The aim of ACART, as a distinct non-governmental forum, is to represent society and to provide an avenue by which society can interact and deliberate upon vexing ethical questions. It also provides a mechanism to issue guidelines, based not on political expedience, but on coherent, rational reasoning. While everyone may not agree with ACART's guidelines, the reasoning behind the guidelines is legitimate because the process is fair and open and the reasons for outcomes are publicly accessible. However, whether in practice this is how ACART makes its decisions is something that will be addressed by examining how ACART developed its guidelines on PGD with HLA tissue-typing.

Ethics of PGD with HLA tissue-typing

It is necessary first to understand the ethical controversies surrounding creating 'saviour siblings' that ACART had to engage with when developing the guidelines. The term 'saviour sibling', made popular by literature such as *My Sister's Keeper*,[76] is used extensively in this debate. However, the term carries with it many connotations, some helpful and others not.[77] For this reason the term PGD with HLA tissue-typing will be used to characterise the debate and 'donor child' and 'recipient' to refer to the direct participants. Also, in order to understand the debate around PGD with HLA tissue-typing, and to delineate it from the wider debate on PGD itself, it is necessary to understand what this procedure can and cannot be used for. This section will first provide an overview of what PGD with HLA tissue-typing is and why it is medically important. It will then look at the ethical arguments for allowing or restricting, wholly or in part, PGD with HLA tissue-typing. Finally it will detail how ACART went about the process of ethical debate in developing the guidelines.

73 HART Act 2004, s. 28 (1).
74 NECAHR was a ministerial committee established under the New Zealand Public Health and Disability Act 2000, s. 11.
75 Benson-Pope, D. (25 August 2004) 65 NZPD 15060.
76 Picoult, J., *My Sister's Keeper*, New York: Atria Books, 2004.
77 Jones, D. G., *Designers of the Future: Who Should Make the Decisions?*, Oxford: Monarch Books, 2005, at p. 36.

What is PGD with HLA tissue-typing?

The major histocompatibility complex (MHC) is found in most vertebrates. In humans it is called the human leukocyte antigen (HLA) system.[78] It is vital to the human body's immune response.[79] The human immune system uses HLAs to distinguish between cells or cellular materials that are foreign to the body (antigens), from those produced by the body itself. HLAs normally cause transplanted organs or cells to be identified as something 'non-self' and so the immune system attacks them. However, if the organ or cell, such as bone marrow or stem cell, to be donated is an identical HLA match, then the immune system will not be triggered. This is why having an HLA-matched donor is crucial to organ and cell transplants. However, the chances of unrelated donors and recipients having such an HLA match are very small. Even if a specific HLA match is found, the treatment has a low level of success and has a high level of associated morbidity or poor survival times.[80] Putting this into perspective, using haematopoietic stem cells (HSC) from an unrelated donor compared to a related donor doubles the risk of the recipient dying.[81]

While the probability of an HLA match might be low, the potential benefits of finding one can be high. There are several severe diseases that are able to be treated using tissues from HLA identical donors. These are set out in Figure 9.1. The numerous conditions and especially their severity means that finding an HLA matching donor is potentially life-saving.

Due to the low probability of finding an HLA match from an unrelated person, people unsurprisingly turn to relatives as a potential source. One option available to parents with a sick child with a condition in Figure 9.1 is to conceive more children naturally and hope that the resulting child will have an exact HLA match. The chance of this is 3/16, which is quite low. This is because each individual inherits half of their HLA tissue-type from each of their parents.

A more accurate means to ensure that a resulting child will be a HLA match is by using PGD with HLA tissue-typing, which is a relatively simple procedure. Embryos are created in vitro, and at the blastomere stage of development (where the embryo consists of between six to ten cells usually

78 Horton, R., Wilming, L. and Rand, V., 'Gene map of the extended human MHC', *Nature Reviews*, 5 (2004): 889–99, at p. 889.

79 For more information about HLA, see: Beck, S. and Trowsdale, J., 'The human major histocompatibility complex: lessons from the DNA sequence', *Annual Review of Genomics and Human Genetics*, 1 (2000): 117–37; Wolf, S.M., Kahn, J. P. and Wagner, J.E., 'Using preimplantation genetic diagnosis to create a stem cell donor: issues, guidelines and limits', *Journal of Law, Medicine and Ethics*, 32 (2003): 327–39; Parham, P. and Ohta, T., 'Population biology of antigen presentation by MHC class I molecules', *Science*, 272 (1996): 67–74; Hedrick, P. W. and Kim, T. J., 'Genetics of complex polymorphisms: parasites and maintenance of the major histocompatible complex variation', in Sing, R. S. and Krimbas, C. S. (eds), *Evolutionary Genetics: From Molecules to Morphology*, Cambridge: Cambridge University Press, 2000, at p. 206.

80 Grewal, S. S., Kahn, J. P. and MacMillian, M. L., 'Successful hematopoietic stem cell transplantation for Fanconi anemia from an unaffected HLA-genotype-identical-sibling selected using preimplantation genetic diagnosis', *Blood*, 103 (2004): 1147–51, at p. 1149.

81 Ibid.

Malignant diseases

- chronic myelogenous leukaemia
- acute lymphocyte leukaemia
- acute myelocytic leukaemia
- juvenile myelomonocytic leukaemia
- chronic lymphocytic leukaemia
- non-Hodgkin lymphoma
- Hodgkin lymphoma
- multiple myeloma
- neuroblastoma

Non-malignant diseases

- severe aplastic anaemia
- paroxysmal nocturnal hematuria
- hemoglobinopathies (e.g. thalassemia, sickle-cell disease)
- immunodeficiencies (e.g. SCID, Wiskott–Aldrich)
- inborn errors of metabolism

Other possible indications

- autoimmune disorders
- solid tumours
- tolerance induction for solid organ transplantation

Figure 9.1 Diseases able to be treated using tissue from HLA identical donors
Source: based on Wolf, S. M., Kahn, J. P. and Wagner, J. E., 'Using preimplantation genetic diagnosis to create a stem cell donor: issues, guidelines and limits', *Journal of Law, Medicine and Ethics*, 31(3) (2003): 327–39.

around three days after fertilisation) one or two cells are removed. The DNA from these cells is removed and amplified by polymerase chain reaction (PCR) or, in more recent times, fluorescence *in situ* hybridisation (FISH) which allows the HLA compatibility to be assessed.[82]

Ethical controversies surrounding PGD with HLA tissue-typing

This procedure is potentially life-saving for existing children, but is also ethically controversial. Fortunately the ethical controversies that surround PGD with HLA tissue-typing can be distinguished from some of the broader moral questions that are inherent in PGD itself, such as the fear of eugenics and enhancement. As the previous section on the science of PGD with HLA tissue-typing outlines, the sole use of the procedure is to select an HLA match for someone else who is sick.

This section will outline the various arguments for and against restricting this procedure. Aside from the 'pro-life' position, which views any manipulation or destruction of human embryos as morally wrong, there are two main objections to using the procedure itself: that PGD with HLA tissue-typing harms the welfare of the resulting child, and that the procedure treats such children as a mere means to an end and 'instrumentalises' them. Other objections relate to which conditions are serious enough to justify using the

82 Gavaghan, C., *Defending the Genetic Supermarket*, New York: Routledge-Cavendish, 2007, at p. 6.

procedure, who can be a recipient, and what tissues can be used. These objections are aimed not at the procedure itself, but the choices that PGD with HLA tissue-typing creates, and how these choices should be regulated.

Harm

The first main objection is that PGD with HLA tissue-typing harms the welfare of the resulting child. This argument claims that there are significant risks to the child and thus the procedure should be severely restricted or even banned depending on how serious the harm is. This is because PGD with HLA tissue-typing need not provide any benefit to the resulting child, and may expose the child to dangers both in the process and also in having tissue removed. Based on the harm principle, it is argued that there are not enough benefits to outweigh the risks of the procedure and so the embryos should not be screened unless the disease possibly affects them.[83] However, what the risks of the procedure are to the resulting child is not entirely clear. There are three possible sources of harm: the procedure itself, the removal of tissue, or the psychological or other harm associated with being a donor.

The first possible harm is that the embryo might be affected in development because of one or two cells being removed. However, this risk of harm does not seem to be substantial if it even exists.[84] Additionally, many children are born using PGD and the removal of cells does not seem to affect the resulting child.[85] Another possible area where harm might exist is in the treatment of the resulting child. Here the child might be the subject of medical invasions and removal of tissue, which, because it could lead to pain and suffering, could clearly amount to harm. However, the most common tissue sought from children born using PGD with HLA tissue-typing are the haematopoietic stem cells that are removed from the umbilical cord. As this involves no invasive surgery, there is no harm to the child. However, other sources of tissue, including bone marrow and regenerative tissue, might involve the donor child being subjected to pain and so be harmed. In medical practice, in order to be able to remove these tissues, it might be expected that the parents would have to show that such a procedure is in the child's best interests, since this is the usual requirement for medical interventions in respect of children. In reality, it may be hard to establish whether such a procedure is in a child's best interests. It is more likely that the analysis will be based on a consideration that it is not against the interests of a child, rather than it being in his or her best interests. This may depend on an evaluation of both the physical consequences and the psychological impact of donation, or of a failure to donate. In any case, it is highly improbable that anybody involved in pre-implantation procedures

83 Devolder, 'Preimplantation HLA typing', at p. 583.
84 Liu, C.K., '"Saviour siblings"? The distinction between PGD with HLA tissue typing and preimplantation HLA tissue typing', *Bioethical Inquiry*, 4 (2007): 65–70, at p. 69.
85 Ibid.

would have any role to play in what happens to a born child, and different legal requirements are in place when proposals to remove tissue for donation arise. These considerations act as a check to the argument that potential harm to the child should be a reason for not permitting PGD with HLA tissue-typing at all, but arguments about these kinds of possible harms to a donor child may still influence what restrictions are put in place on the use of the procedure.

The final argument concerning possible harm is that the procedure will lead to psychological harm. It is claimed that children might be psychologically harmed if they were to find out that they had been conceived in order to save someone else and also that they would be harmed by experiencing mental trauma (as distinct from physical pain) in being subjected to medical procedures. However, others argue that not allowing HLA tissue-typing could cause psychological harm to any born child, as s/he will experience the loss of a relationship if the intended recipient dies and it is therefore in his or her interests to be a donor. If HLA matching is not allowed, then the donor child may not be born, which leaves open the argument whether it is better to exist, than not exist at all. The harms here are largely speculative. A movie such as *My Sister's Keeper*[86] shows the potential for serious harm when a child is valued solely as a donor for others. Such a scenario does not eventuate if parents see the 'donor child' as a child in its own right. The potential psychological harm to the 'donor child' cannot be totally removed and does leave room for a precautionary case-by-case approach to ensure that each particular child's interests are not likely to be subverted.

'Instrumentalising' children

The second argument against permitting PGD with HLA tissue-typing is that it may allow parents to commodify or instrumentalise their children. This is based on Immanuel Kant's categorical imperative that a person should always be treated as an end and not merely as a means to an end.[87] The argument goes that because parents are intentionally selecting the embryo for a certain characteristic that is for the benefit of someone else, and which is not valuable in and of itself, then the parents are treating the embryo and resulting child as a means, rather than as an end. However, this argument misses the fact that Kant's imperative states that people should not be treated 'merely as a means'.[88] The categorical imperative can be transformed from a negative command, into a positive one of 'act always so that you respect every human being, yourself or another, as being a rational creature'.[89] A focus on the parents' actions, rather than the parents' intentions, is best because 'how one is treated by others over

86 Cassavetes, N., *My Sisters Keeper* (2009).
87 Kant, I., *Groundwork of the Metaphysics of Morals*, Denis, L. (ed.), Abbott, T. K. (trans.), Peterborough: Broadview Press, 2005, at p. 87.
88 Ibid.
89 Donagan, A., *The Theory of Morality*, Chicago: University of Chicago Press, 1977, at p. 65.

the course of one's life is more morally significant than the reasons for causing one to exist'.[90] Most parents who use PGD with HLA tissue-typing are motivated by compassion and love for their first child, and so it would be reasonable to assume that they would show equal respect in the way that they treated the donor child.

The concern about treating a donor child solely as a means is more likely to be realised in two ways. The first is if the parents selected an embryo and later had an abortion to collect the foetal stem cells. Once approval is granted for parents to use PGD with HLA tissue-typing, and the selected embryo is implanted, the future parents' decisions are outside of ACART's control. However, law prohibits having an abortion solely for this reason.[91] The second possibility is that the parents adopt out the resulting child once the necessary stem cells, bone marrow and other tissues are collected. However, yet again this lies beyond the scope of ACART's authority, and is governed by the law of adoption whereby the adoption is required to be in the best interests of the child.[92] Both scenarios are implausible,[93] and anecdotal evidence suggests that parents of children created using PGD with HLA tissue-typing are loving and do not treat their children solely as means.[94] It would be unwise to deny all PGD with HLA tissue-typing based on implausible situations, but it could be useful to consider any possible restrictions to prevent these situations from occurring.

Other ethical arguments

Aside from these two main arguments for banning or severely restricting PGD and HLA tissue-typing, there are several other ethical arguments that lead to calls for restrictions on who can use the procedure and how the procedure should be used. The first of these is based on the harm principle, and argues that while PGD with HLA tissue-typing should be allowed, it should only be allowed where the recipient's condition is sufficiently serious. This is where any possible harm to the embryo and resulting child would be outweighed by the serious condition suffered by an existing child; less serious conditions would not be able to justify placing the embryo and resulting child at risk of harm. The problem with this argument is that it requires the risk of harm to be quantified (and quantifiable) in order to weigh it against conditions suffered by existing children. Quantifying the predicted risk is difficult, particularly since it seems that the risks are at most minimal or even non-existent.[95] Further,

90 Glannogan, W., *Genes and Future People: Philosophical Issues in Human Genetics*, Oxford: Westview Press, 2001, at p. 120.
91 Crimes Act 1961, s. 183. Such an abortion would not be within the exclusions set out in s. 187A.
92 Adoption Act 1955, s. 11.
93 Devolder, 'Preimplantation HLA typing', at p. 584.
94 Ibid.
95 Liu, C. K., '"Saviour siblings"?', at p. 69.

as noted in Figure 9.1 above, most conditions that can be treated using tissues from an HLA tissue match are objectively relatively serious, and so the possible harm to a child selected as a tissue match will generally be outweighed by the actual serious disease being suffered by his or her sibling.

Another ethical argument surrounds what can be removed from a donor child. This has implications for restricting what a donor child can be created for. This ethical debate is not restricted just to PGD with HLA tissue-typing, but applies to removing organs from someone for the benefit of another. Where there is difficulty is where the procedure involves taking regenerative tissue, or an organ such as a kidney, where some pain and harm is caused. Here, the parents are placed in the position of having to decide what is best for the donor child and the recipient, if that recipient is also their child. Although, as noted, an analysis of the best interests of the donor child may in fact need to be replaced by a test of what is not against the interests of that child, what remains contentious is the level of harm, actual or potential, that the parents are required to take into account. For instance, there is no lasting harm (in a physical sense) in the removal of regenerative tissue like bone marrow, but there is the potential for harms due to the surgery, like infection. This is something parents have to weigh up and is uncontrollable by ACART. If, for instance, parents wanted to use PGD with HLA tissue-typing to conceive in order to harvest stem cells from the umbilical cord and consent was given, it is impossible for ACART to prevent the parents from later seeking to use bone marrow or a kidney, although this would be governed by existing law.

The third possible restriction is who a recipient can be. It is seemingly non-contentious that if PGD with HLA tissue-typing is allowed, a sick sibling can be a recipient, but what about parents or cousins or even friends.[96] In siblings, having an identical HLA match is quite possible (3/16 chance an embryo would be a match), but in the case where a parent would be the recipient this probability is reduced to 1/200.[97] Despite this low chance, there have been reports of a child's stem cells taken from their umbilical cord saving a father's life.[98] Due to this possibility, and because there is no actual harm incurred by the embryo or a resulting child in harvesting stem cells in this way, there seems little or no reason to restrict the recipients to siblings. Having a firm rationale for this is important, as in other cultures, including Māori culture, the idea of a family is larger than the Western conception of family.[99]

The only possible reason for preventing parents from becoming recipients is the potential conflict of interest caused by a parent putting their own needs before the best interests of their child. This concern could easily be overcome

96 Although here there is the problem of high morbidity and low success mentioned earlier.

97 Devolder, 'Preimplantation HLA typing', at p. 585.

98 De Greef, P., 'Baby Redt Leven Vader Met Bloed Uit Navelstreng [Baby saves life of father by cord blood]', *De Volkskrant*, 29 October 2001, at p. 1.

99 Metge, J. and Ruru, J., 'Kua Tutu Te Puehu, Kia Mau: Maori aspirations and family law policy', in Henaghan, M. and Atkin, B. (eds), *Family Law Policy in New Zealand*, Wellington: LexisNexis, 2007, at pp. 49–51.

by requiring an independent guardian for medical procedures where the recipient is a parent. Preventing parents from receiving tissue is outside ACART's jurisdiction, which only applies when the PGD procedure is carried out.

From the above discussion it can be seen that there are many arguments against PGD with HLA tissue-typing. However, a strong argument in favour of PGD with HLA tissue-typing is the idea of procreative liberty, which requires that procreative autonomy should be respected unless harm is shown.[100] These ethical arguments for restricting, partially or completely, PGD with HLA tissue-typing need to show that there would be harm to the embryo or resulting child. There will always be the possibility of some harm, but the issue is whether or not the harm is sufficiently lasting to justify removing the choice for parents. This question is exactly what ACART is designed to decide.

How ACART turned theory into practice

This section examines how ACART applies the theoretical process to the ethical controversies described above in the practice of creating guidelines for PGD with HLA tissue-typing.[101]

On 6 July 2007 ACART released a discussion document entitled 'Advice on aspects of assisted reproductive technology: a consultation paper on policy issues'.[102] This wide-ranging discussion document focused on several areas, including PGD. This document was sent out to 272 individuals and groups that had previously registered an interest with ACART, a press statement was released and the consultation process was advertised in all major metropolitan newspapers. Two months later submissions closed, with ACART receiving 46 submissions on all of the issues covered in the discussion document.

Following this consultation, ACART prepared draft guidelines for the use of PGD with HLA tissue-typing that were publicly released in July 2008. These guidelines incorporated some of the concerns that submitters had voiced. In relation to what level of severity of medical condition sufficiently justified the use of PGD with HLA tissue-typing, the draft guidelines left this decision up to the clinical team and prospective parents' judgement.[103] ACART thought that PGD with HLA tissue-typing should not be restricted to just siblings, but should also be available to close relatives such as cousins, subject only to the approval by the Ethics Committee on Assisted Reproductive Technology (ECART).[104]

100 Gavaghan, *Defending the Genetic Supermarket*, at p. 12.
101 The current guidelines regulating PGD with HLA tissue-typing were created prior to ACART by the National Ethics Committee on Human Assisted Reproduction (NECHAR). For discussion of these guidelines see Snelling, 'Law and regulation', in Human Genome Research Project, *Choosing Genes for Future Children*, at pp. 232–42.
102 www.acart.health.govt.nz/moh.nsf/indexcm/acart-news-home (accessed 12/01/2012).
103 ACART, Consultation on Draft Guidelines of the Use of Preimplantation Genetic Diagnosis with Human Leukocyte Antigen Testing, July 2008, at p. 6.
104 Ibid.

After the draft guidelines were released, further public consultation was undertaken with submissions closing two months later. These submissions essentially mirrored the opinions set out in the earlier ones. In response to these submissions, further draft guidelines were created, with the most notable change being the restriction of the use of PGD with HLA tissue-typing to genetic siblings of the embryo only. At the time the exact reasons behind this were not clear, but this change was later justified by ACART on the basis that 'the use of PGD has implications for the whole family. Restricting the use to genetic siblings within a family minimises the complexity of relationships.'[105] A copy of these revised draft guidelines was then sent to the Minister of Health for consultation. The Minister of Health (Hon. Tony Ryall) subsequently referred the draft guidelines to the National Ethics Advisory Committee (NEAC) for comment. This was in part because the Minister was 'uneasy with the whole area of policy work on assisted human reproduction' and 'finds it hard to see how . . . he can make policy decisions that will make for clear and agreed improvements in the sector for New Zealanders'.[106] Here the Minister of Health viewed himself as being in control of the guidelines.[107] However, there is no statutory basis for this assumption.[108] ACART was given deliberative autonomy because the area was seen as too specialised for politicians to make appropriate policy about.[109]

The NEAC report on the draft guidelines, which was in response to the Minister's request, found that the draft guidelines were mostly 'reasonable'; that is, they could be rationally justified.[110] However, NEAC did say that the consultation and provision of reasons could have been better, especially in showing the application of the s. 4 principles. NEAC also considered that the guidance given to ECART, which ultimately had to apply the guidelines, could have been better in determining whether PGD with HLA tissue-typing was the best option, whether the degree of severity of the condition justified using PGD with HLA tissue-typing, and what other tissue aside from cord blood could be used.[111]

Following this report, ACART addressed these issues. The Advisory Committee did not fully accept some of the recommendations, especially those concerning the provision of guidance to ECART because 'there is always a fine balance between getting clear policy parameters into the guidelines and ensuring the guidelines are not too prescriptive and do not restrict the role of ECART unnecessarily'.[112] However, ACART did amend the draft guidelines

105 ACART, *Agenda and Meeting Papers*, 13 August 2010, at p. 48.
106 Moore, A., 'Talk on tissue-typing', ACART Meeting (27 November 2009).
107 See also Ryall, T. (16 November 2010) 668 NZPD 35884.
108 Snelling, 'Law and regulation', in Human Genome Research Project, *Choosing Genes for Future Children*, at pp. 256–7.
109 Chadwick, S. (25 August 2004) 619 NZPD 15058.
110 NEAC, NEAC Analysis: ACART Draft Guidelines on Preimplantation HLA Tissue-Typing, 31 August 2009.
111 Ibid.
112 Email from Rumball, S. to Moore, A. regarding NEAC's report (31 August 2009).

to provide some more details around what tissue could be used, as well as some guiding factors to assist in assessing the severity of the condition. In relation to the criticisms levelled at the consultation process and providing reasons for the guidelines, Sylvia Rumball, the Chair of ACART, admitted that both of these posed 'an ongoing challenge'.[113] However, consulting every time a change was made to the guidelines as NEAC suggested 'would not be very efficient'.[114] At the end of 2011, these draft guidelines were waiting for the Minister of Health to accept them before they are issued.

Analysing how well ACART turned theory into practice

As Albert Einstein is reported to have said, 'In theory, theory and practice are the same. In practice, they are not.'[115] This is especially true regarding how advisory committees work. In order to evaluate how well ACART turned theory into practice in creating guidelines for PGD with HLA tissue-typing, it is necessary to analyse two of the specific criticisms levelled against the Advisory Committee by NEAC. These were directed at the adequacy of ACART's consultation – in other words at how deliberative and reciprocal they had been – and how transparent the Advisory Committee's decision-making had been.

In relation to the consultation, for significant issues such as PGD with HLA tissue-typing, ACART is statutorily obligated to provide a discussion document, consult the public, and take their submissions into account. As described above, there were two periods of consultation: one following the release of a broad discussion document (the omnibus consultation), the other following the release of the draft guidelines on PGD with HLA tissue-typing (the specific consultation). The omnibus consultation asked for views on the proposed guidelines for PGD with HLA tissue-typing, and whether these adequately addressed the needs, values and beliefs of Māori. The specific consultation asked whether the key issues had been identified and adequately addressed in the draft guidelines, whether there were points that could be better reflected and whether any improvements or clarifications were needed. Clearly these are broad questions aimed at allowing people to express their opinion on a range of issues, but because they were so broad, NEAC viewed them as an inadequate consultation on some specific issues. For example, changing the test for treatment options from PGD with HLA tissue-typing as being the only available treatment option, to simply the option most likely to have a successful outcome, was in NEAC's opinion 'not clearly raised at any stage in ACART's consultation'.[116] While the issue may not have been 'clearly

113 Ibid.
114 ACART, *Agenda and Meeting Papers*, 13 August 2010, at p. 48.
115 This is a quote often attributed to Albert Einstein, although it is also attributed to Lawrence Peter 'Yogi' Berra and Jan L. A. van de Snepscheut.
116 NEAC, NEAC Analysis: ACART Draft Guidelines on Preimplantation HLA Tissue-Typing, 31 August 2009, at p. 12.

raised' the questions provided ample opportunity for people to write submissions on any area of the proposed guidelines and on whether any further clarification was needed. So this criticism comes down to whether it is the role of an advisory committee to ask specific questions that may be too limited, or to allow the public to raise issues they see fit. In fact, there is no reason they could not do both.

Another area that ACART did not specifically consult on was who should determine the severity of the condition that justifies using PGD with HLA tissue-typing. Indeed, this was one area on which submitters raised issues, some arguing that objective criteria should be provided, and even 'ECART expressed concern that the draft guidelines appear to leave [ECART] with no role on this significant issue'.[117] The reason ACART did not consult the public about this was that it held that this issue was best decided by clinicians and prospective parents.[118] While this recognises the procreative liberty principle, it goes against the structure of the HART Act 2004, which does not allow ACART to make decisions without consultation. This is because, under the HART Act 2004, the Advisory Committee is required to take submissions into account,[119] and predetermination precludes this from occurring. While there is no requirement to follow what submitters say, there is an obligation to be open to their views. The reality is that a differently constituted ACART could well come to different conclusions on who should decide the severity of the condition that justifies the use of PGD with HLA tissue-typing. The degree of latitude that will be given to parents to make their own decisions comes down to the views of the committee, rather than statutory principles.

Taking this criticism into account, for the most part the consultation process fulfilled the statutory requirements. While in hindsight consultation can always be better, sometimes issues cannot be anticipated in advance and 'this is probably an unavoidable feature of the process, and so criticism of it is unjustified'.[120] So the general criticism of ACART's consultation seems misplaced and ACART did, in this respect, turn theory into practice.

Turning to the second criticism, the transparency of ACART's decision-making, this poses, as Rumball admits, an 'on-going challenge'.[121] The difficulty lies in 'making ACART's thinking transparent and accessible'.[122] While ACART makes available the discussion documents, public minutes, and reports

117 Ibid., at p. 15.
118 Email from Rumball, S. to Moore, A. regarding NEAC report (31 August 2009).
119 HART Act 2004, s. 39. The phrase 'take into account' has been held to be synonymous with 'have regard to' and means that the submissions must be 'considered and given due weight, as a guide in the decision making process, but there remain[s] an ultimate discretion' (*Staunton Investments Ltd* v. *Chief Executive Ministry of Fisheries* [2004] NZAR 69, at p. 75).
120 Jones, D. G., 'Discussion of the NEAC Report', 26 November 2009.
121 Email from Rumball, S. to Moore, A. regarding NEAC report (31 August 2009).
122 Ibid.

to the Minister of Health 'these mechanisms do not always allow for ACART to present detailed arguments and full reasoning for a particular position'.[123] Gareth Jones, a member of ACART, explains that providing clarity and transparency for the reasoning underlying proposed policy changes 'is a difficult task for any committee, and is made extremely difficult by the requirement that reasoning be sufficiently detailed, yet sufficiently simple, for all audiences to understand'.[124] However, this difficulty is not an excuse, and Jones says in an earlier article that '[i]t is crucial that any advisory committee seeking to engage with the public uses clear reasoning to arrive at its advice and makes this reasoning visible'.[125]

One option that Jones proposes in relation to transparency is 'providing a statutorily-derived framework that can structure reasoning and its clear expression'.[126] Without this framework the danger is that the decisions will be based on each member's different experiences and backgrounds, and arguments become 'a multitude of opinions and anecdotes'.[127] In part, this statutory framework already exists in s. 4 of the HART Act 2004, which provides ACART's guiding principles. As Andrew Moore says, 'ACART has a duty to give publicly available and credible thought to the legal and ethical relevance, and, where relevant the implications, of the s. 4 principles.'[128] One cannot do this by 'bare assertion' as ACART often does by listing at the beginning of each document the principles and stating that '[t]hese guidelines have been developed from the principles of the Act'.[129] Instead, Moore proposes that ACART shows how it has been guided by these principles in a publicly accessible way.[130] This might be difficult, as several of the principles are 'vague and ambiguous',[131] and even if ACART used them the 'Advisory Committee could adopt a variety of possible meanings' and so 'reach very different conclusions'.[132] For example, regarding the development of the guidelines it is unclear how, when ACART restricted the use of PGD with HLA tissue-typing only to genetic siblings, it was guided by the principle of respecting Māori values which include the view that the family unit (*Whanau*) is broader than genetic relations. This uncertainty is one of the reasons for ACART forming a working group to look at what it means to respect Māori values and traditions in the field of assisted reproductive technologies.

123 Ibid.
124 Jones, 'Discussion of the NEAC Report'.
125 Jones, D. G., King, M. R. and Whitaker, M. I., 'Who gets born? How did the New Zealand's Bioethics Council arrive at its recommendation', *New Zealand Medical Journal*, 122(1294) (2008): 84–91, at p. 89.
126 Ibid.
127 Email from Forman, J. to Baynes, V. regarding the Informed Consent Working Group (14 May 2009).
128 Moore, 'Talk on tissue-typing'.
129 ACART, *Advice on Aspects of Reproductive Technology* (July 2007), at p. 9.
130 Moore, 'Talk on Tissue-Typing'.
131 Martin, 'HART failure', at p. 33.
132 Ibid.

Despite the difficulty that the content of the principles presents, attempting to explain how the principles have been applied would possibly help to avoid concerned parties' feelings of dissatisfaction or being ignored. For example, it is unclear how ACART applied the principle that requires ACART to treat with respect different ethical, spiritual and cultural perspectives. Many religious groups have traditionally been concerned that creating and destroying embryos is akin to 'Playing God'.[133] ACART is required to consider this spiritual perspective under s. 4 of the HART Act 2004. However, it is not clear in practice how to balance the respect for this religious and ethical perspective, while at the same time applying the other principles that clearly envision and condone the use of assisted reproductive technologies. One proposal is that ACART should explain that it is proceeding from a liberal presupposition and, 'if this is the case, and this [has] been made explicit, the dissatisfaction of some of those involved in the consultation may . . . [be] avoided'.[134]

In relation to transparency, the criticism of the decision-making process seems justified. Explaining how ACART has been guided by the statutory principles could be a way of making decisions more transparent. ACART could release a document accompanying the draft guidelines that provided 'reasoned analysis of the decisions reached, including the scientific basis, the differing perspectives taken into account' and possibly even the 'opportunity for dissenting individual members to record and append their comments to the final decision'.[135] Were ACART to make its decisions understandable, this would go a long way to making each decision 'a publicly acceptable solution to dilemmas on which opinions may differ'.[136]

Conclusion

ACART is a statutorily created advisory committee that is tasked with creating guidelines and giving advice on assisted reproductive technologies in New Zealand. This chapter has addressed how ACART has done this in relation to regulating PGD with HLA tissue-typing. What became clear in developing its guidelines is that there is no clear social consensus on the use of PGD with HLA tissue-typing. There are those who oppose it outright, and those who support it with little or no restriction, and others in between these positions. No hard scientific evidence has been produced to say that the procedure is harmful to the health of an unborn child or the interests of a donor child. The families most affected are small in number, but the outcome is important to them. The key factor throughout the process is the political ramifications. Despite all the consultation that takes place and the good faith consideration

133 Henaghan and McLean, 'Main findings', in Human Genome Research Project, *Choosing Genes for Future Children*, at pp. 7–9.
134 Jones *et al.*, 'Who gets born?', at 88.
135 Henaghan and McLean, 'Main findings', in Human Genome Research Project, *Choosing Genes for Future Children*, at p. 11.
136 Warnock, M., *An Intelligent Person's Guide to Ethics*, London: Duckworth, 2006, at p. 118.

of the principles of the HART Act 2004, the decision-making process is open-ended in nature and ultimately the Minister 'is the final arbiter' who 'wields considerable power'.[137] The decision becomes a political one, rather than an ethical, legal or personal one. That may be inevitable, given the reality that if there is a sufficient degree of societal discomfort or protest against a certain use of new technology, it is most likely going to be a decision for the government of the day. Those who want to use or provide PGD to select for the appropriate tissue-type must educate both the politicians and the public as to the benefits of the procedure. Fear of the unknown and movies such as *My Sister's Keeper*[138] fuel a climate resistant to moving forward too fast. Autonomy of choice is at the mercy of a sea of public uncertainty and anxiety. While ACART is not a perfect vehicle for navigating such a sea, it does link the public with the politicians and proves an educational vehicle for slowly moving forward.

The underlying irony of the entire process, which is difficult to put out of one's mind as a member of ACART, is that as a society we give parents a vast array of choices as to how they bring up their children; from what they eat, to how they are disciplined. Yet, when it comes to choices about an embryo that will have life-saving potential for another child in the family, we require guidelines to be drawn up and for an ethics committee to vet each decision. It is difficult to see any coherent rationale for the erosion of the power of parental decision-making at this point, but not at other stages that are likely to put children at more risk of harm.

137 Snelling, 'Law and regulation', in Human Genome Research Project, *Choosing Genes for Future Children*, at pp. 256–7.
138 Cassavetes, N., *My Sister's Keeper* (2009).

Conclusion

Sheila A.M. McLean and Sarah Elliston

When making policy in areas as sensitive and emotional as human reproduction, regulators and legislators are likely influenced by their perception of public opinion and what public policy should embrace. In each of the countries considered in this narrative, which were selected primarily because of their similar jurisprudential traditions and because – unlike the United States – there has been legislative activity specifically targeted at this area, legislators have tended to adopt what might be called a precautionary approach and indeed, there may be expectations that they ought to do so. It has, for example, been said that:

> Many of the decisions about what to regulate or to legislate about depend on the approach taken with regard to the balance of harm and benefit or potential harm and potential benefit. It has become fashionable to specify that authorities (whether that be Governments, agencies, industry, watchdogs etc) should take a 'precautionary approach' or adopt the 'precautionary principle'.[1]

This principle, which is widely used in debates on the environment, has been described as follows:

> Simply put, the precautionary principle (PP) calls for the world to take action to make products, environmental activities and technology safer, healthier and accountable to everyone.[2]

Expressed in this way, the principle seems unexceptionable. It is self-evident that we would wish products, technologies and activities to be as safe as they can be. However, one negative implication of this principle is that it can be used as a means of stifling innovation in the face of anxieties – whether or not

1 HCSTC, Fifth Report of Session 2004–5, *Human Reproductive Technologies and the Law*, vol. 1, HC 7–1, 24 March 2005, p. 22, para. 47.
2 See www.ehow.com/about_5184467_definition-precautionary-principle.html#ixzz1nackJtpt (accessed 27/02/2012).

realistic – about *possible* harms from *potential* developments. There have been criticisms in the UK of the 'excessive use' of a precautionary approach in regulating assisted reproductive techniques,[3] and we would suggest that this observation could be made in respect of regulation in many, if not most, of the jurisdictions considered in this volume. This kind of approach taps into public and regulatory fears about the advances in science and can in itself generate further distrust, or fear of so-called slippery slopes.

While science has contributed to making human life easier, more bearable and longer than previously, there is, in some quarters at least, suspicion about its goals and the way in which it is regulated. For example, a report by the (UK) Office of Science and Technology (OST) and the Wellcome Trust found that:

> There is concern about the effectiveness of the regulation of science, and the qualitative research found that participants saw regulation as being very secretive and bureaucratic. Having some idea of the end product brings more faith in the regulatory system – hence some respondents were more positive about engineering and technology than about science. Seven out of ten agree that:
>
> Rules will not stop researchers doing what they want behind closed doors
>
> But only a third believe that:
>
> Science is getting out of control and there is nothing we can do about it
>
> And two out of five agree:
>
> The speed of development in science and technology means that it cannot be properly controlled by Government.[4]

These findings clearly demonstrate the ambivalence sometimes shown towards science and scientists. On the one hand, people believe that it (or they) cannot be fully controlled, while on the other holding out some hope that control is indeed feasible. In any event, the precautionary principle is by no means uncontroversial. One of the problems that a review of UK regulation conducted by the House of Commons Science and Technology Committee (HCSTC) identified is that there are different interpretations of the precautionary approach that are used by various groups to seek to achieve specific goals. Indeed, the role of such arguments as part of the political process of influencing regulatory agendas has been documented in a number of chapters in this book. The HCSTC promoted a particular medical/scientific understanding of the precautionary principle and contended that in this sphere it had never meant 'proceed only where there is evidence of no harm'; rather that:

3 HCSTC, *Human Reproductive Technologies and the Law*, vol. 1, p. 117, para. 263.

4 *Science and the Public: A Review of Science Communication and Public Attitudes to Science in Britain, Office of Science and Technology*, London: Wellcome Trust, October 2000, para. 4.26.

> [i]n clinical practice it means proceed cautiously and in a manner amenable to ethical oversight and clinical audit while there is no evidence of sufficiently serious harm or potential harm to outweigh benefit or potential benefit, while being vigilant in looking for unintended and otherwise adverse outcomes.[5]

As a result, it concluded that 'alleged harms to society or to patients need to be demonstrated before forward progress is unduly impeded'.[6] Nonetheless, one author at least sees some potential (if somewhat cynical) benefits to the use of a precautionary approach, saying '[i]n one sense . . . the precautionary principle might have some utility. If we apply the precautionary principle to itself – ask what are the possible dangers of using this principle – we would be forced to abandon it very quickly.'[7]

When the science in question relates to 'making babies', ambivalence can coalesce into something more forceful, with more than seven out of ten people interviewed for the above study into public attitudes to science agreeing that '[p]eople shouldn't tamper with nature'.[8] Leaving aside the question of what is so inevitably 'good' about nature – which after all gives us conditions such as cancer, which we are generally happy to use scientific knowledge to try to prevent and treat – the possibility of intervening in the 'natural' process of reproduction is anathema to some individuals and groups. Thus, assisted reproduction in and of itself is wrong; nature should be left to run its course, and if this means condemning hopeful intending parents to childlessness, so be it. This view is often associated with certain faith groups, from whose perspective all life is a gift from, and controlled by, a god whose will is supreme and who has a plan for each of us that may or may not involve parenting. Even from a more secular perspective, the *Report of the Committee of Inquiry into Human Fertilisation and Embryology* (Warnock Report) described the response to the birth of the world's first *in vitro* fertilisation (IVF) baby, Louise Brown, as a mixture of:

> pride in the technological achievement, pleasure at the new-found means to relieve, at least for some, the unhappiness of infertility, and unease at the apparently uncontrolled advance of science, bringing with it new possibilities for manipulating the early stages of human development.[9]

This leads directly from the precautionary principle to an exploration of slippery-slope arguments. As is evident from the OST/Wellcome Trust Report,

5 HCSTC, *Human Reproductive Technologies and the Law*, vol. 1, p. 22, para. 47.
6 Ibid., 'Conclusions and recommendations', p. 175, para. 3.
7 Anon., 'Beware the precautionary principle', Social Issues Research Centre, www.sirc.org/articles/beware.html (accessed 22/02/2012).
8 Ibid., para. 4.9.
9 *Report of the Committee of Inquiry into Human Fertilisation and Embryology* (Warnock Report), London: Stationery Office, 1984, at p. 4.

there does seem to be some unease about the possibility that science will create its own momentum and will inevitably take us to places we do not want to, or should not, go. The notion that scientists will 'do what they want behind closed doors' carries the implication that at least some of this work, of which the public generally may be unaware until a technique has been successfully developed, will have unwanted or unacceptable consequences. In the area of human reproduction, this fear is perhaps at its most acute. The anxiety that science might allow for the birth of animal–human hybrids or the cloning of armies of dictators entered the public consciousness through popular literature and the media. However unlikely these outcomes may be, the unease that the mere possibility generated has probably tainted attitudes to certain areas of research and techniques developed from it and, in turn, has created an atmosphere in which the precautionary principle seems – to some at least – entirely appropriate. Doctors and scientists are accused of 'playing God' and legislators and regulators are encouraged to intervene to prevent the seemingly inevitable slide down the slippery slope towards Armageddon. Almond, for example, says '[e]ver since the development of the first atomic weapons . . . people have been aware that scientific advance divorced from ethical sensitivity is a Frankenstein'.[10]

Making policy in this area, in the face of these and other, perhaps less extreme, concerns can be very difficult. In liberal Western democracies, such as the countries we have considered in this volume, the tradition of a relatively 'hands off' approach to the role of the state vis-à-vis its citizens can seem inappropriate in the area of human reproduction, and therefore to be worthy of challenge. The assumption that essentially private matters – such as reproduction – are not the concern of the state seems especially vulnerable when medicine and science offer not just the opportunity to circumvent fertility problems but also to choose what kind of children to have. Fox, for example, argues that 'advances in biotechnology give special reason to rethink our liberal commitments. Liberal arguments about liberty, equality, and harm to others will not do when it comes to practices that seek to remake nature.'[11] The state, therefore, may on this argument have a legitimate role in shaping and controlling the decisions that intending parents can make. In a limited defence of the so-called 'nanny state', Calman says that 'the state has a duty to look after the health of everyone, and sometimes that means guiding or restricting people's choices'.[12] Even the relatively liberal report from the (UK) Science and Technology Committee conceded that 'assisted reproduction and research involving the embryo of the human species both remain legitimate

10 Almond, B., 'Philosophy, medicine and its technologies', *J Med Ethics*, 14 (1988): 173–8, at p. 173.

11 Fox, D., 'Retracing liberalism and remaking nature: designer children, research embryos and featherless chickens', *Bioethics*, 24(4) (2010): 170–8, at p. 178.

12 Calman, K., 'Beyond the "nanny state": stewardship and public health', *Public Health*, 123 (2009): e6–e10, at e9.

interests of the state', albeit with the caveat that '[r]eproductive and research freedoms must be balanced against the interests of society but alleged harms to society, too, should be based on evidence'.[13]

For others, however, reproduction is an essentially private matter, even when it requires medical assistance, and the state should not intervene to prevent intending parents either from gaining access to the necessary technology or from using all of the technology at their disposal, particularly pre-implantation genetic diagnosis (PGD). This argument, as we have seen in some of the earlier chapters, is based on the concept of reproductive liberty; the idea that in the absence of evidence of harm, people should be free to make their own decisions about whether and when to reproduce and what kind of children to have. In fact, as Jochelson notes:

> The debate over the limits to state intervention and extent of individual freedom weaves through the history of public health. In the simplest terms, it divides between interventionists and libertarians. For interventionists, governments promote freedom for individuals by creating opportunities and leveling out inequalities in society. For libertarians, minimal government is the best way to protect individual freedom, which is about not being interfered with by others.[14]

This is no less true in the arena of assisted reproduction. For policy makers, then, the fundamental issue is which ethical position should be adopted.

As we have seen, most of the jurisdictions we have considered have opted for a legislative response that assumes that some restrictions are appropriate. In other words, the emphasis on reproductive liberty that so dominated human rights rhetoric in the aftermath of the negative eugenics prevalent in the late nineteenth century and early twentieth has not been fully translated into policy. Not only may people be denied access to the technology, and therefore denied the opportunity to parent, but even those accepted as suitable to receive the technology may find the choices that could flow from this to be limited by state policy. So, how does policy come about?

While we might wish to believe that public policy is based on proven facts and shaped in a rational and deliberative manner, this is by no means a given. Page says:

> Insofar as they arise from conscious reflection and deliberation, policies may reflect a variety of intentions and ideas: some vague, some specific, some conflicting, some unarticulated. They can . . . even be the unintended

13 HCSTC, *Human Reproductive Technologies and the Law*, vol. 1, para. 46, p. 22.

14 Jochelson, K., 'Nanny or steward? The role of government in public health', *Public Health*, 120 (2006): 1149–55, at p. 1150.

> or undeliberated consequences of professional practices or bureaucratic routines.[15]

Policy may also be, as Walsh says, 'peculiarly open to distortion by political and social ideology'.[16] The presumption that people should not be totally free to obtain access to assisted reproductive technologies, or the unfettered use of the options it makes available, seems to reflect (at least) a social ideology that prioritises speculation about the kind of parents people will be, or the kinds of decisions they will make, over reproductive liberty itself. In most of the arguments in favour of limiting choice (apart perhaps from those based on faith) dominant anxieties are about the welfare of future children, fitness for parenting or the creation of 'designer babies'.

To be sure, the welfare of children is a legitimate interest of the state; hence, there are laws in place that seek to protect children from abuse or neglect. However, it is surely problematic for the state to regulate in an effort to balance the possible welfare concerns of potential future children with the deeply felt desire of people to reproduce. This is especially true where the outcome of the decision concerns whether or not technology should be used so that such a potential future child can be conceived. Equally, fitness for parenting is a concept intimately linked with the compulsory sterilisation programmes of the early to mid-twentieth century, and is – in any case – not a test that those who can reproduce naturally have to meet before becoming parents. Of course, it might be objected that assisted reproduction *is* different from natural reproduction because although we cannot prevent people in the latter case from reproducing, we can – perhaps should – attempt to ensure that people are suited to parenting when third-party (sometimes state) involvement is necessary and regulation is feasible. While this argument may have an immediate appeal, it should be remembered that unblocking fallopian tubes and reversing vasectomies also require third-party involvement, are done with the aim of restoring reproductive capacity, but do not require evidence of parental fitness. On what grounds, therefore, would those who require more advanced technologies be required to jump this further hurdle? The mere fact that we *can* limit choice is not a sufficient justification for doing so. Nevertheless, while reproductive decisions might reasonably be regarded as essentially private, whatever the context in which they arise, it seems that the temptation for states to interfere in them where they arise in connection with IVF and associated techniques has been irresistible, at least in the majority of the jurisdictions we consider here.

As to PGD specifically, objectors often use emotive language about 'designer babies' and 'parental acceptance' to show why its use should either not be

15 Page, E. C., 'The origins of policy', in Moran, M., Rein, M. and Goodin, R. E. (eds), *The Oxford Handbook of Public Policy*, Oxford: Oxford University Press, 2006 (paperback, 2008), pp. 207–27, at p. 207.

16 Walsh, P., 'Principles and pragmatism', *Medical Law Review*, 3 (autumn 1995): 237–50, at p. 237.

permitted or should be limited. Each of these has been canvassed already in this manuscript, but they bear brief reconsideration here. People seeking to use PGD (and they remain relatively rare) will often already have experience either of having a child affected by a genetic condition, or may have knowledge that such a condition is present within the family. The desire to avoid the birth of a child with certain disabilities is probably derived both from concern for the quality of the future child's life and anxiety about their own ability to cope with such a child, perhaps particularly when another affected child already exists in the family. The effort to avoid such births, however, has been criticised as not demonstrating the love that parents should have for their children, no matter what. Of course, it could equally be argued – and we would agree – that parental love is also evident in decisions to avoid future suffering for a child as well as in concern for their existing children.

Nonetheless, the argument that parents should be willing to accept whatever child they are fortunate enough to have is commonly used by the opponents of PGD. The notion of parental virtue is thereby introduced to cast doubt on the intentions or morality of those who would seek to prevent the implantation of an embryo known to be affected by a particular condition. A virtuous (good) parent would not make choices of the sort that PGD makes possible. To say that such an argument is naïve is, perhaps, an understatement. There is no rule of thumb that tells us what a 'good' or virtuous parent would or should decide. Is a virtuous parent one who chooses not to know that the child they are attempting to conceive may suffer and die young, or one who uses technology to avoid such suffering by choosing to have a different child?

Further, in support of their claim that the slippery slope really does exist, opponents of PGD will point to the next stage in 'designing' babies: the creation of a child who can provide matching tissue to save the life of an existing, but ill, child. This, they might argue, instrumentalises the child and shows it inadequate respect. Again, these arguments have been raised elsewhere in this volume, but it should be restated that while the precautionary principle might suggest that such choices should not be permitted because the child may be harmed, there is no evidence to support such a gloomy, and not entirely logical, conclusion.

Another argument that will be considered briefly here is the not uncommon one that PGD is just another form of eugenics, and on that basis alone it should not be offered as an option. It also follows on this account that we disvalue people already living with disability by selecting against embryos with the same characteristics. In effect, proponents of this argument equate non-implantation of specific embryos on the grounds of potential disability with the sterilisation programmes of Nazi Germany and some disability rights activists see such choices as discriminatory and demeaning for people living with disability. The first point can be cleared up relatively easily. The Nazi sterilisation policies (and those which existed in the United States and elsewhere) were formulated by government and backed by state coercion – they were not based on the free and informed choice of intending parents. The denial of reproductive liberty, and the abuse that inevitably flowed from it, was the actual harm. No liberal supporter of PGD would wish to see it used as part of a mandated state programme; rather, they would emphasise the need for a free and uncoerced choice by intending parents. Of course, eugenics – for historically valid reasons – has a bad reputation, but as the HCSTC said: 'If ensuring that your child is less likely to face a debilitating disease in the course of their life can be termed eugenics, we have no problem with its use'.[17]

As for the second issue, it bears repeating that preferring to implant an unaffected embryo as opposed to an affected one in reality does not disrespect people already living with the condition. In choosing, for example, not deliberately to have a child suffering from a condition that would prove fatal early in its life, intending parents do not lose concern or compassion for those who are born with the condition. If intending parents could shape a future for their children that guaranteed the best possible health, or the absence of a specific disabling condition, might they not reasonably wish to do so? Making such a choice does not imply that they become aggressive, hostile or dismissive in respect of people who have the same condition; merely that, where choice is available, some might reasonably want to avoid the situation arising.

It is interesting to note that exactly the opposite concerns have arisen where people seek to use PGD in order deliberately to select an embryo for implantation that has a genetic make-up associated with a potentially disabling condition. Such possible choices have attracted even more widespread condemnation, perhaps reflecting the fact that, contrary to the fears expressed above, many people do think it is legitimate and even morally virtuous to seek to avoid having children that may be affected by disability. However, although it often seems to be ignored, this runs up against the same objections to imposing state controls on the kinds of children that people can and should choose to have as are raised by the earlier examples. Again, people who wish to select an embryo because it has a genetic condition linked with disability are most likely to do so because they have direct experience of the condition. They will be in no doubt that any children they might have with the same condition have as much potential for a good life as anyone else's. They may go further and argue that a child without the condition might pose greater challenges to them as parents in providing what they consider appropriate care and support within the family and its social network. The extent to which a state is justified in regarding such views as so irresponsible as to be impermissible is surely open to question. On a liberal account, it would be necessary to demonstrate harm before state intervention would be legitimate. Given that the selected embryo only has the potential to be a child with that particular disability this poses distinct problems, as demonstration of harm to a future child would require it to be established that the balance of risks and benefits lies in avoiding its existence.

17 HCSTC, *Human Reproductive Technologies and the Law*, vol. 1, p. 55, para. 116.

Finally, using PGD for sex selection on non-medical grounds has widely been dealt with by legislative prohibition, although the reasons for this may be regarded as far from convincing. For example, the UK's Human Fertilisation and Embryology Authority stated that one of the major arguments justifying a prohibition on this practice was the public response to consultation which, in its view, had indicated 'considerable alarm among consultation respondents that children selected for their sex alone may in some way be psychologically damaged by the knowledge that they had been selected in this way as embryos'.[18] Leaving aside the fact that the numbers who responded to the consultation were extremely small, such justifications have not passed by entirely without notice. The HCSTC was robust in its disapproval of this stance, commenting that '[t]hus the most persuasive argument was not that there was evidence of harm but that there was evidence of concern about harm. This is not a satisfactory use of evidence to support policy advice.'[19] It concluded that although sex-selecting embryos raised ethical issues concerning the creation and destruction of embryos which warranted some caution, in the absence of convincing evidence of psychological harm to children, arising from having been selected for sex, or wider demographic impact concerns, '[t]he onus should be on those who oppose sex selection for social reasons using PGD to show harm from its use . . . On balance we find no adequate justification for prohibiting the use of sex selection for family balancing.'[20] Despite this, its recommendation was not followed in the subsequent legislation.[21]

However, if, as the HCSTC suggests, the onus of demonstrating harm from the use of PGD is on those who oppose its use, this hurdle would seem hard to overcome, at least at this stage in the clinical application of PGD. It must be recognised that it may be much more difficult to demonstrate certain types of alleged harm than others. Detecting that an embryo carries genes associated with medical illness or disability may well not enable accurate prediction of the extent to which a child will be affected. Even where the prognosis is reasonably clear, there is still room for a substantial difference of opinion over whether the effects on the child should be regarded as 'serious', and in consequence, whether an embryo should or should not be used for treatment. Another set of possible risks relates to safety concerns: that interventions upon embryos have the potential to cause them damage or affect their development, with a consequent reduction in successful live births or an increase in birth defects. Some kinds of harm may not be detected immediately, but would depend upon long-term studies of children born using these techniques, and possibly their own children, and establishing the existence of such risks may require many years of data collection. By way of comparison, the drug

18 Ibid., p. 121, para. 272.
19 Ibid.
20 Ibid., p. 64, para. 143.
21 Human Fertilisation and Embryology Act 2008, amending and supplementing the Human Fertilisation and Embryology Act 1990.

diethylstilboestrol (DES) prescribed for pregnant women at risk of miscarriage from the 1940s to the 1970s, was found to have a number of adverse effects upon the women themselves and their children, such as the risk of developing forms of cancer. However, it also affected these women's daughter's reproductive systems leading to increased risk of pregnancy loss and other complications.[22] Research suggests that additional health problems may be suffered by the third generation, that is, grandchildren of the women for whom DES was prescribed.[23] The existence of many of these adverse effects clearly could not be established until years after the drug was originally taken, and research is continuing. There is similarly an inevitable difficulty in establishing at the present time whether diagnostic procedures undertaken on embryos carry any significant health risks to children or subsequent generations. The same concerns arose when IVF was developed and we are still less than 40 years from its first successful clinical use. As the HCSTC put it: 'The safety of assisted reproduction has been a matter of conjecture, since even the earliest children born using IVF are still only young adults.'[24] In commenting on the use of novel techniques in assisted reproductive techniques (ART), an independent working group, set up by the UK's Medical Research Council at the request of the HFEA, wrote that:

> Although there is widespread acceptance, based on experience, that current ART procedures are generally safe, the evidence for this, particularly in terms of long-term safety, is relatively weak when compared to other similarly well-established clinical techniques. Too little is known about the basic mechanisms of early human development – whether natural or assisted – about interactions between the mother and her growing baby, or about the overall risks and benefits of ART to draw firm conclusions about whether a new treatment may have any unforeseen adverse consequences.[25]

While the understanding of human development may have moved on since this report was drafted, many questions remain. However, it would seem that, despite some residual concerns and objections, much of assisted reproductive technology – perhaps especially IVF – has become accepted in each of the jurisdictions addressed here, and of course in many others. Indeed, for many, IVF is a routine medical procedure, requiring only the availability of relevant resources and the agreement of individuals/couples and clinics. For this reason, regulation is muted, with its focus being primarily on safety and quality rather

22 Hoover, R. N. *et al.*, 'Adverse health outcomes in women exposed *in utero* to diethylstilbestrol', *New England Journal of Medicine*, 365 (14) (6 October 2011): 1304–14.

23 National Cancer Institute, Factsheet: Diethylstilboestrol (DES) and Cancer, www.cancer.gov/cancertopics/factsheet/Risk/DES (accessed March 2012).

24 HCSTC, *Human Reproductive Technologies and the Law*, vol. 1, p. 19, para. 36.

25 Medical Research Council, 'Assisted reproduction: a safe, sound future', London, 2004, p. 2.

than an examination of the acceptability of the procedure. The same cannot, however, be said of PGD.

Here also, questions of safety and quality inevitably arise. It is of course impossible to state with any certainty that new procedures carry no risk, and even if some risks are found to exist, what is at issue is a risk–benefit analysis. While proponents of the precautionary principle would point to the lack of evidence as requiring a cautious approach, a liberal account would prioritise reproductive liberty unless and until evidence of harm is found. How a risk–benefit analysis is calculated will, of course, depend on which interests and concerns are prioritised. This, in turn, as we have seen in relation to making public policy, will depend on many factors, including the personal morality of legislators and regulators and their views as to what is, and is not, acceptable or important.

On this point the MRC may be seen to have adopted a view that is commonly taken, one that prioritises concerns about child welfare:

> Throughout their deliberations, the subgroup worked on the basis that the mother's health and well-being are important, but the health of children, who have no choice about how they are conceived, must be the overriding concern in demonstrating whether ART treatments are safe and effective.[26]

However, in reality, it seems that there was a certain level of ambiguity towards this prioritisation of child welfare, since the Report concluded that:

> Waiting to assemble enough information on long-term safety and efficacy to conduct exhaustive ART safety assessments would cause unnecessary delay and prevent rapid feedback to patients and their doctors. It would be more productive to focus initially on critical safety issues from conception to six months old, taking a healthy single live birth as a the key indicator of a technique's efficacy.[27]

Nevertheless, the MRC report recognised that improving data collection and access to information to enable long-term research on the outcomes of assisted reproduction are necessary to an informed assessment of risks and it recommended that a number of steps be taken to enable such research to take place.[28] Changes in both the practical processes and the legal requirements for recording information and making it available to researchers were put in place.[29]

26 Ibid., p. 9.
27 Ibid., p. 10.
28 Medical Research Council, 'Assisted reproduction: a safe, sound future', 2004.
29 See for example 33D and 45 (1) to (3A) of the Human Fertilisation and Embryology Act 1990, as amended by the Human Fertilisation and Embryology Act and the Human Fertilisation and Embryology (Disclosure of Information for Research Purposes) Regulations 2010.

In respect of the balancing of risks and benefits concerning health risks to children who may be born as a result of the use of ART, the approach that has been taken in the countries discussed has generally been to permit the use of PGD in some circumstances, despite the difficulty of establishing the level of long-term risk, if any. As discussed elsewhere in this volume, evidence relating to short-term health risks so far does not appear to indicate particular causes for anxiety. Accordingly, while the issue of safety of PGD remains current, the focus of concern may be seen to have shifted: notably from the *safety* of the procedure to the *reasons* for using PGD and its possible effects on children and the wider society. Here, the evidence base for determining whether any risks exist is at least as, if not more, limited. Establishing the existence or not, for example, of a negative psychosocial impact on children born as a result of assisted reproductive techniques poses significant challenges in devising appropriate studies and recruiting sufficient numbers to enable meaningful analysis to take place. Similarly, possible effects upon demographics or more abstract fears such as a change in social views about disability or the possible commodification of children may be even harder to establish or quantify. Nevertheless, as we have seen, concerns about such risks often appear to pave the road to prohibitive regulation.

Part of the problem here is that the number of people who may wish to use ART, while not insignificant, will be a minority of the population and those seeking to combine it with PGD will be even fewer. The use of speculative fears, even those that are alleged to be shared by society at large, to dictate the terms on which individuals may exercise choice should always engender the utmost caution. This is especially true where what is involved is the choice to engage in what is an area of private and highly significant decision-making: namely, whether to seek to establish a family, and in some cases, what kind of family to have. That reproduction is an area of critical importance to individuals and couples seems so obvious as to scarcely require comment here, and it is recognised in international instruments, such as the Universal Declaration on Human Rights.[30] However, the kinds of decisions that could be made as a result of the availability of PGD are beyond the range that was previously available to intending parents and will still be inapplicable to the majority who have no need of ART to procreate or who do not have specific reasons to seek to determine the genetic makeup of their children. Concerns that those who wish to have the opportunity to utilise PGD will make 'wrong choices' may suggest that those who wish to use PGD have different – unacceptable or inappropriate – ways of approaching decisions about founding a family from those who do not. They may also be based on a perception that because these are not the kinds of decisions that most people are faced with, or are able to make, they should not be available to anyone. This required acceptance of the

30 Adopted by the United Nations General Assembly on 10 December 1948. Article 16 concerns the right to marry and found a family.

status quo is reminiscent of arguments that mandate acceptance of childlessness for those who cannot procreate without medical assistance, and has generally been rejected.

Of course, it can be argued that the existence of choice is not an unmitigated benefit to individuals and, furthermore, that decision-making may be influenced by many factors. As has been said in respect of prenatal diagnosis, 'the very fact that a test is offered by doctors tends to suggest to a woman that its use is warranted and desirable'.[31] The exercise of choice may therefore be affected by third party views and pressure may be brought to bear to decide in particular ways. Nevertheless, it is one thing to seek to influence a person's choice, it is quite another to exclude certain matters from choice altogether.

Concluding reflections

As was suggested at the beginning of this chapter, it is possible that the concerns seemingly aroused by PGD stem in some part from a sense that science is progressing without the ethical scrutiny that many intuitively believe necessary, and that the kinds of decisions available to intending parents go beyond what virtuous parents should either want or make. This lurking unease is the result of apprehension based on assumptions that do not, it has been argued here, withstand robust scrutiny, and threatens the pursuit of reproductive liberty – a principle that has become increasingly important over the last century or so.

The final question then must be: what is it about PGD that has resulted in such regulatory interest? Given that – even as its possible scope continues to expand – PGD remains a relatively rare procedure, it may seem that legislative interventions are disproportionate to any harms that may result from its use. Indeed, as is clear from this narrative, it is the more unusual potential applications of PGD that now ground the remaining objections to its use at the discretion of intending parents. That is, issues like sex selection for non-medical reasons are now at the forefront of the debate about PGD, particularly for those who oppose a liberal approach to reproductive choice, including in some cases access to assisted reproduction itself. The tactic is to home in on the most extreme example that could be imagined and then use it to show the danger of the enterprise being permitted at all, even if the basis for objection is entirely speculative and rests on assumptions of dubious validity. What this form of argument does, then, is to seek to engage people's innate anxieties about just where science may take us. Additionally, it appeals to a latent sense of discomfort with the reproductive enterprise being structured or manipulated as opposed to 'natural'.

Even if this is an intelligible response, it requires justification. The liberal project that prefers state non-intervention in essentially private matters

31 King, D. S., 'Preimplantation genetic diagnosis and the "new" eugenics', *Journal of Medical Ethics*, 25 (1999): 176–82, at p. 177.

provides a formidable objection to regulatory efforts based on speculation, anxiety or moral distaste. It also, by clear implication, requires us to question whether or not the law is an appropriate mechanism in this area. As Caulfield *et al.* argue:

> Too often, we believe, the search for a regulatory response to certain scientific developments has led governments to adopt simple bans and prohibitions . . . Using the law in such a manner is, however, frequently an inappropriate means of regulating behaviour in this complex and dynamic area.[32]

In other words, the knee-jerk response to innovation is often to use the law to impose moral values, even though these values may change over the years and may, in any case, be illegitimate. In addition, while it is clearly the case that individuals will be guided by their own moral values, it is less clear that concerns for 'public opinion' or some aggregation of supposed moral values are in themselves sufficient justifications for preventing others, who do not share these values, from making choices that *for them* are morally appropriate. One major problem with the anti-liberal approach is that it imposes the views of one group on another. The liberal approach, on the other hand, coerces nobody and provides liberty for those who wish to exercise it in ways that others would not choose to.

Of course, were it clear that using PGD causes actual and significant individual or social harm, then even the liberal account might support state intervention, but compelling evidence to support this does not yet appear to exist. Perhaps it may become available in the future, and certainly it would be appropriate to keep a watching brief. For the moment, arguably, the harms most intimately connected to PGD are the restrictions imposed on its use.

We do not claim that all regulation is inappropriate, however. Manifestly, there are genuine individual and community goals served by requiring that PGD is offered safely and effectively by people with relevant expertise and in accordance with the existing legal rules concerning consent to treatment. Maintaining these standards may require state intervention. However, whether or not such intervention is a necessary or even a helpful tool in other areas must be moot. Too often responses are prohibitory rather than permissive, conservative rather than liberal.

In the long run, it does not seem unreasonable to trust people to make decisions that are appropriate for them and their families in conjunction with their medical advisers. Many of the small number of people who would seek access to PGD will either be aware of a potential genetic problem within the family or may already have an affected child and there is no reason to suppose that the decisions they make will be harmful, immoral or unethical.

32 Caulfield, T., Knowles, L. and Meslin, E. M., 'Law and policy in the era of reproductive genetics', *J Med Ethics*, 30 (2004): 414–17, at p. 414.

If and when harm can be shown to result from allowing intending parents this freedom of choice, it may well be time for the law to intervene in a reasoned and appropriate manner. While the first generation of children born following PGD is still relatively young, to date there seems no reason to believe that the process itself causes harm. Nor is there evidence that significant numbers of people want to use PGD and far less is there evidence that they would wish to do so for what can be deemed to be 'inappropriate' reasons. While there may be some uses of PGD to which some will continue to object – for example, social sex selection – the importance of reproductive liberty should be the primary moral principle underpinning regulatory responses; not speculative fears, knee-jerk reactions, moral distaste or unreflective majoritarianism.

Index